# THE
# MORAL AND POLITICAL PHILOSOPHY
# OF DAVID HUME

# THE
# MORAL AND
# POLITICAL
# PHILOSOPHY OF
# DAVID HUME

By JOHN B. STEWART

Columbia University Press

NEW YORK AND LONDON 1963

# PREFACE

WHEN about ten years ago I began the work that has produced this book, I knew far less about the thought of David
Hume than about that of some other political philosophers,
for Hume's political theory is not readily accessible. He wrote
no major treatise on the subject comparable to Aristotle's
*Politics,* Locke's *Second Treatise,* or Rousseau's *Social Contract,* so that one has to rummage through one work after
another. Moreover, each of his works has its own specific purpose: the argument of one, therefore, does not dovetail directly
into that of another. And, perhaps most discouraging, Hume's
political ideas are expressed in the "moral philosophy" terminology of the eighteenth century, a terminology that we find
dull and disengaging. Nevertheless, I saw that Hume had a
high, if often unexplained, reputation, and this made me
curious.

Besides, Hume seemed to stand at the juncture of several
important questions. First, what is the relation between the
tradition of Natural Law, which is criticized by Hume, and
the principles of economic and social organization advocated
by the classical economists of the eighteenth and nineteenth
centuries? Second, what is the relation between the rise of
classical economic theory and the new interest in history, two
developments in which Hume played a fairly important part?
Third, what is the explanation for the fierce aversion to religion
especially characteristic of eighteenth-century intellectuals?
And, fourth, why is Hume ranked, with a fair show of evidence,
as both a conservative and a liberal?

As I read and wrote I made, of course, many decisions which
give this book the shape and character it now has. I want to
refer to only two of these; and I do this only because by doing

so I may disabuse the reader of certain expectations that he might very reasonably entertain. Early drafts of some chapters, especially Chapter II and Chapter V, contained many references to the views and interpretations of Hume put forth by leading scholars, but, on reflection, I determined that thereby I was frustrating what I gradually had come to believe was the proper purpose of my work. I had discovered, I thought, a high degree of consistency in the whole corpus of Hume's writings. This unity, I concluded, should be displayed at all costs. Consequently, I pruned from those chapters my own excursions into the learned controversies. From this decision there followed a second. I should deny myself the privilege of commenting on any of Hume's views, however accurate or perverse they might seem to me, except when by doing so I could call the reader's attention to the implications of an argument or assumption. The task I undertook was to bring forth Hume's theory to the modern reader. I have tried to stay in the background. More could have been done, and something else could have been done; but this is what I proposed to do.

Perhaps, therefore, I may be excused for mentioning here that there are some aspects of Hume's thought that I find unsatisfactory. He makes the Platonic error, I think, of overstating the effects of knowledge; and, consequently, he makes the ignorance of "the vulgar" the great obstacle to order and happiness in the world. The more somber analyses of St. Augustine and Thomas Hobbes, which exempt no man, be he vulgar or philosophic, and deny the possibility of continuing order and happiness to mankind, no matter how enlightened, ring far truer in our own century. His theory of history, as I have tried to show in Chapter XI, seems inadequate. If he had been consistent in employing one basic theory of historical change—one basic set of what Collingwood called "absolute presuppositions"—we could not protest; instead, he now employs one theory, and now another, thus exposing himself to the criticism that although he sighted and skirted a continent, for polemical reasons he preferred to remain afloat. Finally, whatever the wrongs done in the name of historical religions,

Hume's denunciations seem unrealistic and, therefore, uncharitable. The application to his own view of a little more
of that "moderate scepticism" which he commends might have
been salutary. Even assuming his own views on both theology
and revealed religion—to allow him the ground most advantageous to himself—those denunciations are unwarranted because they fail to take adequate account even of the mere
pragmatic value of religious rites and dogmas. Perhaps what
is most annoying about his treatment of "popular religion" is
that he did not rise above the Enlightenment fad of deriding
the beliefs of the people, but exploited that fad for the sake
of popularity in a certain circle.

I am stating my own views on these points, not because they
are worthy of consideration, but to assure that the reader of
the chapters which follow will be alert to detect any misinter-
pretations of Hume's views in these particulars that may have
crept in despite my care.

I think I should explain why I have quoted extensively in
my footnotes from the *Essays* and the *History of England*.
The edition by Green and Grose of the essays, the only satisfactory modern edition, is very difficult to find. The *History*
fills eight volumes, and although it is pleasant reading, I doubt
that many students nowadays are prepared to take the time to
mine out the passages of a theoretical nature.

I am grateful to the Syndics of the Cambridge University
Press for permission to quote from J. G. A. Pocock's book,
*The Ancient Constitution and the Feudal Law* (Cambridge,
1957).

While writing this book I have anticipated again and again
with pleasure the opportunity its publication would give me
of expressing my gratitude to my teachers in politics and philosophy. At Acadia University I had the privilege of studying
under the late H. F. Scott Thomas and the late T. M. Dadson,
as well as under that judicious philosopher, R. MacGregor
Fraser, and a very exact historian, R. S. Longley. At Columbia
University my debts are innumerable, but I cannot refrain
from mentioning two great teachers, Reinhold Niebuhr and

the late Franz L. Neumann. The book never could have been written without assistance of various kinds from the officers of Barnard College, The Rockefeller Foundation, Columbia University, and St. Francis Xavier University, and to them all I record my thanks for their understanding. I had many useful conversations with Herbert A. Deane, Columbia University, while I was writing several chapters; and he made a careful reading of most of the completed manuscript.

JOHN B. STEWART

*Ottawa*
*June, 1963*

# CONTENTS

# ABBREVIATIONS

All page references to Hume's works are to the editions listed here, unless otherwise indicated in the reference.

*Abstract*          *An Abstract of a Treatise of Human Nature, 1740: A Pamphlet hitherto unknown by David Hume.* Reprinted with an Introduction by J. M. Keynes and P. Sraffa. Cambridge, 1938.

*Dialogues*          *Hume's Dialogues concerning Natural Religion,* 2d. edition. Edited with an Introduction by Norman Kemp Smith. Edinburgh, 1947.

*Enquiry* I          *An Enquiry concerning the Human Understanding.* Edited and introduced by L. A. Selby-Bigge. Oxford, 1902.

*Enquiry* II          *An Enquiry concerning the Principles of Morals.* Edited and introduced by L. A. Selby-Bigge. Oxford, 1902.
(The two *Enquiries* are bound together in this edition.)

*Essays*          *Essays, Moral, Political, and Literary.* 2 vols. Edited, with Preliminary Dissertations and Notes, by T. H. Green and T. H. Grose. London, 1912.

*Letters*          *The Letters of David Hume.* 2 vols. Edited by J. Y. T. Greig. Oxford, 1932.

*History*          *The History of England; A New Edition, with the Author's last Corrections and Improvements.* 8 vols. London, 1778.

*Natural History*          *The Natural History of Religion.* Edited with an Introduction by H. E. Root. London, 1956.

*New Letters*          *New Letters of David Hume.* Edited by Raymond Klibansky and Ernest C. Mossner. Oxford, 1954.

*Treatise*          *A Treatise of Human Nature.* Edited by L. A. Selby-Bigge, Oxford, 1951.

# I

## INTRODUCTION

> I am, or rather was (for that is the style I must now
> use in speaking of myself, which emboldens me the more
> to speak my sentiments) ; I was, I say, a man of mild
> dispositions, of command of temper, of an open, social,
> and cheerful humour, capable of attachment, but little
> susceptible of enmity, and of great moderation in all
> my passions.
>
> "My Own Life," Essays, I, 7–8

H UME'S greatest merit as a philosopher was originality:
whatever he turned to—epistemology, natural theology, economics, political theory, or history—he worked through for
himself. He strove to escape the despotism of words, to ascend
from the level of words to that of meanings, to make words the
vehicles, not the gaols, of thought. This is why the profundity
of his writings is now deemed beyond dispute, even by those
who would never agree for a single moment with his conclusions.

We detract nothing from Hume's right to fame when we admit that he was a man of his age and his country. Many of the
questions with which he struggled are perennial: they are questions that are dealt with anew by each generation because no
answers, however true, are adequate unless a man has achieved
them for himself. Each man comes to these questions from his
own standpoint, and with his own presuppositions and emphases, and what his standpoint shall be is largely a matter of
his time and place. Hume was a man of eighteenth-century
Scotland.

That country was then undergoing extremely rapid transformation. Throughout the four or five previous generations,
at least from the union of the crowns in 1603, although Scotland was drawn closer and closer to England in her political,

economic, and ecclesiastical developments, the main foci of interest were in England, and Scottish thoughts and deeds were
of only minor importance. But in the eighteenth century a new
outlook and a new zeal grew up which, in the short space of fifty
years, transfigured the minds of Scotsmen and the face of Scotland, and put Scottish engineering, agriculture, medicine, economic thought and institutions, political philosophy, and letters
in the vanguard of European civilization. Hume had a highly
original mind; yet it must be conceded that he wrote in an
atmosphere calculated to arouse and evoke the qualities of such
a mind.

Politically, in the eighteenth century the Scots were busy
learning how to employ the mixed constitution of Great Britain
for their own benefit. After the unhappy first seven years of the
Union, those Scottish leaders who did not eliminate themselves
from the ordinary game by Jacobitism seem to have been
chiefly, and openly, interested in the fruits of power. It was
assumed by them that the government was to be supported, and
that their fidelity was to be rewarded by laws favourable to
Scotland and by appointments profitable to themselves. Before
1746 there was some uncertainty as to which of two connections,
the Argathelians or the *Squadrone Volante*, was to serve as the
liasion between Scotland and the government, but after 1746
the Scottish bloc was united, supporting the ruling Whigs until 1760 and the ruling Tories after 1760.[1] Scottish politicians,
who had stifled their own sentiments and ignored the national-
ism of the majority of their people, when they consummated
the union of 1707, and who had been initiated into cynicism
by the English attitude to Scotland's interests, regarded British
politics largely as a matter of Ins and Outs, and were eager to
support the Ins, whoever they might happen to be in terms of
English prejudices, in return for laws advantageous to Scottish
agriculture, manufacturing, and trade, and for jobs and pen-
sions. This simple strategy, together with the electoral system
that prevented vulgar sentiment from frustrating the strategy,
was, as Elie Halévy comments, "one of the weapons she [Scot-
land] employed to conquer England."[2] Almost inevitably, as

Hume learned from personal experience, Scottish politicians were neither loved by the governments nor respected by the oppositions. His pleas for the abandonment of obsolete political ideologies are an eloquent statement of the political "realism" at that time prevalent in ruling circles in Scotland.[3]

Probably even more important as an influence on his thinking than the play of politics, was the contemporary transformation of Scotland's economy. Throughout the seventeenth century Scotland had suffered the worst of both worlds: she had payed for the union of the Scottish and English crowns by enduring governmental neglect of her interests and business at home and abroad; the Thirty Years War had destroyed her trade with the Baltic countries; the wars of Charles II ruined her trade with the Low Countries; and the wars of William III cut her off from France. Moreover, by the Navigation Act, she was excluded from anything like full access to the English market and from the new imperial trade. It was chiefly their awareness of this intolerable situation that made Scotland's political leaders press for the closer union of 1707.

By the time of the union her trade had shrunk to a mere trickle.[4] A desperate attempt finally had been made, through the Darien Scheme, to overcome the effect of the Navigation Act by obtaining a strategically located trading base overseas. But the Scheme failed dismally: not only was Scottish access to world trade unimproved, but an investment valued at somewhat over one-third of Scotland's entire currency had been lost, and a stunning blow had been sustained by her merchants.[5]

Contrary to expectations, the immediate economic effects of the union were bad. The colonies now were open, but the Scottish merchants lacked the resources to plunge heavily into this trade immediately. At the same time, the trade with France was cut off; the heavy salt tax blighted, almost obliterated, the fishing industry; and Scotland's chief line of manufacturing, the spinning and weaving of wool, suffered from competition with finer English goods. It is easy to understand why Scots, who suffered so much from mercantilism, both before and after 1707, soon became bold practitioners of "free trade," and also earnest advocates of its legitimation. But after a while legitimate commerce began to increase: from about 1730 a fresh wind was blowing. The process seems to have begun with the tobacco trade. In 1724, according to Henry Hamilton, 4,192,-576 pounds of tobacco came to the Clyde, and of that total about 3,053,570 pounds were exported. By 1758, Glasgow had become the leading British port in the trade. In 1771, fully 47,268,873 pounds of tobacco were brought into Scotland, and 45,588,720 pounds were exported. Almost as important was the new linen yarn and cloth industry. In 1728 the Board of Trustees for Manufactures, set up in the previous year by Parliament to encourage production with money due to Scotland by the terms of the Treaty of Union as compensation for assuming a share of the English national debt, hitherto unpaid, stamped for sale 2,183,978 yards; in 1750, 7,572,540 yards; in 1760, 11,747,728 yards; and in 1771, 13,466,274 yards.[6] These figures, however spectacular, must not be allowed to obscure the new industriousness that spread throughout the people, and expressed itself in the introduction of sound buildings, good roads and bridges, comfortable furniture, and better clothing.[7]

Throughout the century the basis of the economy was still agriculture, and new attitudes and aspirations were making themselves felt here, too. Subsistence farming, which over the years had made the face of the land naked, bleak, and ugly, and the lower orders poor, lazy, and tolerant of dirt, was gradually supplanted by scientific farming. Throughout the first half of the century no dramatic improvements were made. Nevertheless, these were the years in which foreign ideas and designs were being studied, in which cautious experiments, deemed mad by some and impious by others, were being made by the energetic nobles and gentry, knowledge was being propagated by the Society of Improvers in the Knowledge of Agriculture, and the notion of a new way of rural life was spreading from one landowner to another.[8] The vast metamorphosis of the Lowlands and of some parts of the Highlands that took place between 1750 and 1790 is understandable only when it is remembered that preparations had been underway throughout the previous fifty years. The "run-rig" system was abandoned; instead, plots or "mailings" were combined into large farms and let out on long leases to "substantial tenants." The manuring and liming of the soil became standard practices. Clover and fine grasses were introduced, as were turnips and potatoes. New methods and machines for fanning, threshing, and grinding grains were adopted or invented. Hundreds of millions of trees were planted in hedges, groves, and forests across the hitherto naked land. After both the 1715 and the 1745 risings, the government gave a good deal of attention to the construction and repair of roads leading into the fastnesses of the country. As the economy became productive, a need for commercial arteries came to be felt, and the answer was the Turnpike Act of 1751, which initiated a programme of highway building that was to continue for half a century.

Indirectly but closely connected with this new economic activity were certain notable changes in religion in Scotland. The Act of Union had confirmed the status of the Kirk as the Church of Scotland, established in 1690, but the strong religious genius of the Scots soon produced diversity. What is important for our purposes is that the religious differences of the eighteenth century paralleled somewhat the line of social cleavage between the nobles and gentry and the labouring poor. The policies of Charles I and Charles II had discouraged men of outstanding ability and education from entering the Presbyterian ministry. It is not surprising, therefore, that although popular religion in Scotland lost some of its militancy, it remained highly dogmatic and enthusiastic throughout much of the eighteenth century. In contrast, as soon as the nobles and gentry had turned from politico-religious wars and intrigues and had begun to spend their time and energies in agriculture and commerce, they began to favour a more generous, less assured style of preaching, with somewhat more attention to refined morality and somewhat less to dramatic conversion, the joys of the elect, and the agonies of the damned. As if to meet the demand, Francis Hutcheson (1694–1746) and William

Leechman (1706–85), among others, at Glasgow University particularly, were busy training young men in the new philosophies and the more humane theology.

The practical point on which conflict occurred was the "calling" of ministers. In 1712, as part of a general attempt to weaken the hold of Presbyterianism, "unalterably secured" only five years before, lay patronage, abolished in 1690, was restored; thus the nobles and gentry were put in a position to promote the Moderate cause even in resolutely Evangelical parishes. By the middle of the century the Moderates had achieved a majority in the General Assembly of the Church, and they numbered among their leaders some of the most notable men in Scotland's history: William Robertson, historian and Principal of Edinburgh University; Robert Wallace, scholar and eminent preacher; Hugh Blair, author of *Lectures on Rhetoric;* John Home, whose play, *Douglas,* caused one of the most acute ecclesiastical tremors of the century; and Alexander "Jupiter" Carlyle. But even in this period of Moderate dominance, this "Midnight of the Kirk," the Evangelicals (or "High-flyers"), although lacking both votes and notables in the Assembly, were far from negligible, for the people at large retained their old tastes and loyalties, as the great Disruption (1843) would eventually demonstrate.

Hume's writings on religion fit into this scene. His Calvinist upbringing, in which salvation was either a matter of predestination or of dramatic conversion, neither of which he found understandable, rather than a slow curing of the soul, led him to treat religious questions primarily as logical questions. Because he refused to accept the fashionable deistic answers, he became an advocate of "moderate scepticism" and revealed religion. And when he turned his attention to the beliefs and practices of popular religions, both historical and contemporary, he found much that he thought required explanation.

Although he stayed at a discreet distance from almost all the great arenas of public life until he had completed his writings, and although he never wrote as a party spokesman, Hume's thought, obviously, did not take place in a vacuum; indeed, it can be argued that it was his extraordinary sensitivity to, and interest in, the economic, intellectual, religious, and political transactions of his own day that prompted his thought. He was a Scot, a Lowlander, by birth a Presbyterian, and a member of the gentry; and he was a man of the eighteenth century. Many of the questions with which he grappled are perennial, but the ways in which he took them up, and the answers he gave, are those of an eighteenth-century Scot, a man born a Presbyterian, and a member of the Lowland gentry.

Unlike Thomas Hobbes and John Locke, he was not caught up as a participant in great political events. He was born in 1711, and therefore was too young to become involved in the conflict of opinion attending the last crises, in 1714 and 1715, of the English constitutional revolution. The illness that caused his death in 1776 had begun before Great Britain was shaken by the Revolution in the American colonies and in Europe, and by the industrial revolution. The years between were comparatively peaceful and quiet, disturbed only by the Jacobite rising of 1745, by fairly remote foreign wars, and by the squabbling of the political parties at Westminster. Hume lived in a time when an able thinker could avoid political entanglements if he chose. Only in the years after 1763, after he had completed his philosophical works and the *History of England*, was he drawn into public affairs. Up until then he had lived as a writer, almost as a solitary writer. His philosophical interest seems to have been aroused early, and thoroughly, at some time between 1723 and 1725, while he was still a student at the University of Edinburgh. The twenty years after he left the university were given over to reading, thinking, and composing, chiefly at his family home at Ninewells, near Berwick. Early in 1734 he spent a few months at Bristol as a merchant's clerk, but he soon gave this up, determined to succeed as a man of letters, and went to France, where he spent the next three years writing, chiefly at La Flèche, in Anjou. In September, 1737, he returned from France, and passed sixteen months at London, polishing the first two books of his projected *Treatise of Human Nature*, and in negotiations with publishers. The books,

"Of the Understanding" and "Of the Passions," were brought out late in January of 1739, and the following spring Hume returned to Ninewells. There he resided until 1745. In the autumn of 1739 he wrote his *Abstract of A Treatise of Human Nature,* a kind of blurb which was published anonymously early in 1740. In November, 1740, the third and final book of the *Treatise,* the book, "Of Morals," appeared. Then, in 1741, he brought out a volume of fifteen essays. In 1742 he published a volume of twelve essays. The following three years probably were spent in recasting the first book of the unsuccessful *Treatise,* in mining out some of the argument in "Of Morals," in composing the two religious works published much later, and in thinking through the argument to be expounded in the economic essays.

The four years 1745 to 1749 were disrupted. In 1745, after his candidacy for a professorial chair at the University of Edinburgh had failed because of the unpopularity of his religious views, he obtained his first post, other than that of a Bristol clerk, when he was appointed as the companion to the mad Marquis of Annandale. This employment was terminated after a little more than one year had elapsed.[9] But he was immediately invited by his kinsman, General James St. Clair, to accompany him as private secretary on an expedition against Quebec. After several months of waiting at Portsmouth and Plymouth, the expedition was called off, and the fleet was redirected against the coast of Brittany. By the fall of 1747 he was back in London. Then, after a visit to Scotland, he accompanied General St. Clair, again as his private secretary, on a diplomatic mission to the courts of Vienna and Turin. The only major work published in this period was *Philosophical Essays concerning Human Understanding,* the revision of "Of the Understanding," which came out in 1748.[10]

By early summer 1749, he had returned to Ninewells, and there he remained until the marriage of his older brother, John, in 1751. He and his sister, Katherine, then moved, first to Berwick, and later to Edinburgh. In that year he brought out *An Enquiry concerning the Principles of Morals.* The following year saw the publication of his famous *Political Discourses*, in which he treats chiefly of economic questions.

The ten years between 1752 and 1762, during which, with the exception of a fourteen-month sojourn in London in 1758–59, he remained at Edinburgh, were given over mainly to assiduous research and writing on the history of England. The only philosophical work published in this period was the *Natural History of Religion*, which appeared in the volume, *Four Dissertations*, in 1757.

During all this early period his life, like that of a professor, was remote from contemporary politics. Naturally, he was interested in events, and, given his close friendships with Scotland's leading lawyers and politicians, undoubtedly he was extremely well informed, but no cause, except that of moderation, enlisted his practical support. His writings, both the theoretical works and the *History of England*, are remarkably free from partisan political bias. When the former were criticized, much of the animus of the criticism was religious, for religion was a subject on which Hume did have strong and controversial views. His *History* comforted neither the Whigs nor the Tories, and therefore drew cries of denunciation from both camps.

In 1763 he was chosen unexpectedly by Lord Hertford, the new ambassador to France, as secretary to the embassy. At first he performed his duties without either the title or the appointed stipend, but later, through the efforts of Hertford and Hume's friends in London, he was given both. For a few months, after the recall of Lord Hertford, he served as *chargé d'affaires*. In January, 1766, he returned to England: on this occasion he brought with him Jean-Jacques Rousseau, thus embroiling himself in the most unpleasant, unseemly commotion of his entire life. From February, 1767, until January, 1768, he served as undersecretary of state, northern department. After leaving office, he lingered a while in London, but in 1769 he returned to Edinburgh, where he resided until his death. During this final period, although he was not busy with distracting appointments, no new works, except one essay, were added to the corpus of his writings. In 1779 the *Dialogues concerning Natural*

*Religion* were published by his nephew; but these had been written long before.

Hume's disengagement from practical affairs during the productive, early period of his life must not be permitted to mislead us. For Scotland, those years, as we have seen, were years of profound intellectual and religious change, of vast economic and social reorganization, and of political reorientation; Hume was so profoundly concerned by these developments that we may regard him as the chief advocate of the new Scotland, even as the chief advocate of the new Britain.

He is often described as a "moral philosopher." This is a term which, with the division and subdivision of subject matter in modern universities, has lost its meaning. When applied to Hume, it does not mean that he was a moralizing philosopher. Early in the nineteenth century, Hegel, in his introduction to the *Philosophy of History*, sought to state clearly the difference between the realm of external nature and the realm of *geist*.[11] The same distinction is made when Hume is called a "moral philosopher." In common with his contemporaries, he assumed that the basic division in the fields of knowledge is that between physical and moral subjects. As a moral philosopher, he had taken as his province not merely private conduct, not even private and public conduct, but all kinds of purposeful activity consequent to human judgments of good and bad. By "moral subjects" he meant what we might call "historical subjects," those treating of subject matter in which the changes that take place, and that are described in histories, are traced not to physical causes, but to "human" causes. Moral subjects are what we, for lack of better terms, probably would call, "the humanities" and "the social sciences." They are the subjects that treat of human action in private or in civil conduct, of human expression or production in the arts, and of the standards by which such action or expression is evaluated. The concern of the moral philosopher, the range of subject matter encompassed by "moral subjects," is neatly summarized by Hume himself in his essay, "Of National Characters." Therein he argues that the characteristics of different professional groups, such as merchants and soldiers, are results of moral, not physical, causes. He writes:

By *moral* causes I mean all circumstances, which are fitted to work on the mind as motives or reasons, and which render a peculiar set of manners habitual to us. Of this kind are, the nature of the government, the revolutions of public affairs, the plenty or penury in which the people live, the situation of the nation with regard to its neighbours, and such like circumstances. By *physical* causes I mean those qualities of the air and climate, which are supposed to work insensibly on the temper, by altering the tone and habit of the body, and giving a particular complexion, which, though reflection and reason may sometimes overcome it, will yet prevail among the generality of mankind, and have an influence on their manners.[12]

As a very young man he had become discontented with the condition of the sciences. Many of the philosophers (scientists), misled by ignorance or ulterior interest, discharged their energy in winning mere rhetorical victories, and instead of bringing enlightenment, thereby cast a dark, sulphurous smog over their own minds and those of others. The vulgar, consequently, tended to regard the sciences as useless and contemptible.[13] Hume thought he could help to remedy this sorry situation. He thought that he had discovered how men understand the subject matter of all the sciences.

It is clear that the two writers who contributed most to his thought were Isaac Newton and Francis Hutcheson. The former, following Bacon and others, had given all philosophers a sound example by seeking to do no more than to observe and to describe the operation of the objects he studied. He had not sought to make judgments (of reality) beyond the scope of the human understanding. The latter had emphasized the contribution made by human nature in the (value) judgment of beauty. It may have been that "the new Scene of Thought" that Hume says opened up before him was illuminated by the idea that the answer to the question of how we can reason about the world around us, a world which, according to Newton, we know only by observation, may be that our judgments of reality, like our judgments of value, arise in part from human nature.[14] In any case, this is the fundamental argument of Hume's first published work, *A Treatise of Human Nature.*

What is needed in all the sciences, physical and moral alike, Hume proposes, is critical reappraisal, followed by careful reconstruction. Since the sciences are systems or provinces of human knowledge, they take their forms and limits from the nature of human beings. To be accurate they must be in conformity with the principles on which the human mind operates. They can encompass no knowledge attainable only in ways alien to, or beyond the capacity of, the human mind. If the sciences are to be improved, human nature—man, the knower—must be studied.

In some sciences human nature enters only as the knower. The sciences, men's knowledge of the objects known, depend on the subjects of knowledge, on the men who know the objects, but also on objects which are known. In the case of these sciences—Hume mentions mathematics, natural philosophy, and natural religion—the objects are independent of man. But in other sciences—Hume names logic, morals, politics, and criticism—human nature enters as both the subject and the object of knowledge, as both the knower and the known.[15] It is with this second group that Hume chose to deal in his *Treatise.*

His emphasis on man as knower explains the great concern for method shown by the subtitle of the *Treatise*, which is, "An ATTEMPT to introduce the experimental Method of Reasoning into MORAL SUBJECTS." It is by "the experimental method," as Newton showed, he contends, that men know the natural world, and this method, and no other, should be employed by both physical and moral philosophers.[16] All that a philosopher can do to know nature, either human nature or external nature, is to observe it so as to be able to describe it, and to observe any changes so as to be able to say what the causes of any particular effect are. It is no detriment of "the experimental method" that it only discovers what things do, not what their essence is, for just what the essence of nature is, human beings cannot know, and this is as true of human nature as of external nature. We must notice that for Hume "the experimental method" does not require that the philosopher (scientist) contrive cases, instances, or experiments; rather, it entails only the exact observation of cases, either contrived or fortuitous.

Hume is careful not to submerge the difference between moral and physical subjects. The nature studied in physical subjects is only part of nature. The nature studied in moral subjects, too, is only part of nature. Both are the same in that they are natural, i.e., part of the same universe. Each is different from the other in that one is physical, and the other moral, and this difference has to be taken into account in the use of the method. Answers to questions about physical subjects can be achieved by designing tests and experiments, and provided that the procedures are reliable, the laboratory report will be reliable. But since consciousness can cause changes in human conduct, reports on moral subjects cannot be collected in this casual way.[17] Rather, we must rely chiefly on the data supplied by our own daily observations and in histories.

At some time, early in his life, Hume may have projected a kind of encyclopedia of all the sciences.[18] This would have comprised three main parts. The first would discover the principles by which men know all that they know. Then, on the one hand, would be a set of books, each treating of one of those sciences into which man enters only as a knower, e.g., mathematics, natural philosophy, and, possibly, natural religion. And, on the other, would be the "moral sciences," those in which he enters as both knower and known. This third part, treating of morals, politics, and artistic behaviour, would be subdivided into three levels: first, the description of motivating feelings; second, the discovery of the way in which judgments of value are made; and, finally, a book on each of the main fields in which value judgments are fundamental, i.e., morals, criticism, and politics.

Whatever his early aspiration, when he was ready to begin publishing, he had limited his endeavours to those sciences which "more intimately concern human life," that is, he excluded entirely the second of our three parts. In the first of the two books published in 1739, "Of the Understanding," he gives us the first of our three parts: therein he treats of man's cognitive faculty. In the second, "Of the Passions," he gives us the first of the three levels in the third part: therein he describes the motivating feelings. Hume, in his Advertisement, writes: "The subjects of the understanding and passions make a compleat chain of reasoning by themselves." While "Of the Understanding" explains how men know, the second book, "Of the Passions," treats of the second of the two contributions that human nature makes to the complex which he designates as "morals, politics, and criticism." The passions native to man, directed and refined by the creative power of knowledge, find their expression in the facts, laws, and standards studied by moral philosophers. These two books go together in that both are more fundamental than, and provide the raw materials for, the activities studied in the moral sciences.[19]

In the Advertisement he promises, provided only that his labours are rewarded by public approval, to proceed "to the examination of morals, politics, and criticism," and announces that this "will compleat this Treatise of human nature." Eventually, he published only one more book in the *Treatise*, the book, "Of Morals." However, his threefold promise and the title of the one book that did appear can lead to misunderstandings about the structure of the *Treatise*. At the start of the book, "Of Morals," he commented sadly: "Without this advantage [the great interest men naturally have in moral questions] I never should have ventur'd upon a third volume of such abstruse philosophy, in an age, wherein the greatest part of men seem agreed to convert reading into an amusement, and to reject every thing that requires any considerable degree of attention to be comprehended." [20] In the short autobiography, "My Own Life": he writes that the *Treatise*, a juvenile work, "fell dead-born from the press, without reaching such distinction, as even to excite a murmur among the zealots." This evidence seems to suggest that when Hume returned from France he was prepared, or at least thought he was prepared, to publish a vast work, a work resembling a giant, spreading tree in its

structure, and that he abandoned the project because the failure of the books published in 1739, followed by the failure of
"Of Morals," published in 1740, forced him to conclude that an
unknown writer could not win fame or even an audience among
the learned, let alone the conversible world, with long, studious
tomes. His Advertisement, this argument runs, foretells of at
least three books beyond the first two. Only one was published.
Surely, therefore, "Of Morals" is only one-third of what we
were led to expect.

It seems probable, however, that "Of Morals" contains the
greater part of what Hume had planned to write. When we
read the book carefully we find that it contains, not the examination of a single moral subject, as the title read together with
the Advertisement might lead us to expect, but discussions of
three different kinds of conduct. Besides, it is clear that Hume's
treatments of these three kinds of conduct—personal conduct,
economic conduct, and conduct in the state—are not intended
as independent pieces. "Of Morals" is primarily an exposition
of Hume's theory of value judgment.

Very early in his life, probably when he was about eighteen,
and probably under the influence of Hutcheson, he had come to
think that he had discovered a principle that would enable him
to construct a complete and unified system encompassing all
moral (mind) subjects. Judgments and acts have two sets of
causes. Judgments are formed about many different kinds of
things, and acts are of as many different kinds. The nature of
the different things judged and found good or bad—economic
"goods," works of art, charitable or malicious acts, the laws
made by a government—enter into the judgment. Each thing
judged is judged according to its kind. The acts that men do to
acquire and promote what they find "good," and to avoid what
they find "bad" or "evil," are of different kinds, suitable to the
particular goods or evils they have in mind. Concentration on
the different things approved and sought, or disapproved and
avoided if possible, leads to the recognition of different moral
subjects, such as economics, politics, ethics, and aesthetics, and
to subdivisions within these. Hume voiced no objection to such

specialization. What did annoy him was the bewilderment prevailing among philosophers about what is meant by "good" and "bad," or by "virtuous" and "vicious," and he thought that he had come to know how this bewilderment could be overcome. The second set of causes producing a judgment and an act is common to all judgments and all acts: judgments are made by men, and acts are done by them. The common set of causes is what we call "human nature." It is because their own nature is as it is that men call many diverse things "good," and it is because of their own nature that they desire what they call "good." Hume, in short, had decided that the theory of judgment applied by Hutcheson to beauty only was valid for all value judgment. This was the principle that he hoped to demonstrate by applying the experimental method to moral subjects.

"Of Morals" was written to set forth the general principle that Hume thought explained all value judgments in all moral subjects; namely, that virtuous or good conduct in all kinds of relations among people is conduct useful or agreeable to the actor or to his associates. He treats personal conduct, economic activity, and political conduct not as independent topics but as the evidence bearing out this basic principle. In short, "Of Morals" is the second level of our third part: it shows how judgments of value are made.

It may be that Hume never settled down to draw together into separate books his thoughts on politics, criticism, and ethics. If he did, what happened is that he, perhaps deliberately because he was too discouraged to plan to continue the *Treatise*, or perhaps unavoidably because of the demands of his undertaking, used much of his basic material on politics, ethics, and criticism in the exposition of his theory of value judgment. The one listed moral subject slighted in "Of Morals" is criticism: the book contains only two or three comments on the agreeableness of wit. It is clear, however, that Hume believes that his principle applies in the arts, too. Since this book deals chiefly with conduct, rather than with production or expression, the absence of a more extensive treatment of criticism is not surprising. In short, although it does not conform to what seems to have been the original plan, although it seems truncated because the parts of the third level are subsumed in the second, the *Treatise* is complete in its essentials.

It is the greatest of Hume's works. Unlike the other, later works, it stands in some parts unpolished, and in others without its full development, a kind of Carcassonne of thought in which the builder had lost his joy, but not before the keep had been completed and the main towers and walls had been erected. His later philosophical works are lesser, not because his genius declined, but, because, although presented as separate edifices, they are structures anticipated or implied in the *Treatise*. Without a thorough change of mind, he could neither rear towers higher than those in "Of the Understanding," nor produce a work which did not depend on the *Treatise*. Its nearest rival is the posthumous *Dialogues concerning Natural Religion;* this, however, although the genre is different, is a work central to the original undertaking and forecast in the introduction to the *Treatise*.

Hume's disappointment with the fate of his great work did not end his search for wisdom; rather, the search was over, although a good deal of consolidation and elaboration was still required, when he gave up the *Treatise*. By 1740 he had worked out his theory of "moral subjects"; thereafter, in one way or another, he put that theory before the public. In other words, his later writings are not radically new undertakings; instead, they can best be understood as applications and extrapolations of the principles set forth in the *Treatise*.

In the first of the essays which he brought out in 1741 he made it clear that hereafter he would perform the role of "a Kind of Resident or Ambassador from the Dominions of Learning to those of Conversation; and shall think it my constant Duty to promote a good Correspondence betwixt these two States, which have so great a Dependence on each other." [21] In this capacity, as an ambassador between the two elegant parts of mankind, the learned and the conversible, he was both active and successful. The volume published in 1741 contained fifteen essays. The next volume, published in the following year, contained twelve more. In the new edition brought out in 1748 he added three more. Then, in 1752, in the volume entitled, *Political Discourses*, came twelve pieces. Three more were added later, two in 1758, and one in 1777, thus bringing the total number of those published to forty-five. Of these, eight, all from the volumes published in 1741 and 1742, were subsequently dropped in later editions. This great collection of essays can be fruitfully studied apart from the *Treatise;* but they are most easily understood when treated as extensions and applications of the tenets set forth in "Of Morals." After the *Treatise* itself, these essays are the most important source of Hume's social and political thought.

Even before his success as a writer had been fully established by these essays, Hume had begun to salvage as much as possible from the *Treatise*. He surveyed it, and succeeded in separating out two major independent works, the *Philosophical Essays concerning Human Understanding*, which appeared in 1748, and *An Enquiry concerning the Principles of Morals*, which appeared in 1751. The former is a popularized version of the first book, "Of the Understanding." It is a composition ostensibly in "the easy style and manner, which draw not too much from life, require no deep application or retreat to be comprehended, and send back the student among mankind full of noble sentiments and wise precepts, applicable to every exigence of human life." [22] The latter, in contrast, is not a simplified version of "Of Morals"; rather, it is based on only one part of the argument in that book. One of his *Four Dissertations*, of 1757, is a précis or summary of the remnants of the second book, "Of the Passions." These three works contain little that is new, but since, in them, Hume takes especial care to keep his arguments brief, and to write simply, they are often helpful to the reader who easily may become lost in the intricacies of the *Treatise*.

Similarly, both Hume's major works on religion rise out of the *Treatise*. In 1737, after his return from France, he wrote from London to his cousin, Henry Home, later Lord Kames, that, "I am at present castrating my work, that is, cutting off its nobler parts; that is, endeavouring it shall give as little offense as possible." [23] This clearly refers to the passages used in 1748 in the *Philosophical Essays concerning Human Understanding* under the titles, "Of Miracles" and "Of a particular Providence and of a future State." It may also refer to some of the material used in the *Dialogues concerning Natural Religion*. In any case, in 1751 he wrote to Gilbert Elliot about the argument in the *Dialogues;* and his letter shows that that work was even then almost in its final form. Among the essays published in 1741 is one, "Of Superstition and Enthusiasm," dealing with the causes of two forms of erroneous belief. The work, *The Natural History of Religion*, published as one of the *Four Dissertations*, stems from that early essay.

Moreover, his vast *History of England*, which by reason of its scope and artistry seems an entirely independent work, when examined closely will be found, as we shall see in chapter 9, to be inspired by an argument drawn directly from the third book of the *Treatise*.

Intellectual and religious insecurity, emphasis on the natural sciences, a new commercial and industrial way of life, and the conduct of public business by institutionalized parties—all these are standard features of the modern western world. Hume was present when this world was being ushered in, and felt challenged to expound all its main features in a summa of the moral sciences. Although this great work was never completed, the *Treatise* and his subsequent writings constitute a system of thought which is not only highly unified, but quite valuable as a description of the rock and the sand on which our modern world is built.

# II

## BELIEF: FALSE AND

## AUTHENTIC

The sole end of logic is to explain the principles and
operations of our reasoning faculty, and the nature of
our ideas.

*Treatise*, p. xix

"O F THE Understanding," the first book in Hume's *Treatise of Human Nature*, of all his works has been the most carefully examined by modern writers on philosophy. No protest can be made against this particular concentration of attention, for the book is both the most basic and the most difficult of his works; indeed, it stands prominent among the most profound works in all philosophical literature. Besides, this book can be studied quite successfully even if the other two parts of the *Treatise*, the books, "Of the Passions" and "Of Morals," are ignored. This does not mean, however, that the student of Hume's moral and political theory—and Hume was primarily a moral and political theorist—can ignore "Of the Understanding" on the ground that it belongs peculiarly to, and interests only, the metaphysicians and epistemologists.

In it Hume seeks to explain the experimental method of acquiring knowledge, and advocates that this method be adopted deliberately by all scientists (philosophers). He writes, not to begin, but to complete a revolution in thought. The experimental method, the method of learning by which men rely on either fortuitous or contrived experience, he argues, is no peculiar fad taken up by a few natural philosophers; rather, what those philosophers have done is to revert to the method by which all men ordinarily acquire knowledge, more or less accurate, about the physical and moral worlds around them. This basically is the method we all use to learn the nature of men and of things. Even those thinkers who, in their closets, seek a knowledge more esoteric than experience can produce, resort to experience, and are content with its results, as soon as they have put down their pens and come forth. The only innovation made by natural philosophers such as Newton is that they have carried this familiar method into the learned sciences, and therein have applied it consciously and, therefore, carefully. They have transformed it into experimentation. In "Of the Understanding" Hume tries to show the fundamental importance of learning by experience, tries to distinguish experience from the other ways of acquiring knowledge, and tries to have its limits accepted as inherent and inevitable; consequently, the book, an attempt to explain the experimental method and its epistemological implications, becomes a full-fledged treatment of the knowing faculty. Accordingly, it commands the attention of modern metaphysicians and epistemologists. But it is important to the student of Hume's moral and political theory also. First, the standards of artistic judgment, the political system, and the system of morals prevailing at any time are for Hume the products of the passions and of knowledge, and much of this knowledge comes to men, hitherto generally unconsciously, through experience; therefore, the process by which those systems and standards come into existence, and change, cannot be explained if "Of the Understanding" is ignored. And second, the book sets forth the method which Hume proposes should be used, not only in the natural sciences, but in the study of human nature proper and in the ancillary sciences of morals, politics, and criticism.

This book, and the later revision, *An Enquiry concerning Human Understanding*, are complicated works, rich with proofs, compelling in clarity, and with passages of unsurpassed philosophic prose. Their basic argument, nevertheless, can be stated baldly. It is that there are five, and only five, basic ways of knowing: intuiting, remembering, fancying, demonstrative reasoning, and believing. These five, and especially demonstrative reasoning and believing, should be distinguished clearly

from one another.[1] By believing, as a result of experience, we
have ideas which are beliefs, and such beliefs ought not to be dis-
paraged by closet philosophers, who, while they yearn for
knowledge beyond the ken of human beings, rely on these beliefs in their mundane affairs. Outside our intuition and remembrance, all our knowledge about human beings and the rest
of the world past and future is made up of beliefs. The rise of
authentic beliefs and the rise of false beliefs—an authentic
belief is not necessarily correct, and a false belief might turn
out to be correct—ought to be understood. This is the argument we must now explore.

In the first of the four parts which constitute "Of the Understanding" Hume analyzes perception at the most elementary
level. Here he begins the exposition of his own theory of knowledge, which is set forth fully in the third part. But here, and in
the second part, he is also demolishing, without much announce-
ment, the foundations on which were based the rationalistic
theories of morals and politics current in the eighteenth century.

Knowing is perceiving, in Hume's language. We are aware
of nothing, we know nothing, other than the perceptions we
perceive. What is not perceived is not known.

Immediately we must make two general comments. The first
is that Hume never tries to compare perception (the function
of knowing) with anything else. He never treats it as a variety
—to be related to the other varieties—of some more inclusive
operation. Perceiving for him is the one and only way of knowing. Any reader, he assumes, will recognize what knowing in
general is. Hume's description of knowing, therefore, is always
analytic, the indicating and naming of the different methods of
knowing, which sometimes, but not always, are confused by the
ordinary man. And the second comment, a corollary of the first,
is that the differences discovered by his analysis do not—and we
should not permit them to lead us to think that they do—destroy the unity of knowing. We are dealing with the different
ways of knowing (perceiving). At the ultimate level the differences disappear.

Hume seems to have written the first part in "Of the Understanding" as a convenient portal by which his system might be entered.[2] In this he is almost too successful. What he says there seems so perspicuous, and the terse manner in which it is said seems so conclusive, that even the reader who persists with constant attention through the arduous, winding passages to the end of the book may still think of those first pages as an adequate synopsis of Hume's thought. Perhaps the most deceptive passage in the entire *Treatise* is the first paragraph, wherein Hume refers to the difference between "impressions" and "ideas."[3] He seems to say that impressions (feelings) and ideas (thoughts) are vastly different, that impressions have none of the characteristics of ideas, and that ideas have nothing in common with impressions. The sharp contrast is reduced somewhat by the reference to ideas as "the faint images" of impressions, but it still remains great. If in reading the book this opening paragraph is treated as an adequate, although abbreviated, statement of Hume's theory of the relation between impressions and ideas, almost everything in the third part, in which he seeks to explain how we understand "reality," and in its sequel, the fourth part, wherein he shows why errors have been made by earlier philosophers, would have to be abandoned as unintelligible.

The paragraph is misleading in two important ways. First, it seems to imply that we are not thinking when we are perceiving an impression, as we are when we are perceiving an idea. Hume does not treat this point directly, but what he says in "Of Abstract Ideas" makes plain his assumption that there is no such difference between impressions and ideas.[4] Thought is not excluded from the perception of an impression, and feeling is not excluded from the perception of an idea. Both feeling and thought are involved in every perception. We know whatever is known as an impression, i.e., we know it as a sensation or a passion. We know it by one or more of the five senses, or, if it is a passion, we feel it as anger, joy, etc. But we are seldom totally submerged in the feeling, and lost in it. We also know it with some degree of objectivity, i.e., as being a particular kind of impression, one resembling certain other impressions which we remember, and differing from others. We probably call it by its own name, and can say intelligibly that we have a feeling of coldness, sweetness, joyousness, or pride. When for the first time we hear a bell ringing in the distance, we at once detect that this sound is not that of a drum or bugle, which fortunately we already know from experience; if somebody explains the new sound to us, and tells us the name of its cause, a bell, we thereafter recognize that sound. If we see a white disc, we recognize that it is neither blue nor a cube. When we begin to feel anger or weariness, we relate these feelings to others, such as disgust or sadness, and can say that we are weary or angry. Similarly, when we perceive an idea, we have an appropriate feeling. If we read that Agamemnon felt love or hatred rise within him, we know fairly well what or how he is supposed to have felt. Hume does not separate feeling and thinking, and thus leave the former blind and the latter empty. Second, the paragraph can easily be misread as stating that ideas cannot have any of the vividness that makes us accept a perception as convincing or reliable.[5]

However, again and again in the *Treatise,* Hume insists that "impressions and ideas differ only in their strength and vivacity." [6] They "differ only in degree, not in nature." [7] His repeated references to ideas as "images" of impressions does seem to suggest a difference in nature between them, but we must recall that he also speaks about ideas of ideas as "images." [8] That is, the word, "image," is not to be taken as meaning that feeling and thinking are separate. It means merely that impressions are prior to ideas in time.[9] It is as impressions that particular perceptions "make their first appearance in the soul." Ideas are *reproductions* of impressions. The distinction to which Hume is here referring is the one we all make between our perceptions of the present, the "here and now," and our perceptions of the unpresent in either time or place. There is no difference between the former and the latter, he argues, except that the former, the "impressions," have a high degree of strength, vividness, or impressiveness that causes us to distinguish between the present and the unpresent—between impressions and ideas—and when this fails, as it sometimes does, we are bewildered.[10]

The second distinction to which Hume calls our attention in his opening pages is that between simple and complex perceptions. Every distinct thing and being in the world—apples, gold, houses, horses—has many different attributes. Nothing that exists has only one characteristic or attribute, e.g., is simply yellow, simply malleable, or simply soluble in *aqua regia*. A particular simple perception, e.g., yellow, can be known only by abstraction, only by divorcing in our minds this one quality from all the other qualities of the thing we are examining.

There is, Hume contends, an exact balance between a man's simple ideas, that is, his ideas (thoughts) of single attributes, and that man's past and present impressions (feelings, either sensations or passions) of single attributes. Nobody can know as an idea any quality or attribute which he himself has not first known as a present perception, i.e., as an impression. But this is not true of complex perceptions. If immediately after we have surveyed a strange city from a high place, we try to recall the prospect of roofs, spires, and avenues so recently spread before us, our idea of it will be defective. Moreover, after we have turned away and have begun to forget, our idea of the city resembles our original perception of it less and less. Or let us consider another experiment. Let us think of—make up by assembling attributes—a very complete griffin, with needle-sharp claws, a mane of bright gold, a voice like a trumpet, and diverse suitable qualities. Each of the ingredients here included —which we may regard as simple ideas, without breaking them down into their constituent attributes—is one of which we have had an impression, but the complex idea, the idea of the whole beast, is not a reproduction of an impression. This is a complex idea to which no complex impression conforms.

Hume is deeply concerned with a third distinction that we all make. This one, the distinction between perceptions of unreal things and fictitious happenings, on the one hand, and perceptions of things and happenings in "the real world," on the other, is Hume's chief topic in "Of the Understanding." We never doubt that some perceptions are reliable, that they give us genuine knowledge. Others we dismiss as "mere ideas." To account for this distinction between the real and the unreal, and thus to define the boundaries of "the real world," beyond which natural knowledge cannot go, is the central problem of epistemology. Hume's argument is that we do not make this distinction by comparing the beings we perceive with another set of beings, called Real Beings; rather, the distinction is made by comparing perceptions one with another. Since all are perceptions, any difference among them must be in respect of some quality not essential to a perception. It is Hume's contention that some perceptions have for us a strength, vividness, or impressiveness that other perceptions lack. This difference is the decisive factor when we take them as reliable or unreliable sources of knowledge about the real world. All perceptions are convincing, to the extent that they are impressive. We never doubt that vivid perceptions are reliable—epistemologically, their vividness and their power to convince us are the same quality.

The reason why Hume begins the *Treatise* by calling attention to the distinction between perceptions of the present ("impressions") and perceptions of the unpresent ("ideas") now is evident. The present, our present, the "here and now"—this is the moment of reality for us. What we regard as present, we also regard as real. When we speak of things and happenings in remote places and times as "real," we mean that if we were at the appropriate place and time those things and happenings would then be present to us. The test of the reality of a perception, its impressiveness, is met perfectly by a perception of the present; and therefore we call such a perception, an "impression." Here, we may notice that the vividness, the feeling of "force and violence," to which Hume refers, is not to be confused with any particular feeling of sensation or passion in a perception. We can, for example, think of Agamemnon feeling anger or love without being led by our idea of him to believe that there ever was a real man named Agamemnon. What Hume is talking about is a "sense" or feeling of authenticity which distinguishes the genuine from the reproduction. He, we may also notice, does not define the words "vivid" and "impressive" except by trying to have the reader recognize the feeling of authenticity which those words denote. Since he has made the evidence of their authenticity inherent in authentic perceptions, this is the only procedure available. The distinction between the real and the unreal is one we all make repeatedly each day. Animals, too, make it. For example, a cat that concludes that, after all, there is no mouse under the sofa knows the difference between a real mouse and a nonexistent mouse. If the factor decisive to the decision were external to the perception, e.g., if to discover whether or not our perceptions are reliable we had to compare each of them with "the real Being and Existence of things, or with their Archtypes," [11] it would be unlikely that busy and ignorant beings, such as we are, acting thoughtlessly most of the time, as we do, could survive. Hume's argument is that some perceptions are impressive for us, while others are not. The former we accept as reliable; the latter we reject. If his readers do not know the difference between a perception which they accept as giving reliable knowledge of reality and one which they do not believe, they will be unable to guess, and he will be unable to tell them what he is writing about. He will be in the position of a teacher trying to define the word "colour" for a child blind from birth.

We never have any doubts about the reliability of our perceptions of the present.[12] We always accept anything present in time and place as real. This is true for both simple and complex impressions. We never doubt that the city we now see, hear, and smell is real. Simple and complex impressions always convince us. Even when in a dream we see a spectre, we regard it as real, while we are dreaming.

It is when we come to our perceptions of the unpresent, to our "ideas," that we distinguish between the real and the unreal. Our simple ideas give us no trouble. We regard every attribute of which we can think, as existing, or at least as having once existed. Every attribute of which we can think has been present with us at some time. But our perceptions of things and happenings which no longer are present, or which have never been present with us—the perceptions which Hume calls "complex ideas"—always require that we sit in conscious or unconscious judgment on them. Some of these perceptions we find impressive, and therefore we regard them as reliable. Others we find unimpressive, and therefore we dismiss them. The latter, unlike the former, are mere ideas, bare and inert, devoid of the power that convinces. If we think of Katmandu, our idea of that city, which we have never seen, is more than a mere idea; so we say that we believe that Katmandu is real. If we think of the Land of Prester John, our idea of that land, which likewise we have never visited, is a mere idea; so we say that we do not believe that the Land of Prester John is real. The former idea has an impressiveness for us that the latter lacks. Now, why is it that the perceptions of some things once regarded as present, e.g., a spectre in a dream, although impressive when seen, and therefore treated as real then, lose their impressiveness rapidly, and became inert, incapable of moving us, quite soon after we begin to think normally again? And how is it that perceptions of some things which have never been present to us, e.g., Katmandu or Merovingian France, are sufficiently impressive to be regarded as perceptions of reality, while other such perceptions are dismissed? This difference in the impressiveness of these ideas has to be explained.

It is a difference of the greatest importance, for it is in the world real to us that we live, and by far the greater part of our reality is composed of what we accept as reliable thoughts. The "here and now" is only the small, moving centre of our field of reality. By thinking, we push out from this centre into the remote past, into distant places, and into the future. The constitution of reality, as known to us, is the basis of most of our instinctive, and all our deliberate judgments and acts. We know, without pausing to calculate about gravity and our anatomy, that we shall be hurt if we walk over the edge of a cliff or fall out of bed, and, without ratiocination, we avoid these happenings. We know without pondering long that under next summer's sun the sands will be warm. We know, as we say, "without ever thinking" that there is no phoenix and no unicorn, that our political opponents will not lose their lust for power, and that there will be no abiogenesis this year or next. We know that coelacanth exist, although we have not had the good fortune to see one, and that the owl will not announce a course of lectures in philosophy. Besides, with the constitution of reality, as known to us, assumed, mere isolated data become items of evidence whether we are at an archaeological site, in the archives, in the laboratory, in the law courts, or in the legislature. When we find coins and inventories at Pylos, we believe that men who stored and traded goods once dwelt there. When, while reading Thucydides, we think about Athens during the Peloponnesian War, we accept the thoughts that come to us as reliable. We believe that a decrease in the discount rate will foster inflation. At the same time we pay little attention to unreliable thoughts, or treat them as amusements. We reject as dreams or delusions even our own remembered perceptions, once we find that they conflict with our basic view of reality, because they then lose their impressiveness. Some thoughts are impressive, and we accept them as true descriptions of real things and happenings. Other thoughts have no strength to convince us.

Although human beings, at least adult human beings attending to their daily affairs, normally are fairly consistent in their decisions as to what is real and what is unreal in the physical world, at times that boundary goes undetected. Then the reality of real things is overlooked, or, more frequently, the reality of unreal things is assumed or asserted. Hume thought that these violations of the distinction might be reduced if the basis of the distinction were shown. For one thing, this might deter philosophers from pretending that their natural knowledge extended beyond the limits of natural reality. Even more common are mistakes of judgment in the moral subjects. All Irishmen are witty. All absolute monarchies are bad. The loss of bullion by a country weakens that country. These are examples of ideas which, although false, darken men's minds and distort policy.

We distinguish between the real and the unreal; yet, because we are not aware of the basis of the distinction we often err where error might have been avoided.

Before we examine Hume's explanation of the fact that perceptions differ so much in impressiveness that some are regarded as perceptions of reality while others are dismissed as unreal, let us turn aside to notice three negative implications of Hume's assertions that all knowing is perceiving, that simple ideas can result only from simple impressions, and that all our complex ideas are made up of simple ideas. First, since we acquire all our ideas of single attributes from impressions, from perceptions of the present, i.e., by experience, we must give up the notion of complex ideas prior to, or independent of, experience. When we come into existence we have only the characteristics of human nature, which include a capacity for perception. The mind at the beginning, as far as ideas are concerned, is a *tabula rasa*. It is through the cooperation of our human nature and the characteristics of the world, i.e., by becoming experienced, that we acquire such natural knowledge as we have. Hume was convinced that his argument that all simple ideas are first acquired in impressions destroyed the notion that there are *a priori* ideas.[13]

Second, according to Hume, we have no idea of "being." When we compare our idea of a fancied Utopia and our idea of a real Utopia, we can discover no difference in the internal relations, or structures, of these complex ideas. The perceptions are different, but the difference is not that in the case of the real Utopia the idea of the Utopia is supplemented by a second idea, the idea of "being"; rather, the difference is a difference in the impressiveness of the ideas of the two cities. This means that if all perceived and perceivable things and beings were annihilated, nothing, no being called "mere being," or "being in itself," would remain. If beyond our perception there are "essences" of any kind, those essences are indeed beyond our ken. We know only either simple or complex perceptions, only simple perceptions known abstractly, or simple perceptions in relation (or combination) with other simple perceptions. We can mention the name of a perception, and anybody who has had a similar perception, who remembers it, and is familiar with our language will recognize what we are talking about. And we can describe the several kinds of relations that prevail between and among perceptions. But, beyond knowing perceptions singly or in combinations (relations), just what knowledge of an essence would be, we have no notion. Accordingly, Hume insists that it is folly to talk about the eternal and immutable laws of being.[14]

The third negative implication, which is connected with the second, is the topic of most of the second part in "Of the Understanding." Hume's argument, here, is that we often treat our ideas of space and time as if those ideas themselves were independently real. That is, we often lapse into Realism. Complex perceptions are systems of related or combined simple perceptions. Each object we perceive is made up of attributes which appear to us in a certain manner, form, or order. Some of the parts of those mountains appear miles apart. None of the parts of this table is perceived as being more than a few feet from the other parts. Some perceptions are perceived before others, some, contemporaneously with others, and some, after others. The word "space" refers to the manner in which many of our perceptions, all those of extended things, appear to us. The word "time" refers to the manner in which all our perceptions, those of both external things and of "moral" activities, such as musical performances, social and political processes, and thinking, undergo change. If all perceptions were annihilated, or if there were only one perfectly simple perception, neither space nor time would remain. These are not two independent beings or things, but instead they are the two fundamental ways of being. Space and time do not exist independently. They are the dimensions of existing beings and things.

For the moral philosopher time is the more important of the two. We know every object as a succession, a progress of perceptions; that is, every object—every tree, every wave on the ocean, every constitution of government, and every man—changes. What we call "time" is the manner of appearance, an observed relation among our perceptions, or, as a musician speaking of one pattern of sounds in a piece would say, the "tempo" of the change. An unchanging object would be timeless; more exactly, it would be eternal. Such an unchanging object would give us the idea of *unity*.[15] It would be one and the same, itself, and without variation. On the other hand, every perception in a succession of completely similar perceptions, although not *specifically* different, is *numerically* different from all the other perceptions in that succession. The perceptions seem exactly the same, but one is the first, another is the second, another is the third, and so forth. It is by means of these two ideas—*unity* (changelessness or complete sameness) and *number* (change or difference)—that Hume explains the important idea of *identity*. When we imagine an unchanging thing surrounded by changing things, and then, illogically applying time (change) to all the objects alike, declare that the unchanging thing remained unchanged through a period of change, we achieve an idea that combines unity and number, and this is the idea of identity, the idea we use when we speak of "individual" real beings, e.g., individual waves, individual trees, or individual men.

The truth is that none of these beings is identical. None is an individual in this strict sense. Every real thing and being changes at some tempo. To overcome the problem of speaking about change, we have resorted to the device of establishing a standard rate of change. We have picked out one quite constant process of change, that of a certain movement of the planets, as our metronome; consequently we rate most changes—for some we find other standards, such as "light years," more convenient —by comparison with that movement, i.e., in terms of hours, days, and years. When compared with this standard, and with many other things, some things—hills, elephants, the British constitution, and oaks—seem everlasting, while others—the fruit fly in the laboratory and the grass of the field—have but a brief day. In either case, however, every thing changes slowly enough to permit us to give some sort of description, although, inevitably, a more or less inaccurate description, of it. Every object, considered at the very present, seems to be identical, i.e., seems to remain as it is. In some cases this fiction can be maintained easily for years, while in others it lasts only a second. This means—the clock forgotten—that the *present* for every thing and being has duration, either short or long. For a mountain the present is long. The present in the life of a man is longer than the present in the life of a butterfly. In other words, it is incorrect to think of the present, as we often do, as a fleeting instant, an advancing line without width, drawn between the past and the future. At any hour there are as many different "presents" as there are objects with different rates of change. Every succession of resembling perceptions gives us both the idea of identity (unity) and the idea of difference (change).

With these three asides understood, we now are ready to return to the main line of Hume's argument, and to advance.

We have noticed that some of our thoughts about remote things and happenings impress us, so that we accept them as reliable evidence of what once was real, is now real, or may be real, while the rest of our thoughts we treat as "mere ideas." Since we know only perceptions, and since it is the impressiveness or unimpressiveness of perceptions that we are trying to explain, this difference must depend on one or more of the relations between these perceptions.[16] It must be that some perceptions are related to others in a certain way, while the others are not so related. Which relation(s) among our perceptions cause some of our ideas to convince us of their reliability? It is in the third part in "Of the Understanding," after he has set forth his introductory statement of the basic elements of knowledge in the first part, and has shown some of the negative implications of his preliminary analysis in the first and second parts, that Hume takes up this crucial question.

There are, he finds, only seven different ways of comparing perceptions in terms of their relations; only seven different relations among perceptions that can be described by thought.[17] We can and do compare perceptions in terms of degrees of the same *quality*, total *number* of units of quantity, *resemblance*, and *contrariety*. We also compare perceptions in terms of their relative proximity to one another in time and in space at a specified time, i.e., in terms of *contiguity*. We compare them to discover whether two perceptions perceived at different hours, days, or years are one and the same—that is, in terms of *identity*. And finally, we speak of them as they are, or are not, causally connected with one another, i.e., in terms of *causality*. As we inspect these seven kinds of relations, we find that four, the first four, are not necessarily independent of our lucubration. We can think of fabulous beasts, and then can speak of them in terms of these four relations. We can compare the colours of a griffin and a yale. We can compare their weights. We can speak of their resemblances. And we can decide that they are not one and the same beast. In none of these comparisons would we come to any block that might lead us to believe that griffins and yales are or are not real-world beasts. The answer to any question we may ask in terms of these four relations depends entirely on how we have made up the ideas compared—in this case, on what attributes we have bestowed upon the beasts we created in our fancy. That answer will be only the result of an analysis of our own constructs.[18] The other three relations, however, refer to the manner or order in which our perceptions come to us; they are the relations which constitute the orders which we commonly call "time" and "space." [19] Since the present is a moment in time and space, the accuracy of any statement about contiguity, identity, or causality could be tested by comparison with the "impressions" we would have if we were present; indeed, we do find that many statements made in terms of these three relations are false. These relations are not dependent on our own mental constructs alone, and therefore they promise to be more helpful in explaining how we know "reality." [20]

We can narrow the field even more. We regard our knowledge of contiguity, e.g., our knowledge of the fixed distance between two neighbouring mountains, as fairly reliable, because we do not expect some cause suddenly to move the mountains closer together or farther apart. We regard our knowledge of identity, e.g., in the case of a process such as the growth of a pumpkin, as reliable, because we expect no cause to convert the pumpkin into something else. In short, both our knowledge of contiguity and our knowledge of identity are instances of our knowledge of natural causality.[21] Causality is the basic "matter-of-fact" relation. Our knowledge of the manner in which things appear and happen, that is, our knowledge of "time" and "space," fundamentally is knowledge of natural causality. The constitution of the real world, as human beings understand it, is a web of different cause-effect sequences.[22] Anything outside the system of sequences, or contrary to it, we do not understand.

We think of each kind of thing or being as having a particular kind of nature, a particular set of qualities or characteristics. We refer, accordingly, to the nature of sea-gulls, to the nature of pumpkins, to human nature, the nature of Englishmen, and even to the different natures of our friends. So certain are we of the fixed attributes and processes of different things and different kinds of things that we refer to the aggregate of things as "Nature." We know the world as cosmic, or orderly.

By the "nature" of any real thing we mean, strictly speaking, the causes and effects to which it is related by natural necessity. Often we speak of the nature of a thing as made up of its "powers," but at best this is a vain circumlocution, and at worst it is evidence that we do not know the limits of the understanding. We never understand or can hope to understand *why* any cause produces a certain effect. When we look at some totally new thing for the first time, we cannot discern its "powers." [23] We cannot say what its effects will be. We understand things only descriptively; that is, to learn the "nature" of a thing we have to wait until we have observed the effects it causes regularly, and then we say that its nature is such that it produces "such and such" effects. The human mind understands changes in terms of *how*, not *why*, they happen. In other words, the human mind has no *a priori* understanding of "natures"; rather, it understands "natures" only *a posteriori*, only as the result of experience. If we say that a variety of apples is sweet, we mean that this variety has been found to give a taster a sweet sensation. If we call a rock hard, we mean that it has been found to be such that flimsy tools will not cause it to shatter. If we call a man charitable, we mean that his past deeds have evinced a charitable disposition, and that we expect that disposition to cause him to behave in the same way in the future.

This knowledge of the physical and moral worlds as orderly is presupposed in all our judgments and acts. It affords the foundation of all our historical investigation, of all our thought of distant places and people, and of all our plans for the future. We presuppose natures and Nature when we step long to avoid a puddle, when we cross a bridge confidently, strike a match, or seed a field. At all times we expect changes or processes, but we expect them to take place within a fixed natural constitution. For example, we expect fire to burn wood at a certain rate, we are sure that lodges are built by beavers, not by bears, and we believe that by calculation we could learn at what hour the sun arose on a specific day a thousand years ago. To say that we know the physical and moral worlds as made up of things and beings with "natures," and the whole as "Nature," means that we know it as a consistent system of due processes, a system in which the same causes always have, and always will have, the same effects. It means that we know it as a system of *natural necessity*.

But what can have made us come to think of the real world as "Nature," as a system of natural necessity, the same at all times and places? How do we come to know the constitution of the physical and moral worlds to any extent beyond our present, or at most beyond our past and present? We now must shift our attention to the ways of knowing to discover how—by what method—we come to know the world as a system of causality, and how we come to know particular instances of causation. This will bring us to the apex of Hume's theory of knowledge.

The knowing of perceptions of the present we may call "intuiting." When we know in this way, we have an "impression." Let us now inspect some things which we invariably regard as causally related, e.g., on the one hand, tinder in a fireplace, a steady draft, and a blazing match, and, on the other, a warming fire. We see that what we call the "causes" and the "effects" are contiguous in place and time, but that they are not exactly contemporaneous. They are contiguous in time, but they are in succession; and this succession is orderly in that the fire never appears in the fireplace before we strike the match. This—their contiguity and succession—we can know by intuition. Yet there are innumerable cases where things are related by contiguity and succession, but are not called "cause" and "effect," e.g., the northward migration of birds and the flowering of daffodils. Things related by contiguity and succession are treated as causally related only if we are sure that the removal of one object necessarily entails the removal of the other, and that the appearance of one necessarily entails the appearance of the other. We think of causes and effects as related by some kind of necessity. The puzzle, then, is to discover what we mean when we say that we know the physical world and the moral world as systems of necessary relations. And to this puzzle our intuition gives us no solution. By seeing, hearing, tasting, etc. we may learn that two particular things are causally related, but this assumes that contiguity and succession are admissible evidence of causation.[24] If they are, and when they are, is exactly what we have not yet established. By intuition we know only what we at the moment have as an original perception. Intuition alone gives us no knowledge of anything beyond our presence.

A second kind of knowing is "remembering." A specific occurrence while yet recent, one that has left the "present" by just now slipping past the arbitrarily placed, grammatical check-point, is still perceived quite vividly, but since we no longer have a present perception, it is the remembered idea that bears some of the original feeling. As more and more happenings intervene, the perception impresses us less and less. It may become so weak and unaffecting that we may even wonder whether our thought is about something real or unreal, about something that did happen, or a mere fancy. It may be forgotten completely. In any case, it is not by remembering that we discover the principle of causality. First, remembrance throws a narrow light down the dark well of our past, picking out some sequences, passing over others; yet, even for men who have lived long and full lives, it gives only particular knowledge, not knowledge of an abiding and general constitution. Remembrance is subjective. We know only what occurred at a particular place at a particular time. It is limited strictly to what was once present to us. Just as it is *our* present that we intuit, it is *our* past that we remember. And second, when we remember having seen the same two things in contiguity and succession again and again, this is no basis for arguing that they will continue to entail each other even within the narrow confines of *our* future, unless we already have established the existence of causality, and have admitted repetition as sound evidence of causal relation. Both intuition and remembrance are useful in particular cases, are useful in discovering particular instances of causal relation between things, but neither explains what a causal relation is.

The present question concerns our reliance on some of our ideas as sources of convincing information about things and happenings that are not now and never were present to us, that is, information about the historical past, about distant places, and, most important, about the future. These ideas, Hume has shown, are impressive because they fit into the system of causes and effects. However, we have not yet been shown how Hume believes that it is possible for us to know causality. Both remembrance and intuition inform us about what we call "the real world," but they give us only particular knowledge, not general systematic knowledge which takes us beyond our past and present. Let us turn to complex ideas not derived directly from our past or present perceptions, but imagined.

The first kind of imagining we may call "fancying." We take simple ideas and assemble them into all sorts of complex ideas: griffins, castles in Spain, fantastic plots against ourselves, golden ages in the past, utopias in the future, and histories of Fairie. In this we are restricted by the limits of our stock of simple ideas, but within these limits we may arrange and rearrange those ideas in any way we like. At one moment we may establish autocracy in our ideal state, and in the next we may

set up absolute democracy, and then we may decide that no
government whatsoever is needed. We may change the colour—
black, blue, purple—of our fancied apples capriciously. In
fancying, there is no fixed or independent relation of any kind
between the ideas which are known. All the relations depend
entirely on our wills. In imagining fancifully, we need pay no
attention to causality. Fancying, obviously, is a way of knowing
perceptions that is very different from the knowing of things
related by natural necessity.

Then there is the kind of imagining involved when we engage
in "demonstrative reasoning." What is involved here is our
knowledge of certain standardized relations, such as the relations among the angles of an isosceles triangle, or between
"two" and "six." Once we have defined (standardized) what we
mean by "isosceles triangle," or by "two" and "six"—probably
we simply accept the contemporary definitions—we must abide
by the consequences, or be absurd. Here we have necessity; all
the angles of an isosceles triangle cannot be unequal; one pair
of the factors of "six" must be "two" and "three." Demonstrative reasoning, however, is not an adequate explanation of our
knowledge of the real world. It gives us only hypothetical information, and the reliability of that information depends on
the validity of the hypothesis which we may or may not be able
to test. If this field is shaped like an isosceles triangle, and if one
side is 150 feet long, and the base 100 feet, we shall need $y$
pounds of grass seed to plant it. If each of six kings has two
crowns, there are twelve crowns in all. The logical accuracy
of the conclusions is easily shown, but the accuracy of the conclusions as statements about reality must be tested. And we can
test the validity of the hypothesis only when intuition and remembrance apply. Demonstrative reasoning, in short, gives us
no basis for going beyond our past or present. Demonstrative
reasoning gives knowledge of necessary relations; but this
knowledge is not inevitably about the real world. What is discovered here is *logical* necessity. It is the origin of our knowledge of necessary relations among real-world objects, the origin
of our knowledge of *natural* necessity, the knowledge which

permits us to think to reliable conclusions about the remote past, the future, and distant places, that we are trying to discover.

The keystone of the mistaken analysis of human understanding prevalent among rationalistic philosophers, according to Hume, is the notion that our thinking about the real world is an instance of demonstrative reasoning. This notion, he finds, is defective in two ways. First, it fails to explain how we acquire the knowledge of natural necessity essential to our thinking about a cause and its effects. We have no *a priori* ideas, so we cannot know causality as an *a priori* idea. And no matter how we inspect any particular cause-effect sequence known by intuition or remembrance, we can discover no basis for saying, *a posteriori,* that *this* cause leads to *this* effect by natural necessity. And second, it fails to explain how we distinguish between true and fictitious ideas.

We have seen that, according to Hume's account, thoughts about garrulous owls, future wars, stateless utopias, and generous deeds done by misers are impressive or unimpressive for us because some perceptions are related by natural necessity, while others are not. But we have not yet considered Hume's attempt to explain how we know natural necessity. He maintains that none of the four ways of knowing that we have examined is a way of knowing the real world as a general and consistent causal system. Two—intuition and remembrance— almost always involve what we call "reality," but these give us only isolated, particular knowledge. Two—the knowing of fantastic and of systematic constructs—involve complete knowledge of their objects, the constructs, but the constructs do not necessarily correspond with what we call "reality." Now, we do perceive the real world as made up of a rapidly changing stream of perceptions, and despite this change, we do perceive these perceptions as related by contiguity in place, by identity, and by causality. But if these four ways were the only ways of knowing, we could not know these relations; rather, we would know the real world only as an unintelligible, incessant flurry, a mere chaos of atomic perceptions. Obviously, there is still another way of perceiving familiar to us all in our daily lives, another way which we have not yet analyzed and named.

The fifth way of knowing, Hume submits, is a way produced by experience, i.e., a way which results from the combination of what hitherto we have treated as separable: the character (or nature) of our real-world perceptions and the character (or nature) of the perceiving mind. This way of knowing, the way we understand the real world, is what Hume calls "believing."

To imagine is to think synthetically or constructively. By imagination, simple ideas are assembled into complexes, and complexes into greater complexes. Already we have noticed two kinds of perceptions produced in this way, fancied thoughts and demonstrable systems. There is, Hume holds, a third way of imagining. By its natural constitution, the human mind tends to move on restlessly from one perception to another, but not erratically and at random. When we do not interfere to think fancifully or in logical systems, it tends to follow "principles which are permanent, irresistable, and universal" to bring up those ideas related to present perceptions by resemblance, contiguity, or by constant contiguity and succession.[25] This is natural imagination. Hume's conclusion is that in addition to fanciful systems and numerical systems of units, there are natural systems of perceptions, systems in which one perception naturally introduces another.

Now—turning from the characteristics of human nature to the characteristics of the perceived perceptions—we already have noticed that many of our perceptions constantly come in contiguity and succession. This, we have noticed, is not a satisfactory basis for reasoning demonstratively from known to unknown instances. But it does correspond exactly with the third of the principles of the natural progress of human thought. "Here, then, is a kind of pre-established harmony between the course of nature and the succession of our ideas; and though the powers and forces, by which the former is governed, be wholly unknown to us; yet our thoughts and conceptions have still, we find, gone on in the same train with the other works of nature." [26] The answer to our whole problem now is clear.

As a result of repeated observations we have become habituated, accustomed, or experienced; and no sooner do we see one of two things which have been constantly related by contiguity and succession than, whether we wish it or not, and whether or not we are aware of it, we tend to think of the other. When we see a fire, for example, we immediately are convinced of the existence of heat. The earlier of the two things we call the "cause," and the later, the "effect." This transition of thought from cause to effect ordinarily is not made consciously, but spontaneously. The locus of the elusive natural necessity in causal relations now has been found. A particular perception, the "effect," follows another, the "cause," in every instance we have known. Whenever, for any reason, we think of the two, we feel what we call "necessity"; yet we neither touch nor know by any of the four other senses anything named "necessity." On the basis of our intuition and remembrance we can say only that in each observed instance, a specific perception followed another specific perception. But we have been forgetting that we inevitably become experienced or habituated, that human nature inevitably participates in human knowing, and is influenced by this participation. The human mind, like a gramophone disc, becomes grooved. We become experienced, and thereafter, whenever a perception of a "cause" appears, we move on by imagination to the idea of the "effect." The effect is expected. Our own feeling of expectancy, not a sensation known by one of the senses, is what we call "natural necessity." [27]

We see lightning in the sky, and we think of thunder immediately, according to Hume, because our imaginations have become habituated. The perception of lightning brings on the idea of thunder. But not only do we have the idea of thunder, but we expect to hear it. Why is the idea of thunder convincing or impressive? Already we know that, as ideas, there is absolutely no difference between the idea of a thing and the idea of that thing as existing. There is nothing about the idea of thunder, as an idea, that makes us regard it as reliable evidence of the immediate future at this moment, just after we have seen lightning, but not as reliable evidence about what to expect to hear tomorrow. Simply to imagine the idea of an effect is not sufficient to make us think of that effect as real. But all our perceptions of the present, we have noticed, are impressive, and therefore convince us. Likewise, impressive ideas also, to the extent that they are impressive, convince us. All strongly impressive perceptions—either "impressions" or impressive ideas—we receive as reliable. We believe them. Now, our perception of lightning is an impression: we believe the lightning is real. This perception, by the natural operation of the imagination, brings on the idea of thunder. But, Hume contends, it does more than that: it communicates impressiveness to the idea of thunder, and consequently that idea convinces us. We do not argue ourselves into this belief; rather, our acceptance of our thought as a perception of the real world is the immediate result of its strength or vividness.

In one or two places Hume says that we believe impressions (present perceptions), and remembered ideas, but generally he reserves the name "beliefs" for ideas of things and happenings never yet present, but made impressive through natural imaginative association with an impression. The definition he gives of a belief is, "a lively idea related to or associated with a present impression." [28] In the *Abstract* he writes: "Our author proceeds to explain the manner or feeling, which renders belief different from a loose conception. He seems sensible, that 'tis impossible by words to describe this feeling, which every one must be conscious of in his own breast. He calls it sometimes a *stronger* conception, sometimes a more *lively*, a more *vivid*, a *firmer*, or a more *intense* conception." [29] When we see lightning, we know, or more specifically, we believe, that we shall hear thunder within a few seconds. Believing is one of the ways of knowing.[30] An idea believed is a *belief*.[31]

Probability [or believing], as it discovers not the relations of ideas, consider'd as such, but only those of objects, must in some respects be founded on the impressions of our memory and senses, and in some respects on our ideas. Were there no mixture of any impression in our probable reasonings, the conclusion wou'd be entirely chimerical: And were there no mixture of ideas, the action of the mind, in observing the relation, wou'd, properly speaking, be sensation, not reasoning. 'Tis therefore necessary, that in all probable reasonings there be something present to the mind, either seen or remember'd; and that from this we infer something connected with it, which is not seen nor remember'd.[32]

We saw earlier that for Hume the three "time" and "space" relations, the "matter of fact" relations, could be reduced to one, namely causality; in short, we decided that the constitution of the world as known to us is a system of causal relations. We now have a complete explanation of how it is that we know reality. Knowledge of perceptions as related by causality and those two other relations dependent on causality, namely, contiguity in space through a time and identity, the only ways we know perceptions as related despite change (time), is the result of our experienced minds working synthetically or constructively under the prompting of the data gained by our direct contacts with the real world. Because the impressiveness of those direct contacts is transmitted to the ideas related with them by causality, we know those ideas as ideas of the real world. This way of knowing is the way produced by experience. "All belief of matter of fact or real existence is derived merely from some object, present to the memory or senses, and a customary conjunction between that and some other object." [33]

Whether or not we shall have beliefs is not a matter of choice: some knowledge of Nature and of the natures of familiar things and people is an inevitable result of living. We do not choose to expect darkness after sunset; that expectation grows on us without any effort on our part. Moreover, beliefs are of vital importance, for it would be impossible to act if we decided never to act without knowledge superior to beliefs. All the knowledge about the future on which we base our acts is made up of beliefs.

We develop this way of knowing so early in life, it is no wonder that we ignore it when first we try to analyze knowing. - Each mind when it begins to be is a *tabula rasa*, without ideas,

but with the nature of a human mind. Each man comes to ex- ✔
pect that the things he repeatedly observes in contiguity and
succession will reappear invariably in contiguity and succession. Human nature being as it is, we are not long in the world
before we begin to regard it as composed of many different
causally related sequences, i.e., of many different, explicable
sequences. We begin, in short, to think of each specific kind of
being—each kind of tree, mineral, plant, or planet—as having
certain attributes or characteristics, which we call its "nature."
The entire realm of beings, we think of as a system made up of
predictables, as "Nature." Once, Hume writes, long before
"the age of maturity," we begin to know some things in this
way, we begin to know everything in this way, for perceptions
resemble each other, and so are naturally associated by the
imagination.[34] We come to regard everything as an effect, even
when we cannot indicate the cause(s). We come to treat the
entire stream of our perceptions as a causally related continuum. This does not mean that we come to view everything
posterior as causally related immediately, as effect to cause, to
everything prior, but that everything posterior is viewed as
related causally to something prior.[35]

The importance of Hume's epistemology now is clear. We
understand the physical and moral worlds by believing, and
our beliefs are the product of repeated experience. Hume's
argument is that "all our reasonings concerning causes and
effects are deriv'd from nothing but custom; and that belief is
more properly an act of the sensitive, than of the cogitative
part of our natures." [36] It is on the basis of beliefs that the
affairs of men, corporations, and nations are conducted. And
belief underlies all our physical and moral sciences. Because we
expect causes to produce the same effects regularly, we propound explanations of geological occurrences, we propose economic policies, and we undertake to design governments for
future generations.

Up to this point in our account of Hume's epistemology, we
have been treating all beliefs as if they were equally strong; but,
as anybody knows, they are not. We often have doubts. The

impressiveness of our ideas about reality varies. Some ideas about things and happenings unpresent we believe with absolute certainty. Others we hold with various lesser degrees of assurance. We can distinguish, Hume contends, between two levels of belief produced by different degrees of regularity, between "proofs" and "probabilities." [37]

Some occurrences we observe taking place with complete regularity: the rising of the sun, the ebb and flow of the tides, the exhaustion of the supply of ink in our pens. The regularity we experience here is perfect; whatever the causes, those causes are unvarying. Here our minds are focused on only one belief (possibility); and accordingly we are unanimous in our expectation. This kind of belief Hume attributes to "proofs." It is because our expectation of regular occurrence is overwhelmingly strong in these cases that we tend to confuse the natural system, in which we believe, with a demonstrable system, which we have constructed as a system; and the result is that we often confuse natural and logical necessity. "Proofs," although implying freedom from doubt, reflect only natural, not logical necessity; for Hume they are different from "demonstrative reasoning," despite what may be suggested by twentieth-century terminology.

Within the frame of these proofs are other lesser beliefs, beliefs with diverse degrees of strength, which Hume calls "probabilities." Many happenings, in both the past and future, we guess about with only limited assurance. All these happenings had or will have causes, and in turn had or will have their effects; but exactly what things did or will interact, i.e., did or will serve as causes, we cannot say. Sometimes we have not yet observed a particular set of causes often enough to have acquired the habit of immediately thinking of a particular effect.[38] This defect can be overcome by further experience. But, second, often the continuum is so complex and intertwined that what apparently is the same set of causes produces different effects at different times. Nothing seems so simple as the tossing of a die with only two different marks; yet some of the influences that operate are so hard to specify and control that the outcome varies. The same is true in both private and public life. The causes running into the immediate future seem stable and limited; but we never quite attain certainty, and even despite a guarded tentativeness, we often are astonished by strange events resulting from our own acts. Here it is not the limited extent, but the lack of uniformity, of our experience that makes our expectancy less than certain.

A third reason why beliefs may remain at the level of probability and not attain that of proof is that the present perception may be only analogous to the previous repeated perceptions.[39] The first two kinds of probabilities result from the weakness of the imaginative connection, established by repeated observation, between the perception of the cause (or effect) present to us and the idea of its effect (or cause). Beliefs based on analogy are less than certain, are not proofs, because the present perception resembles the cause of the effect in question in some ways, but not in others. The present perception, therefore, may or may not be an instance of the kind of cause that produces a particular kind of effect.

These three factors explain why many of our beliefs are somewhat less than absolute in strength, and, given the nature of the understanding, the influence of these factors is inevitable and proper. The beliefs that arise under that influence are authentic beliefs, even although some of them turn out to be incorrect. But we often have false beliefs, that is, beliefs which have arisen, or which have been changed in strength, improperly. There are, Hume finds, at least four ways in which our minds tend to produce false beliefs, i.e., beliefs which, regardless of their accidental accuracy in any isolated case, are illegitimate. It is at this point that Hume's epistemology begins to have practical implications.

The impression with which the idea believed is associated may be somewhat remote—the present, we must remember, is not neatly separated from the past—and therefore is likely to be a less impressive impression than one of the very present moment. Consequently, without a good reason, the belief will be weaker at one time than at another.[40] Again, although an impression may be strong, a long time may have elapsed since we last saw this particular cause and its effect in sequence, so that our idea of the effect is weak. We make all kinds of good resolutions under the influence of recent experiences, but as those experiences become more and more remote, we become careless of the results, and slip back into our old ways.[41] Third, a prolonged chain of accurate thoughts may produce less conviction than a short, and inaccurate chain.[42] And still another kind of improper influence on our beliefs is prejudice, which arises when we assume rashly, on too little evidence, that a group related in one way is also related in another way. Once we have concluded that all Frenchmen lack stability, and that all Irishmen are great wits, these false beliefs can be expunged from our minds only by many contrary experiences.[43]

Beliefs may be acquired artificially, without direct experience, by education. Men transmit beliefs to others, especially the young, thereby bestowing upon them the invaluable gift of past experience if the beliefs are authentic, or thereby twisting their minds if the beliefs are false.[44] The process of education, good or bad, Hume finds, is very effective and very important. It is repetition which accustoms us. In education it is not impressions, but ideas, that are repeated frequently. These ideas, however, are not inert and unimpressive; they are valid for the impressionable young because the young associate these ideas with their elders and others in offices of authority, whom the young accept as creditable sources.[45] "I am persuaded," writes Hume, "that upon examination we shall find more than one half of those opinions, that prevail among mankind, to be owing to education, and that the principles, which are thus implicitly embrac'd, over-ballance those, which are owing either to abstract reasoning or experience." [46] Indeed, so efficient is education that those ideas to which we have become accustomed from infancy become solidly set in our conglomerate of beliefs, and generally neither incompatibility with our other beliefs nor the impact of direct contrary experience serves to exorcise them.[47]

In "Of the Understanding," Hume's chief aim is to give an

accurate account of how the knowing faculty works, and especially to show how we have thoughts that convince us about the future and about the remote past and the far away. His argument is that the understanding has been badly misrepresented by philosophers. We reach in thought beyond our past and our present, not by demonstration, but by imagination charged by experience. Our thoughts of the real world beyond the present are beliefs. Hume does not pretend to invent or discover a new way of knowing. Presumably, these five ways of knowing—intuiting, remembering, fancying, demonstrative reasoning, and believing—have been used throughout all time, and will continue to be used; however, his explanation of believing has practical as well as theoretical importance. A man perceiving in any one of the five ways may err, especially if he is not aware of the dangers peculiar to the particular kind of knowing involved. This is plainest, perhaps, in the case of remembering; because the possibility of mistakes of memory is very evident, men seldom trust their memories very far. It is obvious in demonstrating, also, where it is easy to fall into absurdities in tracing a long chain. As we might expect, it is with the accuracy of our understanding (believing) that Hume is most concerned. Beliefs come about either naturally, by direct experience, or artificially, by education. Either kind of beliefs may be false.

Since we now know the nature of our understanding we can consciously try to exclude false beliefs. First, since no "belief" can be an authentic belief unless the idea involved is tied to the "here and now" by a chain of natural causality, ideas of things and happenings contrary to nature and beyond it must be dismissed. Second, we ought to assure that our "beliefs" are as soundly based as possible. This means that we ought, by seeking experience, by experimentation, to reduce as much as possible the influence of the three proper causes of doubt; that we ought to try to eliminate the distortion caused by the four improper influences; and that we must not be too sure of the accuracy of the ideas we receive in education. Our "beliefs" arise from experience; aware of this, we should try to make our experience as complete as possible.[48] The scientist, Hume tells us, tries to make his believing conform to "the more general and authentic operations of understanding," but the vulgar form "beliefs" wildly. To assist in this self-critical task of checking our "beliefs," he sets down the rules of logic in outline form.[49]

Having expounded his own theory of how we know the real world, and how we can improve our knowledge of it, Hume turns in the fourth and final part of the book, "Of the Understanding," to apply this theory to the classic problems of epistemology. His aim here is not to prove that our knowledge of reality is correct. Such an undertaking would be vain: we would have to have correct knowledge somehow, in order to test the knowledge that we do have! We know perceptions which are more impressive than others, and these we call perceptions of reality. Whether or not we have such perceptions is not the question; for that is a question of fact, and even the most sceptical philosopher probably would admit to having such perceptions. Rather the question is, does the theory of knowledge under examination accommodate all the chief ways we know what we call "natural reality"? Hume is trying to show that his theory does not exclude any province of natural knowledge. And while he is making his survey of the main provinces, he also tries to explain how philosophers, by ignoring the influence of experience, have become muddled, and sometimes, in their desperation, have been led to a sceptical denial of knowledge, a denial which they promptly forget and disprove by their own acts as soon as they have issued from their closets. For our purposes, it may suffice to notice how he deals with two of these classic problems, namely, the problem involved when we speak of ourselves as objects of knowledge, and the problem involved when we speak of external objects of knowledge.

Ordinarily, we make the mistake of speaking of ourselves as if we were absolute units, that is, as if there were entities, called "selves," which persisted unvaried and uninterrupted, despite the normal changes, from birth until death. This is an understandable error.[50] By neither intuition nor remembrance do we know "selves"; rather, what we know is a current of perceptions related by constant contiguity and succession and by resemblance, and distinguishable from the rest of the entire stream of our perceptions. We feel impressions, which bring on their ideas. These, in turn, cause secondary impressions. These, then, bring on their ideas, which, in turn, may cause us to act, and thus may bring on new original impressions. As a result of natural imagination, these perceptions are thought of as a distinct causal sequence extending back to our birth and forward to our death. A mind is an extremely complicated chain of interrelated causes and effects. A mind is analogous to a commonwealth. It, too, constantly loses old members and acquires new ones. A mind, like a commonwealth, by this process, may come to have a new character and disposition. Yet, as with bodies politic, such conversions for better or worse, even of men of unusual experience and extraordinary independence, are likely to be both gradual and slow, and always will be the outcome of the web of prior causes. Any remarkable change, by definition, takes much time, at least in the preparation. Each mind, then, is "a system of different perceptions or different existences, which are link'd together by the relation of cause and effect, and mutually produce, destroy, influence, and modify each other." [51]

But, except on rare occasions, we do not take the trouble to speak of ourselves so carefully. The difference between a single, enduring perception, a perception of numerical identity, and a series of exactly or closely resembling perceptions is detected only if we reason that if perceptions foreign to the series intervene, our perceptions must be an intermittent series, not a single perception. Ordinarily, we are not quick to reason gratuitously. Consequently, in the present case, we ordinarily fail to notice that this succession of causally-related and resembling perceptions is not a "self," an entity enduring entirely without change throughout a period of time. And then, when we have to take the normal developments of aging and any extraordinary changes into account, we compound our error by feigning a new, unknown kind of being, a "self," as the ground of inherence of these changes which, thereafter, we call "accidents." This separation, with its mystery, would be unnecessary if we had been careful to describe ourselves as we are led by experience to know ourselves, i.e., as distinguishable (identifiable) series of causally related perceptions. Fortunately, the erroneous separation has no bad consequences, except for philosophers, who, although they should be able to think of particular minds as chains of causes and effects, dispute rudely and, inevitably, vainly, on the nice and subtle question of whether these unknown beings, "selves," are material or immaterial! [52]

Our ideas of external objects (perceptions of things as external to ourselves)—and the quandaries of those philosophers who mistakenly try to distinguish between perceptions of things as external and objects—come about in much the same way. We sense sensations only as sensations, and not as signs, manifestations, or appearances of another kind of being beyond the sensations.[53] At the same time, sensation provides no basis for reasoning to the conclusion that there is another kind of being, independent of our sensation.[54] Yet we do divide our perceptions into perceptions of ourselves and perceptions of things external to ourselves, such as tables, books, clouds, and trees. Moreover, we do think of these external bodies as continuing when we are not seeing, touching, hearing, tasting, or smelling them.

Again, the answer is that experience has produced this way of knowing the world. Our perceptions (primarily sensations) of books, tables, and clouds come to us with constancy and coherence. When we enter this room we always see the desk, the fireplace, and the window; rather, they are so constant that we hardly notice them when we return to resume our labours. And they have coherence. We always sense them in a certain order. The perceptions of crackling noises and hot red sparks attributed to the fire always are to the left of the perceptions of the window. The desk is always perceived slightly to the right of the window. And when we look up from the desk to the window, we always perceive the pine tree in the meadow as beyond the windowpanes. In short, we have here several identifiable series of causally related perceptions—what we call the desk, the fire, and so forth—each with its own fixed place in a large scheme of causally related perceptions, i.e., in the room. By the synthetic operation of the imagination we have connected our perceptions into a number of identifiable causally related series, and have connected all these series into one causally related scheme. This is how we know the room.[55]

But we do not stop here. We advance to understand these perceptions as making up a world external to ourselves, and composed of enduring and independent things: we do not think that this room ceases to exist when we go into the hall. Our perception of the room, we have seen, always is the same. It always has the same arrangement. It is easy for the mind to explain this unaltered order by the assumption that the chamber continues to exist when it is not perceived. But even more influential in causing us to know it in this way is the constancy of our perceptions. We have entered the chamber many different times, and each time we saw it, heard its echoes, and smelled its bookish smell, there seemed to be no noticeable, at least no unaccountable, change. Because our countless perceptions of the desk over the last twenty years resembled each other so exactly, seemed so much the same, we think of them as one and the same perception. Accordingly, unphilosophical men, i.e., both the multitude and the philosophers when away from their closets, regard what they perceive—in this case, the desk—as enduring even when they are not seeing or touching it. Believing, not sensing, and not demonstrative reasoning, produces our ordinary way of knowing the external world. We perceive perceptions related by constancy and coherence, and this leads us to think of those perceptions as external and independent.

However, many philosophers, once in their closets, ignore the synthetic operation of the imagination, and endeavour to explain why we believe in external bodies in other ways. They remark correctly that each perception, although it may resemble exactly all the others in its series, is a new, numerically different perception. Then, having no synthetic agency to account for the combination of these separate and different perceptions, to avoid the ridiculous conclusion that we know nothing as continuous and independent of human perception, they proclaim that there is a difference between our perceptions and the objects we perceive, and argue that while the former are but momentary, the latter persist.[56] They thus manœuvre themselves into the frustrating plight of claiming to possess two worlds, and being unable to speak of one in terms of the other.[57] One is an inner, subjective world, which is known, but only as a chaos of atomic perceptions. The second is an external, objective world, which is made up of timeless objects, but is unperceived. The truth is that the senses know only sensations. By reasoning, the existence of the objective world cannot be proved, for it is just as logical, and far less complicated, to argue that perceptions are uncaused (inexplicable) as to argue that perceptions are caused by unknown "objects," which, in turn, are uncaused.[58] The truth of the matter is that it is because of the influence of experience on our minds that we think of many of our perceptions as external to ourselves, and as related in the separate causally related series which we call "objects." It is through experience that we come to know (to believe in) external objects.

Certain relations among our perceptions combine with the "permanent, irresistible, and universal" principles of the imagination to bring us to beliefs about the characters (natures) of particular men, and about the characteristics (natures) of external objects. Likewise, it is the expectancy of the experienced imagination that leads us to say that the entire universe is Nature. Moreover, as we have noticed, it is because we have a present perception of the "real world" that we know that nature, human and external alike, beyond our past and present, was, is, and shall be "real."

Hume's logic, his theory of human understanding, and the importance of that theory are now clear. The real world, as known to us, is made up of identifiable beings and things related causally. We understand when we know how the effects follow the causes, but we do not know why any particular effect follows any particular set of causes. Our understanding of the natural world is believing. Experience accustoms us so that our imaginations bring up the ideas associated with our present perceptions, and because of the more or less close imaginative association between the present perception and the ideas, those ideas become vivid or impressive.

Much of our understanding is done subconsciously. When we perceive a cause, we immediately, without striving, think of the most obvious effect. But it is possible to check our beliefs against the rules of logic, and to seek experience deliberately.

Hume describes his theory of the understanding as one of "moderate scepticism." By "scepticism" he means not a specific theory, but an attitude of dubiety evoked by the spectacle of rash reliance on the unexamined powers of the human understanding. Pyrrhonism, or what he calls "excessive scepticism," he, of course, dismisses as fallacious. The Pyrrhonists make the common mistake of failing to see that the understanding makes judgments about the abstract relations of ideas and about the natural world in two different ways. They think of mathematical knowledge as the highest form of knowledge. They concentrate their attention on the prevalent erroneous theories about the senses and about reason; they find that neither can give them mathematical certainty, and then, disinterested in explaining how, in truth, we do know the natural world, they subside into a sour, fruitless idleness. Hume denies the mathematical paradigm of knowledge. The legitimate knowledge of the natural world is beliefs, which are the product of experience. His theory leads to "a more mitigated scepticism," a dubiety that dampens the pride and recklessness of men, and, indeed, he presents his theory as the theory most compatible with this healthy kind of scepticism.[59] First, although their beliefs often are weak, and often are not even genuine beliefs, men tend to be assured, haughty, and obstinate, smug in their own wisdom and judgment, unwilling to brook delay or to admit even the possibility of error. His theory, a theory of "moderate scepticism," he thinks, by making men aware of "the strange infirmities of human understanding, even in its most perfect state, and when most accurate and cautious in its determinations; . . . would naturally inspire them with more modesty and reserve, and diminish their fond opinion of themselves, and their prejudice against antagonists." [60] Second, men tend in their philosophical enquiries to venture out beyond the scope of human understanding. His theory, a theory of "moderate scepticism," he thinks, may lead them to confine their endeavours within appropriate limits.[61]

We gain our more or less accurate understanding of the physical and moral worlds in which we live, by experience; we are all highly dependent on our beliefs, be they authentic or false.[62] But now that we know this, we need not be passive, giving lodging to all the beliefs that crowd in upon us, and to them only. Once we have become self-conscious, that is, once we have become cognizant of the nature of our understanding, not only can we assay the beliefs that offer themselves either in direct experience or in education, but we can invite beliefs by experimentation. We can check our beliefs against the rules of logic, i.e., against the authentic principles and operations of the reasoning faculty.[63]

Hume's logic is relevant to all men: insofar as they increase their genuine understanding by winning more and more authentic beliefs and by jettisoning false "beliefs," they bring their private and public lives more and more into accord with reality. The vulgar are commonly guided by their unexamined "beliefs"; but wise men by beliefs consonant with "the more general and authentic operations of the understanding."

Hume's logic defines the task of the moral philosopher. He must, to the extent that he relies on natural science, find his principles in human nature, for the human understanding cannot reach beyond the world of natural necessity. He must proceed descriptively, that is, in terms of causes and effects, and not make a vain attempt to plumb the depths of human nature. And he must test his conclusions—his beliefs—against the rules of the authentic operation of the understanding. This task Hume himself proposed to undertake.[64] He proposed to discover certain principles of human nature, and to show how these proliferate into those acts, processes, standards, and institutions which constitute morals, politics, and criticism.

# III

## PASSION AND ACTION

But though reason, when fully assisted and improved, be sufficient to instruct us in the pernicious or useful tendency of qualities and actions; it is not alone sufficient to produce any moral blame or approbation.

*Enquiry* II, p. 286

THE human mind, according to Hume, knows the real world beyond the scope of remembrance and intuition by believing. Experience sets up relations between perceptions, so that when we have a present perception we also have a more or less impressive thought of the things and acts related in our minds to that present perception. These thoughts about the unpresent may turn out to be correct or incorrect, but this indefiniteness is essential to their nature as beliefs. What is far more important to us, whether we are considering our received beliefs or are experimenting to achieve new beliefs, is the difference between authentic and false beliefs, between beliefs acquired in the proper way and those acquired illicitly, for in the crucible of practice, authentic beliefs are likely to turn out to be correct, while false beliefs are likely to prove unreliable.

Hume himself is concerned to examine human nature as a cause of judgments and of acts, either private or public, in the fields of morals, politics, and the arts. Already we know how the human understanding acquires beliefs which, whether correct or not, influence our activities. In "Of the Passions," the second book in the *Treatise*, he proceeds to the other part of human nature, to those principles of human nature which, guided or misguided by beliefs, move men to action. In "Of the Passions," a piece published in 1757 in *Four Dissertations*, seventeen years after the *Treatise*, he gives a terse summary statement of his explanation of those principles. In these two works, as in those on the understanding, he is trying to discover the principles, the ultimate processes, what we might call "the constitution" of human nature, beyond which we cannot penetrate. These principles we know as inevitable and invariable; for us they are the principles of nature. Individuals, neighbourhoods, and nations, of course, differ in their characteristic feelings, as in their beliefs, and these differences will have to be explained; here, however, we are not interested in secondary variations, but with the basic feelings. In his account of the passions, Hume accommodates, but does not descend upon, these differences.

Perceptions, he has told us, are known both as impressions (feelings) and ideas (thoughts). The feelings he now divides into two kinds: the "original impressions" or "sensations," and the natural human reactions to the original impressions, which reactions he calls "secondary impressions," "impressions of reflection," or "passions."

Since his analysis of human nature is intended as the foundation of a study of moral subjects, a study of the various kinds of human judgments and the various kinds of acts based on judgments, it is not with original feelings, but with the reactions natural to human beings, the passions, that he is concerned. The sensations, therefore, he chooses to regard as data. For the study of moral subjects it is enough to know that these sensations exist, and that human nature is such that every sensation not indifferent, no matter what its other qualities, is found either "painful" or "pleasant." This difference, according to Hume, is the basis of all moral judgments and acts. Why the painful sensations are not pleasant, and the pleasant painful, cannot be explained. Nor can "painful" and "pleasant" be directly defined; but no reader will need such a definition. The cardinal point is that human beings approve the sources of pleasant sensations, and call them "goods," and disapprove the sources of painful sensations, and call them "evils." [1] It is from this primary judgment, this approval of pleasure and disapproval of pain, that the secondary feelings, the passions, stem. As the relation between the individual man and the goods and evils varies, the two reactions proliferate into a bevy of different feelings—joy or sorrow, fear or hope, love or hatred, pride or humility, desire or aversion—each a feeling suitable to the individual's situation. According to Hume's analysis, these two factors, first, the basic reaction to pain and pleasure, and, second, the various ways the individual may be related to the goods and evils, are the causes of all the many distinguishable passions.

The passions, once distinguished, can be grouped in three main ways. First, they are either calm, in which case, Hume finds, they are often mistakenly called "reason," or violent, and then they generally are called "passions." Second, some are aroused in the individual immediately by original impressions, while others involve certain kinds of relations between the cause of the original impressions and the individual. Hume calls the former, "the direct passions," and the latter, "the indirect passions." And finally, the passions may or may not lead to volition, and thus to action.

Hume's discussion of the direct passions—chiefly, joy and grief, desire and aversion, and hope and fear—is easily described. When we possess a good, we feel the pleasure which causes us to call it a "good," and we feel joy also. Again, if we believe in a future good, the pleasure of which we do not yet feel as a present perception, we feel joy. When an evil is present, certain to come, or highly probable, we grieve. Desire is a passion for goods not presently enjoyed, and aversion is a passion for the removal of evils. Hope and fear rise from thoughts about the future. If we have no strong, dominating idea of forthcoming happenings, so that from a concatenation of happenings we now foresee a good event, and now an evil event, joy and sorrow are mingled, and we are either hopeful or fearful. Passions, unlike thoughts, do not shift lightly. They are sluggish, and die away slowly, so that although our moods do vary with our thoughts, their changes are slower and less extensive. They shift, as if on a shorter radius.[2] Consequently, at any moment our mood may be incongruous with the prospect we survey. When we think that a specific good and a specific evil are equally possible, and think at one moment of the good, and at the next of the evil, the feelings appropriate to the two thoughts, joy and grief, meet and mingle in an uneasy turmoil, not to be properly called either hope or fear. But when we believe in the good result, and think only vaguely of the evil, joy predominates over sorrow. The consequent feeling we call "hope." And, on the other side, as our expectation of evil grows, our mood is influenced less and less by joy, until finally, when joy is gone, fear becomes sorrow.

Those passions called "indirect" by Hume, we might call "social." While the direct passions involve only two factors, an individual and a perceived good or evil, the indirect passions arise through a trilateral process. They are the feelings a man has when he evaluates a person, either himself or some other(s). These feelings, like the direct ones, involve a perceiver, who feels them, and involve good or evil things and attributes, but they also involve the person who has these good or evil things and attributes. This person is the one about whom the perceiver has the feeling. Moreover, the indirect passions come about only in some kind of society, for since evaluation involves comparison, it is impossible to decide that a man is worth much or little without a standard of worthiness. These passions, our feelings about ourselves and others, based on comparisons with the standard of worthiness prevailing within our society, are outstanding as causes of behaviour, and, therefore, are of great importance to the moral, economic, and governmental institutions of every group and nation.

The indirect passions, like the direct, are felt only by individuals; that this is true, as we shall see, inevitably helps to determine the nature and the strength of the passions known and operating in any particular social situation.

Since the indirect passions are the feelings, based on approval of goods and disapproval of evils, with which we regard either ourselves or others, Hume's elementary list contains only four: pride and humility, when we ourselves are the object, and love and hatred, when some other person or group of persons is the object. A twentieth-century writer probably would designate the lesser degrees of these feelings, especially of love and hatred, by less extreme terms, e.g., like and dislike, but if we remember that Hume is employing them to cover four logical possibilities, and is not especially concerned here with the strength of these passions, we can follow him easily. Later we shall come to his discussion of other indirect passions, most notably pity and malice, passions which contain elements of love and hatred, but which arise from somewhat more complex relations between individuals.

The first of the principles of human nature by which we come to have feelings about ourselves and others is "double association." [3] Hume's argument is that these feelings, like the direct passions, have their basis in the primary distinction between pain and pleasure; when we find that one of our attributes or anything regarded as connected closely and constantly with ourselves is the cause of notable pleasure, and so is good, or of notable pain, and so is evil, we feel pride or humility. Here the thought of the cause is so closely related in our minds with the thought of ourselves that when we think of the former, we immediately think of the latter. The first idea is associated with the second, and entails it. But the idea of the cause already is charged for us with a pleasant or painful impression as a result of our original perception of it, and, consequently, when we move on to the idea of ourselves, we find that idea also pleasantly or painfully impressive. Our notably close relation with a good gives us a new pleasant feeling, a feeling of elation, and this we call "pride." [4] Our notably close relation with an evil gives us a new painful feeling, a feeling of dejection, and this we call "humility." Similarly, the other pair of basic indirect passions, love and hatred, are the feeling we know when, as a result of thinking of a good or evil, we are led to think with pleasure or pain of a person other than ourselves.

Each of these four passions involves both an association of ideas and an association of impressions. First, the idea of the cause of pleasure or pain is associated with the idea of one person or a few, not with the idea of everybody. And, second, it is the pleasure or pain of the original impression that determines that we shall think of ourselves with elation or dejection, or of others with the additional pleasant feeling called "love" or the additional unpleasant feeling called "hatred."

The difference between the two pleasant passions and between the two unpleasant ones results not from a difference in their particular causes, but from the different relation between the man who feels the passion and its cause. In the case of pride and love, for example, when he himself is closely related to the good, the result is a pleasing idea of himself, and when another is closely related to it, the result is a pleasing thought of that other person.

The particular causes of pride and love, and of humility and hatred, Hume submits, are much the same: a thing that brings on pride if related to ourself, will bring on love for another person if we consider it as belonging to that person. These particular causes are also innumerable: all sorts of attributes and things will bring on these passions in some degree. But, although the particular causes are natural causes, they are not original causes.[5] That is, each particular cause of pride, for example, does not operate by its own separate principle; rather, it is effective because it is an instance of the general principle that our goods cause us to think of ourselves with pride. This is why the particular causes may vary from one historical period to another. New discoveries and inventions, i.e., new goods, may be added to the causes of pride and love, and may make many old things, once causes of pride and love, causes of humility and hatred.

However, it is possible, Hume shows in discussing the origin of pride and humility, to assemble the particular causes, constant and variable alike, into four groups based on four different relations between men and their goods and evils. (The same grouping, of course, applies in the case of love and hatred.) First, excellence in any attribute of *mind*—in wit, judgment, memory, learning, courage, humour, and, especially, in moral virtue—will make us feel pride (and love). Any unusual and agreeable ability of *body*—strength, agility, poise, skills, and that shapeliness or "beauty" which is taken as evidence of general ability—will have the same results. *Special distinctions* acquired by adventure or accident of birth—the merits of the wines, language, and customs of one's native parish, county, and country, when among strangers; the merits of strange sights and exploits, when at home; the riches, antiquity, and deeds of one's forbears—occasion these passions. And fourth, the goods to which one has a right, that is, *property*—one's clothes, vehicles, houses, furniture, wines and delicacies, sporting equipment, trees, and parks—cause pride and love, and indeed, Hume finds, are the most common causes of pride and love. Abnormal poverty, mean descent, deformity and clumsiness of body, and lack of ordinary grace of mind, especially if the lack takes the form of moral vice, all these cause some degree of humility and hatred. Three important qualities of these causes must be mentioned.

First, every cause that by double association produces some degree of pride or love is a good. It must be a capacity or a thing that also causes, or is capable of causing, a pleasant original impression, for it is on the basis of the fundamental distinction between pleasures, or "goods," on the one hand, and pains, or "evils," on the other, that human beings conduct themselves in the moral and physical worlds. Similarly, every cause that by double association produces some degree of humility or hatred is an evil.

Second, the distinction that men make between impressions as good and evil are made within the limits fixed by their common human nature. Within those limits there are standard and historical and personal differences. Men and women, the young and the old, will everywhere have preferences suited to their sex and age. Tastes vary from clime to clime, from country to country, and even from generation to generation. Finally, there are differences in choice that express the particular nature or character, the particular birth, education, vocation, and circumstances of the individual man or woman. But, even when this variation has been taken into account, the number of capacities and things that all men agree are good and evil is overwhelming. If this were not so, it would be impossible to speak of "human nature."

Third, the outstanding good, be it a capacity or a thing, if it is to produce the social passions of pride or love, must be related permanently and obviously in some special way to the person who is the object of the passion.[6] It will not produce these feelings if, like many great goods, e.g., sunshine, the ability to talk, common lands, and ordinary truthfulness, it does not distinguish the individual from all or most of his fellows. Love is not a feeling that we know when we think of any or every human being. The same is true of hatred. Similarly, we are not always proud or humiliated. The peculiar qualities of the particular person, be they mental, bodily, adventitious, or proprietary, are what is important; otherwise, love and hatred, pride and humility could not be distinguished, i.e., would not exist. And it is the endowment with *excellent* qualities, the outstanding, special goodness of the particular person's conduct, wit, beauty, travels, or possessions, or a combination of such qualities, or the outstanding evil in regard to the same, that creates the feelings of pride or love, or of humility or hatred. Pride and love are implied denunciations of evil. And humility and hatred are implied tributes to goodness.

By double association, the social passions arise from the primary distinction between pain and pleasure. This does not mean that this process of double association is repeated every time we come to have a feeling about ourselves or others. Once the connections between goods and the passions of pride and love and between evils and the passions of humility and hatred have been established by experience, the process, Hume finds, often is reversed. Instead of moving in imagination from goods and evils to the person to whom they are related, we make the transition in the opposite direction. We start by knowing the feelings of another person, and then, with them as evidence, declare his possessions, attributes, and conditions as good or evil. Instead of initiating our knowledge of the other two factors in the triangle in a particular instance by sensation of good and evil, we often initiate our knowledge by "sympathy" with another person.

"Sympathy" is the name Hume gives to what, for him, is one of the most important operations of human nature. It is, he submits, only with great difficulty and, therefore, only rarely, that men can conceal their direct and indirect passions. Sometimes patently and sometimes only by implication, either deliberately or without any desire to produce an effect, in countless ways they express their approval or disapproval of things, deeds, and words which cause them pleasure or pain. By what they say and do not say, by what they do and do not do, by the meaning they give to words, by gestures, by smiles and frowns, by single deeds and the pattern of prolonged action, they reveal their feelings or sentiments. Initially only the signs, the expressions, are known by their fellows. But so much do all men resemble each other in mind and body that the mere intuition of these signs suffices to give them a weak perception (or idea) of the particular passion, and then to enliven that idea immediately, with the result that it comes to rank as a passion.[7] They come to know, that is, to feel, the particular feeling that the observed man is feeling. "Hatred, resentment, esteem, love, courage, mirth and melancholy; all these passions I feel more from communication than from my own natural temper and disposition." This, of course, is not perfect communication. If the man expressing his feelings is a stranger, his modes of expression are certain to be at least somewhat unaffecting. His signs will not evoke the appropriate ideas immediately or exactly, and if he is very strange, the observers, even when they try hard to comprehend, may fail. Again, if the observers are young or of limited experience, they may never have had the particular feelings now expressed in their presence, and so can neither know those feelings nor evaluate their causes.[8]

Sympathy, or, as we might say, "communication," prevents the isolation of the individual. Each man is not separate and independent; all are caught up somewhat in the sympathetic exchange of perceptions; every man is susceptible to the feelings of all those around him. This does not mean that there is multilateral reciprocity among all. Some men are great of character, and have a strong "presence." Their feelings are powerful. They express powerfully their moods, their approbation and disapprobation, their desires and aversions. Such men will dominate, especially if their influence is enhanced by high office, by an established ascendency, and by a wide circle of personal acquaintance. Many others are slight, inconsequential men; yet, despite their lack of importance as individuals, such men can influence the general temper of a village, city, or nation when they are numerous, unanimous, and vocal.

According to Hume, the need for perception through sympathy is one of the greatest reasons why men, like all animals except those "that prey upon others," are sociable. Economic cooperation, as we shall see, produces tangible advantages, but these do not explain the desire for company. "This is still more conspicuous in man, as being the creature of the universe, who has the most ardent desire of society, and is fitted for it by the most advantages. We can form no wish, which has not a reference to society. A perfect solitude is, perhaps, the greatest punishment we can suffer." [9] So much are men dependent on communicated perceptions that when they are without companions their lives become wearisome and worthless to them. They are dependent on others for many of the perceptions which sustain the mind in a tolerable state of animation. Besides, any pleasure, and so any ability or possession that gives pleasure, acquires its worth from the standards prevalent within a society as well as from its own intrinsic quality. And beyond that, a perception acquired through sympathy is known not only as an impression attended by an idea, but as an idea attended by an impression, and by this reflection or doubling, its quality is heightened and its duration extended.[10]

It is to sympathy that Hume attributes the uniformity of taste and ideals commonly found in a community. Within the limits set by human nature considerable variety is possible; yet, while there always are some eccentric individuals, the people of a village, city, and even an entire nation generally display a remarkable uniformity in their temperament, morals, and aspirations, and this, Hume contends, results not from physical causes, such as climate, but from education and sympathy. In one passage he attributes "more than one half of those opinions, that prevail among mankind" to education.[11] In another he argues that to the principle of sympathy "we ought to ascribe the great uniformity we may observe in the humours and turn of thinking of those of the same nation; and 'tis much more probable, that this resemblance arises from sympathy, than from any influence of the soil and climate, which, tho' they continue invariably the same, are not able to preserve the character of a nation the same for a century together." [12] The two moral causes, education and sympathy, work together; indeed, much of the impact of education is derived from sympathy. But whereas education is primarily concerned to establish opinions, which may or may not be correct, by training the young to associate certain ideas, that is, to think in certain ways, sympathy communicates feelings, basically feelings of approval or disapproval. Sympathy, therefore, is both a more subtle and a more ubiquitous guide and control. When our words or deeds are perceived by another, they cause some degree of approval (pleasure) or disapproval (pain), and we, by sympathy, acquire the same feeling. Since we desire pleasure and wish to avoid pain, we soon learn to conduct ourselves in the acceptable manner and style. We may even do more: we may feign virtues, abilities, adventures, and possessions—all things that would cause us pride immediately if we had them—and hide our wants and debilities, in order to enjoy praise, which makes us proud, and to avoid blame, which would humiliate us. The total result is that the members of any group tend to acquire a common character.

Sympathy is the principle of human nature to which Hume refers in accounting for the love of fame, in accounting for our esteem for the rich and the powerful, and in accounting for pity. Fame is desirable because, through sympathy, we know the favourable feelings we cause others to feel.[13] This pleasure leads then, by double association, to the pleasant passion of pride. Infamy has the opposite effect. So great is the influence on us of our reputation that it may annul the humility or pride produced by double association.[14] By sympathy we enter into the sentiments of men made happy by riches and power. Consequently, we hold those men in high esteem, defer to them, and call the particular causes of their happiness, "goods," although we never have felt either pain or pleasure from them directly, and have no prospect of ever doing so.[15] Again, it is through sympathy that we pity the unfortunate, and come to love them to some degree. Love and hatred when brought on by the double association of ideas and impressions result from the goods and evils of others. By sympathy we know somewhat the feelings both of our companions, whom we may also have occasion to love or hate, and of strangers, who otherwise are perfectly indifferent to us. When, by sympathy, we perceive clearly the misery of a stranger, and consequently conceive the whole course of his misfortune, we share his grief, and thus, since our relief depends on his, we come to have an interest in his betterment and future happiness. We become, as it were, partners in his fortune. Now, love, unlike pride and humility, is not a simple feeling, but tends to produce an interest in the happiness of the beloved. This common tendency of pity and love to make us interested in the happiness of other persons causes us to love somewhat those whom we pity.

In the indirect passions, as depicted by Hume, we seem to have the foundations for an idyllic universal society: the common nature of human beings precludes the possibility of any serious discord about what is good and what is evil; the general desire for a good reputation inevitably supports standards of good conduct everywhere; all men love those who enjoy good attributes and good possessions; and, instead of hating the poor, the wicked, or the ill-favoured, we are led through the principle of sympathy to pity them, to try to help or reform them, and to love them. Presumably, all this would happen spontaneously wherever there are human beings. But we have not yet noticed another principle, the inevitable *selfishness of perception*. Always it is a particular individual who thinks and feels. Therefore, mankind is not one great homogeneous society integrated by common values and by love and benevolence; rather, each man is at the centre of his own web of diverse social sentiments, and there are as many webs of those sentiments as there are men. In addition, an individual's feelings towards other persons vary from person to person: some are loved with different degrees of love, some are pitied to different extents, and a few are viewed with more or less envy or even malice. These webs vary in their scope. Some are vast and tie in many people—a king or church leader, for example, will have some concern and favour for all his people. Others, those of magnates, politicians, or military leaders, are of intermediate size. Most are fairly small in their coverage, embracing the members of a single family, a neighbourhood, and a shop or office, and such strands as reach beyond to more remote figures are likely to be feeble. The different webs, of course, overlap. Besides, their limits are never trim, fixed, and certain, and therefore cannot be demarcated easily by law. They will not conform to the boundaries of families, parishes, cities, or even nations. Many stop far short of most legal limits. Others reach beyond them. The indirect passions, far from being general and inclusive, are always particular, varied, and partial. The social and political implications of this theory are obvious.

The fact that it is through his own perceptions that each individual knows both himself and others influences the focus and strength of the passions in three ways. First, it has an effect through familiarity. Our knowing is always interrupted and fragmented; but of all those chains of perception that we call "human beings" it is our "self" that we know best. Now, strange places and strange persons challenge the understanding, and if uncanny, seem hostile, while the familiarity of old scenes and old friends, even if they are inferior in quality, gives us "a satisfaction and ease." We are ready, therefore, to excuse their mediocrity as comfortable, and their minor defects as endearing eccentricities. Similarly, familiarity gives us a basic pleasant feeling about ourselves. We have "a good opinion" of ourselves which can be lost through humility or distraction, but probably only temporarily.

Second, it influences the operation of the imagination. It is natural, we have seen, for the imagination to move from idea to idea along the lines of established relationships. If a man has a twin brother, the blood-relation between them is perfectly reciprocal in the view of a neutral observer: the idea of Rupert is as likely to bring up the idea of Norman as the idea of Norman is to bring up the idea of Rupert. But for Rupert there is an undulation of thought that moves always towards himself, and the same is true for Norman. If Rupert thinks of his brother, he thinks of him in relation to himself, Rupert. But if Rupert thinks of himself, he may have no occasion whatsoever to think of Norman, and indeed he can think of himself even when Norman is miles away or dead. The influence on the passions of this natural bias of thought is most obvious in the case of pride and love or humility and hatred. Rupert, let us say, is proud of his own virtues. He loves his brother dearly because of the latter's famous virtues; and he is made proud because it is his brother who has these good qualities. But if Rupert himself is splendidly virtuous, while Norman is just an ordinary fellow, the former's pride in his own virtue does not cause him to love Norman. Likewise, we are humiliated by the vices of blood-relatives, but do not hate them because of our own vices. Our ideas when we think by natural association about society tend to run in along the radii to ourselves. When our feelings about people arise from the natural association of ideas, our own pride or (much less frequently) humility, is certain to be at the centre of the web of feelings.[16]

Third, the selfishness of perception modifies the effects of the sympathetic communication of feelings. We know (feel) our own feelings, but those felt by someone else can be known only by sympathy. This process will be much easier in the case of friends than in the case of strangers, and when we are receptive we will be affected greatly by them; yet the passions brought on by our own pleasure and pain are almost certain to challenge those brought on through sympathy, and may obscure or distort our awareness of the feelings of others.

Hume mentions three specific instances in which our feelings are modified by the inevitable selfishness of perception: our special sentiments for those "near" to us, our special attitude towards our allies and partners, and the rise of envy and malice.

Those "near" to the perceiver are generally dear to him. We are likely to value highly, to have special affection for, those related to ourselves closely, for example, those related to us by family ties, acquaintance, and similarity of temper and disposition, regardless of the true comparative rating of the goods and evils of those persons. Hume's explanation is interesting. If we withdraw from other people and concentrate our attention closely on ourselves, we soon settle into languor and daze. When subject and object are one and the same, the result is boring idleness, for no mind suffices to occupy itself long at anything like full capacity. When other objects, especially other persons, are present, we are stirred, become involved, and feel a pleasant exhilaration. Any present person will be known somewhat; we shall have some perception, although perhaps only a very faint one, of him. The fainter our perception, the less are we stirred and entertained. Now, the common effect of blood-relation, acquaintance, and similarity of disposition is that we know those close to us in these ways strongly. Our perception of them is lively and impressive. Accordingly, even when they are not causing any pleasant original impression, they stir our minds, and that in itself is pleasant, for it keeps us from *accidie,* some would say from great melancholy and despair.[17] We find them pleasant, and "good"; therefore, we have a special affection for them.

The worth of men, in terms of general standards of goods and evils, is often hidden by our own interests. We tend, for example, to love our allies and partners without regard for their merits except as allies and partners, and to hate our opponents, again without much attention to their true qualities. This is because we wish to win or to gain; by their efforts our allies and partners do good to us and we, by ours, do good to them. From doing good to each other, some degree of love arises. On the other hand, from competition and strife, hatred

arises. In fact, so much are our sentiments guided by our interests that not only do we not always love those related to
goods, and pity those related to evils, but we pay a perverted
deference to standards of good and evil by insisting that the
distribution of goods and evils conform to our interests. In a
war, for example, our enemies are "cruel, perfidious, unjust,
and violent," while our allies, like ourselves, are "equitable,
moderate, and merciful."

If the general of our enemies be successful, 'tis with difficulty we
allow him the figure and character of a man. He is a sorcerer: He
has a communication with daemons; as is reported of *Oliver
Cromwell* and the *Duke of Luxembourg:* He is bloody-minded, and
takes a pleasure in death and destruction. But if the success be
on our side, our commander has all the opposite good qualities,
and is a pattern of virtue, as well as of courage and conduct. His
treachery we call policy: His cruelty is an evil inseparable from
war. In short, every one of his faults we either endeavour to ex-
tenuate, or dignify it with the name of that virtue, which approaches it. 'Tis evident the same method of thinking runs thro'
common life.[18]

If we are forced into bankruptcy, lose in an election, or are
accidentally injured, we are likely to declare those whom we
hold responsible for our discomfort both ugly and vicious.
When we are storm-tossed on the sea, we denounce the waves as
"cruel." When cooler friends protest that our opponents are
not malevolent, and that the waves are magnificent, they thereby
seldom endear themselves to us.

Sympathy, we have noticed, is a principle that can make us
rejoice with the joyous and pity the sad; but it often, Hume
proposes, leads to envy, and sometimes to malice. This remarkable shift is brought on by selfishness.[19] Because the central
place in our perception normally is occupied by ourselves, we
naturally tend to compare our own condition with the fortune of
others. Pity and love for the unhappy, we say, is the result of
an impression of another's grief or fear strong enough to involve our happiness in his to some extent. Comparison, however, prevents this.[20] Instead of forgetting ourselves and enter-

ing deeply into the feelings of another, when we are comparing we move repeatedly from the thought of ourselves to that of the other, and then back again to ourselves. We know his feelings in subordination to our own, and therefore we know them only slightly. We do not give ourselves up to them. Moreover, it is by comparison, not by referring to a neutral standard, that we generally evaluate goods and evils. The great happiness of another makes us uneasy with our commonplace pleasures; and this produces a feeling of envy. Malice goes one step further: it is the unprovoked desire to produce evil to another in order to reap pleasure from a comparison favourable or more favourable to ourselves.[21] Because of the parallel direction of desire in both hatred and malice, we hate those towards whom we feel malicious.[22]

Despite these results, Hume does not yearn for the abolition of the self-orientation of perception, for such an abolition would deprive the individual of the motives of action, and would even destroy him by eliminating the possibility of distinguishing between him and all other beings. The remedy is not the elimination of individuals and the confined systems of feelings which they form around themselves, but the establishment of a system of rights and wrongs.

Both the direct and indirect passions—those feelings we have about goods and evils, and those feelings we have about ourselves and others—may cause us to act. We desire goods as such, and desire to move away from evils as such; similarly, we desire to help those whom we love or pity, and desire to harm those towards whom we feel envious and malicious; but desire and aversion do not stir the will unless we *believe* we can achieve the desired result by activity of mind or body. If we perceive goods that may be achieved and evils that may be evaded, our passions will move us to act.

This assertion brings us to Hume's famous denial of what he calls "the fantastic doctrine of free will." The will, strictly speaking, he reports, is not a passion; it is the connector between the self as judge of goods and evils and the self as actor; it is the medium between our passions and our moral, political, and artistic activities.[23] Hume's argument is that by every act, by every word and deed, a man expresses his character. Between a man's character and his acts—not the events, which will be influenced by additional causes—there is no elastic phase, no chance, no unnatural, noncausal relation. Besides, he contends, nobody believes in "free will"; the heated debates on this question are entirely of verbal or grammatical origins. Hume's argument must be understood in terms of his explanation of "necessity."

What we know as "necessity," when we deal with the natural world, is not an overwhelming power, but only the tendency of the imagination, trained by repeated experience, to move from the perception of a cause to the perception of the usual effect. When we say that we detect "natural necessity," we mean only that we believe that a particular set of causes always is followed by a particular set of effects. In other words, the idea of "natural necessity" has two, and only two, ingredients, the observed constant union of objects, and our consequent expectation; wherever we find these two—the first is invariably followed by the second—we may say that we have found "natural necessity." Now, submits Hume, the union we observe between physical objects is no more constant than that between men's motives and circumstances, on the one hand, and their acts, on the other. Similarly, our belief that men's acts will be comformable with their characters as human beings, as members of their own age group and sex, their vocational group, as members of their nation, and as particular men is just as strong as our beliefs about the physical world.[24] Place a man with a specific character in a specific situation, and his acts will follow by "natural necessity" in exactly the same way as the effects of any other set of causes. If this were not so, if "free will" separated men's characters from their acts, men would do uncaused, totally inexplicable, totally unpredictable acts. That we do not believe in "free will," Hume argues, is evident from the care we take to contrive laws calculated to cause men to behave in certain ways, and by the truth that we praise men for their good conduct and punish them for their misdeeds.[25]

He does not say that the individual has no freedom; instead, what he says is that the individual, having the character he has at any moment, is the immediate cause of his own acts. What causes an individual to feel pain or pleasure depends on the character (or nature) of that individual, which at any moment is a product, within the range possible for human nature, of his education, his direct and sympathetic experience, his station in life, and his interests. What causes him pleasure, he will regard as good, and will strive to attain. What causes him pain, he will regard as evil, and will endeavour to avoid. Within the limits of their physical and moral environments men are free to do what they will to do, but what each man wills is the expression of his character.[26]

Directly connected with this rejection of the doctrine of "free will" is his insistence that there is no conflict between reason and the passions, and his denial of the popular view that acts of passion are necessarily evil, and acts of reason are necessarily good. To follow him here we have only to recall what we already have learned about the understanding. To reason, we have been told, is to form a judgment as to what is logically necessary or naturally necessary. By reasoning we discover the implications of systems, either abstract systems, the consistency of which we establish by fiat, or natural systems, the consistency of which habituation leads us to presuppose. By reasoning we gain information about those systems. But no matter what information we acquire by reasoning about geometric figures or about past, present, or future happenings in the real world, we remain perfectly indifferent to that information unless it causes us present or anticipated pain or pleasure. Only when the basic distinction between painful and pleasant feelings is taken into account directly or indirectly do we make any judgment of good or evil. We are moved to act only by our desire for what we judge to be good, or by our aversion from what we judge to be evil. Our beliefs about reality are important, for they provide us with the prospects which we evaluate, and with much of the information on which we base our plans for acquiring goods and avoiding evils. But if we did not evaluate the things and acts about which we are informed, we would have no interest whatsoever in that information. " 'Tis from the prospect of pain or pleasure that the aversion or propensity arises towards any object: And these emotions extend themselves to the causes and effects of that object, as they are pointed out to us by reason and experience." [27] Judgment of reality and judgment of value are both important human operations. They are not opposed and contending; rather, they cooperate. The former tells us what was, is, and may be; the latter evaluates as good or evil what was, is, or may be.[28]

Men always desire what they find good. But many things and qualities are good, and all cannot be sought at once. Moreover, some entail evils as means or by-products. According to Hume's system, the passions are the immediate causes of acts, and which passion or passions—which desired good or goods—will prove dominant at any time depends on the character and circumstances of the actor. In any choice, the *strong* passions take precedence over the *weak* ones, or supplant them; this does not mean, however, that the *violent* passions overrule the *calm*.[29]

An illustration of the passions that ordinarily are calm, Hume says, in one passage, is "the sense of beauty and deformity in action, composition [of music and poetry], and external objects." [30] In another passage, he says that they are of two kinds, "either certain instincts originally implanted in our natures, such as benevolence and resentment, the love of life, and kindness to children; or the general appetite to good, and aversion to evil, consider'd merely as such." [31] Normally these passions exert their influences without much turmoil or perturbation; but that they are genuine passions is shown by the truth that occasionally they become extremely moving.[32]

What erroneously is thought to be a conflict between reason and the passions in truth is a struggle between violent and calm passions. Since the thinking called "reasoning" ordinarily takes place without much emotional turbulence, the knowing of any calm passion may be mistaken easily for reasoning. When we contrast reason and the passions, we praise the former and suspect the latter, because under the sway of a violent passion we are captivated by the thought of some one good, which, some-how, looms large before us, hiding the prospect of diverse goods stretching out into the future, while under the influence of the calm passions we view goods in their proper proportions. The truth is, not that the word "reason" as used by the careless, as the opponent of the passions, designates nothing, but that it designates the calm passions.[33]

Whether a particular passion will be calm or violent depends on various things. A passion is likely to become violent if the mind is excited by curiosity, by uncertainty, and by either the opposition of others or the opposition of one's own minor, divergent passions.[34] Repetition and habituation have the most remarkable influence. Any new activity of mind or body, whether pleasant or painful, is certain to be most affecting, but when the novelty has worn off, the effect of repetition begins to appear. A facility in the action or thought is acquired and, provided that this passes not a certain degree, a new ease and pleasure result, which may make us indifferent to, or even cause us to enjoy, originally unpleasant experiences. But if habituation becomes too great, the result will be boredom, which is painful. Again, the more detailed and exact a plan or design of the imagination, provided the complications are not extreme, the more it will interest us, and appeal to us; but to stir us, any plan or prospect must be within the range of our experience or comprehension.[35] And the farther from ourselves in place or time any good or evil is placed, the weaker will be our passion.[36]

It is easier, Hume says, to influence a man's conduct by arousing a violent passion in him than a calm one, and this is the normal tactic of politicians, preachers, and legislators. But this does not mean that the violent passions always are strong and the calm, weak; indeed, it is because the efficacy of the calm passions is commonly underrated that "reason" is often pre-sented as the true opponent of the "passions," for obviously the violent passions do not always prevail.

Men often act knowingly against their interest: It is not therefore the view of the greatest possible good which always influences them. Men often counteract a violent passion, in prosecution of their

distant interests and designs: It is not therefore the present uneasiness alone, which determines them. In general, we may observe,
that both these principles operate on the will; and where they are
contrary, that either of them prevails, according to the general
character or present disposition of the person. What we call
*strength of mind* implies the prevalence of the calm passions above
the violent; though we may easily observe, that there is no person
so constantly possessed of this virtue, as never, on any occasion,
to yield to the solicitation of violent affection and desire. From
these variations of temper proceeds the great difficulty of deciding
with regard to the future actions and resolutions of men, where
there is any contrariety of motives and passions.[37]

The circumstances in which a man finds himself or is placed by
those who would influence his conduct are not decisive, for "the
*causes* and *effects* of these violent and calm passions are pretty
variable, and depend, in a great measure, on the peculiar temper
and disposition of every individual." [38]

Hume's theory of the passions is fairly simple. Our judgments of reality are based on feeling, on the impressiveness of
some perceptions and the unimpressiveness of others. The passions, too, are feelings, but of a different kind. While judgment
of reality depends on the impressiveness of perceptions, judgment of value depends ultimately on the difference between pain
and pleasure. All the passions, which are the springs of action,
are nothing more or less than expressions of our approval of
good and our desire for it, and of our disapproval of evil and
our aversion to it. The direct passions—joy or grief, hope or
fear, desire or aversion—are brought on immediately by good
or evil. The indirect passions, our feelings for ourselves and
others, arise through double association, sympathy, and the
egocentricity of perception.

It is not to be thought that Hume credits reason with no important role in determining our acts. Our outlook on the present
is shaped in part by our beliefs, and our outlook on the past
and the future depends almost entirely on beliefs. The reasoning faculty places us in the context of the past, the present,
and the future. Without that faculty we should be caught up in

an isolated present, and enthralled, therefore, by the present goods or evils. With the aid of reason we foresee many goods and evils distributed ahead over many days and years, so that our feelings are ordered, balanced, and restrained by each other, and consequently are calm.

# IV

## MORAL DUTIES

That Faculty, by which we discern Truth and Falshood, and that by which we perceive Vice and Virtue
had long been confounded with each other, and all Morality was suppos'd to be built on eternal and immutable
Relations, which, to every intelligent Mind, were equally
invariable as any Proposition concerning Quantity or
Number. But a late Philosopher [Mr. Hutcheson] has
taught us, by the most convincing Arguments, that
Morality is nothing in the abstract Nature of Things,
but is entirely relative to the Sentiment or mental Taste
of each particular Being; in the same Manner as the
Distinctions of sweet and bitter, hot and cold, arise
from the particular feeling of each Sense or Organ.
Moral Perceptions therefore, ought not to be class'd
with the Operations of the Understanding, but with
the Tastes or Sentiments.

*Essays*, II, 10, footnote

Early in November of 1740, twenty-one months after "Of
the Understanding" and "Of the Passions" had been published,
Hume brought out "Of Morals," the third and last book in the
*Treatise.* By then his youthful hope for acclaim, built up during more than ten years of arduous study, had wilted somewhat under the frosts of neglect. His theories were bold and
ingenious, and carefully expounded; yet his work, it seemed to
him, was ignored by everybody. Accordingly, he begins "Of
Morals" by saying that if it were not that morals is a topic in
which most men are interested because of its great practical importance, he should never have undertaken "a third volume of
such abstruse philosophy, in an age, wherein the greatest part
of men seem agreed to convert reading into an amusement, and
to reject every thing that requires any considerable degree of

attention to be comprehended." What is notable is not his complaint, but his suggestion that "Of Morals" will serve to introduce and promote his entire system: "I am not, however, without hopes, that the present system of philosophy will acquire new force as it advances; and that our reasonings concerning *morals* will corroborate whatever has been said concerning the *understanding* and the *passions*." [1] In "Of the Understanding," he had argued that our decision as to whether or not a perception is reliable evidence of reality results, not from its internal or external relations, but from its strength or impressiveness. Judgment of reality depends not on ideation, but on feeling. Then, in "Of the Passions," he had argued that all the passions arise from the basic distinction, known by feeling, between good and evil. Judgment of value, too, depends on feeling. Now, the effects of the feelings we can state, but why the feelings arise, and why they produce those effects, we do not know. In short, Hume treats both ratiocination and passion as operations of human nature which can be described, but which ultimately, like the progress of a star or the fall of an apple, are beyond explanation by natural philosophy. The cardinal place he gives to impressions (feelings), his insistence on the singular importance of experience (together with its refinement, the experimental method), and his "moderate scepticism" entail and imply each other. These are the main arches of his system of philosophy. What he writes in "Of Morals," as he says, is entirely consistent with that system, and might serve to introduce it.

We have seen that moral virtue is among the greatest causes of pride or self-esteem, and of our love for others, and that moral vice is outstanding as a cause of humility, and of hatred. But exactly what moral virtue and moral vice are, we have not yet been told, for in "Of the Passions" Hume was setting forth his theory of passion, volition, and action, and did not stop to explore the distinction we all make between virtue and vice.[2] In "Of Morals" he reverts to this distinction, and examines it at length.

The casual reader probably will find this book hard to com-

prehend: its title, its structure, and even much of the material
in it, all combine to obscure the basic purpose underlying the
work. Moreover, the reader is likely to be confirmed in his misapprehensions if he assumes, as easily he might, that *An Enquiry concerning the Principles of Morals* is simply a revised
or popularized version of "Of Morals." [3] In the latter book
Hume is seeking to show that it is not what has been called
"reason," but the feelings which, through sympathy, give rise
to the distinction between virtue and vice. His interest is focused on this sympathetic process; all human characteristics
that we come to approve because of this process, he calls "virtues," and all that we come to disapprove because of it, he calls
"vices." [4] "Virtue" and "vice" for him are not limited to "moral
virtue" and "moral vice." The title, "Of Morals," which seems
to imply that Hume is concerned with morality alone, is deceptive. He generally employs the word "moral" with a very
broad eighteenth-century meaning to refer, in contrast to
"physical," to the entire realm of words, deeds, institutions, and
works of art, insofar as this realm is shaped by the minds of
men. This is the realm caused mainly by human nature, the
area in which human nature, in its moral (or mind) aspect, not
its physical aspect, is expressed. Causes independent of men's
minds, i.e., the qualities of the physical universe, also are influential, and set the limits of human achievement. But within
those limits, what men do, either individually or collectively, is
the result of their own moral (mind) characteristics. What
they do is the product of their moral characters. We have just
been told, in "Of the Passions," that one of the causes most influential in producing our feeling for any other person, and
thus most influential as a cause of our conduct towards him, is
his moral character. Our judgment of others is influenced by
their wines, their adventures, and their houses, but also by
their different high or low moral (mind) characteristics. Similarly, the attitude of other people towards us is influenced by
their appraisal of our moral (mind) characteristics. Just as
each person, probably without any great precision, appraises
the gardens and carriages of his neighbours, so he appraises

their moral qualities. Many are found to be men of ordinary and undistinguished virtue; a few are regarded as exceptionally virtuous, and therefore are called "great men"; and some are found deficient in important respects, and are called "vicious." Why this should be, why we should make a distinction between virtuous and vicious moral (mind) characteristics, is Hume's main subject in "Of Morals." The title of the book, however, probably would lead a casual reader to expect a discussion restricted to morality.

The structure of the book, too, is far from helpful. Hume does see that there is a difference between what loosely are called "natural (mind) abilities" and "moral virtues," and he regards these as two kinds of moral (mind) characteristics. In expounding his theory of how we evaluate all moral characteristics as either virtuous or vicious, he begins, not with the "natural abilities," but with the "moral virtues." Besides, he devotes by far the greater part of the book to the "moral virtues," and comes to "natural abilities" only towards the very end. A reader who, in the beginning, misunderstood the title would have no cause to suspect that this is more than a study of morality until he reached the final pages; by then his interpretation of the book probably would be too settled to permit easy revision.

Again, the political parts of the book help to hide Hume's basic argument. In his Introduction to the *Treatise*, he wrote that while our tastes and sentiments are studied in morals and criticism, "men as united in society, and dependent on each other," is the subject matter of politics. But it would have been impossible for him to have written perspicuously about morals without writing about politics. And, since what he has to say on politics—that is, on the artificial moral virtues—takes up over half the book, and is interesting in the extreme, it tends to become the cynosure of attention. The long illustration submerges the main argument.

For these reasons "Of Morals" might be taken as a discussion of moral virtues; actually, it is a discussion of how we evaluate all good human qualities. We need to remind ourselves constantly of the wide significance for Hume of the word "moral," and of his general purpose in "Of Morals," because in this chapter, our own subject is Hume's theory of the origin and content of moral duty. Our interest is restricted to the "moral virtues." Much of the argument with which we shall be dealing, we must remember, has a considerably wider relevance in both "Of Morals" and *An Enquiry concerning the Principles of Morals*.

Our purpose in evaluating a person—either his entire character, or some one of the characteristics which make up his character—is largely practical. We want to know how he is likely to behave in the future, so that we may conduct ourselves suitably. We have no direct practical interest in his past fidelity, probity, or generosity, for both his past and ours are irrevocable. It is his future conduct that concerns us. But because the deeds of the past are done, they can be reviewed, while because the deeds of the future are as yet undone, we cannot know them. This, however, is a situation in which we normally apply causal thinking, for it is one of our beliefs that a man's past acts were in part the effects of his own character, and that his future acts, too, will be in part the effects of his character. We, therefore, evaluate his character—not either his ephemeral past acts, or his unknown future acts—as virtuous or vicious. But a man's character can be known only as it has been made manifest; so, finally, we are thrown back on the evidence of past deeds. These deeds—we must repeat, for Hume is insistent on this point— are not themselves virtuous or vicious, but are called so only because they manifest a virtuous or vicious character.[5]

Our main questions now come into sight. We all assume that we can take a man's past acts as evidence of his character; to each man we attribute various qualities or properties, also called his "characteristics," or his "virtues" (or "vices"), sufficient to cause (him to do) the same kinds of acts again if the same conditions recur. We also assume that every act, in addition to all its other causes, has a motive. These two assumptions imply that each man has his constant or characteristic motives. It is with these, with the characteristics that are motives, not with the other qualities of the mind, that we are concerned when we evaluate a man's "moral virtues" and find him truly virtuous, or fairly virtuous, or so deficient in one or more of the virtues as to be called, simply, "vicious." And when we evaluate a man's motives, we compare them with a standard. The clear implication of this is that there are ways of acting, and therefore motives, suitable to particular occasions, circumstances, and stations in private and public life. The "moral virtues" are the kinds of motives that lead a man to act in the proper ways at the proper times. Here rises a question: What causes us to regard some ways of behaviour as good, and other ways as bad? What is the origin of our standards of virtuous behaviour? What is the origin of our list of the "virtues"? Moreover, when we feel prompted to act in ways incompatible with the standard of good or proper behaviour, we often also feel a desire to live up to those standards. We have, we find, a general sense or feeling of moral obligation. In other words, we find that the morally approved acts and ways of acting are "duties" for us, and that we often do our duties despite contrary desires and aversions. Here rises a second question: Why do we feel a special desire, a desire separate from all our diverse other desires, to act according to the standards of virtue? What has to be explained, then, is two fold: first, the general moral feeling, or "moral sense," which often is our motive when we do those acts called "duties"; and, second, the content of the standards of virtuous behaviour, i.e., the content of duty.

There are eddies—and Hume is especially anxious that we shall see them—beyond which we must pass safely, if we are to follow his explanation of why we distinguish between moral virtue and moral vice and his explanation of why we feel obliged to act virtuously. We must not get caught in circuitous arguments, and give a moral distinction as the cause of all our moral distinctions. The content of duty is to be explained in terms of virtue, and then virtue itself has to be explained—but not in terms of either duty or virtue. "Virtuous" and "vicious" are words that show approval or disapproval, and our present task is to see why any value distinction (entailing approval and disapproval) is made among motives. We are trying to find the crucial difference among motives, that difference which causes men to approve one group of motives, and to disapprove the other group. This difference cannot be that one motive has been evaluated as "virtuous" while another has been evaluated as "vicious."

Hume's warning can be set forth in another way. The words "virtuous" and "vicious"—and "virtue" and "vice"—are not meaningless, and they are not meaningless because they have been used to refer to a difference. This difference is what is important—the words themselves could be interchanged without any substantive change in either our moral ideals or our moral conduct. We consider a man's motives, as evinced by his words and deeds; we find that they win our approval; and then we call them "virtuous." If we want to know what it is that we call "virtue," we must decide why we gave our approval to his motives. Or we may find that one or more of his characteristic motives, as demonstrated by one or more acts, cause our disapproval, and then we call those motives "vicious." Again, if we want to know what it is that we call "vice," we must try to discover what there is about those motives that leads to our disapproval.

We must be careful to notice that Hume is not saying that our moral judgments are mere *ex post facto* comments on acts and motives, and that they never have an influence on private or public affairs. In the first place, he is not suggesting that in everyday life we do not often decide whether or not a particular act is virtuous by comparing it with our preestablished standards of virtue. We often learn that certain acts are duties for us simply by reading the appropriate list of duties. Once the standards of moral virtue—that is, the content of moral duty—have been fixed, those standards have a very beneficial influence. Hume's query concerns the origin and basis of the standards themselves. And, second, he is not arguing that our standards of virtue are not among the common causes of our acts. Men sometimes do acts of virtue because they feel that those acts are their duties. Moreover, they often try to act according to standards, not because of an immediate motive or any sense of duty, but because, for some reason, they wish to appear virtuous, or wish to become virtuous. It is precisely because our standards of moral virtue—our standards of duty—are influential in our daily judgments and conduct that Hume tries to explain why the standards exist.

An act must be virtuous before it can be our duty to do it. It is our duty to do it, because it is a virtuous act. It is not a virtuous act because it is our duty to do it.[6] Similarly, it would be preposterous to say, at this fundamental level, that virtuous acts are those acts done for the sake of virtue, for we have not yet stated what virtue is, as distinguished from vice. The "first virtuous motive, which bestows a merit on any action, can never be a regard to the virtue of that action, but must be some other natural motive or principle."[7] Prior to standards of virtue, and to the sense of obligation to live up to those standards, there must be motives to action of which we approve without referring to standards, and which supply the content of our standards of virtue.[8] If we are to explain the difference between virtue and vice, we must go back beyond the standards to the cause of the distinction between virtue and vice, and to the cause of the standards.[9]

Philosophers before and after Hume have disagreed less about which particular acts are virtuous and which ones are vicious than about why it is "good" to do the former, and to avoid the latter. Three explanations of why motives are divided into two basic groups have been prominent. Since the morally virtuous man is the man who fulfills the moral possibilities of human nature to the highest degree—the several moral virtues are the moral characteristics of such a man—the debate among the philosophers has centered on deciding what the correct description of human nature is. One view is that a true man, one to be approved and called "virtuous," is one who obeys God. It follows from this that God's laws ought to be obeyed, not because of their content, but because they are His commands. Here, moral duties are derived from the religious relation between God as ruler and men as God's subjects. When God's commands are known, the standards of virtue are known. A second explanation is that since men are rational beings, they are morally virtuous when they act rationally, and vicious when they act irrationally. The difference underlying the evaluative distinction between virtuous and vicious acts is that the former are rational, while the latter are irrational. When the prescriptions of reason have been fully discovered, the rules of good conduct will be known. A third view—the one accepted by Hume—is that it is by the feelings that men distinguish between good and evil, and therefore that men are most virtuous when they are most agreeable and useful to themselves and others. The arguments in favour of these three theories are not of the same order: either the second theory or the third can be enveloped within the first without any substantive change. The first often has been developed into the second by philosophers: God has often been treated as the sole cause of reason, which in turn has been treated as the cause of morality.

The task of theological moralists is inevitably the most difficult. For them the validity of moral laws depends, not on their content, but on their origin as commands of a will with an absolute right to be obeyed. Since the true laws cannot be identified by inspecting their content, the decisive question is: Who is the true interpreter or spokesman on earth of God's will? If the divine commission were self-evident to everyone, this question could be answered at once, but since a claim to be commissioned is not its own warrant, attempts sometimes are made to support claims in terms of nature, i.e., nature known by abstract thinking ("reasoning") or by feeling. Another method which at first is promising is the marshalling of historical proofs, but whether or not these are convincing and command our faith depends on whether or not the historical words and deeds seem natural—and that brings us back to nature. Faith not based on evidence may be valid, but is not self-evidently valid, and therefore is inadmissible as evidence that one holds a divine commission to proclaim God's laws.

When, midway through the seventeenth century, Thomas Hobbes set forth his views on the social and political order, he thought it necessary to refute the several conflicting theological

explanations of morality then prevalent—or rather, to prove
that reason shows that the right of interpreting God's will,
whether found engrossed in the Holy Scriptures or in the Creation, to the people of a commonwealth belongs exclusively to
their government, and never to any private person or group.
Hobbes' argument is rationalist, but he makes it relevant to his
seventeenth-century readers by occasionally stating it in theological terms, which neither add to nor subtract from the substance of the argument. That is, he tries to vanquish the theological moralists by posing as one of them, and then making
God the sole cause of the effects on which his own theory rests.[10]
Hume, in presenting his explanation of virtue, spends no time
on theological moralists. His aims, it is true, were somewhat
more literary, even academic, and less desperately practical
than those of Hobbes; undoubtedly, the social level of the audience he hoped to reach was higher. Nevertheless, the contrast
must stand as evidence of a reconstruction in the thought, not
necessarily of the generality of the people, but of the more ad-
venturous sections of the literate in Britain. It was rationalist
moral philosophy, not theological moral philosophy, that Hume
believed would have to be overcome before his own theory could
gain acceptance among his readers. Instead of concentrating
on the relation between God and the passions, which presumably
would have been the seventeenth-century approach, he concentrates on reason and the passions, and traces the distinction between moral virtue and vice primarily to the passions
rather than to reason. It will be helpful to notice briefly his two
famous criticisms of the rationalists, before we turn to his own
view.

Is the distinction between moral virtue and vice based on
reason? Is there "an abstract rational difference betwixt moral
good and evil" which can be known solely by right reasoning by
all rational beings—God, all men, and every other being that
may be? What we call moral virtue and moral vice are very different. Can this difference be stated in a theorem of reason? Is
there an order, constitution, or system of private and public
life which has as its constituent principle a rational distinction

between good and evil—a system of "eternal immutable fit-
nesses and unfitnesses of things"—requiring some acts, and
prohibiting others, so that we may define the virtuous as those
who live by this constitution, and the vicious as those who de-
viate greatly from it? We already have found, Hume reminds
us, that reasoning is the understanding of either demonstrable
or natural systems. If we say, as we have, that every man is an
individual instance of human nature, we say that there is a relation of basic equality among all men, and we say that mankind
is a system of equal units. This will be important, once we have
made the moral judgment, that is, after we have decided that
certain acts, e.g., murder, breach of promise, or acts of charity,
are either virtuous or vicious. But the rational relation itself
leads us to conclude neither that we should seek to destroy all
mankind, nor that we should try to save a single life. This relation is merely a relation among units of a kind of being. It
would be the same if we were talking about fire-logs, onions, or
typewriters, instead of about human beings. Before we have
learned, not by reasoning, but by experience with at least one
typewriter or one human being, the nature of such things, the
statement that all typewriters or all human beings have the
same nature is abstract and unimportant. A command telling
us to operate all typewriters properly has no content until we
know how we ought to operate one typewriter. Similarly, when
it is a matter of treating human beings, a command that we
treat all men alike has no content until we know how we ought
to treat one human being. Hume's argument is that since correct conduct is always conduct appropriate to the nature of the
object involved, correct moral conduct is conduct appropriate
to the nature of human beings. We can have no standard of
moral conduct, and thus no conception of the morally virtuous
man, until we know the nature of human beings. Our standard
of conduct and thus our conception of moral virtue result from,
and are not prior to, or independent of, our knowledge of human nature. And it is by experience, i.e., primarily by our
senses and passions, that we come to know what is good and
what is bad for human beings.[11]

Moreover, a second impossible task confronts the advocates of an "eternal and immutable code" of rational laws, which, quite independent of the desires and aversions characteristic of the nature of those to whom the laws apply, sets forth the ways in which all rational beings, including even God, are obliged to behave. Not only is it incumbent on them to show that the difference between good and evil is a matter of relation, but they must demonstrate the *a priori* necessity by which the code causes good acts. They have to be able to show that a formula of thought not made impressive by any feeling—for they have ruled out desire and aversion as irrelevant—can be important to a will, and that it is logically necessary that every well-disposed rational being be influenced by it. To do this, Hume contends, is impossible, both because an unimpressive relation is unimportant and because the only way that the existence of a necessary connection between a "cause" and an "effect" in the real world can be known is, not by logic, but by repeated experience.[12]

Hume's objections to eighteenth-century rationalist explanations of morality imply his own theory.[13] It is his contention that our standards of moral virtue, our conceptions of the virtuous man, or our lists of the moral virtues—whichever manner of expression we prefer—have their basis in the distinct nature of human beings, and that, therefore, these do not apply to vegetables or brutes, on the one hand, or to God, on the other. They are no more eternal or immutable than is human nature. Moral good and evil are known and distinguished by men. There are only two ways of perception: knowing in terms of relations, and the knowing of feelings. If, as we have seen, the difference between moral good and evil is not a difference between abstract ideas, it follows that it must be a difference known by feeling. This is Hume's view. The basic element in every value judgment is the primary difference between pleasure and pain. And this holds true when we come to evaluate men's characters, or specific attributes of their characters. It is because, human nature being as it is, some motives cause acts which, in a certain way, are found pleasant by men, while others cause acts which, in a certain way, are found painful, that the former are called, "virtuous," and the latter, "vicious." This distinction can be traced back to human nature, and no farther. The difference between pleasure and pain, and therefore between moral virtue and vice, cannot be discovered by an exertion of thought, but only by knowing feelings. What things and acts will cause pleasure and what will cause pain cannot be known *a priori*, but only as the result of learning, i.e., experimenting.

When we say that the distinction between virtue and vice arises from the distinction between pleasure and pain, we do not mean, Hume contends, that when a motive leads to pleasure we *infer* that that motive is virtuous, or that it is vicious if it leads to pain. To say that would be preposterous. Rather, it is pleasure and pain that cause us to make another distinction, the distinction between virtue and vice. The knowledge that an impression, *which qualifies otherwise*, is pleasant and not painful, or *vice versa*—this knowledge itself—is the basis of the consequent moral distinction.[14]

This distinction between pleasure and pain, however, is only the primary distinction in the process of forming a moral judgment. This distinction does not explain fully how the standards of moral virtue applied in private and public life arise. Evaluation as pleasant or painful is essential in moral evaluation, but, clearly, not everything that causes us pleasure is morally good, and not everything that causes us pain is morally bad. A judgment distinguishing between moral virtue and vice is not simply a matter of sensation or passion. If it were, every pleasant thing would be morally good and every painful thing would be morally evil. Rather, the judgment is a matter of a "moral sense." Moral evaluation, as explained by Hume, is marked by four additional causes or conditions, each of which must be present.

First, the pleasant and painful feelings on which the distinction is based are felt through sympathy.[15] All perception, we have seen, is individualistic. We know only the pleasant and painful sensations and passions we ourselves feel. But we come to feel pleasure and pain in two different ways, immediately and by sympathy. If each man felt only the pleasant and painful things that happen to himself, it would be impossible to distinguish between moral and nonmoral evaluation.[16] One man's moral good would be another's moral evil—and such terms, therefore, would be meaningless. But the principle of sympathy frees us from this isolation, for through it we come to feel the reactions to pleasure and pain already felt by those around us. Through sympathy we share, to a degree, the joy, hope, and love, or the grief, fear, and hatred, experienced by any person present with us. It is the pleasure and pain that come to us in this second way, through sympathy, that lead to our moral judgment of the person responsible for those feelings.

Hume, it must be noted, in the *Treatise*, as in the later *Enquiry concerning the Principles of Morals*, holds that it is totally impossible to explain our approval of virtue by calling it an expression of self-love. His argument that our moral judgment depends on feeling sympathetically the feelings of others —the argument he labours to establish in the *Treatise*—is contrary to the self-love theory, and excludes it. His whole explanation of the importance of the principle of sympathy is an implied rebuttal to the self-love hypothesis. He seems to have assumed, in the *Treatise*, that it would be impossible for anybody to fail to see that he was writing to supplant the self-love theory, as well as all other erroneous theories; at least, he is content to dismiss the theory in a sentence or two.[17] In the *Enquiry concerning the Principles of Morals*, he spells out his criticisms at greater length.[18]

Second, genuine moral judgments are made from a neutral (or impartial) standpoint.[19] Although sympathy widens our perception of pleasure and pain, it alone is insufficient to give us a standpoint free from egocentricity. Sympathy, like immediate perception, operates naturally only within a limited circle, only within the circle of those whom we know, and within this, its efficiency varies with the extent of our acquaintance with the men involved. This suggests that our esteem for any virtue and our disapprobation of any vice, although somewhat more extensive, are limited and varied, just as are the affections produced by our selfish interests. Hume finds that this is untrue. Our moral judgment of any man's character, he holds, is not a function of direct sympathy with him or those around him. Moral judgment at its best, that is, when genuine, is completely independent of our direct sympathetic feelings, as well as of our interested feelings. It is independent of time and place, and does not change as the men involved are viewed as living near us, a thousand miles away, or in antiquity; nor does it change as the men involved are our friends, our enemies, or persons indifferent.[20]

The only interest or pleasure that can be viewed in such a way as to meet the requirement of neutrality is that of the person whose character is being appraised, or that of those influenced by him.

Now, in judging of characters, the only interest or pleasure, which appears the same to every spectator, is that of the person himself, whose character is examin'd; or that of persons, who have a connexion with him. And tho' such interests and pleasures touch us more faintly than our own, yet being more constant and universal, they counter-ballance the latter even in practice, and are alone admitted in speculation as the standard of virtue and morality. They alone produce that particular feeling or sentiment, on which moral distinctions depend.[21]

Only the judgment of the impartial, disinterested spectator can be a genuine moral judgment, and a spectator can be impartial and disinterested only when he attends exclusively to the interest and pleasure of the men appraised or those associated with him.

This timeless and placeless viewpoint is possible to us because through sympathy we learn the pleasure and pain caused, both in the short run and the long run, by certain acts; our attention then shifts to those acts; and wherever or whenever we see those acts, or a record of them, we judge the characteristics of the men responsible for them as virtuous or vicious. This abstraction, this shift from a judgment of the feelings we know through sympathy to a judgment of particular *kinds of acts*, permits us to gauge from a neutral standpoint the moral stature of our friends, the moral stature of distant heroes and saints, and the moral stature even of our rivals.[22]

When, in practice, we fail to make accurate moral judgments because of the egocentricity of perception, we are likely to show considerable deference for the moral standpoint in our public utterances, at least.[23]

Third, when we judge a man's moral character we take into consideration his particular role, place, or station. We form conceptions of the acts appropriate to men as fathers, uncles, kings, merchants, neighbours, comrades, samaritans, and politicians, and we judge a man not simply, but with regard to his office(s). Our view of what constitutes a man's duty in any particular role is the result of our learning. We expect from him what we think highly probable or certain, because of our observations of other men similarly placed, and we are disappointed when his motives do not cause him to live up to our expectations.

[We] always consider the *natural* and *usual* force of the passions, when we determine concerning vice and virtue; and if the passions depart very much from the common measures on either side, they are always disapprov'd as vicious. A man naturally loves his children better than his nephews, his nephews better than his cousins, his cousins better than strangers, where every thing else is equal. Hence arise our common measures of duty, in preferring the one to the other. Our sense of duty always follows the common and natural course of our passions.[24]

We now have before us Hume's explanation of the virtues, those attributes of human nature, which when possessed at the optimum level, make up the character of the perfect man. Some of these attributes are approved, through the influence of sympathy, because they please *the associates of the men* endowed with those qualities. Some of them, such as "wit, and a certain easy and disengag'd behaviour," are pleasing because they are immediately agreeable to those associates. Others are pleasing because we have found that such qualities cause results which are agreeable to the associates. Of these two kinds, the latter,

those which are useful, is by far the more important. In this
case it is the effects that are pleasant, and we approve the specific characteristic only because, through the understanding,
we foresee its good effect. It is, incidentally, with qualities of
this kind, those whose good is learned by "reflections on the
tendencies of action," that moral duty is chiefly concerned.[25]
Then—and here we come to two other kinds of virtues—we may
find that some characteristics please us, through sympathy, because they are either immediately agreeable or are the causes of
effects which are pleasing to *the person* endowed with those
qualities. Although sometimes we think of virtues as attributes
of character which give pleasure to the associates of the virtuous man, we find that many have their direct effect only on
that man himself. We praise prudence, temperance, frugality,
industry, enterprise, and dexterity, as well as generosity and
humanity.[26]

In short, the virtues are of four kinds: through sympathy we
reap "a pleasure from the view of a character, which is naturally fitted to be useful to others, or to the person himself, or
which is agreeable to others, or to the person himself." [27] In
the *Enquiry concerning the Principles of Morals*, also, Hume
concludes "that personal merit consists entirely in the usefulness or agreeableness of qualities to the person himself possessed
of them, or to others, who have any intercourse with him." [28]

But, fourth, we must remember that in "moral" judgments
we must restrict our judgment to "moral virtues." This is a
point that Hume—understandably, given his aim in "Of Morals"—leaves undeveloped, so we must examine his comments
relevant to it with especial care. Since the one section in "Of
Morals" in which he discusses this point at any length is one in
which he is trying to destroy the notion that "moral virtues"
and "natural abilities" are totally different, it can be misread
as saying that there is no difference whatsover between them.

Hume believed there were two chief obstacles to the reception
of his theory that our standards of all human virtue are the
result of the pleasure and pain caused by men's characteristics
to themselves or their associates, as known by neutral specta-

tors through sympathy. The first was "the fantastic doctrine
of free will" and the second, the verbal usage, based on that
doctrine, by which we speak of "moral virtues" and "natural
abilities" as if these were two quite different classes, one subject
to causality and the other "free." His aim in the section, "Of
Natural Abilities," is to expose and destroy these obstacles.

He chooses to refer to all human qualities judged from a
neutral standpoint as "virtues." A man who has those qualities
to a high degree is "virtuous," while one who is deficient in them
is "vicious." Hume's main purpose in "Of Morals" is twofold:
first, to show how it is possible for men to have a special kind of
feeling distinct from their self-centered feelings; second, to
show that the distinction we all make between good and bad
characteristics is based on a real difference known, not by reasoning, but by means of this special, this "moral," feeling. For
this purpose his explanation of virtue and vice is sufficiently
precise. The virtues, thus defined, would include not only the
"moral virtues" and the "natural abilities" of the mind, but also
physical abilities; but this does not mean that Hume thinks
that there is no difference between physical and mental abilities,
or between mental abilities and moral virtues. He is prepared to
have the words "virtue" and "vice" restricted to "moral virtue"
and "moral vice," provided that some other pair of terms is
provided to signify all the human qualities judged from a neutral standpoint, through sympathy.[29]

Hume's own view is, first, that human motives are not a matter of mere choice; second, that if they were, we could know
nothing whatsoever about them, because our knowledge is based
on the assumption that there is a causal connection between
acts and motives; third, that no parent, priest, or governor
ever proceeds on the assumption that motives are "free"; and
fourth, that the entire discussion of moral subjects would be
greatly expedited if the true meaning of "free will" were generally acknowledged. If we distinguish between abilities and motives because we think that the former come about by "natural
necessity," while the others are a matter of "free will," our distinction, he contends, is false. Neither a man's motives nor his

abilities are free and uncaused. Every change in either is the effect of sufficient causes. We are not dealing with two different realms; one, a realm of necessity, and the other, a realm of mere choice. Our usage, however, by which we speak of "moral virtues" and "natural abilities," implies that there is an absolute difference. This Hume denies. But to say, as he does, that motives and abilities are not totally different, is not to say that when we examine human behaviour we do not detect evidence of two different, although not totally different, kinds of moral (mind) characteristics. It is not to say, either, that the causes which produce a man's abilities are the same as those which produce his motives. And it does not mean that motives and abilities change and can be changed in the same way. The difference is not that motives are "free," while abilities are under "natural necessity"; rather, it is that motives are in one causal continuum, whereas abilities are in, perhaps not a separate, but a distinguishable, causal continuum. The causes which, by being added or subtracted, influence the motives and the abilities are different. This is the difference between motives and abilities when we speak of them in terms of causality.[30]

The second difference between moral virtue and natural ability is that when we say that a man is virtuous or vicious in respect of his motives, we are speaking about his taste (his sense, feelings, or judgment of value). When we judge a man's abilities only two factors are involved: the abilities and the feelings they cause us through sympathy. But when we judge a man's motives, three factors are involved: our moral judgment, the man's own moral judgment, and the act (or motive) which he judges. We know already that, according to Hume, when we speak of a man as being virtuous in respect of a particular virtue, e.g., charity, we mean that the acts he does in certain specific types of situations cause pleasure to those benefited, and that we, as observers, have a pleasant feeling brought on through sympathy. In addition, we mean that we assume that the man intends to do the charitable acts. He feels, we assume, that it would be good to do those acts, and, consequently, since his understanding leads him to believe that the acts are not impossible, he wills—he is moved by a motive—to do them. His taste, judgment of value, or moral sense is such that he thinks of those future acts, or their results, as good. Within the limits set by his abilities and circumstances, what a man does (or does not do), and how, expresses his judgment as to which acts or works are good, better, or best, and which are bad. They express his taste. Hume summed up his theory felicitously when he wrote that "morals and criticism regard our tastes and sentiments."

This brings us to a question. Why should we ever feel and say that an uncharitable man, for example, is vicious? Why should we expect him to judge that acts of charity are good? Why should we expect him to be moved to do acts of charity? Hume's answer is simple. It is through sympathetic feeling that we have come to know that uncharitable acts are morally painful, and, therefore, are morally bad. We believe—and if the idea were contrary to our experience it would not impress us—that all other experienced people have come to this same judgment, and that, accordingly, they will be moved to some extent by charitable feelings. Our expectations, which probably are seldom exactly correct, are seldom far wrong—otherwise, they would change—although occasionally men who are extraordinarily charitable or uncharitable appear, and then we are surprised. In short, Hume's answer is that we believe, as a result of experience, that others will have much the same feelings (or sentiments or taste) about what acts and works are good and desirable as we ourselves have.

Hume makes it quite clear that he thinks that while a man's natural abilities cannot be changed much, his moral feelings are susceptible to improvement, and also to degradation. There is little that can be done to add to or to subtract from the causes which first produce, and then maintain, the abilities; but a man's value judgment can be altered by the prolonged operation of old causes or the introduction of new ones. Hume refers to such alterations of moral taste in many passages. He seems to have thought of it as happening in at least four ways. First, governments may cause their subjects to behave in specific

ways by setting up rewards and punishments. Once, by the influence of this ulterior motivation, the subjects have become accustomed to acting in those ways, they may come to think of
them as good, and subsequently follow them without attention
to the ulterior rewards and punishments. Second, a man's tastes
are influenced by his beliefs, and these, in large part, are produced by parents, teachers, moralists, and divines. Acts cannot
be judged apart from their effects, but the most important effects of many acts are remote; consequently, any judgment of
these acts will depend on what one believes their results will be.
And many beliefs, as we have noted, are acquired vicariously,
not through direct experience. Any change in a man's beliefs, in
his judgment of reality, however produced, may work a change
in his judgment of value. Third, a man may cause a change in
his own moral characteristics. Pride and humility are brought
on not only by our judgment of our own houses, carriages, and
skills, but by our judgment of our own moral taste. We may,
therefore, for some reason, for example, a desire to reduce our
humility or a desire to enjoy fame, undertake to do good works
in emulation of the virtuous, in order to acquire the good taste
which normally causes those works and acts. "When any virtuous motive or principle is common in human nature, a person,
who feels his heart devoid of that motive, may hate himself
upon that account, and may perform the action without the
motive, from a certain sense of duty, in order to acquire by
practice, that virtuous principle, or at least, to disguise to himself, as much as possible, his want of it." [31]

And fourth, there is that change in moral taste which may be
called "civilization." The conduct of persons in relation to one
another is prompted either by their indirect passions or by their
desire for impersonal (economic) goods. Through sympathy
we feel pain when established expectations in either the sphere
of personal relations or the sphere of civil relations are disappointed. Now, whereas the prevailing pattern of personal relations is quite settled, because human nature is constant, the
pattern of civil relations prevailing at any time is dependent on
human insight into the implicit laws of civil relations and on

customary respect for those laws. In short, while the room for change in moral taste in the sphere of personal relations is small, in the sphere of civil relations—as we shall see in the next two chapters—the room for change is great. As a man becomes civilized his taste (or judgment) as to what is a good or bad act in civil relations will improve.

We now can answer the two questions which we raised at the start of this chapter. What, according to Hume, is the nature of duty? What, according to Hume, do we mean when we speak of "moral obligation"? We have found that we evaluate acts, and thus, motives, from two different standpoints: as interested actors, and as impartial spectators. As participants, we evaluate our acts and the acts of others as good or bad according as they cause us, or seem likely to cause us, pleasure or pain immediately. But we also feel pleasure and pain through sympathy, and thus we are able to evaluate acts and motives, as impartial spectators. Once we have come to think of particular acts as morally good or bad, we desire to avoid the latter in our conduct, and to do the former. These two evaluations, the interested and the moral, do not always conflict. Quite often our own interested desire and our moral desire lead to the same course of action; but when they do conflict, we feel drawn towards alternate courses of conduct, and at such times we become aware of the feeling of moral obligation, the sense, or feeling of duty.

The moral standards also recommend themselves to us because they are steady. Inevitably, the selfish evaluation is shifty and unreliable. We have to turn away from it repeatedly, to orient ourselves even when we are only thinking idly. Likewise, if we are planning or acting with others, the several selfish evaluations of those concerned provide no common foundation for cooperation. Even if we were always to plan and act independently, the inconstancy of selfish notions about what is good and evil would cause so many changes in our aspirations that all success, except what came accidentally, would be impossible.[32]

What is the origin of the content of duty? Why are we drawn to some acts, but not to others, by a feeling of moral obligation?

This question concerns the causes why the persons whose feelings we come to know through sympathy feel as they do. Here, we find, expectation about the conduct of men is most important. There are acts and ways of acting (and, therefore, motives) which are deemed proper to men in certain roles, offices, and relationships. When these roles are fulfilled, those involved are given pleasure, and when they are neglected, they are given pain. Our question, then, is: What is the origin of these diverse standardized relationships? Hume gives a twofold answer. Some, such as the relationship of parent and child, are the manifestation of feelings for other persons, feelings which, as a result of experience, we believe are natural to human beings; that is, feelings which are a part of what we mean when we speak about "human nature." Others, for example, the relationship among traders, are basically the manifestation of feelings for economic goods. The former kind of relationships Hume calls "natural." The latter kind, he calls "artificial." But in each case the relationships are based on what men, having the nature of human beings, find good in men and in the world in which they live, when these are viewed from the viewpoint of an impartial spectator. The content of duty is the outcome of human nature and of mankind's situation.

Moral standards, then, can be, and ought to be, explained strictly in terms of nature. The distinction between morally good works and morally bad works is a result of human feeling, not of human reasoning. The sense of moral obligation is not to be attributed ultimately either to reason or authority.

In seeking to shake the prevailing prejudice that correct standards for public and private life are to be apprehended by ratiocination, Hume wrote: "Reason is, and ought only to be the slave of the passions, and can never pretend to any other office than to serve and obey them." [33] These are derogatory, even contemptuous words. They are an exuberant lunge against the advocates of eternal laws binding on man and God alike. They go beyond Hume's argument. Already we have noticed that the basic difference between moral virtue and vice for him is discovered not by thinking about supposedly eternal and immutable principles of reason, but by attention to certain kinds of impressions. Morality is based on human nature, and arises as a result of feelings known sympathetically. From this, however, we must not conclude that Hume thinks that the understanding makes no contribution to our moral judgment or our moral conduct. By reasoning we come to understand the natural world; thereby, we acquire knowledge about what was, is, and shall be. Such knowledge contributes to morality in four ways.

First, it permits us to form moral standards of general applicability. Without the belief that human beings have a nature that remains constant, we could not acquire standards of general applicability. Second, reasoning is involved in our reflections on the tendencies of characteristics to cause good or evil results, which reflections lead us to call those characteristics virtuous or vicious. Here, again, we presuppose human nature, and believe that the characteristics of a particular man will produce the same results produced by those characteristics in other instances. These are elementary operations, and Hume passes over them without calling our attention to them. The two functions of reasoning in morality that he deals with directly bear not on moral judgment, but on conduct. By informing us of the existence of an object, reasoning may evoke the passions appropriate to that object, and thus arouse us to action. And by informing us of the effects of causes, reasoning may show us the means by which to express a passion. Hume's argument is that there are moral standards appropriate to all men, that these are consequences of human nature, and that reasoning is indispensible in discovering the scope and application of these standards.[34]

Moral judgments, being general, have no assured coincidence with our particular interests, and therefore tend to be calm rather than violent. This is why their influence on us is often mistaken for reasoning. Indeed, no great harm is done, if, following popular usage, we refer to "good moral behaviour" as "rational behaviour," provided that this does not mislead us into the error of thinking that "good moral behaviour" is described and ordained in an immutable and eternal constitution to be expounded to us by closet philosophers.

The process which we have been examining is the one by which moral standards are first introduced. Once a society has acquired the moral standards to some degree, those standards will be transmitted to each new generation largely by parents, teachers, and moralists.

# V

## NATURAL RELATIONSHIPS

## AND CIVIL SOCIETY

Human nature being compos'd of two principal parts, which are requisite in all its actions, the affections and understanding; 'tis certain, that the blind motions of the former, without the direction of the latter, incapacitate men for society.

*Treatise,* p. 493

HUME'S virtuous man, we have seen, is one who is agreeable and useful both to himself and to others. Moreover, it is probable, we have seen, that each man will feel it his duty to be as agreeable and useful as he can in his several moral roles. We now come to Hume's discussion of duties, that is, to his theory of the basic order, structure, or constitution of private and public life.

In "Of Morals" we learn that the roles that everybody ordinarily feels morally obliged to perform can be divided into two groups: some duties fall into what we may call the sphere of "personal" relations, and the rest into the sphere of "social" relations. In other words, in a fully developed order there are two distinct spheres of conduct. The duties of the personal sphere Hume calls "natural"; perfect conduct in this sphere would be the result of perfection in the "natural" moral virtues. The duties of the social sphere he calls "artificial"; perfect conduct in this sphere would be the result of perfection in the "artificial" moral virtues. We shall see later that social conduct is of two kinds: some social activities are economic, while others pertain to the state. We shall also see later that a "civil society" is an order in which both the principles of good economic conduct and the principles of good governance are embodied.

The principles of personal (natural) relations and of civil (artificial) relations are not to be mistaken for relationships existing in the real world. A man alone on an island, if informed sufficiently about the nature and necessitous situation of men, could think out the principles, but his success would not bring the principles into operation anywhere. In the case of the natural relationships, this difference between principles and principles realized is not important: whenever men live together, these relationships will be realized. But the existence of a civil society is impossible unless certain beliefs prevail about other people, and these beliefs do not exist in the beginning. In short, it is important to distinguish between, on the one hand, the *principles of civil society*, and, on the other, *civilization*, the process by which civil society comes into existence. Throughout this chapter we shall be concerned mainly with Hume's analysis of the principles of civility. In the following one we shall turn to Hume's account of civilization.

In no place does he undertake to set forth an exhaustive list of the natural moral virtues; yet, from what he says about them, in several passages, we can obtain a fairly complete view of what he regarded as the correct personal relations among men. For him, many of the most important activities come within this sphere: indeed, the civil sphere is composed primarily of activities auxiliary to those of the personal sphere.

The main personal (natural) relationship is the family.[1] Each pair of parents is a centre from which radii of blood relation reach out to radii from various other centres, and each new couple, in turn, becomes one of the new centres on the palimpsest of time. At first the family is not a moral institution: it is simply a natural alliance initiated by the sexual attraction between men and women, and continued by the love of parents for their offspring, the children's prolonged need for care and protection, natural affection, and by the joys of comfortable acquaintance. Now, if there were no other principles of natural grouping, the degree of affection prevailing among the several members of the populace would be fixed by the closeness or remoteness of their blood relation. But there are other causes of affection, Hume finds, to which the existence or absence of family ties is irrelevant, except when those ties are especially close and strong. Men with neighbouring abodes often find that common interests and long acquaintance make each other's company more agreeable than the company of outsiders. Then there is the great, general need for appreciation and companionship without which men are overpowered by boredom and languor. Consequently, persons of similar temperament and inclinations tend to draw together. From these origins arise friendships, instances of a relationship entailing important moral obligations. Still more extensive in its scope than the feelings which create and maintain families and friendships is a certain natural sensitivity to the happiness or misery of any other man, and even of creatures outside the human species.[2] This sensitivity does not produce any continuing groups, but issues as *ad hoc*, occasional acts to relieve the distressed, to assist "the industrious and indigent," to comfort the afflicted, and to extend "bounty even to the greatest strangers." [3] In one passage Hume summarizes the virtues relevant to the sphere of personal relations as "meekness, beneficence, charity, generosity, clemency, moderation, equity, . . ." [4] In another he summarizes them as "generosity, humanity, compassion, gratitude, friendship, fidelity, zeal, disinterestedness, liberality, and all those other qualities, which form the character of good and benevolent." [5] It is to the personal sphere that Hume assigns all the activities of living, as distinguished from those of making a living.

We saw earlier that the indirect passions—love and pride, hatred and humility—are instigated by many different causes. They are brought on by all the kinds of goods and evils: by a man's moral virtues and vices, by his physical beauty or deformity, by his economic wealth or poverty, and by success or failure in endeavours and adventures. But the rise of these passions, we saw, is not simple. Sympathy leads us to love the distressed and unfortunate. The egocentricity of perception leads us to love ourselves, our blood-relatives, our old friends and partners, and to hate our rivals and competitors and those with whom we compare ourselves. The indirect passions are feelings for human beings, either ourselves or other men and women. It is by these feelings—by love and pride, by hatred and humility—that activities within the sphere of natural morality are caused. A man's acts in this sphere are done because he feels malevolent or benevolent towards the other person or persons involved. Here, the desirability to a man of a single act or a prolonged course of action depends largely on what the other persons are to him. Who they are is of the greatest importance, for while the thought of many men leaves him unmoved, he will arouse himself to help his close relatives, his friends, and those whom he finds in distress; and he will arouse himself also to resist or ruin his personal enemies.

Personal (natural) relations among men—relations based on love, hatred, pride, or humility—are particular, never general, and, consequently, they are both limited in the number of persons involved, and, within that number, unequal. For one reason or another, a man has a different attitude, a different degree of love or hatred, varying from a strong passion to near indifference, towards each other person whom he meets personally: his wife, his nephews, his several neighbours, and the distressed stranger. Natural relations are composed of many different circles, each centred around an individual who is connected by a different tie to each of the other persons with whom he associates in any personal way. Despite this particularity, this sphere is not a moral chaos. There are certain standard natural roles in which a man appears—husband, father, son, friend, benefactor—in relation to one person or a few persons and as a result of one's sentiments. These natural roles become moral roles: the pleasure felt through sympathy by an impartial spectator when the natural role is fulfilled, and the pain felt when it is not performed, give the roles a moral quality, so that a man who is not moved, or not moved sufficiently, to live up to the standards of any one of the natural relationships is accounted deficient in the appropriate natural moral virtue, and to the extent of his deficiency is accounted vicious.

Evidently Hume thought that while the natural feelings

men have for others tend chiefly to peace and concord, the natural economic relations among men, relations based on their common desire for scarce goods, are antagonistic and, therefore, if unrestrained, destructive. From the very beginning of his treatment of civil society he presupposes that this competition must be mitigated, but not supplanted, by artifice. He finds, in addition, that when the destructiveness of the natural economic relation, total competition, has been modified by being brought within a framework of laws, that is, when *society* has been established, three very important positive benefits result. When a man seeks to satisfy his economic needs by his own independent labour, his success is highly unlikely.[6] He can accomplish no great tasks and projects, for his strength is trivial. Second, because he must produce all his necessities by his own efforts, he cannot attain the skill and mastery that come as a result of a division of labour among men, and the consequent specialization of each on the operation for which he is best suited. And since he lives alone, or at best with a few others, he is defenceless against all the perils of independence—sickness, accidents, old age, local droughts, and storms—and cannot rely on assistance from other men temporarily more fortunate. What is needed to overcome these three difficulties is a general division of labour in production, and a method for the distribution of the products.

The remedy is not the introduction of a totally artificial relationship, one from which competition would be excluded entirely, but the introduction of certain basic rules of competition. These rules, which Hume calls the principles of "justice," are three in number; and a group of men competing according to these rules is what he calls a "society."

The first of the principles requires the introduction of private property. There are three kinds of things which cause pleasure, and therefore are desirable: the virtues (goods) of the mind, the virtues (goods) of the body, and the qualities of such possessions as we have acquired by our "industry and good fortune." Now, while the enjoyment of the virtues of the mind and the body cannot be transferred fully to anybody else, the

third kind of goods, external goods, by their nature are completely external to persons, and, accordingly, are loose and
transferable. Moreover, while everybody has a mind and a body,
economic goods, we know, are often, even generally, scarce.
Natural affection among men works, not to solve, but to ag-
gravate this problem.[7] Many goods and services will be provided
within the natural groups as a result of affection, but this does
not suffice, for the number of persons related by feelings strong
enough to sustain the sharing of labour and its products is
very small. Natural economic relations embrace husbands and
wives, and parents and their young children, but beyond that,
where brothers, friends, and strangers are involved, the be-
stowal of goods and services is likely either to be limited to occasional gifts and acts of charity, or not to take place at all
—in short, is likely to be far too extraordinary to prevent
destructive competition and to overcome the three great disadvantages of economic independence. And not only are those
feelings themselves which lead to benevolent actions insufficient,
but they help to make cooperation difficult. Hostile acts rising
from personal, not economic, reasons, especially from envy
and the desire for revenge, inevitably cause some troublesome
conflicts, but such acts and conflicts are no considerable obstacle to cooperation. They are isolated, that is, they are only
occasional and are directed only against particular persons.
The great difficulty is avidity for economic goods for ourselves
and for those whom we love. Each individual seeks the joy and
contentment of those who are important to him, i.e., himself,
his immediate family, his friends, and any others for whom he
happens to have favourable sentiments. This avidity, unlike
personal hostility, is both perpetual and universal; unless overcome, it tends to make men enemies. Besides, it is insatiable. If
bounds are not placed on avarice, the possession of external
goods will be extremely precarious.

The first of Hume's principles of justice—the first rule
modifying competition—is that every man is to be left undisturbed in the enjoyment of his proper possessions. Whereas
before, economic goods were only possessed, hereafter they are

to be owned. Hume's argument is that ownership, by which the use and control of a thing in one, several, or all ways belongs to a specific person or to specific persons, while all others are excluded from using it in conflicting ways, is primarily a relationship between and among persons. It involves a relation between men and things, but it is the relation prevailing between the persons that designates the owner of the particular thing. Ownership is a matter of rights, and rights have their direct effect, not on things, but on men. Since ownership is a mental (moral) relationship, not a physical relationship, none of the innumerable physical relations that a man may enter into with his physical environment makes anything his own. Men eat things. They put fences around the mines they have dug. They can dig, fertilize, and plant fields. They can breathe the air, swim in the sea, and soak up the warm sunshine on the sands. But none of these operations, even if uncontested, alone suffices to establish a title of ownership. And when we turn away from physical facts to natural morality we find no basis there for this first principle of justice, because according to the standards of natural morality, we ought, disregarding all others, to seek goods for those whom we love. This rule of conduct—the rule that every man, no matter how we happen to feel towards him, is to be left undisturbed in the enjoyment of his proper possessions—therefore, must be an "artificial" principle, one that men follow because they have come to believe that it is a useful rule to follow.[8]

The principle that everybody is to be left undisturbed in the enjoyment of his proper possessions requires that there be rights of ownership. Each house, field, and book cannot be the private property of everybody; if such things are to belong to anybody, they must belong to somebody in particular. There is, then, a question of the correct criteria to be used in attributing the ownership of the various economic goods to particular persons. The goods of external nature must be divided and appropriated, for every unappropriated economic good is an invitation to contention. What tests should we use when we have to decide who is to be the owner of a specific house, a specific fish, a mine, a book, a river bed, a well, or any other scarce or unique, desirable thing? We are to make a transition from what, as far as the particular good under discussion is concerned—ownership may already be fixed in the case of most other goods—is merely a *de facto* arrangement to an arrangement which subsequently we will regard as righteous. Our question is: What *de facto* qualification should be accepted as giving a man an adequate claim to be treated as the proper possessor of a good, while other men are treated as malefactors if they take that good? In other words, what nonrighteous qualities should be regarded as foundations for a claim to the rights of ownership?

The rules that Hume sets down are five: present possession, occupation, prescription, accession, and succession.[9] These we may divide into three groups, according to the different situations in which the rules apply. First, the potential owners may, by introducing ownership, be establishing a society where none was before. Here the correct test is present possession. Since we cannot expect to compare satisfactorily the merits of men, in conferring rights to goods, we must be prepared to rely on some external considerations. At the moment there are no rights. Accordingly, there is only one relevant test, namely, the factual relation of possession. In short, the division of goods which existed immediately before the institution of society is to be regarded as the proper division. Right is simply superimposed on factual possession. The distribution of goods remains unaltered, but, while before it would not be wrong to seize a man's possessions, it would be a wrong, a violation of rights, to do so hereafter. The reason, Hume explains, why present possession is a relevant test in this situation is that the relation between a man and a good possessed by him is closely analogous to the relation between a man and a good owned by him, so that given the absence of any overruling consideration, a distribution of rights based on present possession is the distribution most likely to prove generally acceptable.[10]

The second situation is the one in which, although the owners of other goods are known, a particular parcel of goods is without a recognizable owner, either because those goods are newly discovered or because the title cannot be traced. Here again, possession is the primary consideration, and Hume's explanation again is that possession and property are relations so analogous that one is easily mistaken for the other. But here (present) possession is not enough. The rule applicable to new-found goods is occupation (or first possession), because *first* possession always engages our attention more than any subsequent instance—the third, eleventh, or the seventeenth instance —of possession.[11] And the rule to be applied where no title from first possession can be traced—such cases will be numerous in any place settled for more than four or five generations— is prescription (or long possession), because of the effects of custom. A man's possessions come to be associated with himself in his own thinking, and in the thinking of others. Men, for the most part, prefer the familiar to the strange: custom "not only reconciles us to any thing we have long enjoy'd, but even gives us an affection for it, and makes us prefer it to other objects, which may be more valuable, but are less known to us." [12] Men are likely to be more deeply aggrieved by the loss of their houses, fields, and trees than by not receiving far more valuable things which they have never known. Here we must notice that occupation and prescription are imperfect tests.[13] They are based, not on some prior right, but on a factual relation with the world of time and space, and both time and space run on. Possession must be "stable" if it is to constitute occupation, but, while a fish in the creel ordinarily causes no doubts about ownership, whether or not a fish nibbling the bait is to be regarded by other fishermen as taken is a nice question. In addition to such questions based on cause-effect chains, there is the problem of limits of extension. Where anything without narrow and comprehensible limits, such as a newly discovered continent, as contrasted with an islet, is involved, the question of the exact area to be regarded as occupied as the result of a landing, or even of a large settlement, is not susceptible of neat, logical solution. Again, long possession is not a complete test; it gives only a relative, not a specific, criterion. In these two instances the rules need to be supplemented by precise limits posited arbitrarily, but within the understandable, by a common authority.[14]

The third situation is the one in which the goods in question are the products of goods already owned by somebody, or are goods whose former owner has died. In the first case, when new goods proceed from goods already owned, as do "the fruit of our garden, the offspring of our cattle, and the work of our slaves," the rule to be applied is accession.[15] In the latter case, the descendants of the deceased are to succeed to the rights. Hume's argument in favour of accession and succession changes significantly from the *Treatise* to the *Enquiry concerning the Principles of Morals*. In the earlier work he holds that they are correct rules chiefly because—in addition to the general usefulness they share with the other rules—they are directly useful to society. Somebody has or has had a right, and by accession the owner of a cause acquires its effect; this is easily understood. But more important is the truth that men will be more diligent when they believe that the future fruits of their present labours will belong to themselves. By succession the descendants (effects) acquire the goods to which their parents and forebears formerly had rights. This, too, is very understandable. But two other truths are even more important. First, here the social order and the natural order overlap, and any rule of society that runs against the current of natural affections will cause turmoil. This rule, on the contrary, follows the usual course of the will. And, second, by running with natural affection, from those confined affections the rule draws a benefit for society at large; for inheritance makes men "more industrious and frugal" than they would be if the recipients of their estates were to be persons indifferent or even unknown to themselves, and this is in "the general interest of mankind." But in the *Enquiry*, as amended in 1753–54, while still holding that accession and succession encourage industry, he explains these and his other rules primarily in terms of their acceptability to the human understanding. He writes:

Were a society formed among several independent members, the most obvious rule, which could be agreed on, would be to annex property to *present* possession, and leave every one a right to what he at present enjoys. The relation of possession, which takes place between the person and the object, naturally draws on the relation of property.

For a like reason, occupation or first possession becomes the foundation of property.

Where a man bestows labour and industry upon any object, which before belonged to no body; as in cutting down and shaping a tree, in cultivating a field, &c., the alterations, which he produces, causes a relation between him and the object, and naturally engages us to annex it to him by the new relation of property. This cause here concurs with the public utility, which consists in the encouragement given to industry and labour.

Perhaps too, private humanity towards the possessor concurs, in this instance, with the other motives, and engages us to leave with him what he has acquired by his sweat and labour; and what he has flattered himself in the constant enjoyment of. For though private humanity can, by no means, be the origin of justice; since the latter virtue so often contradicts the former; yet when the rule of separate and constant possession is once formed by the indispensable necessities of society, private humanity, and an aversion to the doing a hardship to another, may, in a particular instance, give rise to a particular rule of property.

I am much inclined to think, that the right of succession or inheritance much depends on those connexions of the imagination, and that the relation to a former proprietor begetting a relation to the object, is the cause why the property is transferred to a man after the death of his kinsman. It is true; industry is more encouraged by the transference of possession to children or near relations: but this consideration will only have place in a cultivated society; whereas the right of succession is regarded even among the greatest Barbarians.

Acquisition of property by *accession* can be explained no way but by having recourse to the relations and connexions of the imagination.[16]

The reason, according to Hume, for adopting rules for the assignment of rights is that thereby, since subjective judgment about who shall enjoy goods is supplanted, possession is made stable and secure. Inevitably, there will be times when these rules, and the positive laws made to supplement them, will fail to show that any party has a sound and exclusive right to a particular article or estate. But so important is it that the stability of possession be not endangered by a resort to subjective discretion, that it is quite correct, Hume implies, for judges to pretend in such instances that they see a good and absolute title where, in truth, there are only conflicting claims.[17]

It is evident that the five rules selected by Hume are regarded by him as the correct rules—in the *Enquiry concerning the Principles of Morals*, if not in the *Treatise*—because the distribution of goods they will produce is the one he thinks least likely to be questioned. The aim of the economic system is general prosperity. The driving force within the system is human avidity. When property is introduced, avidity is not extirpated; rather, the great desire for external goods is then channelled into ways vastly more fruitful for each and every man. Men will remain avaricious as long as it is the individual who perceives pleasure and pain or as long as external goods are scarce. What is accomplished by the establishment of property is that avidity for short-term goods is checked by avidity for greater long-term goods. Now, since avarice is quite general, there is no need to discriminate among men according to their virtues, when rights to goods are assigned. The economic system will work regardless of who owns any particular field or factory: as far as ownership is concerned, men are sufficiently alike to be treated as interchangeable. Accordingly, since no specific assignment is dictated by the economic system, provided that whatever the assignment, it is stable, the only criterion to be used in selecting rules is their acceptability to men, and, therefore, the stability of their results. The five rules given by Hume are the ones that men will follow most readily. They do not clash with, but instead are based directly on, the natural pattern of human thought and sentiment. Of all possible distributions, the one produced by these rules is the least likely to be violated.

The rules are to be applied equally, but they will not assign rights to an equal amount of goods to everybody. This, however, is irrelevant: the end to which the establishment of property is a means is not equality of goods but that security of possession which will permit a general increase in the wealth of the entire society. It is true, Hume finds, that the resources of the earth are great enough, if developed by arts and industry, to supply everybody with all the necessities of life, and even most of its comforts. But the disadvantages of enforcing equality would far outweigh its advantages. Even if all outward goods were once distributed equally, the different degrees of activity, care, and industry of men would soon bring about a new inequality. And if the persons who possess these virtues to a high degree were restrained, the very end for which society was established would be frustrated. Moreover, the task of enforcing equality would probably corrupt the government, for it would be a task so onerous that any government required to assume it probably would soon become a tyranny.[18]

Besides, if we are talking about arrangements contrived with an end other than stability and consequent prosperity, it must be remembered that the ideal arrangement would not be one in which every man would have a share of goods equal to the share of every other man, but one in which goods would be bestowed upon men in proportion to their genuine merit. This task, however, would overstrain human ability dangerously. A man's true merit is far from obvious, and, in addition, the discernment of men is certain to be distorted by conceit and interest; so we must conclude that true merit can be judged only by a god. It is precisely to abolish the inevitable conflicts which result from subjective judgments about who should enjoy goods, that property is introduced. The rules for the distribution of rights to goods are blind to the virtue of the men who get goods under them, but they do achieve the purpose for which they are suited, i.e., the maintenance of a stable order of possession in which men can be efficiently industrious, and, consequently, prosperous.[19]

Private property is necessary for prosperity. Rules of dis-

tribution are necessary if there is to be private property. Hume
has based his five rules for the ownership of goods on human
nature. The rights of private property are not merely the result
of human legislation, and it would be unwise for any government to alter the consequent distribution in ordinary circumstances.[20]

The second principle of justice follows from the first.[21] The
five criteria on which private property is to be based are blind
and general: they assign rights without taking into account
either the different needs or the different capacities as suppliers
of goods and services of the men who, under them, will become
owners. Men differ in abilities, and, besides, each can attain a
higher skill when he specializes in a single line of production;
different places and regions have specialties because of geographical and traditional causes; the needs of one man or of the
inhabitants of one place are never restricted to two or three
goods; nor is the need for any one good unlimited—a man can
use only so much wine, clothing, or equipage. The second principle, then, is one permitting particular adjustments in the as-
signments, adjustments not made blindly, but by individuals
aware of their own particular needs and desires. But this adjustment is only to be such as will not jeopardize the stability
and peace prerequisite to the prosperity which is the end of the
society. The first principle prescribes private property. The
second authorizes trade. It is that rights over goods may be
transferred from one person to another by consent, and only by
consent. By acting in this way, men can continually adapt the
assignment of goods to suit the condition of demand and supply
prevailing at any time. Exchange by consent, and only by
consent, is the principle which underlies the market. This principle makes the goods produced by the division of labour available to all producers. The first of Hume's principles gives
society the character of an association of owners. The second
gives it the character of a market.

Still another rule is dictated by the nature of men and the
nature of their circumstances.[22] A third principle is necessary
if men are to be as "serviceable to each other, as by nature

they are fitted to become." [23] The principle that rights to things may be transferred by consent does not provide an adequate basis for all the trading that is desirable. It provides no foundation for contracts. Accordingly, if it were left unsupplemented, there could be barter involving the rights to specific commodities—the right to *these* five gallons of wine—but there would be no deals involving the rights to specified quantities of a commodity, e.g., *any* five gallons of this wine. Indeed, there could be no agreement involving future performance of any kind, whether this be the future delivery of a house, a sum of money, or a sack of wool, or the future performance of acts and services. This would be especially serious in the case of services requiring work during a long period of time. Trade would be restricted to barter in which both parties simultaneously transferred both the right to the goods and the goods. The remedy is the principle that promises are to be regarded as inviolable. This is the third and last basic rule of economic competition.

Here it is necessary, Hume finds, to distinguish between two kinds of acts. Not all relations are "social." Not all acts are those of persons eager to acquire things and services for themselves, and prepared to make a return for them.[24] Acts motivated by parental love, by generosity, or charity are those done without any expectation of a reciprocal service. But since there is no patent difference between many social (economic) acts and many natural acts, a generous deed could easily be mistaken for an act done in anticipation of a return, and *vice versa*. To mark the difference, a formula of words, "the promise," is used. It is the introduction of a "promise" that shows that an act is done with a utilitarian intent. On this principle—that promises are to be regarded as inviolable—much of the business of society depends.

These three great principles—that each man is to be left undisturbed in possession of the goods he acquires under the rules, that the rights to things and services may be transferred only with the consent of the owner, and that men are to keep their promises—constitute the rules of competition. These are the limits that any just man will respect in his economic relations with others. These are the constitutional laws of society.[25]

Inevitably Hume's ethical thought will be misinterpreted unless his narrow use of the word "justice" is kept in mind constantly. For him justice is not the whole, nor even the greater part of virtue. A just man may be vicious in his behaviour towards his family and friends, and may be uncharitable. The man who acts justly treats all men as equal associates in the economy. The man who is virtuous in his personal relations behaves in different (unequal) ways towards a limited number of particular persons. In society men are related mediately; the men involved in a transaction are involved only because they are first related, as producers, shippers, dealers, or consumers, to desirable things and services. Adam Smith makes the same point aptly: "It is not from the benevolence of the butcher, the brewer, or the baker that we expect our dinner, but from their regard to their own interest. We address ourselves, not to their humanity, but to their self-love, and never talk to them of our own necessities but of their advantage." [26] On the other hand, the natural relationships and the economic relationship, society, are different: vice results if justice is corrupted by affection, and if legalistic equality is carried over into the sphere that should be ordered by family love, by friendliness, and by charity. To observe justice is the obligation of a man, not as a member of a family, a friendship, or humanity, but as an associate in society. Virtuous natural relations are limited and unequal. Virtuous social relations are general and equal.

At this point we must notice that in Hume's theory a "society" and a "civil society" are not the same. A civil society involves a government. Society, a simpler kind of relationship, sometimes can exist where there is no government. Justice is highly useful; once men become aware of this, their confined interest will make just conduct attractive to them. Soon they will come to feel morally obliged to act justly. But in certain circumstances the combined strength of long-range selfish obligation and moral obligation is likely to prove insufficient to restrain violent passions for the short-range gains that can be made by theft or breach of contract. These obligations then will need to be supplemented by a new kind of obligation, the desire to gain rewards promised, and to avoid punishments threatened, by a government.

From what has been said it might appear that a government prepared to enforce justice is an impossibility. There is nobody who has an innate, immediate interest in enforcing the principle of justice generally. And the propensity to prefer the contiguous to the remote, based on the egocentricity of perception, is common to all men; all, although they prefer the greater good when thinking abstractly, tend to see present goods as more important than future goods, when they are acting. But there is a solution. A man or a few men can be given an artificial place, role, or station designed so that they have an immediate interest in just conduct by all others, and so that they themselves have nothing to gain by acting unjustly. They can be placed outside, independent of, the economy; they, therefore, will have no good reason to be unjust themselves, and they will have nothing to gain, and all to lose, by the unjust acts of others.[27] They can discourage such acts by establishing among their subjects an order of positive rights conformable to the three principles of justice, and by providing penalties for violations of that order. A man's interest in acting justly because of his sense of the utility of just conduct and his sense of moral duty, when combined with this new interest, his desire to avoid the government's punishments and to gain its rewards, is far less likely to be eclipsed by the violent passion caused by smaller but closer goods than when economic interest and moral duty stood alone. Rewards and punishments, especially if precisely defined, certain, and prompt, give the subject a short-term interest in acting justly, an interest that is likely to outbalance the short-term attractiveness of theft and of breaking contracts.

It is obvious that a few can never overpower the many; however, since all the many are seldom tempted to injustice at once, the few can depend on at least the passive approval of their acts when they punish particular wrongdoers. It is by the establishment of a few in a position to execute the principles of justice that men pass into civil society.

We may say, then, that for Hume a civil society has two distinguishable aspects. The first is society, a relationship made up of individuals, each participating in the competitive economy as an owner of desirable goods and services. The second is made up of individuals participating, either as governors or as the governed, in a state. The first of these aspects can exist in some circumstances without the second; but in other circumstances the state will be needed to supplement society. The two together constitute "civil society." It is clear that for Hume the three principles of justice are the fundamental laws of civil society. The state is an auxiliary, secondary order which has no sufficient purpose other than the provision, through rewards and punishments, of ulterior supports for those three primary principles. Society, according to Hume, is founded on property, trade, and contracts. When governments are introduced, their primary task is to support property, trade, and contracts.

In no place does Hume set forth explicitly, and examine one by one, a set of principles of governance comparable to the principles of justice. Just behaviour and governance for him are not equally important kinds of activity: a government exists mainly to promote the observance of justice. Accordingly, once he has explained the need for a government, it is sufficient for him to say that citizens are to obey their proper governments, and then to set down the tests by which citizens can best ascertain who are their governors. But by analyzing what he says in the *Treatise*, and rounding out what we find there from the various other works, we can put down four principles of governance which can be safely attributed to him. These four principles of governance and the three principles of justice, we may say, make up the principles of civil society. They are the principles of "civility."

A state, according to Hume, is a relationship which combines individual liberty and authority; and a good state is one in which a proper balance is maintained between these two essential elements.

The first of the principles of governance is that the subjects should obey their proper governor(s). Many men may claim that they could govern well, and, indeed, it is probable that many of the claimants are correct; yet there can be only one government. To exclude subjective discretion, rules are needed by which it may be ascertained which of them is the proper governor. The right to rule in a certain place, like the right to possess certain fields, houses, and ships, belongs to someone or to some group only because, for one reason or another, the commands of that man or group are recognized as law by enough people. A state, like a society, is not an external object, as is a mountain; nor is it a natural group, like the family. On the contrary, a state is an institution, a kind of play instituted as a means for the attainment of an end.[28] The only valid reason for the establishment or the maintenance of any institution is that it has what is considered a good effect on behaviour; and, in fact, the only reliable evidence of any institution's existence is the effect it has on behaviour. In the case of states, this effect takes the form of obedience to the commands of a specific man or a specific group, as commands of the government.

The second principle is that the government is to do its job. Hume's theory is strictly individualistic and, therefore, egalitarian. The government has no independent purpose, goal, or mission of its own; rather, it exists only to advance the common purposes of all its subjects. Hume's whole interpretation of human existence and conduct is nonteleological or nontechnical in style. He does not begin by trying to enunciate a general purpose for the fulfilment of which all mankind or the chosen were created. Accordingly, since his theory does not include a transcendent purpose, it includes no real body politic. This means that he does not begin with a real body politic, a body ordered for the attainment of the ultimate purpose, and then proceed to treat of men as the performers of different roles, parts, or offices, i.e., as unequal members whose separate wills and acts are necessarily fragmentary and incomplete when not coordinated with that ultimate purpose. On the contrary, he begins with individuals—men who perceive—set in a world inhabited by individuals. For him the individual is the original or genuine unit. These individuals, being human by nature, desire certain goods. They act to fulfil their own purposes. Because many of the goods they seek are not plentiful or interchangeable, to permit cooperation a government is needed to maintain property and contracts. The government is a means, not an end, in relation to its subjects. Moreover, because the men who make up the state are regarded, not as the unequal members of a real body politic, but as individuals, they are regarded as equal. As hunters, philosophers, or artisans, they are unequal. Here, as associates in civil society, they are equal; therefore, the government ought to govern in the interests of all.

The activities of governments considered legitimate by Hume are of four kinds. The basic one concerns the principles of justice. First, a government will have to execute them. By this, Hume means that the government will have to punish violators of the principles. Second, it will have to decide when such violations have taken place.[29] And third, in some instances—for example, the fixing of the length of the term of long possession which is to be regarded as establishing a right—it is to supplement the principles.[30] All these activities we probably would call "executive," for although decisions are made in cases and for the establishment of tests, these decisions are merely means to secure justice. This executive activity ordinarily is the most important: the maintenance of the condition in which a general economic system can operate is the chief and the only sufficient reason for the institution of a government. Although there are, as we have seen, other important kinds of activity—the activities suitable to the family, friendship, and humanity—since economic activity is the only kind that, by its nature, tends to involve men generally and is not spontaneous, the standards of this activity are the only ones that need to be enforced by a common agency. The maintenance of property and of contracts is the chief end of governments.[31] This does not mean, however, that any existing government will confine its activity to the "social" sphere. But the enforcement of some of the duties in the sphere of personal relationships is never the primary or sufficient reason for the existence of a government.[32] There will, then, be laws forbidding attacks upon the person, as well as against violations of property and contracts. Here again, the appropriate function of government is strictly executive: it is to enforce standards of conduct—natural duties, in this instance—which are prior to the government. The third kind of activity requires more initiative. A government may properly require its subjects to participate in, or contribute to, common undertakings, such as the construction of bridges, harbours, and canals, which would not be built without public motivation and coordination. It can properly require them to contribute to the maintenance of the established religion.[33] The need for the fourth kind of activity is strictly a consequence of the existence of a state. Since the governmental aspect of civil society involves not only the legal relations among the governed, but also the legal relation between the government and the governed, the government, in preserving the state, will be obliged to define its own rights, and to maintain them against internal subversion and against foreign enemies. It, therefore, may require its subjects to contribute to, and to participate in, the erection of ramparts, the outfitting of fleets, and the control of armies.[34]

The third principle of governance is that in performing these four activities, the government is to be neutral, equal, and impartial in its penalties, judgments, positive laws, and initiated activities. Natural liberty, in short, is not to be restricted beyond that degree necessary for the maintenance of the society and the state. When a government restricts natural liberty beyond the point defined by the rules of natural and civil duty, it is ruling unequally, and is exploiting the generality of its subjects for the illusory benefit of the rulers and their partners. Such exploitation Hume calls "slavery," not governance. The median position between a condition of complete natural liberty and a condition of slavery is true civil liberty. When a government swings too far in one direction or the other, it ceases to govern.

The fourth principle is that the government is to govern in as calculable a manner as possible.[35] This covers at least four points. First, the positive laws are to be as specific as possible, both when they declare the acts or kinds of acts which are prohibited or required, and when they fix the rewards and punishments for fulfilling or breaking the laws. Second, *ex post facto* "laws" are logically impossible. Third, the laws specifying the kinds of acts that are illegal are to apply generally to all citizens, and are not to be changed frivolously. And fourth, the powers delegated to the subordinate agents commissioned to apply the laws are to be specific and limited.[36] The main task of governments is to influence the acts of their subjects. Retroactive or unpublished laws cannot have this kind of effect. A certain degree of incalculability is inevitable whenever any new case has to be decided, but the range or *vires* of those delegated to make decisions in such cases should be as narrow as possible; that is, the incalculability should be a mere run, the narrower the better, in the ice-pans of calculability. Moreover, calculability in the possession and exchange of goods is the chief end of government; when the government itself increases uncertainty, it contravenes its own purpose.

The first of these four principles assures the maintenance of a government, and the other three maintain individual liberty. In a good state a proper balance is maintained between the first and the other three. The need for individual liberty is more fundamental to men than the need for authority, but the need for authority must not be ignored, for when there is no authority, and only individual liberty, their condition may be destructively competitive.

The result, Hume argues, if men live without a government, is not necessarily totally chaotic. Because of the uniformity of human nature, a set of standard relations among men will emerge. Whether or not this condition of "natural liberty" will be tolerable depends on the supply of economic goods available and on the demand for those goods, that is, on the intensity of the competition. Between the tropics, or while men still live by hunting and fishing, the condition of "natural liberty" probably is quite pleasant; but whenever it becomes necessary to produce goods, not simply to seize them, "natural liberty" becomes unsatisfactory. Production requires planning and industry, and these require calculability; yet, the prevailing shortage of goods makes irresistible the temptation to ignore the rights of others.

The purpose of introducing governance is not to supplant individual initiative, but to increase it by insuring that men can safely follow the patterns of personal and social conduct suitable to human beings. The proper function of governments is to provide confirming support to the personal and social relationships. Governments have no missions aside from the purposes of individuals; in relation to those purposes their task is that of an auxiliary, namely, to permit the implicit economic order and the implicit personal orders to develop as fully as possible. The purpose of governance is to increase the liberty of the individual by replacing "natural liberty" with "civil liberty." When the balance of authority and liberty is improper, true governance disappears: if authority becomes ineffective, a reversion to "natural liberty" threatens, and if authority becomes too active, the result is the extirpation of liberty.[37]

In discussing the Magna Charta, Hume provides a convenient summary of his view of the proper civil liberties. He deals initially with the clauses favourable to the lords. He then proceeds:

These were the principal articles, calculated for the interest of the barons; and had the charter contained nothing farther, national happiness and liberty had been very little promoted by it, as it would only have tended to encrease the power and independance of an order of men, who were already too powerful, and whose yoke might have become more heavy on the people than even that of an absolute monarch. But the barons, who alone drew and imposed on the prince this memorable charter, were necessitated to insert in it other clauses of a more extensive and more beneficent nature: They could not expect the concurrence of the people, without comprehending, together with their own, the interests of inferior ranks of men; and all provisions, which the barons, for their own sake, were obliged to make, in order to ensure the free and equitable administration of justice, tended directly to the benefit of the whole community. The following were the principal clauses of this nature.

It was ordained, that all the privileges and immunities abovementioned, granted to the barons against the king, should be extended by the barons to their inferior vassals. The king bound himself not to grant any writ, empowering a baron to levy aids from his vassals, except in the three feudal cases. One weight and one measure shall be established throughout the kingdom. Merchants shall be allowed to transact all business, without being exposed to any arbitrary tolls and impositions: They and all free men shall be allowed to go out of the kingdom and return to it at pleasure: London, and all cities and burghs, shall preserve their ancient liberties, immunities, and free customs: Aids shall not be required of them but by the consent of the great council: No towns or individuals shall be obliged to make or support bridges but by ancient custom: The goods of every freeman shall be disposed of according to his will: If he die intestate, his heirs shall succeed to them. No officer of the crown shall take any horses, carts, or wood, without the consent of the owner. The king's courts of justice shall be stationary, and shall no longer follow his person: They shall be open to every one; and justice shall no longer be sold, refused, or delayed by them. Circuits shall be regularly held every year: The inferior tribunals of justice, the county court, sheriff's turn, and court-leet shall meet at their appointed time and place: The sheriffs shall be incapacitated to hold pleas of the crown; and shall not put any person upon his trial, from rumour or suspicion alone, but upon the evidence of lawful witnesses. No freeman shall be taken or imprisoned, or dispossessed of his free tenement and liberties, or outlawed, or banished, or any wise hurt or injured, unless by the legal judgment of his peers, or by the law of the land; and all who suffered otherwise in this or the two former reigns, shall be restored to their rights and possessions. Every freeman shall be fined in proportion to his fault; and no fine shall be levied on him to his utter ruin: Even a villain or rustic shall not by any fine be bereaved of his carts, ploughs, and implements of husbandry. This was the only article calculated for the interests of this body of men, probably at that time the most numerous in the kingdom.

It must be confessed, that the former articles of the Great Charter contain such mitigations and explanations of the feudal law as are reasonable and equitable; and that the latter [above] involve all the chief outlines of a legal government, and provide for the equal distribution of justice, and free enjoyment of property; the great objects for which political society was at first founded by men, which the people have a perpetual and unalienable right to recal, and which no time, nor precedent, nor statute, nor positive institution, ought to deter them from keeping ever uppermost in their thoughts and attention.[38]

In any discussion of governance the principle that the people are to obey their proper governor must be noted first, for where it is not observed, there is no government. The other three principles constitute a standard by which to measure the quality of any government. This relation we must bear in mind as we consider the question, What tests should we use when we have to decide who has a right to govern?

The answer to this question, according to Hume, does not need to be complicated by a discussion of the best form of government.[39] No person, or body of persons, has an inalienable right to govern. In the constituting of a state, the only formal consideration is that the government is to be removed as far as possible from the economic competition among the governed. This does not mean, as we shall see later, that Hume thinks that the probabilities are equal that all forms of government will serve well in all circumstances. There is no incompatibility between any form and the principles of governance; consequently, there is no formal way of answering our question. It, therefore, has to be answered in terms of the political conditions prevailing at the time.

Here we need to distinguish between only two situations: we may be casting an absolutely new political order, or we may be choosing among rival candidates for an old office. If the latter is the case, any one or more of five criteria must be taken into account in deciding which claimant should succeed. But if not, that is, if none of these tests applies, there is only one way by which the rightful ruler can be ascertained, because there is only one way in which there can be any ruler in such a situation. Where nobody has obedient followers, nobody has a political claim to obedience. In such a situation, since there is no political power to compel obedience—if there were, we should turn at once to the five other rules—a government can be instituted only by the unanimous consent of the first subjects. Since nobody has political power, nobody can win recognition as ruler by exhibiting sufficient ability to enforce his commands —his own natural ability is insufficient to distinguish him. Accordingly, there can be recognition only if a man, not because of the strength of his political following, but probably because of his natural abilities, already has been voluntarily designated as the ruler. The answer to our question here, then, would be: Only he (or they) designated initially by all can have a right to rule. This answer, clearly, is one that would be relevant only at a moment when all ties of old loyalty were entirely dissolved. Moreover, even if it ever was adequate, it would be so for only a moment, because as soon as a government had been created by this method, at least one of the five other tests immediately would become applicable.

The first of the five rules normally applicable in deciding who is to be obeyed in any state is long (and continuing) possession of authority by a man, a dynasty, or a group.[40] Failing this, present possession acquired through usurpation and present possession acquired through conquest are adequate tests. The fourth rule, one which both interest and the natural operation of the imagination make important, is succession, by which a prince acquires the throne which had been rightfully occupied by his father. Since the prince probably has been associated with royal authority for years, to think of him exercising authority is easy. Besides, "The presum'd consent of the father, the imitation of the succession to private families, the interest, which the state has in chusing the person, who is most powerful, and has the most numerous followers; all these reasons lead men to prefer the son of their late monarch to any other person." [41]

Finally, it may be that there are fundamental laws which determine who shall be the governors, and also the process by which they shall govern. Such fundamental laws, except where they embody one of the other rules, i.e., succession, are effective because since men are accustomed to those laws, they assume that those laws are righteous.[42] The basis of all these tests is not that they will point out the ablest men, but that, by reason of taking cognizance of the associations made naturally by the human mind, they point out the men whose right to rule is least likely to be doubted. Therefore, it can be said that, if the abilities of the candidates are not vastly unequal, the rules point out the men most likely to be able to maintain peace and prosperity.

Although rights to economic goods and rights to govern are alike, according to Hume, in that neither depends ultimately on prior right, but on a factual situation, these two kinds of rights are not on the same level: rights to govern are to be regarded as far more questionable and precarious than rights to economic goods. There are two causes why this is true. The rules to be used ordinarily in assigning rights to goods, we have noticed, are not absolutely final: it is possible to conceive circumstances so abnormal that it would not be correct to refuse to alter the distribution of goods produced by the rules, but almost always, these rules can be relied on to produce the best possible results.[43] They are rules devised to produce, not prosperity, but the conditions in which industrious men will produce prosperity. Moreover, there are many owners, so the occasional assignment of goods to lazy or miserly men will have only trivial results for the whole society. In contrast, the right to govern a society is given to only one government. The tests as to who should be given the right to govern merely point out the most acceptable candidate(s). They do not show conclusively who, in the event, will be the best governor(s). That depends on the virtue of the one man or the few. But evidence about a man's character cannot be assayed without admitting subjective evaluation and possible disagreement; besides, such evidence, even if appraised most objectively, cannot be the basis for a proof or even for a statement of high probability about the future, when only one man or a few men are involved. The tests show who among the candidates is most likely to be, at least initially, the governor whom the subjects will feel most obliged to support and obey. The ultimate result, when no longer prospective, may be far from satisfactory. Second, rights to govern are means, means to the performance of the work of a government, and the main task of governments is to assure that property and contracts are respected.

We may conclude, then, that whereas ordinarily only one question is relevant when rights to goods are being weighed—who under the rules has the best title?—in the case of rights to govern, two questions must be asked. First, who has the best *prima facie* title? To this question, Hume's answer is clear: the present possessor of the crown.[44] Second, is the present government governing well? A state, we have noted, is an admixture of natural liberty and authority: when either is aggrandized improperly, the state is threatened. Moreover, it is impossible to define the exact point at which natural liberty and authority are correctly balanced, for what is enough authority in one period may be too much or too little in another. The correct balance is a question on which differences of opinion will arise perpetually, and on which men of learning and discernment, not addicted to hysterical speculation, may be expected to disagree. It is possible to see a portent of chaos in every relaxation of authority. It is possible to see a threat of slavery in every reduction of individual liberty. In short, the extent to which a government conforms to the second, third, and fourth principles of governance is of great importance. No government will ever be perfect. Even the best at times will fall somewhat short in respect of one or more of these principles. This is to be expected. But it is possible for a government to fall so far below the perfect that, although it may still act as a government to some degree, obedience to it no longer is good.[45] Unfortunately, there is no formal method by which it can be discovered and shown that a government has ceased to be a proper government. This must remain a matter of individual judgment.[46] A wise man, however, while striving for the perfection of the government, will not set the mark separating a qualified and a disqualified government too high. Generally, he will rely exclusively on the five (or six) rules to show him whom he should obey; and, we already have noticed that under those rules, present possession is the best title.

Rights in property and rights to govern are far from being the same. Titles to goods do not need to be examined in terms of their results, for we can rely confidently on the enterprise of the many owners to produce prosperity, if justice is maintained. But the decisive test of a government's right to rule is the quality of its rule. Whereas it would be bad, in terms of both utility and morality, to permit thieves to keep their spoils, it would be bad, in terms of both utility and morality, to attempt to overthrow a usurper or a conqueror who is ruling well, and to replace him with a "legitimate" pretender.[47] And although even sloth and indolence do not annul rights in property, the failure of a government to perform its role expunges its rights entirely.

Hume, we have noticed, refers to the virtues of civility as "artificial moral virtues." He does so not to suggest that justice and governance are unimportant, not to suggest that they are not genuine moral virtues, and not to suggest that they are not based on principles independent of human caprice; instead, his aim is to call attention to the truth that justice and governance differ from the "natural moral virtues" in four main ways.

First, whereas the basic cause why men do acts of benevolence is the feelings they have for others, the basic reason why just and obedient conduct by the citizen is good is that such conduct leads to an increase in economic goods. As far as the actor is concerned, acts of benevolence are good *per se*, but just and obedient acts are good only as means. The family, the friendship, and humanity are relationships based on the feelings human beings have for others; but society and state are relationships among men which result from their common desire to acquire external goods. Consequently, respect for property and contracts, and respect for political authority, unlike family

love, friendliness, and charity, are not inevitably important to
men. It is possible, Hume argues, to imagine conditions in
which respect for property and contracts would be useless, or
even harmful. A change in human nature would alter the list
of artificial virtues as well as the list of natural virtues—if
avidity were purged from human nature, the need for property
would disappear. But a change in the mere external circumstances in which men live, while it would not alter the natural
virtues, would alter the list of artificial virtues. Such a change
might make "the cautious, jealous virtue of justice," [48] irrelevant or even harmful, and the same would be true of governance. If the supply of external goods were to decrease so
drastically that the chance that men would perish from a lack
of necessaries while the rights of misers to their hoards were
guarded became as great as the chance of perishing in the disorders that acts of injustice might precipitate, the utility of
justice would vanish.[49] Or if, on the other hand, all goods were
to become so plentiful that everybody could have as much of
everything as he wanted, separate holdings would become a
nuisance.[50] In both these cases a man could be perfectly virtuous, even if not studious to protect property and contracts.
Hume mentions these extreme possibilities only to show that
justice is an artificial virtue. He does not mean to imply that
the supply of goods ever will become generally so scarce or so
plentiful that the need for property and contracts, the institutions prerequisite for cooperative production and extensive
commerce, will vanish. He must not be interpreted as suggesting that the need for government, the buttress of justice, ever
will cease in any large and complex society.

Second, since justice and governance are means to general
peace and prosperity, their rules are to be applied equally and
blindly. When justice is established, men are to cease making
their own judgments about the desirable distribution of economic goods, and are to accept as proper that assignment produced by the general rules. Only by refraining from subjective judgment can men achieve the necessary stability of
possession. When justice is established, men separate those

acts towards others which are motivated by their feelings for themselves and others from the acts which are motivated by a desire for external goods; and whereas the former acts continue to be based on love and hatred, and pride and humility, the latter, thereafter, are guided by a set of rules applied equally to every person. The short- or long-term relationships which result from the natural acts are immediate. But economic relations among men are mediate: men who share only a common, competitive desire to obtain goods from a common supply are interested in each other only as possessors or potential possessors of goods and services. Their primary relation to each other, therefore, is similar and equal. That variety or partiality by which natural relationships are shaped is irrelevant here. When men behave civilly, they behave not according to their feelings, but as equal individuals.[51]

Third, both societies and states exist only where they have been established. Families, friendships, and humanity are relationships which arise directly from normal human feelings, but justice and governance restrain spontaneous conduct. The long-range value of property, contracts, and governments might be obvious to an informed observer, but since all these restrain men, their introduction needs explanation.

There is a fourth reason, one closely connected with the third, why good conduct in civil society is "artificial," and this is that civil society has a history. It is the result of change. While the natural relationships are the result of natural feelings, the moral duties of civil society become obligatory only when the principles of justice and governance have been realized, that is, only when men, as the result of some historical cause, have come to believe that acts conforming to those principles are good. Civil society is the result of an advance in men's beliefs. It is the result of the civilization of men, a process by which they come to know that justice and governance are both usefully and morally good.

Provided that these four important differences between the two sets of virtues (or duties) are remembered, Hume is quite willing to have the "artificial" virtues called "natural"; indeed, after he has explained the differences, he himself sometimes calls justice and obedience "natural," and even refers to the principles of justice as "laws of nature." [52]

To state the principles of civil society is not to explain how groups organized according to those principles come into existence. We must distinguish carefully between the principles of civility and the process, civilization, by which men come to know the principles. Throughout this chapter we have been concerned mainly with the principles. We now turn to civilization.

# VI

## PAST CIVILIZATION

> For a Custome taketh beginning and groweth to per-
> fection in this manner: When a reasonable act once
> done is found to be good and beneficiall to the people,
> and agreeable to their nature and disposition, then do
> they use it and practise it again and again, and so by
> often iteration and multiplication of the act it be-
> cometh a *Custome;* and being continued without inter-
> ruption time out of mind, it obtaineth the force of a
> *Law.*
>
> Sir John Davies, *Irish Reports* (1612) *

THE family, the friendship, and humanity are relationships
that come into existence immediately, as products of the feelings
which normal men have for themselves and for others. Since
these relationships are based directly on the constitution of
human nature, and arise directly therefrom, they are called
"natural" by Hume. They result from acts done, not as means,
but as good in themselves. This being true, once the feeling of
moral obligation in general has been explained, it is no problem
to explain the origin of the feeling of obligation involved in
the natural moral duties. These duties are rooted in, and are as
old as, human nature. Moreover, assuming that human nature
remains unchanged, the several natural relationships, and
therefore the sense of duty appropriate to each, will not change
much. These relationships will have little or no history.

The truth is more complex, however, when we come to the
society and the state. We cannot speak of the principles of
justice and governance as "immutable and eternal" because
they are the result of human nature and man's necessitous condition; yet we believe that both human nature and man's con-

* Quoted by J. G. A. Pocock, *The Ancient Constitution and the Feudal Law*
(Cambridge, 1957), p. 33.

dition will remain constant. In other words, since the three principles of justice and the four principles of governance are based on human nature and the circumstances in which men find themselves, we may assume that those principles, if followed, always will prove to be the most efficient means to the external goods men desire. These principles are the constitution of the best possible society and the best possible state. A society in which the principles of justice were followed perfectly would be a genuine or true society. A state in which the principles of governance were followed perfectly would be a genuine or true state. But genuine societies and genuine states, or, more realistically, faulty societies and faulty states, do not spring up spontaneously. The ends are desired, but first both the advantages of a cooperative division of labour and the efficacy of justice and governance as the prerequisites of cooperation have to be learned. Next, a pattern of just behaviour has to be established. Only thereafter will men come to feel morally obliged to act in accordance with the principles of civil society. The relationship among men that is called "society" is good only as a means; and before it can come into existence men must come to believe that conduct in conformity with the principles of justice is useful (good). Similarly, before states can come into existence, some men, at least, must have come to believe that conduct in conformity with the principles of governance is useful. Even the most virtuous men, before they have acquired such beliefs, do not feel obliged to act in conformity with the principles.

Our question now is, How do the principles of justice and governance come to be realized? How do men come to act—and to feel morally obliged to act—in accordance with these, the principles of civility? In short, how do men become civilized?

In the absence of obligation of any kind, the principles would remain valid, but they never would be put into practice. What we now must explain is how, according to Hume, men come to feel obliged to act civilly. This raises some of the stock questions of political theory: Was there once a "State of Nature" in which justice was not practiced? Was this "State of Nature" terminated by a contract whereby men agreed to follow the principles of justice? Can a society exist without a government, and are governments founded on contracts?

The principles of justice and governance, Hume shows, are brought into operation by the creation of "rights." Each field, house, and book, we have noticed, must be owned by some particular person or persons. Similarly, if there is to be a government in a place, there has to be one rightful ruler, or one group of rightful rulers, distinct from the populace. Already, we have examined the tests Hume sets down for use in discovering the men to whom we should attribute rights of these two kinds. But we have not yet examined his views on the nature of "rights."

He does not undertake to give a complete analysis of rights; yet it is clear from his discussion of both ownership and authority in many passages, that for him the evidence of the existence of a right is *recognition*. We may say that ownership exists to some extent whenever men, without being forced to do so, refrain from taking goods which otherwise they would take. That is, a right to goods may be said to exist whenever men recognize another—because of a relation *previously* established in their minds, regard that other man—as the proper possessor of a particular parcel of goods, and therefore, without testing the grounds of his possession, refrain from disturbing him in his use and enjoyment of those goods. An authority, we may say, exists to some extent, whenever men obey another without being forced to do so. That is, a right to govern may be said to exist whenever men recognize another—because of a relation *previously* established in their thinking, regard another—as their ruler, and therefore heed his commands without testing the grounds of his authority on each occasion. A "right" exists, then, only as a result of a prior step, the previous establishment in the minds of men of a connection between a man and those goods or governmental powers that consequently are to be known as his.

According to this theory, all rights in civil society, either to goods or to rule, are founded ultimately, not on antecedent right, but on either opinion or presupposition. When a title is traced, sooner or later a point is reached at which that title may be said to begin, and before which it did not exist. The title came into existence, was created, or established, at a specific moment by an act of cognition. Before that moment there were only *de facto* considerations. All the tests to be applied when we are first attributing ownership or authority concern, not rightful relations, but nonlegal relations. Did this man first clear this field? Is this man the son of the man who first cleared this field? Is this man the one who is most able (perhaps because others already think of him as the *de jure* ruler) to compel obedience? From the mere *de facto* to the *de jure*, a jump is made. Society and state are plays, each with a vast cast. Rights appertain to relationships. Once in a role, part, or office, a man has rights. Society and state, unlike the family or humanity, are artificial relationships. Prior to the casting of the society and of the state a man can be described only in terms of his abilities, his nonlegal connections with external goods, and his biological ties to other men. The various tests we have reviewed show which of these nonlegal considerations are important when we are making either a wholesale casting, or a partial recasting. Once a man is in a role, we, as a result of either opinion or presupposition, attribute to him all the rights that appertain to his role.

The principles of civility outline the constitution of both a genuine society and a genuine state. They imply the rights of men as owners and contractors, and as governors and as subjects. A group of men becomes civilized when rights conforming to the principles are instituted among them. Our question: How do the unchanging principles of civility come to be realized? can be restated as: How do men come to opine or to presuppose that they themselves and others have the rights appropriate to society and state?

In examining Hume's theory of the civilization of men, his theory of the realization of the principles of civility, we, of course, must distinguish between the beginning of society and the beginning of the state. Civilization is not to be thought of as a process impossible without a government. The task of governments is to promote the attainment of a high degree of civility, but Hume argues, we shall see, that men do not need governments to learn the rudiments of justice: they can live in society without a government. Besides, to some extent, governments are results of civilization. In tracing Hume's theory of how civilization has taken place and does take place, we shall begin by examining his description of the discovery of the principles of justice, and thereafter we shall turn to his description of the introduction of governance.

The principles of justice, we know, are three in number. But the institution of only two of these, the first, concerning respect for rights to external goods, and the third, concerning the careful performance of one's contracts, needs explanation. The other one, that rights to goods are to be transferred *intra vivos* only by consent, does not impose a restraint; rather, it relaxes somewhat the rigidity introduced by the first principle.

There are three basic interrelated questions that must be asked. How does Hume account for the first knowledge of the usefulness of justice? How is society possible without a government? Why do men come to feel morally obliged to respect the principles of justice?

It is his contention that the family is the primary agency by which men are civilized, and that the discovery of the rudiments of justice is as old as the family. Individuals live together in the family; consequently, they come to know the advantage of cooperation. And, at the same time, they are made acquainted with the idea of ownership, without which cooperation is impossible. The family is as old as mankind, and its principle, natural affection, always has been inadequate to maintain concord among its members. Parents share their possessions, and have no compelling need for laws of property; but their children and grandchildren, as they grow to independence within the family, increasingly need a guide other than mutual affection in their use and enjoyment of external goods.[1] At the same time, parents have never been unable to see that the only way to prevent troublesome clashes among their offspring is to assign the use of each scarce good to a specific child, and to

promote respect for property through their own superior force
and natural authority. The nature of the promise, too, is
learned in the family, although, given parental leadership in
cooperative undertakings, less use will be made there of contracts than of property. Once this has been done, once family
affection, as the ordering principle, has been found insufficient,
and has been supplemented to a degree by blind, equal justice,
the group, to that extent, takes on a social character.[2] As the
generations pass, the family becomes more and more extensive,
bonds of affection constantly become weaker, and society becomes more and more important. Property and contract are
first introduced—although undoubtedly the property relationship and the contractual relationship are not thought out abstractly—by persons so situated that they can see the observance of justice in particular instances as a means to their
ends, but who are disinterested, as their children are not, and
who at the same time naturally have the authority and power
to enforce respect for ownership and contracts. The family
group tends to become a small society, as affection is supplanted by justice as its principle. Indeed, for Hume, the family
is somewhat like a small civil society: The parents are in a
position to see that justice is good, and to enforce it. The
family, however, differs from civil society in that parents, unlike governors, acquire their roles through the operation of
biological laws and through affection.

The practice of justice within the family depends mainly on
the impartiality and power of the parents: each child is encouraged to think of just acts with approval and of unjust acts
with disapproval, but it is the parents who are outraged by
thefts and by broken promises, and it is because of parental
enforcement that each child can be fairly sure that the others
will respect ownership and promises. Nevertheless, it is possible,
Hume argues, for men to live in a society without guidance or
coercion by either parents or governors; that is, they can live
peacefully in groups more extensive than the natural influence
of parents, and can do so without a government. Therefore, he
must show how two great changes in men's thinking come

about: first, how each man, or, at least, almost every man, can possibly come to believe that it would be good to act justly if by doing so a man did not expose himself to the exploitative injustice of others; and second, how it is possible for all, or at least almost all, to come to believe that others will act justly. In showing how these beliefs first originate, Hume relies mainly on the influence of experience.

When a man, already made acquainted with the fruits of cooperation within the family, now moved by what seems to him to be in his interest, has acted unjustly a few times, and has found repeatedly that thereby he has deprived himself of the benefits of cooperation, his beliefs undergo a change. His ideas of the immediate goods to be gained by a thoughtless seizure lose some of their compelling attractiveness. As this happens, the self-restraint which when guided by the principles of justice leads to distant, great goods comes to be approved. The man undergoes a conversion. His evaluation of acts changes. While hitherto he has refrained from things said to be "owned" by others, and has kept his promises chiefly because of parental influence, he now begins to think of ownership and of contracts with approval even when these are contrary to his *prima facie* interest. He comes to know that just conduct is good conduct in exactly the same way that he comes to learn that fire can cause pain. He acquires a belief: the idea of an unjust act ceases to be attractive and he is repulsed by the thought of unjust behaviour by either himself or others. The more experienced a man is, the stronger will be his belief that justice is useful.

Such an experienced man will feel drawn to act justly by his own long-term interest, but this feeling of selfish obligation will be overpowered and ineffectual if he believes that his fellows do not believe in justice. It will influence his conduct only if he believes to some extent that his fellows also believe, more or less strongly, in justice. This belief about his fellows comes about, Hume argues, quite understandably through *convention*. The principles of justice are the same for all; therefore, it is not merely one man, but all, who by becoming experienced come to believe that just conduct is useful. Through their experience all come to think alike. But they are not automatically aware of this agreement. Now, the presumption always is in favour of justice: each man, unless overwhelmed by some immediate good, wants to act justly in order to be able to enjoy the fruits of society, and will do so unless this desire is overpowered. We may conclude, then, that each experienced man is likely to act justly, unless too severely tempted, even when he is far from being absolutely sure that others will act likewise. In short, there will be adventures in justice, and the result of these adventures is that all within the community gradually come to believe that all, or at least the large majority, of their fellows normally will act justly, and will come to have beliefs about when and to what extent justice is to be expected in the conduct of each of their different neighbours. If a community were to begin *de novo*, at first the principles of justice would be put into practice only hesitantly; nevertheless, being useful, they would not lie dormant, but inevitably would manifest themselves in men's acts. Although false starts and disappointments would be common, given the ultimate attractiveness of justice, these fumbles would never prevent the eventual realization of a society; instead, by depriving the unjust man of the benefits of cooperation, they would impress upon him the desirability of acting justly in the future. Initially, the principles of justice would be applied rarely in contacts with strangers, but regularly only within the small communities composed of the few people near one, the few with whom one was learning the value of justice and the ways of cooperation. One would expect just conduct only from particular men, only from those whom one knew. If, at some point, economic reasons sufficient to prompt a desire for an expansion of the society became effective, the enlargement—in the absence of a government—would proceed initially only by hesitant, exploratory steps, for, when dealing for the first, or the second, or third time with strangers, each man's belief that a particular stranger believed strongly in the usefulness of justice inevitably would be weak. But, presumably, when, by reason of extensive experience, men came to believe not merely that particular men have learned that justice is good, but that all men have learned this, when they have come to expect not only their neighbours, but even total strangers, to act justly, the size of societies could increase rapidly.[3]

Men, placed by nature in families, come inevitably to know the desirability of limits on competition. By common, although often separate, experience they come to believe that justice is the prerequisite of cooperative competition. By experience with one another they come to expect each other man, and, in truth, all men, to act justly in some degree. Experience produces both similar beliefs and mutual confidence. The result is a strong feeling of selfish obligation, based on selfish interest in the fruits of cooperation, to act justly. This, then, is the first force which makes society, a relationship founded on the three principles of justice, possible. The members of a society did not introduce justice because they disliked their previous condition, then envisioned the peace and prosperity they could enjoy by cooperating, and then thought out the principles of justice; rather, they were conducted into society by experience. Their beliefs were implanted in them by experience. Nor is their initial obligation to act justly the result of a promise made among themselves; instead, it is the outcome of experience and convention. The public enunciation of common beliefs—the statement as a "Convention" of the contents of a convention—may be useful in establishing the existence of common beliefs, but this is not fundamental, for whether or not one takes a Convention seriously, and abides by its terms, depends mainly on one's beliefs. That is, Conventions are descriptive, not prescriptive: they depend for their force on the prevailing conventions.[4]

It is only by becoming embodied in the beliefs of men that the principles of justice enter the historical world. Civilization is the process by which, by becoming experienced, men undergo a change in their beliefs, so that instead of being attracted by immediate goods, they seek goods that can be achieved only in societies. According to Hume, the fundamental reason why men come to feel obliged to act justly is that they come to believe that just acts are in their own interest.

Justice is highly useful to mankind, but justice is also morally good. Perfect societies, societies in which there is complete conformity by all to the principles of justice, are virtually impossible; yet the conduct of men would conform far less closely to the principles if justice were not, in addition to being good in utilitarian terms, a moral virtue. The feeling of moral obligation, Hume finds, often causes just acts when utility alone would fail to produce this result. Justice, we must notice, coincides with the interest of men as individuals, as the equal and undifferentiated members of society, but not always with the interests of every particular man in every particular instance. Justice is useful to all men because if it were ignored completely, they could enjoy none of the good results of association. But since in practice each single unjust act, or even a prolonged series of such acts, is far from likely to destroy a society, a tempted man is not confronted with a simple choice between, on the one hand, a good to be obtained by acting unjustly and, on the other, the survival of society. He has a deep interest in the preservation of the society, but the situation often is not such that this interest is pitted against his interest in the fruits of injustice. In short, if the continuation of society is taken for granted, it well may be that unjust acts are extremely useful for a particular man at a particular moment. Moreover, in addition to an interest in injustice based on strictly selfish considerations, interests arising from the natural relationships may promote injustice. Justice may require that our virtuous relatives and friends be stripped of rich possessions, and that this wealth be transferred to lazy, miserly, stupid, strangers. Justice may require that contracts disastrous for our families and friends be performed. In short, although their ultimate interest is promoted by just conduct, there are times when, because this truth is obscured, men may be drawn by their interests to theft and breach of contract.

At this point, we must remember the effects of sympathy. General adherence to the principles of justice permits cooperation, and cooperation leads to a vast increase in the enjoyment of economic goods, and in the enjoyment of such other goods as are dependent on the availability of economic goods. The effect of general neglect of the principles is scarcity and privation. As actors in a complex economy, we may not heed the tendency of our unjust acts because, being absorbed in our short-run interest, we never think of, or we dismiss the thought of, the collapse of our society. But when we view unjust acts from the standpoint of impartial spectators, we feel, through sympathy, the pain of all those discomfited thereby.[5] Consequently, what initially was felt as good by the wrongdoer, and as bad by the others, comes to be known to us as evil. Similarly, just acts, initially only useful, come to be known as morally good. The mere idea of an unjust act comes to cause us pain, and we are repulsed by it. The idea of a good act becomes attractive. We come, in short, to feel drawn to respect rights and to avoid wrong. A man who is not drawn to act justly because he sees that it is in his interest to maintain society may well be drawn to act justly, contrary to his selfish interest and his interest arising from the natural relationships, because of his feeling of moral obligation.

When a society is small and poor, a distinction between these two kinds of goodness and these two kinds of obligation—between utilitarian good and moral good and between the obligation of interest and moral obligation—probably will not be made, Hume argues. The situation being simple, the causal connection between an unjust act and the disintegration of the society will be obvious. If great riches are absent, the temptation to forget the importance of society will be slight. The difference is detected and is of practical importance only in larger groups, such as tribes and nations, especially if they are wealthy. In such situations, men often will act justly, not because they are able to see that justice ultimately is in their interest, but because of morality.

Many men in established societies undoubtedly think of justice as good and of injustice as evil chiefly because of the recommendations of their parents and teachers and the exhortations of moralists. But this does not show, Hume contends, that justice is an invention of educators, politicians, and divines; rather, it shows only that sound moral beliefs can be transmitted. The truth is that the belief in justice is founded on utilitarian good, and that because justice is useful to all individuals, this belief is seconded and confirmed by a moral judgment. By the acquisition of the double belief that justice is useful and morally good, men become civilized, and the stronger their belief is, the more civilized they are. Once a beginning has been made, once a tradition of civility has been started, it will, of course, be strengthened and continued from generation to generation by education and habituation.[6]

Hume's theory leaves no place for a State of Nature. For him the society is an inevitable consequence of the family, and therefore, since the family is as old as mankind, the society is as old as mankind. Each family gradually becomes a small society, and in the proper circumstances, these small societies merge. The two chief aspects of human nature are the feelings and the understanding. Whereas the natural relationships arise from our feelings for human beings, society is an artificial relationship. It is a relationship that will not exist unless it is thought useful. Hume did not object to the description of the condition that would prevail in what ordinarily had been called the "State of Nature" as a method of displaying the advantages of society and, ordinarily, of civil society.[7] But any such "State of Nature," he insists, must be regarded as an abstraction, as a "mere philosophical fiction" achieved by consciously setting aside the human ability to understand, the ability to acquire beliefs about what is good—in terms of both utility and morality—and must not be regarded as a reconstruction of the earliest historical era. He himself uses this tactic hardly at all, and in no place does he undertake to describe in detail a "State of Nature" based on his own analysis of the passions. But in his discussion of the natural moral virtues, we have—provided that the natural relationships are not too greatly distorted by the removal of the fruits of society—the main features of such a condition. It would be no golden age; but neither would life be, as Thomas Hobbes said, "solitary, poore, nasty, brutish, and short." Natural feelings would produce and sustain families and friendships. The natural increase of families would produce neighbourhoods. Occasional acts of humanity would be done. The chief disadvantage would not be hostility among men, but rather the general scarcity of a secure and bountiful supply of economic goods; for although there would be occasional outbursts of anger caused by personal disagreements, the very absence of great and unequal stocks of goods would entail a reduction of the occasions on which avidity, the most fecund cause of strife, would express itself. When the only goods are primitive tools and weapons and the carcasses of animals, there is little incentive to take what somebody else already has. But such a "State of Nature," he argues, never existed. Instead of thinking that once there was an era when men did not believe in justice to some degree, an era in which relations among men were entirely the result of love and hatred or pride and humility, and that at a specific moment, because of the prevailing discomfort, a full-blown society was superimposed on the natural relationships by an act of reason, we should acknowledge that there never was a time when the rudiments of a social order were not needed and when the capacity to understand the means of satisfying that need was not present. We must not make the mistake of thinking that prior to a certain, unknown date, justice was entirely unknown among men. And we must not overlook the truth that the basic work of civilizing men is performed, not by governments, but primarily by the family and secondarily by the neighbourhood. Whether we are thinking of an early era before the introduction of governments, or of the conditions which would prevail if governments were suddenly abolished now, we should see that although conditions would be primitive, a total disorder, an Hobbesian "war of all against all" would not prevail.

Hume's insistence that there never was a State of Nature entails the rejection of the social contract theory as a basic explanation of why men feel obliged to act justly. But even if there once had been a State of Nature, the contract theory, he contends, would have been inadequate as an explanation of the beginning of society. Primitive men could not reason abstractly, and therefore could never formulate so complex an idea as an associating principle.[8] And even if they could, two other problems would still remain to be solved. First, they would have to overcome the natural tendency each man has to see his own immediate good as the paramount good when he is deeply engrossed in business. And second, they would have to be fairly sure that other men also would act justly. Once a government exists these two problems can be solved fairly easily. But Hume is not prepared to say that society is never possible without a government. His own theory, based on the inculcation of a belief in justice, does not involve these problems.

His theory requires that instead of thinking of the history of civilization as neatly divided into two great parts, one, the State of Nature, in which there is neither justice nor governance, and the other, the period of civil society, we should think of civility, at some level, as timeless. The basic step in the civilization of men is not one that was taken long ago, but rather is one that is repeated in the experience and education of each child.

Justice is logically prior to governance: the only valid reason for supporting a government is that it helps to maintain society. Moreover, it is Hume's theory—in his early works, at least—that, to a degree, justice can be actualized without governance. Accordingly, we have dealt first with his explanation of how men come to know justice. We now turn to his theory of the actualization of the four principles of governance.

In poor communities the principles of justice will not be used to a high degree: economic relations will be based mainly on the first principle, on the second to only a slight extent, and hardly at all on the third. Since there is little or no far-flung trade, the scope of the power of the natural leaders will be as extensive as the market. In such a situation, justice, insofar as it is needed, can be maintained by the obvious interest all have in it, by their sense of moral obligation to act justly, and by such enforcement as parents, chiefs, and elders can provide. The pressure to be unjust will be controllable by interest, by the

moral sense, and by natural authority. But once the first principle of justice has been made the means by which to amass
considerable amounts of goods, and once the second and, especially, the third principles have become—or seem likely to become—the foundations for an extensive division of labour and
an extensive market, justice will break down if no enforcement
is provided other than that provided by those men naturally
preeminent. The dangers inherent in unjust conduct are often
very hard to see when the economic system is large, complex,
and apparently solidly established. The value of just conduct is
dubious when one is dealing with men afar off, with men whose
respect for justice is uncertain. The authority of natural leaders is too strictly local and personal; they themselves are too
directly involved in economic business to be always just to all,
and they have no military forces constantly at their disposal.
A new kind of obligation is needed if men are to act justly in
these new circumstances.[9]

It is clear, Hume argues, that the need for a government is
not a result of the wickedness of men. Avarice can lead to both
good and bad results. When life is simple, men will succeed in
being just without the promises and threats introduced by a
government. That is, many men, moved by a desire for external
goods, will act justly because they see that this is the best way
to satisfy their needs, or because of moral obligation, or both.
But perception, we know, is selfish. When great and unequal
wealth has been accumulated, and when the market comes to
embrace men totally unknown to us, our ability to see our long-
run good often proves inadequate. It is this change in the circumstances that brings on the need for a government.

Whenever these new circumstances develop, any impartial
observer will see that a government is needed. From this, however, we must not conclude that once and wherever these circumstances appear, men think out the four principles of governance, and then, guided by those principles, proceed to establish
governments over great societies. The rise of a need for a
government does not cause men to begin following all the principles of governance at once, or to observe any one of them

perfectly; rather, men first have to come to believe that conduct conformable to the principles is good, and this belief is not likely to be strong from the very beginning, or to arise at the same time for each and all the four principles. Only as men come to accept as good, conduct conformable to the principles do the principles become effective. They come to know these principles only under the hard tutelage of their needs and circumstances. In the early period, given the great desirability of some kind of government, even if inept and rudimentary, the principle pushed to the fore is the first, namely, that somebody is to be obeyed as governor, and that all within the society are to obey the same man or the same group of men. The first principle to be realized is that one government is to be obeyed by the entire society. The other principles come to be known later and consequently.

Did the first civil society, the first society under a government, come into existence by consent, or was it the product of political power? Hume's answer to this question, we shall find, is not the same in his later essays as in the *Treatise*. He is consistent in tracing the origin of political power to consent. Since in the *Treatise*, he equates the origin of political power with the origin of civil society, his answer therein is that civil society began by consent. Later he separates these two origins, and, therefore, is able to trace—as he does more and more—the rise of civil society to the use of political power.

It is his theory, we have noted, that every right to govern is founded ultimately, not on antecedent right, but on prior fact. A right to govern exists when men recognize a particular man as their ruler. Now, most men recognize their rulers on the basis of opinion. The thought that he whom they think of as their ruler may not have a perfect claim, even the best claim, to rule never comes to them. But occasionally there are times when, because there are contending claimants and pretenders, the primary question—Are there *de facto* reasons why hereafter I should recognize this man as my ruler?—does arise for a few men. It is as a guide in making this decision that Hume puts down his set of five considerations, namely, long possession, present possession, conquest, succession, and positive laws. All these criteria, however, are political. All these considerations are important because they are evidence that any claimant who has one or more of these points in his favour already has some supporters or followers. Already, it may be assumed, he is recognized as their ruler by some men. All these tests apply only where at least some men feel civil or political obligation. These tests imply that somebody already is distinguished from all others, except rival claimants, not merely by his particular natural abilities and connections, great or small, but also by the support which he can command from at least a few others.

If, then, we ask how the first right to command came into existence, the answer cannot be that the ruler was accepted because one or more of these five tests pointed him out. These tests assume the prior existence of a right to command (the prior existence of political inequality) ; and it is the origin of a right to command (or, the origin of political inequality) that has to be explained. Moreover, the first right to command can never have been caused by natural inequality, for no degree of superiority in strength, wisdom, charity, or justness, within the limits of human nature, is sufficient in itself to make other men recognize the superior man as their ruler. The answer can only be that the first right to command was the result of the tacit or express consent of all the first subjects. Besides, the only reason why each original subject should consent to be ruled is that he had come to believe that under the circumstances of the times it was in his own interest that he and the others be under a ruler. The only possible origin of the first group united by a common allegiance is unanimous consent. The superior natural qualities of one man undoubtedly influence the choice of the particular man who is to become the ruler, but it is the choice, not his abilities, which may have gone unremarked for years, that introduces his right to command. The only possible reason why anybody should ever recognize any particular person as his ruler in a period in which there is no prior political claim of any kind is that one already has designated that person as him to whom thereafter one will render obedience.

Hume maintains that the immediate cause of obedience of the first subject to the first ruler could have been only the earlier consent of the subject to obey that man as ruler, and that therefore the origin of the first political group in any place, the first group united by obligation to obey a common ruler, could only have been the unanimous consent of all the original members of that group; yet he insists that even if these groups were large, these acts of unanimous consent must not be thought of as contracts. Correctly speaking, no political union can ever be founded on a contract. Contract is an act in the sphere of society. It is an act between men in their relations as owners of economic goods and services, not between men as prospective members of a political group. Consequently, contract is logically irrelevant and inappropriate to the sphere of political activity. The only reason why anybody would ever be led to think of political relations as founded on contract would be the erroneous notion that justice is a virtue, not because it is useful to men, but because it is prescribed by "reason" or by a divine law; whereas, we know now that it is virtuous to be just, and that it is virtuous to obey one's good government because each of these two kinds of behaviour is highly useful. Since both justice and obedience are regarded as good for the same reason, nothing except mystification is accomplished by using one as a logical foundation for the other.

If, at this point, we ask whether or not Hume believed that the first civil societies were founded, albeit mistakenly, by the making of an original contract, we find that we are brought back to our main question, Did the first civil society come into existence by the consent of the first civil associates, or was it the product of political power? Hume's answers to these two questions go together, and as one changes, so does the other.

In the *Treatise* he insists that governments are far from being as important as writers such as Thomas Hobbes say. If the circumstances are suitable, men will act justly even where there is no government. It is only a change in the circumstances, an increase in the wealth or in the complexity of affairs, that makes the competition so keen that a government is desirable. Indeed, he submits, so much are men inclined to justice by their interest and moral sense that the first introduction of governance probably is to be traced not to injustice within a society, but to clashes with aliens. There are fewer deterrents to conflicts between strangers than between associates, and, therefore, less wealth would suffice to unleash avaricious strife between the former than between the latter. Once a society becomes embroiled in a struggle with another society, it needs a government to conduct an equal and orderly war effort and to plan its martial strategy. The military camp, he submits, is to the state what the family is to the society. It is there that men first learn the advantage of having a single authority. Moreover, once civil or political authority has been set up, it may easily be continued into times of peace. Or, if not continued, the memory of its efficacy provides the associates with a ready answer for the troubles that arise if "by the pillage of war, by commerce, or by any fortuitous inventions, their riches and possessions have become so considerable as to make them forget, on every emergence, the interest they have in the preservation of peace and justice." [10] It is to the military origin of governments, rather than to familiarity with the rule of patriarchs, that Hume attributes the monarchical character of all early governments. When enemies approach and close in, the desirability of a combined, cooperative effort is plain and general. The need, and its solution, can be seen without any great perspicacity. At such times men begin to follow the commands of those distinguished by courage, skill, strength, or other relevant virtues.

Not only are men able, according to the *Treatise*, to live in society without a government, but, instructed by experience in wartime, they are able deliberately to establish governments— by an invalid "contract"—whenever changes in their circumstances warrant this. Because society, at some level of perfection, is historically prior to civil society, the principles of justice are known to some extent before governments are established. Consequently, the promise or contract would be a fairly common institution in the everyday transactions of men. It would be surprising, therefore, if men did not resort to the contract when they were about to establish a government. The principles of justice are "antecedent to government, and are suppos'd to impose an obligation before the duty of allegiance to civil magistrates has once been thought of. Nay, I shall go farther, and assert, that government, *upon its first establishment*, wou'd naturally be suppos'd to derive its obligation from those laws of nature, and, in particular, from that concerning the performance of promises. When men have once perceiv'd the necessity of government to maintain peace, and execute justice, they wou'd naturally assemble together, wou'd chuse magistrates, determine their power, and *promise* them obedience." [11] Besides, "the voluntary consent of men must here have the greater efficacy, that the authority of the magistrate does *at first* stand upon the foundation of a promise of the subjects, by which they bind themselves to obedience; as in every other contract or engagement." [12]

By 1748, Hume had come to think of the "original contract" in much less formal and specific terms. He implies then that the origin of government is not to be thought of as having been quite as deliberate as the *Treatise* suggests. In the essay, "Of the Original Contract," first published in that year, he writes:

When we consider how nearly equal all men are in their bodily force, and even in their mental powers and faculties, till cultivated by education; we must necessarily allow, that nothing but their own consent could, at first, associate them together, and subject them to any authority. The people, if we trace government to its first origin in the woods and desarts, are the source of all power and jurisdiction, and voluntarily, for the sake of peace and order, abandoned their native liberty, and received laws from their equal and companion. The conditions, upon which they were willing to submit, were either expressed, or were so clear and obvious, that it might well be esteemed superfluous to express them. If this, then, be meant by the *original contract*, it cannot be denied, that all government is, at first, founded on a contract, and that the most ancient rude combinations of mankind were formed chiefly by that principle. In vain, are we asked in what records this charter of our liberties is registered. It was not written on parchment, nor yet on leaves or barks of trees. It preceded the use of writing and all the other civilized arts of life. But we trace it plainly in the nature of man, and in the equality [* or something approaching equality], which we find in all the individuals of that species. The force, which now prevails, and which is founded on fleets and armies, is plainly political, and derived from authority, the effect of established government. A man's natural force consists only in the vigour of his limbs, and the firmness of his courage; which could never subject multitudes to the command of one. Nothing but their own consent, and their sense of the advantages resulting from peace and order, could have had that influence.[13]

In the last edition of the essays, published in 1777, he inserted a paragraph immediately after the one quoted above, and in this the idea of an "original contract" is almost explicitly denied. The paragraph reads:

Yet even this consent was long very imperfect, and could not be the basis of a regular administration. The chieftain, who had probably acquired his influence during the continuance of war, ruled more by persuasion than command; and till he could employ force to reduce the refractory and disobedient, the society could scarcely be said to have attained a state of civil government. No compact or agreement, it is evident, was expressly formed for general submission; an idea far beyond the comprehension of savages: Each exertion of authority in the chieftain must have been particular, and called forth by the present exigencies of the case: The sensible utility, resulting from his interposition, made these exertions become daily more frequent; and their frequency gradually produced an habitual, and, if you please to call it so, a voluntary, and therefore precarious, acquiescence in the people.[14]

In the essay, "Of the Origin of Government," first published in 1777, he presents an account of the realization of governance brought about by the discovery of the benefits of governance. But, although this ideal account is far less simple than what is outlined in the *Treatise*, Hume immediately proceeds to modify it drastically, and insists that the actual origin of civil societies is piecemeal and slow, with no place in the process for a deliberate "original contract." He writes:

But though this progress of human affairs may appear certain and inevitable, and though the support which allegiance brings to justice, be founded on obvious principles of human nature, it cannot be expected that men should before-hand be able to discover them, or foresee their operation. Government commences more casually and more imperfectly. It is probable, that the first ascendant of one man over multitudes begun during a state of war; where the superiority of courage and of genius discovers itself most visibly, where unanimity and concert are most requisite, and where the pernicious effects of disorder are most sensibly felt. The long continuance of that state, an incident common among savage tribes, enured the people to submission; and if the chieftain possessed as much equity as prudence and valour, he became, even during peace, the arbiter of all differences, and could gradually, by a mixture of force and consent, establish his authority. The benefit sensibly felt from his influence, made it be cherished by the people, at least by the peaceable and well disposed among them; and if his son enjoyed the same good qualities, government advanced the sooner to maturity and perfection; but was still in a feeble state, till the farther progress of improvement procured the magistrate a revenue, and enabled him to bestow rewards on the several instruments of his administration, and to inflict punishments on the refractory and disobedient. Before that period, each exertion of his influence must have been particular, and founded on the peculiar circumstances of the case. After it, submission was no longer a matter of choice in the bulk of the community, but was rigorously exacted by the authority of the supreme magistrate.[15]

While in the *Treatise* the unanimous consent of the associates given at one decisive moment in an invalid "original contract" is the first origin of civil societies, Hume increasingly in his later writings depicts civil societies as products which arise from the interplay of political forces. In other words, he emphasizes increasingly the extent to which the actualization of the principles of governance comes about, not by human insight and design, but rather, accidentally, as an unanticipated consequence of less worthy human strivings.

It is important to notice that this change could be made without a modification of his theory of authority. At the end, as at the beginning, he can argue that, aside from the acceptance of a ruler because he meets one or more of the five tests, the only basis of recognition is the prior consent of the subject. But he changes the stage of civilization at which he introduces authority. In the *Treatise* he seems, when he comes to tell how civil societies came into existence, to have assumed that separate well-defined societies already exist as data. Therein he assumes that the need for justice already had produced considerable societies. Consequently, he writes as if the most advanced of these societies, each at a specific moment, had converted themselves into civil societies by establishing a government. The most likely device by which to explain how such conversions were effected was the invalid "original contract." Hume, in short, therein assumed the existence of "societies," and then applied his theory of the origin of authority to them: since each of these societies existed, but had no government, each could acquire a government only by the unanimous consent of all the associates. In his later writings, especially in the paragraphs published in 1777, societies no longer are treated as the obvious entities to which to apply the theory of the origin of political authority. The result is that the origin of political authority, and therefore the origin of the interplay of competing authorities, can be pushed back far beyond the stage at which there are great societies, back to the moment when two or three men first take another man as their leader. No ponderous device, such as an "original contract," seemed necessary to explain such a tentative alliance among small bands of savages. Whereas in the *Treatise* considerable societies precede the start of politics, in the later writings such societies are in large part the products of politics. A reader of the *Treatise* would be led to think that the first civil societies originated in unanimous acts of enlightened self-interest. He would be led to think that when political authority was first introduced, it inaugurated civil societies comparable to modern Britain or France. Consequently, he would be led to think that human reason, according to Hume, is a great force in history. A reader of the later works would never think of the historical process as so logical or of human conduct as so deliberate. He would never doubt that, not at one moment, but only by slow, perhaps imperceptible gains, effected by force, habituation, and education were even the most primitive of the early kingdoms established.

In both his versions of the origin of civil society Hume finds that obedience to the ruler comes to be an important moral duty.[16] In the first, once insight into the usefulness of having a ruler leads men to take a particular man as their ruler, and thereafter to recognize him as ruler, the perils to all threatened by acts of disobedience produce pain through sympathy, and the benefits to all entailed by acts of obedience produce pleasure through sympathy. Consequently, ideas of acts of disobedience come to have a painful, repulsive impression, and ideas of acts of obedience come to have a pleasing, attractive impression. The government may have been introduced by an invalid "original contract," but the contract is not necessary to explain why men think that it is morally good to obey. The danger to all of acts contrary to the commands of the government selected by the original civil associates soon leads men to call such acts "evil." In this early version, the genuine moral obligation to obey—as distinguished from the ill-founded moral obligation produced by the illusory contract—develops only after the introduction of the civil society. In the second, and later, version, since the first leaders were only chieftains, the moral obligation to obey existed before there was any union that might properly be called a "civil society."

It is remarkable that in neither of these accounts does Hume move directly from the utility of obedience to the morality of obedience. In the second account, the moral obligation to obey the government in a civil society is to a small extent a matter of direct utility and to a large extent a matter of custom and education. In the former, more notably, it would have been logically possible to proceed from the general insight into the utility of transforming the society into a civil society to a moral judgment favouring obedience and condemning disobedience. However, Hume does not propose that this is what happened. The government might not survive long enough for the moral judgment to develop, so the use of a promise or contract, an act which already had a moral status, is suggested by Hume as the invalid, but effective, means by which the time gap is bridged. Even in his first account, then, Hume is not prepared to say that a stable government could have been established and maintained with general insight into its utility as its sole foundation.

The account with which we have been concerned hitherto, the account of how the rudiments of justice and governance are realized, is unhistorical—not in the sense that this process never takes place, but because it takes place always. The causes which operate to civilize men in this way are always present and are always the same: if at any moment the rudiments of justice and governance were forgotten, these causes immediately would begin to reinstate civility, and would carry it up to, but not beyond, a certain level. In the *Treatise*, wherein he is mainly concerned to show that the characteristics of human nature produce all the natural and artificial relationships, and thus all the related virtues, Hume concentrates on this basic process. At this level, however, the principles of civility would be far from completely realized; men would still be far from being completely civilized. Hume's theory needs a second account, an account of an historical process, a process superimposed on the basic, repetitious (or timeless) one, a second process in which men are led to know more of the principles of civility and led to believe in them more and more deeply, or in which, perhaps, at times they become less civilized. Such a process, unlike the basic one, would be the subject of a history of civilization. In the *Political Discourses*, published in 1752, we find references to just such a history. There Hume treats of the past civilization of men as a process made up of three overlapping stages. Each of these three stages is the result of a different way of labouring, and the transition from one stage to the next is brought about by changes in the way men labour. This assignment by Hume of the cardinal place in historical causation to changes in the way of labouring is not surprising. Society and then civil society, for him, are primarily systems of relations among men brought on by their relations to external goods. It is by acquisitive and productive action, i.e., by labour, that men establish a relation between themselves and their external circumstances. "Every thing in the world is purchased by labour; and our passions are the only causes of labour." [17]

The first of these stages is the savage or primitive period. Men then get the necessities of life chiefly by seizing other living creatures. They live mainly by hunting and fishing. Their only important possessions are simple tools and weapons, which all can acquire easily. Eventually, where circumstances are suitable, these savages gain enough knowledge and skill to be able to cultivate the soil, thus ushering in the second or agricultural stage. While in the primitive stage there were only natural differences among men, the new form of labour, tilling, leads to an inequality of permanent possessions, and thus to social inequality. In his essay, "Of Interest," Hume writes: "When a people have emerged ever so little from a savage state, and their numbers have encreased beyond the original multitude, there must immediately arise an inequality of property; and while some possess large tracts of land, others are confined within narrow limits, and some are entirely without any landed property." [18] In the essay, "Of Refinement in the Arts," he says: "In rude unpolished nations, where the arts are neglected, all labour is bestowed on the cultivation of the ground; and the whole society is divided into two classes, proprietors of land, and their vassels or tenants." [19] The obvious difficulty is overcome when, "Those who possess more land than they can labour, employ those who possess none, and agree to receive a determinate part of the product." [20]

Even in the savage stage, a few skilled men may spend part of their time fashioning weapons for their fellows, in return for a part of the kill or catch. In the agricultural stage, this specialization is certain to increase. Local craftsmen—weavers, tailors, smiths, masons, and carpenters—appear. These, like the lords, receive their pay in goods. But this manufacturing and trading must expand greatly before we can correctly say that the third stage, in which the economy is a mixed one, partly agricultural and partly manufacturing and commercial, has been attained.[21] The first impetus to a shift from an agricultural economy to a mixed economy ordinarily is given by importers. They bring goods produced in one culture or in one geographical region into another. Thereby they make a good profit. They also begin a reformation of the domestic economy, for once the taste for novel and refined goods, or luxuries, has been aroused, more and more labour is shifted from the land and is devoted to the refining of local goods, i.e., to manufacturing, and to the distribution of domestic and foreign luxuries.[22]

While families relied for their goods largely on their own households and the local craftsmen, most of the population was dispersed throughout the countryside, and most men lived out their lives within the circumference of their farms and villages. Now they gather into the great manufacturing and shipping centres. Formerly, the division of labour was rudimentary and local, and required the use of little or no money.[23] Now, with the rise of manufacturing and trade, specialization advances rapidly, so that more and more people, living and working in more and more distant places, are involved. Money becomes the common denominator of all services and commodities. By its circulation it integrates farms, factories, and ports into one great market. The number of artisans multiplies. Entrepreneurs and manufacturers spring up in every community. Lay professionals, especially lawyers and physicians, become common. The division of labour becomes greater and greater, and productivity increases. And all this is possible because of merchants, a race of men who, like money, draw together all the separate parts of the economy.[24]

The principles of justice—the conditions of association— are the same always and everywhere. But all men will not necessarily form a single society; the extent of each separate society will depend on the economic needs of the times. Similarly, the degree to which the principles are put into practice at any time will depend on the nature of the economic possibilities of that time. In the first or savage stage of civilization, men will learn to follow the rules that the proper possessions of others are to be left undisturbed and that rights to goods are to be transferred only by mutual consent. The third rule, concerning contracts, will be less useful then, and therefore will be used less. In the agricultural period, also, property and barter are the outstanding economic institutions. It is in the third period, when men have learned to take advantage of an extensive division of labour, that contract first becomes prominent. In short, it is in a commercial economy that the principles of justice are most fully actualized.

The principles of governance, likewise, are the same always and everywhere; but the extent to which they are actualized depends on the stage of economic development. In the savage stage, Hume speculates, selfish utility and sense of duty are probably sufficient to produce enough conformity to justice to maintain society. The population in any one place will be small and well acquainted. The strain on natural affection and on ownership will be slight, for the implements of hunters and fishermen are few and are easily fashioned.[25] Hume proposes that here governance will not always be needed. "The state of society without government is one of the most natural states of men, and must subsist with the conjunction of many families, and long after the first generation. Nothing but an encrease of riches and possessions cou'd oblige men to quit it; and so barbarous and uninstructed are all societies on their first formation, that many years must elapse before these can encrease to such a degree, as to disturb men in the enjoyment of peace and concord."[26] Indeed, wherever, as in the tropics, men never have felt the need to amass wealth, civil society has never been established.

What is the reason, why no people, living between the tropics, could ever yet attain to any art or civility, or reach even any police in their government, and any military discipline; while few nations in the temperate climates have been altogether deprived of these advantages? It is probable that one cause of this phaenomenon is the warmth and equality of weather in the torrid zone, which render clothes and houses less requisite for the inhabitants, and thereby remove, in part, that necessity, which is the great spur to industry and invention. *Curis acuens mortalia corda.* Not to mention, that the fewer goods or possessions of this kind any people enjoy, the fewer quarrels are likely to arise amongst them, and the less necessity will there be for a settled police or regular authority to protect and defend them from foreign enemies, or from each other.[27]

But in an agricultural economy, where the land is unequally divided and the population is large, a government to enforce the first principle of justice will be needed.[28] The need in a third-stage society, where men are engaged in both agriculture and manufacture, and where there is much commerce, will be far greater still, for there will be great accumulations of wealth, constant movement of goods from one distant place to another, complicated transactions, constant reliance on weights, measures, and currency, many, many contracts, and, withall, a large population, a major part of which will dwell in cities.

When we try to relate the rise of governance to the three-phase economic development, we find that it is only in the last or commercial stage that governments become truly worthy of that name. In the hunting and fishing stage political unions may be set up, but these inevitably are fairly small, and they are temporary. In the agricultural stage, the existence of property in the land, together with poverty, makes constant governance necessary, but this falls far short of the four principles. Each lord governs his people, but neither the lords nor their subjects have an interest in or an aptitude for anything more than the mere rudiments of governance. The poor and ignorant peasants are slavish. They know only how to obey commands. The lazy, bored lords rule capriciously, according to their moods—sometimes they are harsh, sometimes they are indulgent—and never dream that this is not best. Besides, the units of civil obedience are too small. The lords have no unquestionable common superior. The result is a shifting compromise: the tenuous reign of a king over semi-independent barons. The paucity of commerce makes efficient, centralized governing impossible. The prevailing ignorance of the standards of governance makes the thought of centralized governance dreadful. And the fear of constant quarrels and wars makes the complete independence of the lords unacceptable. The outcome is an uneasy, unsatisfactory balance between royal and baronial power.[29] Clearly Hume considered the late Middle Ages as providing the perfect illustration of the governmental difficulties of the second, or agricultural, stage.[30]

It is interesting to notice that Hume thought of the rise of the great monarchies, in early times and in the sixteenth century, as occurring when commerce, although not yet great, was beginning to destroy agricultural localism. The great virtues of these monarchies was that they embodied the principle that the members of a society should obey a single government. They were the result of a growing belief in the value of one government, and they habituated and educated the people in that sound principle. Once considerable governments had been established, the scene was set for the discovery of the three other principles of governance, and in this, these monarchies themselves were the hard tutors of mankind.[31] The early absolute monarchies, with all competing, independent authority destroyed, tended to degenerate into slavery. The king himself, of course, was absolute and unlimited in his power. Given the ignorance of the times, that was bad enough, for the exertion of great arbitrary power is always "somewhat oppressing and debasing" to those subject to it. But when, because of the size of the population or the territory, the king could not do all the work of governing, and therefore needed assistants, the governmental machinery then created was inspired by the genius of absolutism. The king's power was taken as the model for the power of all his major assistants. They were created in his image. Full authority was delegated to them. They were set over provinces and territories wherein they ruled as absolutely as if they themselves were kings. The notion of establishing a system of general laws, and of dividing the labour of applying those laws in such a way that each minister has defined power coextensive with his specified duties, and beyond which he cannot go legitimately, is alien to the experience of a barbarous king, and is too difficult to be discovered independently by an ignorant man unconstrained by necessity. "All general laws are attended with inconveniences, when applied to particular cases; and it requires great penetration and experience, both to perceive that these inconveniences are fewer than what result from full discretionary powers in every magistrate; and also to discern what general laws are, upon the whole, attended with fewest inconveniences." [32] Consequently, the vicegerents appointed in early times are absolute and unlimited except in relation to their royal master, and his control over them is exerted capriciously. The result is that the people are ruled in either a harsh or a careless, incalculable manner. Arbitrary power, while better than utter chaos, is "altogether ruinous and intolerable, when contracted into a small compass; and becomes still worse, when the person, who possesses it, knows that the time of his authority is limited and uncertain. *Habet subjectos tanquam suos; viles, ut alienos.* He governs the subjects with full authority, as if they were his own; and with negligence or tyranny, as belonging to another. A people, governed after such a manner, are slaves in the full and proper sense of the word." [33]

But if it is commerce that makes it possible for kings to reduce the great landholders, it is commerce that destroys capricious absolutism. Absolute royal government, which supplanted baronial power, in turn, is likely to be followed by republican or constitutional government. When commerce has developed sufficiently, a fairly large, wealthy, and intelligent new group of men, quite different from the two classes in which society was divided in the strictly agricultural period, appears. Many of the diligent peasants will have become substantial men. The merchants and entrepreneurs in manufacturing will have grown influential. Remember, says Hume, in speaking of British politics, that, "The lower house is the support of our popular government; and all the world acknowledges, that it owed its chief influence and consideration to the encrease of commerce, which threw such a balance of property into the hands of the commons." [34] Moreover, the minds of men, by practice in the arts and in trade, and by conversation, will have been made capable of devising complex processes of governance.[35] In such circumstances a republic is possible. Besides, the abuses of monarchical power drive men to revolt, and to establish republics. Here the true art of governing a society is first discovered: the second, third, and fourth principles of governance are realized. Because the power to govern belongs to no one person in a republic, but has to be assigned and reassigned among several magistrates, an orderly governmental machine with powers appropriate to each part has to be worked out. In their beginnings, the only check on the magistrate or magistrates may have been the periodic elections by the people, but after a time the need for constitutional law, restricting each magistrate to certain duties or offices, must become obvious. "It may happen, that a republic, in its infant state, may be supported by as few laws as a barbarous monarchy, and may entrust as unlimited an authority to its magistrates or judges. But, besides that the frequent elections by the people, are a considerable check upon authority; it is impossible, but, in time, the necessity of restraining the magistrates, in order to preserve liberty, must at last appear, and give rise to general laws and statutes." [36] The result is a restraint on the magistrates both in relation to each other, and in relation to the populace. A republic infallibly gives rise to law. "Though a republic should be barbarous, it necessarily, by an infallible operation, gives rise to LAW, even before mankind have made any considerable advances in the other sciences. From law arises security: From security curiosity: And from curiosity knowledge. The latter steps of this progress may be more accidental; but the former are altogether necessary. A republic without laws can never have any duration. On the contrary, in a monarchical government, law arises not necessarily from the forms of government. Monarchy, when absolute, contains even something repugnant to law. Great wisdom and reflection can alone reconcile them. But such a degree of wisdom can never be expected, before the greater refinements and improvements of human reason." [37]

Once republics have introduced the practices of defining the

power of each public officer, of governing the conduct of their
subjects by calculable laws, and of treating all their subjects
equally, the general utility of this kind of governance becomes
evident. As soon as the general interest that all have in this
improved mode of governing becomes evident, the practices take
on a moral character, so that governments that live up to these
standards regularly are thought of as virtuous, and any violators are likely to be denounced as barbarous, irrational, and
wicked. But these standards of good governance are not confined to the republics in which they are first introduced; inevitably, they spread into and influence even remote monarchies. The result of this may be that if one were to inspect the
government of some modern monarchy, such as France, Hume
submits, he would find that although constitutionally the king's
power is as full and absolute as that of any barbarous king,
both he and his ministers act as if there were strict limits on
their power. They respect the attained standards of civilized
governance. The art of good governance has been adopted. As
a result general laws have been established. The servants of the
Crown responsible for executing the laws have clearly defined
powers, and may not act *ultra vires.* "It may now be affirmed of
civilized monarchies, what was formerly said in praise of republics alone, *that they are a government of Laws, not of Men.*
They are found susceptible of order, method, and constancy, to
a surprizing degree. Property is there secure; industry encouraged; the arts flourish; and the prince lives secure among
his subjects, like a father among his children." [38]

Relations between men as members of a family, a friendship,
or humanity express the feelings for others natural to men as
human beings. The innumerable good acts which appertain to
these relationships are not done because they are useful to the
actor, but are the result of all the causes of benevolence towards
others. Therefore, there is no history of the realization of the
natural moral virtues. Social and political relations among men,
in contrast, are results of their feelings for economic goods.
These relations, being motivated basically by their usefulness,
do not come into existence spontaneously. Although the three

principles of the most useful economic relations and the four
principles of the most useful political relations could have been
reasoned out at any time, these principles become embodied in
action only when men become aware of the disadvantage of acting in other ways. The actualization of the rudiments of justice
is almost inevitable. On the other hand, neither the actualization of justice to a high degree nor the actualization of governance is inevitable, but rather, depends on circumstances. Accordingly, much of the realization of the artificial virtues has
a history. Since the principles of justice and the principles of
governance are the principles of civil (nonemotional) relations
among men, this history is the story of the civilization of mankind.

Civilization, we must remember, according to Hume, is not a
conversion which men impose upon themselves. They do not
argue themselves into believing that action conformable to the
principles of civility is good. Civilization is not a self-conver-
sion that self-conscious men undertake and achieve. It happens
to them, and many highly civilized men, although they show
by their daily acts that they believe in the acts conformable
to the principles, would have trouble in stating the principles.
Civilization is not a matter of chance, nor, at least in the past,
has it been the outcome of human effort. The principles of
justice and governance outline the most useful relations among
men; by experience and by education in the beliefs previously
acquired by others through experience, men come to accept
those principles. This process is slower than the one by which
men come to have beliefs about the physical universe, because
the occasions for experience are fewer, but provided that education is not interrupted, some degree of civilization is almost
a certainty. To live in the world is to become civilized.

Society and state are artificial relationships. They are plays
with vast casts, and nobody has an exclusive claim to any particular role in either. Once the plays have begun, there are two
ways in which men can regard them, and participate in them.
Those who understand their artificial nature can distinguish
between any actor and the character he bears. They see that

whatever rights to goods a man happens to have, appertain to him by virtue of his role in the economic order, and that whatever rights to rule a man happens to have appertain to him by virtue of his role in the state. But this, presumably, does not cause them to throw up their own roles, and to demand that they be recast as men of great wealth and authority. They see that society and the state are beneficial to all, so they are ready to pretend that the actors really are the characters. They presuppose that Henry is the king, and that Giles is a noble, and that Allan is a great landowner—this is the supposition upon which civil society rests for them. But such men are few in number. It never occurs to most men, born in civilized places, that society and state are artificial. They grow up into an ongoing play. They learn that Henry, the king, is to be obeyed and that Allan's riches are not to be seized. They do not come to know that civil society is like a game with places or offices which men take up. We may say, then, that particular men have their roles (and rights) in society and state, either by *presupposition* or *opinion*. Those who understand civil society deliberately ignore the actors, and focus their attention on the characters; so that thereafter when they are confronted by any member of civil society, they behave towards him according to his preestablished role. They recognize him not as the actor he is, but as the character he is playing. In contrast, the multitude accept the play at face value. They, too, recognize Henry as their king, and Allan as their landlord, but in their case, recognition is the consequence of opinion.

# VII

## ECONOMIC POLICY AND CIVILITY

> Moral reasonings are either concerning particular or general facts. All deliberations in life regard the former; as also all disquisitions in history, chronology, geography, and astronomy.
>
> The sciences, which treat of general facts, are politics, natural philosophy, physic, chemistry, &c. where the qualities, causes and effects of a whole species of objects are enquired into.
>
> *Enquiry* I, pp. 164–65

IT IS often possible, Hume proposes, to reason accurately about the effects of political institutions and public policies. The conclusions thereby attained, of course, are not demonstrably true; they are beliefs, but so, too, are the conclusions formed in the physical sciences. Yet the rules of political science, it must be admitted, are far more difficult to discover than those of physical science. First, there is the problem of variability. Human nature in its fundamentals is the same always, but even the people of neighbouring countries frequently are very different in national characteristics, and there are great differences between barbarians, whose human nature is undeveloped, and highly civilized men. The physical conditions in which men live—whether the place is or is not fertile, mountainous, or temperate in climate—influence their conduct. The size of the population, too, is important: already we have seen how, by determining the demand for goods, it can influence the need for a government. And political factors, such as the size of the country and the form and maxims of its government, factors which themselves can be altered politically, influence the effects of policies and institutions. Second, there is a shortage of data. Because the subject matter of political science is highly

variable (historical), the number of sets of causes that have
been observed frequently enough to permit conclusions at the
level of either "high probability" or "proof" is comparatively
small.[1] Nevertheless, it probably is possible, Hume argues, to
lay down quite accurate rules for specified conditions, provided
that the outcome to be predicted depends on a number of persons sufficiently large to submerge the peculiarities of particular persons and to allow the motives normal to the time and
place to have their effect.[2] For example, says Hume, it is far
more difficult to reason accurately about foreign affairs, a
field in which single persons are highly influential, than about
the operation of the economic system and the changes in the
structure of society. "The depression of the lords, and rise of
the commons in ENGLAND, after the statutes of alienation and
the encrease of trade and industry, are more easily accounted
for by general principles, than the depression of the SPANISH,
and rise of the FRENCH monarchy, after the death of CHARLES
QUINT. Had HARRY IV. Cardinal RICHLIEU, and LOUIS XIV. been
SPANIARDS; and PHILIP II. III. and IV. and CHARLES II. been
FRENCHMEN, the history of these two nations had been entirely
reversed." [3]

Already we know the three principles of justice and the four
principles of governance. But can we discover anything more,
certainly not as basic, but perhaps also highly important, about
the conduct of economic and political affairs? Hume's answer
is affirmative. Although it is difficult to be sure about the outcome of any particular transaction, it is possible to discover
principles which are valid generally in "politics, trade, economy,
or any business in life." He writes: "But however intricate they
may seem, it is certain, that general principles, if just and
sound, must always prevail in the general course of things,
though they may fail in particular cases; and it is the chief
business of philosophers to regard the general course of things.
I may add, that it is also the chief business of politicians; especially in the domestic government of the state, where the
public good, which is, or ought to be their object, depends on
the concurrence of a multitude of causes; not, as in foreign

politics, on accidents and chances, and the caprices of a few persons." [4] Since these principles can be discovered, politicians should strive to learn them, and should make them the foundations and cornerstones of their policies.[5] In this chapter and the three that follow we shall be concerned with Hume's beliefs about the effects of various kinds of political institutions and public policies, and with the recommendations he makes pursuant to those beliefs.

Eight of the twelve political discourses published in 1752 reveal a strong practical intent. Of these, seven deal with economic questions, and one is on foreign policy—a significant apportionment of attention.[6] Hume, as we shall see later, was fairly contented with the constitutional and religious arrangements prevailing in Great Britain; at least, he was hoping for no major improvements other than those consequent to the more general acceptance of the prevailing settlement. But the government, by its actions in relation to the economic activities of the people, and in relation to the foreign affairs of the state, was displaying, he thought, a stubborn ignorance of both the general principles of political economy and the history of civilization. His aim in these eight discourses is to destroy misconceptions, and to discover mistakes in economic and foreign policy derived from those misconceptions. His main subject is the important role of economic commerce, i.e., manufacturing, scientific farming, and trading, in the attainment of high civility.

The prevailing economic policy revealed, he thought, a blindness to the advances made in Great Britain and on the continent during the previous three centuries. During that period, the country and its neighbours had undergone a slow transition from the second phase of civilization, in which the activities, governance, and ethics of men were determined by agricultural production for local consumption, to the third phase, in which farming and manufacturing were increasingly caught up in a great national and international network of specialization and exchange. This truth, and its promising implications, he argued, ought to be seen by the British government, and made the basis of national policy. He did not question openly the belief that domestic and foreign economic policy ought to have as its chief aim the attainment or maintenance of a high level of national strength, but he insisted that, as a result of ignorance, many of the ways in which this was being done were either useless or impedimental. Still too influential was the old notion that imports ought to be restricted and staple trades jealously nurtured and protected to keep the balance of trade as favourable, or as little unfavourable, as possible, so that the nation could make money, or at least not lose too much money. Consequently, the people and the government of Great Britain still found it difficult to see clearly that the surest way to enhance the nation's strength was to free enterprise from most mercantile restrictions, and to encourage commerce to grow and spread. The number, ability, and character of the people, not mere money acquired or retained by a favourable balance of trade, are the ingredients of national strength: in the modern world, it is not the filling of coffers, but the growth of a large, skilful, and industrious populace, the kind of populace created by commerce, that increases national strength.

Correct thinking about policy is impossible, he contends, until money and wealth have been clearly distinguished. To show that these are different, Hume analyzes the logical results of the presence of different amounts of money in a static economy. He shows that, as money, precious metals have only a relative value. They serve as a standard of value, in terms of which the relations among the values per unit of all the commodities on the market can be expressed. And they serve as a symbol, with varying significance, convenient in the exchange of goods and services. The quantity of money in a country at any time is of no importance within the domestic market: if the supply of commodities and services, and the demand for them, were the same as at some previous moment, but the quantity of money in circulation were double or quadruple what it had been at that previous moment, the only difference would be that all prices and wages would be expressed in figures double or quadruple those used at the earlier moment. Or if the quantity of money were only a tiny fraction of what it now is, the only effect would be that all prices and wages would be expressed in proportionally smaller figures. The effects, in short, would be only mathematical.

This distinction made by Hume between money and wealth does not mean that the flow of money within a nation or among nations is of no economic importance to him. He was quite ready to accept the common view that the rate of interest paid on borrowed money in a country is "the barometer of the state" —low rates being regarded as a sure sign of flourishing prosperity, and high rates as a sign of weakness and danger. For him, this proved the great superiority of a highly commercialized economy. It is not, he argues in "Of Interest," the amount of money available in a country that determines the interest rate there. Borrowed money is the symbol of borrowed purchasing power. What determines the rate of interest is the supply of saved purchasing power, the extent of the demand to borrow it, and the size of the profits to be made by investing the savings in other ways.[7] The symbolic value of the money is merely a result of the ratio between the number of tons of monetary metals and the real goods available. Wealth remaining constant, if the amount of money is doubled, the value or symbolic meaning of the money is halved; therefore, the percentage rate of interest will remain exactly what it was.

Changes in the interest rate are caused by changes in real, not in symbolic, things. In an agricultural economy, with few or no great merchants, the rate inevitably will be extremely high. The peasants will have no savings, and only a few extraordinary landlords will be frugal. At the same time, most of the lords will be prepared to squander the income of many future years to secure a temporary release from their present, dull idleness. In sharp contrast, where commerce has increased, and is flourishing, not only will there be many merchants, but there will be a new ethic. A man naturally is uneasy and discontented when idle. In an agricultural society there will be a strong emphasis on aristocratic, useless amusements.[8] In a commercial society there are many opportunities for the useful occupation of the mind and body. This in itself will alter the style of a culture; but the influence of commerce does not stop there, for, says Hume, if the employment you give a man "be lucrative, especially if the profit be attached to every particular exertion of industry, he has gain so often in his eye, that he acquires, by degrees, a passion for it, and knows no such pleasure as that of seeing the daily encrease of his fortune." [9] Commerce makes men industrious and saving. Accordingly, the diligent merchants in a commercial society will have available vast stocks of wealth in the form of the prevailing money to be invested either in new commercial ventures or as loans.[10] Now, the rate of profit and the rate of interest vary together; if the interest rate seems too low, these merchants will put their money back into commerce, thus increasing competition, decreasing prices, and reducing profits, or if competition among the merchants already has produced a low rate of profit, many will be ready to lend their money for interest, and this will bring down the interest rate. In short, both a low rate of profit and a low rate of interest are the effects of extensive, well-developed commerce. Here we have a proof, "little inferior to a demonstration," that a nation with well-developed manufactures and trade is far healthier and stronger than one without commerce or with only feeble commerce.

If we examine a dynamic economy, an economy growing over a time period, we shall find that money, in the short run, does flow into the country where much manufacturing is being done and where merchants are enterprising. This flow, like the interest rate, is an indicator of the comparative economic standing of the countries involved. But the inflow of money must not be regarded as the cause of the low interest rates that will prevail in the more highly commercialized country; rather, the flow is a concomitant effect, with the lowering pressure on the interest rate, of the condition of the economy.

When we analyze Hume's account of the effects of commerce on national strength, we find that his argument for commerce has three interrelated parts. The proprietors of land and their tenants, from whose fields and labour the necessities of life must come, will never exert themselves gratuitously to produce a surplus. On the contrary, they live—not choose to live, for they have no other prospect before them—improvidently, in lax idleness. The earth remains rough and comparatively barren; or worse, it is robbed of its fertility by abuse. No exertion is made to acquire new skills and knowledge. Men live languidly, spending their time in savage sports or drunken indolence. The prevalent sloth and barbarity cause poverty: even the necessities, which with a little more care and work would become abundant, are scarce. Production remains near the subsistence level.[11] But the picture brightens when luxuries, introduced by trading and manufacturing, come upon the scene. The gentry and their tenants, energized by the touch of commerce, begin to become industrious, and undertake to study agriculture as a science. They become diligent, and practice to improve their fields, livestock, seed, fertilizers, and implements. The immediate end to which they are drawn by their desire for goods is the creation of a surplus stock of necessities to be exchanged for the luxury goods for which they have learned to feel a demand. This surplus is all important: it is the strength of the nation. Its size is the measure of the labour that can be diverted to other purposes.

Normally, the surplus labour of a commercialized country is spent in commerce, that is, in manufacturing, importing, and marketing the luxuries, in retailing the necessities, and in advancing the liberal arts. But in time of war, real or apprehended, the government may divert the "superfluous hands" to the purposes of the state. "The encrease and consumption of all the commodities, which serve to the ornament and pleasure of life, are advantageous to society; because, at the same time that they multiply those innocent gratifications to individuals, they are a kind of *storehouse* of labour, which, in the exigencies of state, may be turned to public service." [12] At such times, by taxing the consumption of goods, especially luxuries, the consumption and production of them can be reduced. The hands thus released will seek employment in the expanding armed services.[13] In the meantime, the farmers, having once become industrious, still have their well-tilled fields, sturdy beasts, and science. They continue to produce the surplus, at least in the short run, although they now receive fewer luxuries in return, and this surplus of necessities maintains the fleets and the armies.[14]

It must not be thought that the amount of labour in a country can be measured simply by counting the populace, for labour is productive capacity. It is not to be reckoned only in terms of the mere number of hands or heads, but also in terms of the skill, temperament, morals, and mobility of the men. In all these respects the labour of a commercial nation will be better both in peace and in war than that of a nation composed of dragging peasants and some gothic barons. The great supply of efficient labour available is Hume's first reason why a commercial nation is a strong nation.

The second reason is that much less coercion is needed to concert the power of a modern nation for public purposes when that nation has been commercialized. Would it not be preferable to return to the maxims of ancient policy, and draw off a large surplus from the husbandmen immediately, without providing luxuries as bait, so that the nation's surplus hands could be employed, not just occasionally, but incessantly, in winning new dominions and martial glory? Hume's reply is that the efficacy of such a policy depends on the spirit of the people, and that in modern times a policy which sought public good directly, not indirectly thorough private good, would be perverse.[15] Human nature is not stereotyped: it does allow and include many different varieties of individual and national characters. But the types near the limits of the sweep of possibility are rare, appearing only as the result of the prolonged operation of very unusual circumstances. The ancients, especially the citizens of Sparta and early Rome, to whom modern moralists look back with deep sighs, as they lament the selfishness and the luxury of their own times, were rather extraordinary.[16] They had become patriotic in the extreme; indeed, among them, patriotism often was regarded as the greatest of the virtues. Their leaders, in shaping public policy, could rely on this spirit of patriotism.

For them, accordingly, the fostering of luxury and of commerce would have been only an unnecessary distraction. The virtues valued by modern men, however, fall nearer the middle of the sweep, so we may say that moderns are more "natural" than the ancients. Of this the governors of modern states should take cognizance. In addition, they should appreciate that they cannot reform and render extreme the values that motivate their subjects. "Sovereigns must take mankind as they find them, and cannot pretend to introduce any violent change in their principles and ways of thinking. A long course of time, with a variety of accidents and circumstances, are requisite to produce those great revolutions, which so much diversify the face of human affairs. And the less natural any set of principles are, which support a particular society, the more difficulty will a legislator meet with in raising and cultivating them. It is his best policy to comply with the common bent of mankind, and give it all the improvements of which it is susceptible." [17]

The less conformity there is between the spirit of the people and the policy of their government, the more coercion the government must use in executing its policy. Modern men, unlike the ancients, being quite normal, are more individualistic than patriotic. A policy requiring constant public service from husbandmen could be carried out only by swarms of intrusive government agents, constantly using force, and even at that, only with disastrous, even ludicrous, inefficiency. A nation with commerce is a nation most agreeable to ordinary human nature; accordingly, a policy based on the logic of luxurious rewards will be far easier to apply, and, therefore, will be far more likely to succeed, than one founded on inappropriate ancient examples, however admirable these may appear in books.[18]

The third beneficial effect of commerce on national strength is that it makes it possible for the government to galvanize and manage more of the strength of the entire nation. While each family relies largely on its own members and on local craftsmen to produce the goods they want, the nation may be one state, but there is little substance behind that legal unity. There is a myriad of local economic units, and these are held together merely by a common allegiance. The government can tax these local systems only awkwardly, by taking such surpluses as they have in the form of commodities and military service, neither of which is applicable to many of the needs of a government.[19] But when the people are caught up in one great commercial system, and most of their labour at some point is translated into money, the government, by money taxes on consumption, can draw upon the productive capacity of the entire populace.[20] These tax moneys can then be used to buy the specific goods and services required by the government whenever and wherever they are needed.

Although commerce had spread throughout Britain and the neighbouring European countries, the British public and, worse, its leaders, Hume found, had not as yet managed to understand either the nature or the promise of this momentous change. Some moralists, overlooking the truth that commerce supplants an ethic of sloth with an ethic of industry, were still reluctant to give their approval to an economic system based on manufacturing and on extensive domestic and foreign trade, based, that is, on the natural human desire for luxuries. And the government paid little or no attention to valid economic principles; instead of allowing and fostering the growth of commerce, it clung blindly to remnants of an indefensible earlier policy, ludicrous in theory and, if effective, barbarous in practice. For the increase of the genuine wealth of the British nation, Hume makes three recommendations.

The least important of these—it hardly deserves to be ranked with the others, so little emphasis does he give it—is that where possible, the government, any government, should follow an inflationary monetary policy. The amount of money in a static economy, we have seen, is of no importance, for where the quantity of gold and silver is high or low, wages and prices will be proportionately high or low. But a decrease or increase in the supply of money over a time period, i.e., "in the real world," will have a drastic effect on the business and prosperity of a nation. This is because the adjustment of wages and prices to the new high or low level takes place, not instantaneously, but gradually. There is a time lag. When new money comes into the hands of entrepreneurs and merchants, they hire more workmen at the going wage. If workmen become scarce, the employers require an increase in labour in return for higher wages. In either case, more money is taken to the market by the workman when he goes to buy commodities, and since prices are still unaltered, he succeeds in buying more goods. The husbandmen then increase their production to meet the increased demand, and without an increase in prices acquire more money, which, in turn, they spend on more manufactured goods. The whole system receives a boost, and all gainfully employed men are made busier. The entire kingdom becomes more vigorous. The entrepreneur shows greater industry. The merchant is more enterprising. The workman eats and drinks better. The husbandman follows his plow with a spring in his step. Conversely, when money decreases, a depression of business and morale sets in. Workmen, having less money, buy less because prices have not dropped, and consequently, the husbandman and all his suppliers feel the pinch. The result is an increase in poverty, beggary, and sloth. Because of these multiplier effects of both inflation and deflation, it is a good policy for a government to seek to increase the currency slowly and constantly.[21]

Hume's second and third recommendations appertain to international relations. Since they are complementary, they can be expressed as one; namely, that Britain, instead of pursuing a pointless, ruinous policy of warring with her neighbours, especially France, should interweave her commerce with theirs.

He found that the people and politicians of England retained a spirit far too bellicose and fierce. The former are transported by rage at the mere thought of the French, while the politicians cynically foster this attitude, and exploit it to enhance their own popularity. In the discourse entitled "Of the Balance of Power," which in the first edition of *Political Discourses* he placed immediately after "Of the Balance of Trade" and immediately before the two discourses "Of Taxes" and "Of Public Credit," [22] Hume argues that Britain is prodigal in her warring. The English like to think that their "speculatists" first discovered the principle of the balance of power, a principle so obvious that many of the abler politicians of antiquity followed it, even if it was not then expressed as a maxim. This principle justifies British care to prevent a universal Bourbon monarchy; yet the danger of such a hegemony should not be exaggerated. Unfortunately, the principle of the balance of power is being used to justify folly: it is being used as the good reason, concealing the real reason, for waging war. England, animated by a passionate, barbarous ardor for war, rushes to arms without precise and worthwhile aims, and once begun, the wars are prolonged uselessly. "Here then we see, that above half of our wars with FRANCE, and all our public debts, are owing more to our own imprudent vehemence, than to the ambition of our neighbours." [23] So woodenly is the policy of opposing the French followed that Britain's allies exploit her: "All the world knows, that the factious vote of the House of Commons, in the beginning of the last parliament, with the professed humour of the nation, made the queen of HUNGARY inflexible in her terms, and prevented that agreement with PRUSSIA, which would immediately have restored the general tranquillity of EUROPE." [24] Besides, a policy of holding and waiting would be enough to check the French, for that enormous monarchy will soon collapse of its own weight and growing inefficiency.[25]

This senseless warring is far worse than useless: it jeopardizes the structure of British society. The best taxes, Hume argues, are those geared to the economic activity of the country, that is, those "levied upon consumptions, especially [consumptions] of luxury." If imposed carefully, such taxes tend to make the populace more, not less, industrious; moreover, they cannot be imposed arbitrarily, for when the tax rate is pushed too high, consumption and, thus, government revenue, decline. The disadvantage of other methods of taxation is that they depend for their safe moderation largely on the uncertain wisdom of politicians and rulers.[26]

Now, the prevailing practice of the English is to fly into a war whenever party politics or the humour of the populace recommend this, and to pay for this extravagant folly by mortgaging the future through vast increases in the national debt. The ultimate result of this practice could have been foretold from the beginning: taxes upon consumptions soon prove inadequate to service the debt; [27] taxes on possessions are then introduced, and these are increased as the national debt mounts with each new war, until finally the tax on land comes to be eighteen or nineteen shillings on the pound, and all the revenues of the state, or what is then the same thing, almost all the income of the nation, belongs to a class of *rentiers*. From this perilous situation a despotism might escape by taxing the annuitants heavily or by declaring the state bankrupt. A popular government, however, is likely to be impeded from breaking its fetters so simply, by political factors.[28] The calamitous final outcome in Britain, therefore, will be that the bulk of the populace, by reason of the thoughtless military adventures of the present, deprived of all gain from its labour, will lose its morale and industry, and consequently become an easy victim of the enemy.[29]

From the first, Hume's chief reason for opposing increases in the national debt was the debilitating effect on the spirit of the people of distortions in society brought about by excessive taxes. In 1764 he added six new paragraphs to the discourse, "Of Public Credit," amplifying his basic argument. One of these reads as follows:

In this unnatural state of society [brought about by oppressive taxes on possession], the only persons, who possess any revenue beyond the immediate effects of their industry, are the stockholders, who draw almost all the rent of the land and houses, besides the produce of all the customs and excises. These are men, who have no connexions with the state, who can enjoy their revenue in any part of the globe in which they chuse to reside, who will naturally bury themselves in the capital or in great cities, and who will sink into the lethargy of a stupid and pampered luxury, without spirit, ambition, or enjoyment. Adieu to all ideas of nobility, gentry, and family. The stocks can be transferred in an instant, and being in such a fluctuating state, will seldom be transmitted during three generations from father to son. Or were they to remain ever so long in one family, they convey no hereditary authority or credit to the possessor; and by this means, the several ranks of men, which form a kind of independent magistracy in a state, instituted by the hand of nature, are entirely lost; and every man in authority derives his influence from the commission alone of the sovereign. No expedient remains for preventing or suppressing insurrections, but mercenary armies: No expedient at all remains for resisting tyranny: Elections are swayed by bribery and corruption alone: And the middle power between king and people being totally removed, a grievous despotism must infallibly prevail. The landholders, despised for their poverty, and hated for their oppressions, will be utterly unable to make any opposition to it.[30]

Britain's relations with her neighbours, especially France, Hume found, were characterized by hatred and suspicion. The result was frequent, expensive wars, which by piling up the national debt, distorted the structure of British society and, thereby, threatened to make Britons hopeless and apathetic. Only ignorance of the truth that society is primarily an economic relationship, so that trading, not warring, is the most natural and, therefore, the most advantageous relation among societies, could lead to such folly. Hume's third recommendation is that the government remove all those restrictions on the flow of international trade designed merely to preserve a favourable balance of trade. This seems to run contrary to his first proposal, for, presumably, in many countries free trade would lead to a loss of money and the consequent depression of business and industry. But Hume, we must remember, does not advocate absolutely free trade. What he recommends is not the abolition of all restrictions on trade, but the abolition of restrictions inspired by bullionism.[31] There is no reason, therefore, why the benefits of both recommendations could not be gained by judicious adjustments: the benefits of an inflationary monetary policy would help to overcome the short-run disadvantages of freer trade in many countries, and freer trade would be beneficial to all in the long run.

His criticism of restraints on international trade designed to avoid an unfavourable balance of trade is that the bullion thereby retained, if any, is of slight importance when compared with the benefits lost.[32] The purchase of goods produced at a natural advantage in other countries will increase the prosperity of those countries, but this is no reason why such goods should not be imported. On the contrary, the prospering of foreign countries enables them to buy the products of a country such as Great Britain. The extension of international trade increases the manufacturing and trade in all the countries involved, and enables them all to become good customers of each other. Moreover, this extension permits men to use and enjoy the full bounty of the earth. A refusal to buy and sell, flies in the face of nature: it deprives mankind of "that free communication and exchange which the Author of the world has intended, by giving them soils, climates, and geniuses, so different from each other." [33]

Nor is there any reason for most nations to fear the long-run effects of an unfavourable balance of trade. If a nation's economy is undeveloped, bullion will be lost, but that is no great misfortune, for it is the condition of the economy, not the supply of gold and silver, that constitutes strength. Actually, it is precisely the shift of bullion to the busier country that operates to the long-run advantage of the other. The inflow of money drives up prices and wages there, with the result that the prices of the products of the more prosperous country will rise, and the demand for the products of the other nations will increase. The ultimate consequence is that they, too, attain flourishing commercial economies.[34]

No nation, except perhaps the Dutch, Hume proposes, need fear that it will find itself with no part to play in international trade. The removal of artificial obstructions, it is true, will cause some lines of production to die out, but others, in which the country has a natural advantage, will flourish in their place. The diversity in the resources of the several countries, produced by nature, together with the diversity in the skills and interests of the several people, produced by moral causes, assure that all nations willing to work will find a place in the international division of labour.[35] Even the Dutch, who lack natural commodities, may continue to flourish by providing services, as brokers, carriers, and merchants, an employment in which, by reason of their long experience and established connections, they are extremely competent.[36] Besides, even if a nation, after it once has become commercialized, were to drop out of international trade because of a lack of commodities, it would still be able to retain a flourishing domestic commerce.[37]

Although Hume exerts himself to leave no doubts about the good effects of commerce on the strength of a nation, he has other arguments in favor of the expansion of manufacturing and trade. The argument from national interest he seems to have pressed chiefly for the benefit of the public and its leaders. The other arguments, amounting to an assertion that a commercial economy is most "natural" since it develops human nature to its highest, are far more fundamental; these Hume himself seems to have found more important.

In the essay, "The Sceptic," published in 1742, ten years before his *Political Discourses*, Hume expounds briefly the sceptical view on the attainment of happiness. Human nature being what it is, men require pleasure to be happy, but even more necessary to their happiness is business. Moreover, some kinds of business, being less dependent on external circumstances, are more conducive to happiness than are others. He sums up: "According to this short and imperfect sketch of human life, the happiest disposition of mind is the *virtuous;* or, in other words, that which leads to action and employment, renders us sensible to the social passions, steels the heart against the assaults of fortune, reduces the affections to a just moderation, makes our own thoughts an entertainment to us, and inclines us rather to the pleasures of society and conversation, than to those of the senses." [38] On this analysis of the virtuous (or happy, or perfect) man Hume relies in his defence of luxury and, thus, of commerce. Constantly, he inveighs against sloth and indolence—these he seems to have regarded as the greatest vices. The more slothful and indolent a man is, the less does he deserve to be classed as a human being. A society with a slothful, indolent way of life is most unlikely to produce virtuous, true men, men with all the highest qualities of human nature. Human nature being what it is, the desire for luxuries is the most potent motive to activity shared by the generality of men. Moreover, a luxurious society will not be busy merely in manufacturing and in trade; it will also be busy in the liberal arts. In a luxurious and commercial society, men will be most likely to be happiest. In other words, a luxurious and commercial society is most conducive to the development of the highest potentialities of human nature.

It is in "Of Refinement in the Arts" that Hume expounds most clearly the causal connection between a commercial society and virtuous character. Therein he proposes that human nature is such that men are made happy by three things: pleasure, action, and repose. Some difference in the exact balance of these suitable to different individuals can be discerned. The customs of a people and the education and examples by which the young are influenced modify the values of the young greatly. Nevertheless, it can be said confidently that the most natural of men, those near the middle of the sweep of human variation, will want far more pleasure and action than repose.[39] The most obvious characteristic of a commercial economy, wherein there is as much manufacturing and trade as agriculture, or perhaps more, is its productivity. Great quantities of the necessities are grown. Great quantities of luxuries are manufactured or imported. Goods—and it is the consumption of goods that is pleasure—abound in such an economy. Besides, not only are there more goods, but they can be enjoyed by a far greater part of the people. Rural lethargy and inevitable rents no longer exclude the bulk of the populace from sharing in the surplus riches of the nations. The division of labour, combined with commerce, make luxuries available and cheap. It also distributes purchasing power. This is highly commendable, for great economic inequalities among the citizenry weaken a state, but even more important is the truth that, "Every person, if possible, ought to enjoy the fruits of his labour, in a full possession of all the necessaries, and many of the conveniences of life. No one can doubt, but such an equality is most suitable to human nature, and diminishes much less from the *happiness* of the rich than it adds to that of the poor." [40]

But commerce increases action as well as pleasure. In a second-stage (or agricultural) society all is dullness. There the peasants are stolid, languid, and bovine. They live in ignorance, superstition, and poverty, and when not prodded by the bailiff or starvation, in horrible stupor and idleness. Their lords, having become *rentiers*, are no better: a few of them may live quietly and abstemiously, but most try to abate their deadly stupid boredom by lavish expenditures, by warring, by hunting, by taking part in ostentatious pageants, and by going on excursions devised as pastimes. Those most odious vices, gluttony and drunkenness, are rife. The young are brought up to emulate the depravity of their elders. Into such a stagnant culture commerce comes like a cleansing tide: it sweeps away much of this barbarism, and introduces a new ethic far more agreeable to human nature. For this change it is the merchant who is chiefly to be praised, for it is he who creates the opportunities for gain which make men industrious. By sending goods and money throughout the land, he expels fecklessness and boredom, and introduces business and diligent application. This is very commendable: "There is no craving or demand of the human mind more constant and insatiable than that for exercise and employment; and this desire seems the foundation of most of our passions and pursuits. Deprive a man of all business and serious occupation, he runs restless from one amusement to another; and the weight and oppression, which he feels from idleness, is so great, that he forgets the ruin which must follow him from his immoderate expences." [41] Repose, we must remember, "like sleep, is requisite as an indulgence to the weakness of human nature, which cannot support an uninterrupted course of business or pleasure." Repose contributes to happiness only when alternated with action. When it is unduly prolonged, it becomes stifling and wearisome. Accordingly, it is only in a commercial society, never in an agricultural society, that rest makes a sure contribution to human happiness. Men there are full of business. They enjoy the goods they produce. They enjoy, also, the action of their minds and bodies, that "quick march of the spirits, which takes a man from himself, and chiefly gives satisfaction." [42] They grow in skill and vigour. The manner of their living is natural. By honest endeavour they satisfy the natural appetites of human nature, and, being busy, they have no time or need for prodigal perversions.

A money economy is not only an economy of the greatest pleasure and activity for the greatest number, but it is also the economy most conducive to the liberal arts and to leisure. The minds of men, once aroused from stupor and enervation by the desire for attractive luxuries, do not rest there. Their new healthy energy asserts itself on every side. It develops the sciences. It improves the arts. A sound philosophy makes itself felt everywhere. In addition, commerce draws men into towns and cities, where good conversation and emulation in skills and virtue free them from their ancient dreads and false beliefs, as well as their stupid mediocrity. Beyond that, by producing an economic surplus, it permits the society to invest in beauty and sublimity far beyond the standards of mere necessity.[43]

It also improves relations among men, for by cooperation and association their rough edges are buffed, their tempers lose their rural wildness and become urbane and humane. Their suspicions and hostilities die away. At the same time, contrary to the Latin writers, morality is improved, not depraved.[44] Any increase in libertine love, under the name of "gallantry," which may occur is outweighed by the decline in gluttony and drunkenness. Rage is supplanted by martial skill, discipline, and honour. It would be easy to prove, Hume submits, that "these writers mistook the cause of the disorders in the ROMAN state, and ascribed to luxury and the arts, what really proceeded from an ill modelled government, and the unlimited extent of conquests." [45]

It is in cities and in nations with commerce, we have seen, that the principles of governance are first extensively discovered and applied. While neither of the two agricultural ranks, the landowners or the labouring poor, is suited to governing, commerce nurtures a "middling rank of men, who are the best and firmest basis of public liberty." [46] Such men have no hope to tyrannize over others, and they themselves will not submit to enslavement. To secure their property, and to prevent tyrannical behaviour by either the king or the aristocracy, they demand that government be conducted by equal laws.[47]

Perhaps what is most notable about Hume's entire discussion of public policy is how bare and exposed, stripped of grandeur and mystery, it leaves the dynastic or national state. His theory of obligation and of the role of governments, when placed beside those of Hobbes and Locke, is of a different species, but it is within the same genus. He plays the game in a different way, but it is still recognizable. Like Hobbes and Locke, he does not begin by assuming the existence as a datum of a body politic, preestablished, and set apart from all others by laws or language or divine origin, or by a special mission, by the true religion, or by the divine right to rule in a certain country bestowed on a particular family, and then proceed to show the different places and functions within that body of the several members or classes of members. His thinking begins with men as (equal) individuals, not as members. The task of the government is to maintain property and contracts among these individuals, and to restrain dangerous hysteria.

He overlays his logical analysis with history. Human nature accommodates considerable variation; accordingly, different nations have different geniuses and different manners of living. These differences, presumably, a national government cannot ignore. But the basic task of one government is not different from that of any other merely because it is based on a particular tradition of belief or because the means used must be suitable to its subjects.

The fundamental individualism of Hobbes, Locke, and Hume implies universalism: if any distinction, e.g., the distinction made manifest by the existence of a separate dynastic or national state, is introduced between each and all, its introduction can be explained only in terms of some secondary consideration, such as the benefits to be gained by having smaller, simpler governments. But both Hobbes and Locke ordinarily treated the particular state as the universal political whole. For them the whole of mankind, the universal political whole implied by their primary emphasis on human nature, was too remote and unimportant. Their interest was confined almost entirely to the relations among subjects, and between the subject and his government. Relations with those outside the commonwealth were "external" relations; and they were almost entirely relations conducted by governments. But Hume's awareness of the expanding international market of his times brings an enlarging society before him. He finds that relations among men, aside from those between a man and his family, his friends, and the distressed, are mainly economic. All men need economic goods, and since the natural world varies greatly from place to place, men will be happier, more civilized, and better governed when those goods are produced by a world-wide division of labour. When the needs of men inherent in their common human nature, and the different skills, resources, and climates naturally available in different places are reckoned together, the result points directly to a world-wide division of labour and to world-wide commerce. The world is the natural economic unit. Any more confined economic system is irrational and perverse. On the one hand, relations between men as members of families, as friends, etc., are restricted and local. On the other, as producers and consumers of goods, men are dependent on the earth, and since the earth is one, their economic systems, unless contained within artificial barriers, tend to merge into one great system. The ecumenical order is the world market. The state is no longer high and mysterious; rather, it is left pinched between the family, the neighbourhood, and other strictly local groups, on the one hand, and the universal market, on the other.

Here we must move carefully. It is plain that both the state and the world figure as "the whole" in different places in Hume's works. Sometimes he writes in terms of the former, and at other times he thinks in terms of the latter. He assumed that the governance needed to enforce justice would be provided by dynastic and national governments. In no place does he protest against the belief that a government's domestic and foreign economic policy ought to have as its chief aim the attainment of a high level of national strength. He does not advocate absolutely free trade. At the same time, however, his individualistic theory points beyond national or dynastic boundaries.

In the case of the enforcement of justice there is no problem in reconciling his universalism with the existence of several governments. Although, or rather because, the principles of justice are everywhere the same, there is no reason why they should not be enforced by separate governments. This is convenient in view of the size of the world, its large populace, and the diverse conditions and traditions that prevail. Besides, the states exist, and people are accustomed to obeying the government of their own state.

When we turn to the relation between his basic theory and his assurances that international commerce will improve national strength, no such simple reconciliation is possible. Ostensibly he desires national strength; yet never does he fit national strength into, and show its relevance to, his general argument. It would be hard not to believe that the effects of commerce on men's minds and their way of life interested him incomparably more than the effects commerce may have on the military potential of a state. Certain considerations support this conclusion.

He was prepared to glide over the truth that the short-run effect on a country of increased international commerce—the effect most likely to concern politicians—might be a loss of money, an economic depression, and a decline in relative strength. He was prepared, likewise, to glide over the other truth that if none lost in the long run, and the absolute strength of all was increased equally, their relative standing would be exactly what it had been at the start.

In his analysis of human nature Hume does not mention military achievement and glory as goods inevitably desired by men; at times, he finds, men may be heroic and bellicose, but this is not the most natural human temperament. Similarly, although he had an anthropological interest in local ways and manners, he did not see in these any evidence of dynastic or national missions and purposes. Let us recall that for him deep personal loyalty to the reigning kings in Britain would have meant respect and admiration for the first three Georges, and that patriotic zeal for Great Britain would have required love for "the barbarians on the Thames" and hatred for "the most civilized nation in Europe." It is understandable that a Scot, born four years after the marriage of convenience of 1707, did not have to be a Jacobite to forego such "gothic" emotions.

Again, he makes it plain that wars, when they do occur, are in their very nature degrading. The nexus between the growth of commerce and an increase in national strength is the assumption that the war which tests national strength comes after a long period of peace. During that peace, a momentum has been built up in commercial circulation, so that the fields and stocks and the skill and industriousness of the people have been improved. War has a dissipating effect on the commercial momentum. At first, if the money flow is increased by the opening of the treasury, and because of the increase in the price of luxuries, the husbandmen may work harder. But the longer the war, and the greater the share of the surplus labour fed into it, the sooner its true influence on civilization will appear. The husbandman, unrewarded, becomes lazy, and produces a surplus of commodities only when coerced. Presumably, the artisans lose their skills and their industrious habits, manners decay, and the liberal arts atrophy. It would seem, according to Hume's theory—quite aside from the disastrous effects of a staggering national debt—that a war continued long enough would reduce men to their primitive sloth and barbarity.

Hume's theory of civil society is based on the presumption that the natural economic relation among men is competition. Unrestrained competition is destructive and fruitless; because of this, he proposes, men institute an artificial relationship, society, in which competition is to be limited by the associates' rights as owners of goods and, consequently, by their rights as traders and contractors. But provided that these rights are respected, the best economy, Hume believes, is one in which all men are caught up in the competitive production and marketing of goods and services: thereby not only are more goods supplied, but men lead healthier (happier) lives. In "Of Morals" he shows the need for artificial limits on competition; in his *Political Discourses* he shows that governments should not intervene in society arbitrarily, that is, beyond the enforcement of the fundamental rules of society.

# VIII

## MONARCHIES AND REPUBLICS

The true rule of government is the present established
practice of the age.

*Essays*, I, 468

THE political theory of Thomas Hobbes is centred around
the origin and the rights of governments; while he attempts to
describe men outside the state, his description, by emphasizing
contention and hostility, is primarily an argument to justify
governance. John Locke gives us a view of a far less disordered
State of Nature, but his concern is with the function, the structure, and the limits of governments. In other words, neither
gives us an extensive analysis of the orderly and continuing
relationships among men outside the state. In strong contrast,
Hume explores those relationships; indeed, he is more interested in the origin and structure of the economy than in the state.
It is not surprising, therefore, that for him, a theorist who is
more of an economist than a writer on governments, the work
appropriate to governments is chiefly preventative: the main
task of governments is, primarily, to discourage acts that
would violate the rules of the economy (or society), and, secondarily, to discourage acts contrary to natural morality.

Various relationships, he contends, are implied by human nature and the circumstances in which men ordinarily live. Some
of these—the family, the friendship, and humanity—come into
existence spontaneously. One relationship, the economic relationship, "society," is a means to goods, and it is with this relationship that governments should be chiefly concerned: governments are needed chiefly to prevent acts inimical to the
growth and maintenance of extensive societies. Governments
are to help to create rights to goods. They are to enforce rights
to goods; that is, they are to discourage theft. And they are to

promote the performance of contracts. Thereby they make possible an extensive division of labour and a corresponding increase in trade. In addition, governments will supplement, but
not shape, the main structure of the economy by establishing
bridges, ports, and the like. The natural relationships can
flourish without support by a government, but any government
will make some laws to promote respect for the duties apper-
taining to these relationships: for example, in any civilized
nation there will be laws prohibiting murder and the neglect
of children. Moreover, governments ought to resist forces that
imperil their authority or disturb seriously the serenity of
public life. This means that governments must not neglect
foreign policy, and, indeed, that they may occasionally have
to wage defensive wars. It means, too, that they may have to
act to check epidemics of destructive, false beliefs among their
peoples.

Now that we know the tasks of governments and something
of the way in which they are to be performed, we are ready to
notice what Hume thinks can be said about the advantages and
disadvantages of the basic forms of government. An ideal government would be one that would do these tasks in an impartial,
calculable, and prudent way. The state, made up of the government and the governed, is something like a play. In the
*Treatise* Hume explains the rudiments of the state; that is,
he shows how, by freeing one or more men from the economic
competition of society, governance is possible. Whether the
part of the governor(s) will be played well or badly, however,
depends largely on the qualities of the man or men to whom
it is given, and on the influences and pressures working on
him or them. No gods, only men, all more or less unsuitable because more or less susceptible to the misleading blunders and
influences common among their fellows, are available for the
role of governor(s). No one family, and no particular established rank of men, has an independent, indefeasible right to
rule because of special, innate qualities. Accordingly, the question of the best form of government is not one to be answered
simply and conclusively by pointing out the family or order

whose qualities, and therefore, claims, are constantly preeminent, but rather, is one to be answered only in terms of probable efficiency. What form of government, by reason of its influence on the selection and on the conduct of the governor(s), is most likely to produce the best governance under the prevailing circumstances? To follow Hume's answer to this question, we must bear in mind constantly his views on the factors that will influence a man's ability to reason accurately, his views on political parties, his views on the influence of the moral standards of the times, and his views on the connection between property and political power.

Presumably, the men most able to rule, according to Hume's general theory of the understanding and the passions, are the "moderate sceptics," that is, men who are highly self-conscious. Because they know the nature of the human understanding, they appraise their own beliefs with extreme care. They are keenly aware of the egocentricity of perception, so their violent passions soon become weak. Moreover, by the whole course of their lives, their outlook is elevated and, thus, extended; as objectivity increases, subjectivity decreases; and the result is that their view of the past and present is fair and good-humoured towards all, and that their ambitions are tempered by modesty and charity.[1] Unlike "mere men of the world," they are not enslaved to material goods or worldly vanities.[2] Such men will know the principles of justice, the principles of governance, and the best maxims applicable in economic, constitutional, and religious matters; nor could they, if they were governors, be easily led to ignore this knowledge.

In what rank or order are "moderate sceptics" most likely to be numerous? Although men are not born equal in respect of their potentialities, innate abilities are broadcast indiscriminately throughout all mankind, so that such regular differences between the several ranks within any society are to be traced chiefly to the different education and vocational activities of the members of each rank.[3] "Moral causes," not "physical causes," fix the character of the different groups, ranks, and professions, and thereby even the disposition which each man receives from the hand of nature is altered.[4] Hume considers it evident that "poverty and hard labour debase the minds of the common people, and render them unfit for any science and ingenious profession." [5] Their beliefs remain opinions and are fragmentary because they lack the self-consciousness requisite to the deliberate testing of beliefs and to the formulation of principles. Many of their opinions are correct, so "the people" cannot be dismissed as foolish; yet, although they can judge quite accurately the qualities of men whom they know, they are incapable of dealing with questions of policy.[6] Moreover, they are susceptible to waves of hysteria and enthusiasm, especially when gathered in large multitudes.[7] The middling ranks, unlike the "labouring poor," are capable of thinking beyond particular cases; they can form principles. But men of this kind—they abound in England—are seldom sufficiently cool and careful to achieve true principles. They, accordingly, are far more ardent and self-assured, and, therefore, far more dangerous politically, than the bulk of the populace. Professional men are regarded as clever and industrious by Hume, but he attributes no great love of wisdom to them. The philosophy that distinguishes the "moderate sceptics," we must remember, "requires youth, leisure, education, genius, and example to make it govern any person." The rank in which Hume seems to have found these requirements in combination most frequently is the "landed interest." Members of this rank, by education and experience, can come to form true principles.

While Hume's theory of knowledge is vastly different from Plato's, there are remarkable similarities between the characters of Hume's "moderate sceptics" and Plato's philosophers; however, while moderate sceptics clearly are the men best suited to govern, Hume, unlike Plato, does not propose a constitution in which the rulers are selected because of their philosophy, nor does he argue for the purposeful rearing of philosophers. Presumably, if such thoughts ever crossed his mind, he dismissed them because of the impossibility of developing a certain method for selecting the genuine philosophers, and because a regime so little supported by the ordinary principles of au-

thority would be unlikely to survive. He has no project for an
ideal state in which all the governors will be true "moderate
sceptics," but this does not mean that he thinks that the characters of the men likely to become governors under a particular
form of constitution is a matter of little importance; on the
contrary, the degree of probability that the governors placed
in office will be virtuous to a high degree is one of the most
important elements in his estimation of the different types of
governments.

The likelihood that a government will promote impartial
governance by restraining parties is a second factor on which
he concentrates attention. According to his theory, a highly
developed society is an extensive system of economic relations.
The three principles of justice are the constitution of society.
A true society is an order of equality; in it, in contrast to the
family, the friendship, and humanity, men appear as equals
or individuals. In a true civil society, a society under one government, each man is a citizen, an equal citizen, and all irrelevant differences are disregarded. A party is a social or political
group formed between the individual and the whole. Such
groups are the results of a more or less serious division or partition of civil society; at best, they are a threat to good government; at worst, they break the state into two or more separate
fragments. The chief task of a government, we have been told,
is to enforce the three principles of justice. This task is one
most likely to be performed best by a neutral government, by
governors interested selfishly, because of their unique position,
in the enforcement of justice equally in all cases. Parties are
likely to cause bad governing, either by leading to the control
of the government by one of the parties, or by causing the
government to veer about in its policies and make decisions accidentally, i.e., by compromise among the parties. We find
Hume denouncing the creators of parties vigorously:

As much as legislators and founders of states ought to be honoured and respected among men, as much ought the founders of
sects and factions to be detested and hated; because the influence
of faction is directly contrary to that of laws. Factions subvert

government, render laws impotent, and beget the fiercest animosities among men of the same nation, who ought to give mutual assistance and protection to each other. And what should render the founders of parties more odious is, the difficulty of extirpating these weeds, when once they have taken root in any state. They naturally propagate themselves for many centuries, and seldom end but by the total dissolution of that government, in which they are sown. They are, besides, plants which grow most plentifully in the richest soil; and though absolute governments be not wholly free from them, it must be confessed, that they rise more easily, and propagate themselves faster in free governments, where they always infect the legislature itself, which alone could be able, by the steady application of rewards and punishments, to eradicate them.[8]

But, be it noted, this condemnation is aimed chiefly at men who originate parties. Undoubtedly, all parties are potentially dangerous, but some are less harmful than the evils they check. Some arise from madness and a lust for power, and for them Hume has only contempt; others, however, are more soundly based, and can be condoned, perhaps in some circumstances even approved. The basic causes of partition ordinarily are present in every civil society: all that can be expected of the best government, therefore, is not that these causes will be uprooted, but that the growth of virulent, destructive factions will be prevented. The causes of the different kinds of political parties are examined by Hume in the essay, "Of Parties in General," published in 1741.

Political parties, he finds, arise from either personal or real causes. The former are held together, and are divided from the other members of their state, chiefly by friendly feelings among the partisans, and by hostility for the others. These parties, if purely personal, have no goals. Their members, like the fans of modern sport teams, are loyal to them primarily for the sake of contention and struggle. Their great cause is that men enjoy the camaraderie of a party, and enjoy engaging in exciting conspiracies, ploys, and contests, and perhaps battles, against an opposed party, while they readily forget that thereby they tend to weaken, perhaps even to destroy, their state. Parties of the second kind come into existence because of a common aim. They arise from, and, at least initially, are united mainly by, the interests, the principles, or the loyalty for a particular man or dynasty shared by the members and opposed by others. But most parties, Hume finds, once started, are held together and inspired not by either personal or real causes alone, but by both. Neither of these two kinds of partitioning forces is ever likely to exist for long or to be effective without entailing the other. "It is not often seen, that a government divides into factions, where there is no difference in the views of the constituent members, either real or apparent, trivial or material: And in those factions, which are founded on the most real and most material difference, there is always observed a great deal of personal animosity or affection." [9] Parties formed merely for the sake of excitement—they are most commonly found in small republics, such as those of antiquity or renaissance Italy—soon acquire also interests, principles, and dynastic claims. Likewise, members of parties united by common interests, principles, or dynastic claims almost from the first begin to love their comrades and to hate the opposition.

The word "interest" is used in this connection, by Hume, with two meanings. First, in any society there are various groups, each of which is likely to desire priority and special favour from the government. These groups are of diverse kinds. Some are mainly economic: the several groups in the economic division of labour may become antagonistic; for example, the landed interest and the trading interest in Britain might separate, and become opposed, although at present they enjoy concord.[10] Again, the farmer and his landlord may discover different interests.[11] Other interests are less strictly economic, and have a legal ingredient: each of the different legal orders, such as the nobles and the commoners ("the people"), have their own special and opposed goals. Other divisions are vocational: soldiers, scholars, merchants, lawyers, and priests have distinct concerns, and men in each of these callings are likely to stand amazed at the relentless zeal with which those in the others apply themselves. Although the collapse of the civil society would be a catastrophe for all, each of these groups has an interest distinguishable from that of all the others, and perhaps, in some circumstances, contrary to some or even all of them. In a constitutional government, all these differences will lead to contention on the political level; but this is not entirely deplorable, for where there is no contention, it probably means that one or two of the groups, the most arrogant and strongest, have gained control of the government—and this is despotism.[12] "Of all factions, the first [those arising from interest] are the most reasonable, and the most excusable." [13]

Second, some men have an "interest" in offices of power, profit, and prestige.[14] The partition may have as one of its causes the conflicting interests of those who enjoy and those who wish to enjoy offices. Interest in office, in itself, Hume finds, is not entirely bad, for it is chiefly on the pleasure that rulers and their assistants get from their varied rewards, that we must depend for the enforcement of the principles of justice and governance. Troubles begin, and parties of interest arise, when men become hopeful of dislodging the incumbents and ensconcing themselves in their places. "Interest," in this second sense, being confined to a few, could hardly become the cause of a mass party, unless supplemented by an appeal more relevant to the populace at large.

The partition of states into parties more or less vehemently opposed because of disagreements on religious or constitutional principles, "especially abstract speculative principles," Hume finds distinctly modern. Parties of principle "are, perhaps, the most extraordinary and unaccountable *phaenomenon*, that has yet appeared in human affairs." [15] But Hume's condemnation of them is not wholesale, for principles, he argues, are of two kinds. Some general ideas or principles have practical implications, so that it is easy to understand why men disagreeing on such ideas should fall into separate political parties. But hostility, leading often to civil war, between parties caused by vain disagreements, by disagreements that lead to a difference, not in actions, but only in orations, can be understood only when it is remembered that, since men's minds inevitably are very unstable on speculative questions, they are particularly moved by the opinions of others on such questions. When those around them propound the ideas that they wish to believe more strongly, they feel comforted and easy. But when the ideas propounded by their neighbours confirm their own gnawing doubts, they feel disturbed, and fly into a fury. Mass religious parties, such as those prevalent in England and Scotland during the seventeenth century, says Hume, illustrate this tendency.[16]

Parties from affection are those caused by the conflicting desires of different groups to have their country ruled by different dynasties or men.

When, bearing in mind these three *real* causes, especially "interest," we remember that men have a propensity to form *personal* parties, and often will do so upon the slightest appearance of any real difference, it becomes evident that the partition of the state into parties is almost certain whenever the governors are recruited from the general populace. Moreover, once the personal element underlying a partition has become strong, the parties are likely to become traditional, so that old alliances will continue from generation to generation, flourishing long after the original real differences have disappeared.

Another point, mentioned in reference to ecclesiastical parties in "Of Parties in General" and used extensively in the essay, "Of the Parties of Great Britain," is that the several causes, all of which are to be found in various degrees behind most parties, are almost certain to have a different importance for the great leaders of the parties than for the several levels of their followers. In the case of ecclesiastical parties, says Hume, the priests are moved principally by interest; while their followers are inspired by principles.[17] The leaders of political parties are guided occasionally by principles of immediate practical importance and hardly at all by speculations. Although it is ordinary in both private and public life for those who support another for any reason to come to have affection for him, the great supporters of kings and pretenders are generally impervious to any high degree of personal devotion: such ties are unlikely in the case of men of "an elevated station and liberal education, who have had full opportunity of observing the weakness, folly, and arrogance of monarchs, and have found them to be nothing superior, if not rather inferior to the rest of mankind." The conclusion is that, "The *interest*, therefore, of being heads of a party does often, with such people, supply the place both of *principle* and *affection*." [18]

It is among the less opportunistic lower ranks that principle and affection have their influence. Here, be it noted, we are not much concerned with the bulk of the parties, for in each case it will be found that most join in "they know not why; from example, from passion, from idleness." [19] But those just below the great captains of faction think in terms of principles, both true principles and speculative principles. Gentlemen of some experience and education may be "converted to true principles, by time and education." That is, they may come to see that governance always involves a balance between individual liberty and authority, and that although remedial action may at times be desirable, this should not be drastic or sudden unless the regime has swung dangerously towards either chaos or slavery. Their true principles, however, whether emphasizing the need for individual liberty or for authority, may easily be changed into extravagant, speculative doctrines by men less sceptical and less circumspect. They become absolute maxims, on which no sensible man in any party would ever think of acting, such as those of an unquestioning passive obedience to divine right kings and of the absolute right of revolution because of an original contract, maxims which are of importance only to "pulpit-declaimers, and to their deluded followers among the vulgar." [20] Speculative principles, it would seem, make their greatest appeal to, and are most in vogue among, "that middling Rank of Men, which abounds more in ENGLAND, both in Cities and in the Country, than in any other Part of the World." Such men, unlike "the slaving poor," have "Curiosity and Knowledge enough to form Principles, but not enough to form true ones, or correct any Prejudices that they may have imbib'd." [21] Affection influences all save the great captains of faction: once men have enlisted in support of a man or a house, they acquire an affection for that man or dynasty.

It is evident that Hume thought that parties are a threat to good governance, and that he thought that the causes of parties cannot be eliminated; therefore, the less chance a constitution gives to a party to acquire unchecked irresponsible control of the government, the better that constitution.

Another important factor bearing on the evaluation of forms of government, Hume assumes, is the prevailing distribution of property. While society and state are distinct orders, each exerts an influence on the other. A certain type of government is best suited to each of the three stages of economic growth— anarchic democracy to hunting and fishing, feudal monarchy to agriculture, and representative republican government to commerce—and changes in the form of government will tend to follow changes in the economy. At the same time, there is no doubt in his mind that governments can promote, delay, and for a time, at least, even reverse the development of society by their policies. Moreover, in common with many seventeenth- and eighteenth-century writers on politics, he has not the slightest doubt that a man's economic status plays an important part in determining the extent of his influence on the conduct of other men. Although he cites Harrington, he is far from satisfied with his formula that "the balance of power depends on that of property." As Mr. Pocock has shown, Harrington was thinking in terms of the feudal system, arguing that property gives military and, therefore, political strength to its owners. Hume finds that Harrington's view has much validity—he quotes it without modification in discussing mediaeval England [22]—but must not be taken as totally accurate for all circumstances. First, the formula applies chiefly to representative governments, that is, to forms in which the different ranks, orders, or professions within the society participate in the government. There are three causes which contribute, in degrees varying from time to time, to political authority: the opinion of the ruled that the rule of those giving

them commands is in the general interest; second, the opinion
that the governors have a right to rule; and third, the opinion
that those giving commands have a right to property (and thus
have an economic means by which to exert their wills). It is
quite possible, Hume argues, for an established constitution to
continue unchanged for a considerable period, maintained
chiefly by opinion of right to rule and, perhaps slightly, by
opinion of interest. Such a government will not be supported
by the third principle of political authority, but neither—
evidently, this is Hume's assumption—is it opposed seriously
by those men who have authority because of their property.
Where the different ranks or interests are represented in the
government, the formula is more helpful: an economically
strong order is likely to make its legal power as extensive as
its economic influence. But even where this is true, the formula
falls short of the whole truth, because the political power conferred by a vast amount of property divided among many men
may be far less than that conferred by one-quarter or even one-
tenth of that property concentrated in the hands of one man.
In short, a form of government may be quite satisfactory even
although those who hold office under it are not the great
owners; yet, ordinarily in a representative constitution, some
degree of conformity, probably a high degree, will be necessary
if the constitution is to prove viable.

A factor extremely influential on the operation of forms
of government is the prevailing moral standards. Men feel
obliged to do the good acts that are expected of them by their
contemporaries. They feel a moral obligation to conform to
the standards of their times. This is true of governors as well as
of private citizens. Besides, governors are likely to be eager to
win fame, especially among posterity, as virtuous men and
memorable rulers. Here, then, is an historical consideration of
great importance which may be decisive in determining whether
a particular government will or will not succeed. A form which
in one moral climate will lead to bad governing may prove excellent where other standards prevail.

The primary distinction employed by Hume in his comments

on forms of government is that between absolute governments and "free" (or constitutional) governments. In the latter, the power to govern does not belong to one man or one group, but is divided in a known way; while in the former, it is unlimited and absolute, because undivided, and is rightfully possessed by one man or one group.[23] Although "free" governments, which ordinarily are republics, have made a greater contribution to the civilization of men than have absolute governments, which ordinarily are monarchies, the usefulness of these two basic forms in modern, civilized nations, he finds, is fairly equal. The republican form is generally preferable, but this is not always true, and it would not be true in England, he submits, if the mixed form now prevailing there were to be dissolved.

Hume attains this balanced conclusion by considering those different characteristics of each of the two forms that would tend to make for good or bad governing—measured against the ideal—in various historical circumstances. In early times, at least after the rule of the first kings, however motivated, had shown the advantages of having some kind of government, or at least had accustomed men to living civilly together, "free governments" were superior, for it was in free governments that the art of governance was discovered. It was in the early kingdoms, and by the power of the kings, that civil relations among the governed, based on common subjection, as against the natural relations which prevail within families or tribes, were first introduced among men. But it was in republics that the importance of calculability in the conduct of the government towards its subjects was learned. In modern times, however, the high standards of governance generally prevalent make it probable that governance in a modern absolute monarchy will be just as calculable as governance in a republic. Knowledge of the art of governing has spread, and governments which do not practice the art are scorned as irrational and hated as immoral. Consequently, in monarchies general laws are now established. The servants of the Crown responsible for executing these laws have clearly defined powers, and may not act *ultra vires*. "It may now be affirmed of civilized monarchies, what was formerly said in praise of republics alone, *that they are a government of Laws, not of Men.* They are found susceptible of order, method, and constancy, to a surprizing degree. Property is there secure; industry encouraged; the arts flourish; and the prince lives secure among his subjects, like a father among his children." [24] In modern times, then, a monarchy can be quite as good as, and often better than, a republic. Each form has both an advantage and a disadvantage, as we shall see immediately; and whether a republic or a monarchy will be better depends, in modern times, on whether in a particular instance the advantage is outweighed by the disadvantage.[25]

The essential characteristics of absolute monarchy are that the king's legal power is full or complete and that he acquires his office by inheritance. Absolute monarchy embodies the first principle of governance almost exactly: in theory, a government is to be distinct from its subjects, and the hereditary king, in fact, has no institutional dependence on his people. This is the form which permits the government to be most independent of the diverse economic, religious, and regional interests prevalent within civil society.[26] In short, because it best fulfills the first principle of governance, it has the best chance, in terms of institutional structure, of fulfilling the second principle, namely, that the government is to be neutral and impartial. Since an hereditary monarch is not drawn from among the citizenry, but has a separate and public status from his birth, he is not inevitably implicated in the competition and the jealousies within society, and there is ground for a *prima facie* presumption that he will be impartial. Hume's reasoning on this point can be illustrated by his objections to elective kingship in either a monarchy or a mixed government. If the chief magistrate were to acquire his office by election, dangers would arise, he argues, from two sources. First, the people would be split into factions before, during, and after each election, and the consequent fears and enmities would invite dissidence and even civil strife. Second, a chief magistrate selected among the people, "will carry into the throne all his private animosities and friendships, and will never be viewed in his elevation, without exciting the sentiment of envy in those, who formerly considered him as their equal. Not to mention that a crown is too high a reward ever to be given to merit alone, and will always induce the candidates to employ force, or money, or intrigue, to procure the votes of the electors: So that such an election will give no better chance for superior merit in the prince, than if the state had trusted to birth alone for determining their sovereign." [27] The only restraints on an absolute king are informal: the pressure to respect local tradition, the pressure to observe the prevailing standards of good governance, and his comprehension of his own position and true interest.

If absolute monarchy has its strength in that the ruler can be fairly independent of the partial interests within society, it has its weakness in that the ability of the man who becomes king is largely accidental. There is no way of assuring that those of royal birth will be especially wise and able. It is possible, of course, that a prince may be notable for his discretion and intelligence. If he is mediocre, he still may appreciate his own interest, and consequently be a successful ruler. But he may be too stupid to evade false beliefs, so that he endangers his peace and that of his kingdom by becoming entangled in the clash of rival interests; or he may be lazy, so that he fails to control his lieutenants. In fact, Hume finds, modern kings, while not extraordinarily virtuous or intelligent, given the comparatively high standards of governance now prevalent, are not likely to rule in a mischievous, unequal manner.[28]

Nevertheless, it is true that the dependency of absolute monarchy for its success on "the casual humours and characters of particular men" and on the standards of the times is a great defect in this form of government.[29] In a republic, the simple form of "free" government, this defect is not present, for the magistrates are elected and the power to rule is divided. This reduces the accidental element. But it does so at the cost of establishing an institutional tie between the government and the society, and thus creating the problem of preventing the private and partial aspirations which exist within society from having a deleterious effect on the making of the laws and on their execution. This is why Hume repeatedly insists that the design of the constitution is especially important in a republic. It may be true of monarchy to say: "Whate'er is best administr'd is best." But in a republic those who participate in governing are also members of society. They share, therefore, the selfish partialities inevitable within society. They are liable to use public power for their individual purposes, or they may form parties and work for group interests. Fortunately, however, human conduct is fairly regular and predictable; accordingly, it can be influenced to produce a calculated effect. The writer of a constitution does not have to rely on private virtue. By skilful devising, it is possible to establish a constitution in such a way that while governmental offices are filled by election, the men elected to those offices are prevented from using them for selfish purposes. "Effects will always correspond to causes; and wise regulations in any commonwealth are the most valuable legacy that can be left to future ages. In the smallest court or office, the stated forms and methods, by which business must be conducted, are found to be a considerable check on the natural depravity of mankind. Why should not the case be the same in public affairs?" [30] "So great is the force of laws, and of particular forms of government, and so little dependence have they on the humours and tempers of men, that consequences almost as general and certain may sometimes be deduced from them, as any which the mathematical sciences afford us." [31] Ways can be devised to assure that republics will have able men in their offices, and that these men will use their power impartially.

Accordingly, while a badly constituted republic will be worse than most absolute monarchies, a well-constituted republic will work better than even those absolute monarchies that are reasonably fortunate in their kings. Since the quality of a republic is susceptible of control by men, whereas that of a monarchy is a matter of accident, we may conclude that when the two forms are compared abstractly, the former is better than the latter.

The forms have effects other than those involved directly in the quality of governance. Free governments are more conducive to the growth of commerce. It is not that private property is especially insecure in monarchies; indeed, private property is as secure in a civilized monarchy as in a republic. But the spirit of monarchy is hardly conducive to commerce.[32] The values emphasized by a monarchical system quench the commercial spirit.

Again, the poverty of the common people is a natural, if not an inevitable, result of absolute monarchy. In such a government the rich can conspire to throw all the burden of taxation upon them. Nevertheless, to say that riches are an infallible result of free governments is to go too far.[33]

We find that the arts are encouraged more in a civilized monarchy, and the sciences more in a free government. It was, as we have seen, in republics that calculable government was first introduced, and it was there, consequently, that the arts and sciences were first cultivated. But once the monarchies had become civilized, by imitating the republics, they too began to make advances in arts and sciences.[34] However, to be successful in a republic one must look downward to gain the suffrages of the people. This requires that a man make himself useful by his industry, capacity, and knowledge. But to be successful in an absolute monarchy, one must look upwards to win the approval of the king and court. This requires chiefly that a man make himself agreeable by his wit, complaisance, or civility. Again, republics are more likely to allow advances in moral philosophy and enlightenment than are absolute monarchies.[35]

Absolute monarchies are somewhat better than free governments, Hume finds, on another point, namely, their long-term financial policies. In neither case is a bad policy inevitable, but the constitution of a republic or a mixed government makes the evasion or abandonment of such a policy far more difficult than in a monarchy. This is one point on which their dependence on "the casual humours and characters of particular men" gives an advantage to monarchies.

Now that money can be borrowed at low rates, it is tempting, Hume contends, to mortgage the future to pay for the excitement of a present war, and once such a policy has been adopted by a republic, it is increasingly difficult to abandon it, and it becomes more and more disastrous as its effects multiply. There are some advantages to commerce and industry, but the disadvantages to the state are great. There is no real chance of sacrificing the thousands to the millions by declaring the government bankrupt, for in a republic there are bound to be many ties between the politicians and the financiers. The only recourse is to invent new and bad taxes. The ultimate outcome may be that posterity will degenerate and that the natural structure of society will be decomposed.[36]

Those who benefit chiefly by bad policy in raising money for public purposes, whether by taxation or by the sale of bonds, he finds, are financiers, and certainly not the king, the nobility, the peasants, and the artisans. In an absolute monarchy there is no necessary tie between this breed of men and the government. Accordingly, if the government has adopted or is tempted to adopt a policy of bad taxation or of borrowing, this folly may be prevented or stopped by the rise of an enlightened king or minister. Moreover, if as a result of past errors the king is deeply indebted, he may declare himself bankrupt and thus avoid imposing oppressive taxes on his people.[37]

In the essays published in 1741, Hume emphasizes again and again the need to prevent any partial interest from acquiring unrestricted control of the power to rule. It would be a mistake, he submits, to assume in private life that all men are either angels or knaves; yet that they are knaves is a fair assumption in public life. Especially when men are gathered in a group united by a common aspiration, they become uninhibited. Hume here seems to be thinking more of different legal orders, such as nobles and commons, than of opposed economic professions or classes. "When there offers, therefore, to our censure and examination, any plan of government, real or imaginary, where the power is distributed among several courts, and several orders of men, we should always consider the separate interest of each court, and each order; and, if we find that, by the skilful division of power, this interest must necessarily, in its operation, concur with public, we may pronounce that government to be wise and happy. If, on the contrary, separate interest be not checked, and be not directed to the public, we ought to look for nothing but faction, disorder, and tyranny from such a government." [38] In another essay he writes: "All absolute governments must very much depend on the administration; and this is one of the great inconveniences attending that form of government. But a republican and free government would be an obvious absurdity, if the particular checks and controuls, provided by the constitution, had really no influence, and made it not the interest, even of bad men, to act for the public good. Such is the intention of these forms of government, and such is their real effect, where they are wisely constituted: As on the other hand, they are the source of all disorder, and of the blackest crimes, where either skill or honesty has been wanting in their original frame and institution." [39]

Hume seems to have regarded two points as most important in the contriving of a republican constitution. First, the inhabitants should not be expected to govern themselves; rather, they should be governed by representatives. There are two reasons for this. If the inhabitants were the government, the constitutional processes demarcating their different capacities, as government and governed, would be severely strained, and probably would fail. The governed and the government, contrary to the second principle of governance, would be the same men. Consequently, the government would not have the neutrality of a spectator, but would contain within itself all the diverse interests and opinions present within the populace, and would attain decisions largely through accidents of caprice and compromise. In addition, the individuals who make up that large part of the populace known as "the people" do not have the qualities essential to good rulers. Hume's argument, we have noted, is not that the people is a monster to be driven, but that the people can be led. The people, he finds, are increasingly better informed and more civilized. Nor are they more selfish than their betters; the opposite may be the case. But it remains true that they lack the desire, knowledge, and time to engage extensively in the intricate work of governing. And they are susceptible, especially in large cities, to the arts of demagoguery.[40]

Second, again to promote neutrality, every precaution should be taken to discourage the elected representatives from acting as one party, as opposed to the represented, or from breaking up into contending parties. The men who are made governors or magistrates in a free constitution, no matter how virtuous they may be in their private lives, may be assumed to be knaves in politics. They are infected more or less by zeal for their own selfish interests. The task of the maker of the constitution is to construct the government—dividing the power and making one house and office a check upon another—in such a way that each of these knaves must use the share of the power assigned to him not in his own interest, but to make general laws and then to execute them fairly.[41]

Hume's insistence in these essays, published in 1741, on the importance of a carefully devised constitution is a suitable introduction to his own constitutional project, published in 1752, in *Political Discourses*, under the title, "Idea of a Perfect Commonwealth." His aim in this piece is moderate: to revive discussion of this important topic so that some ideal will be available to guide politicians both in making minor and piecemeal alterations in existing constitutions, and in case, at some time, in some country, there happens to be an opportunity for the creation of a wholly new system.[42] His scheme is not to be adopted wholesale in the place of any established constitution, since even a perfect ideal constitution is inferior to an imperfect, but established constitution, for it is not by reason, but by opinion that most men are ruled.

According to his proposal, a country the size of Great Britain and Ireland is to be divided into one hundred counties, and each of these into one hundred parishes. The primary electorate in each parish is to be based on a high property qualification: only freeholders of £20 a year and householders worth £500 are to vote. These men in each parish are to meet annually to elect, by ballot, one freeholder of the county as their county representative. The one hundred county representatives in each county are to participate in national legislation, and are to serve as electoral colleges. In the latter capacity, the representatives in each county are to elect annually, by ballot, from their own membership, ten county magistrates and one senator. The one hundred senators thus elected constitute the senate of the commonwealth. Any senatorial candidate who receives more than one third of the votes in his college, but is defeated, is made a member of the commonwealth court of competitors for one year.

National laws are to be made by the vote of the separate counties, each county being represented on minor bills by its ten magistrates, and on major bills by its one hundred representatives. A majority of the one hundred counties is needed to enact a law. Every bill must be debated first in the senate; but even if defeated there, must be sent down to the counties to be voted on, if ten senators request this procedure. The court of competitors may initiate a bill, and if it is rejected by the senate, may have the bill sent down to the counties.

The system of representation is to be reviewed and corrected in the first year of each century.

The senate is to have the entire executive power of the British king. Each new senate is to elect, from its own membership, "by an intricate ballot," certain officers: a protector who will have the ordinary duties of a head of state, two secretaries of state charged with foreign affairs, six councils, each composed of five senators, for state (or foreign) affairs, religion and learning, trade, laws, war, and admiralty, and a seven-man commission of the treasury. No council has any power to make executive orders other than such power that may be delegated to it by the senate. When the senate has not delegated executive power on a topic, that topic must be dealt with by executive order only by the senate itself.

The protector, the two secretaries of state, the five members of the council of state, and any group of five or more men appointed by the senate are to possess dictatorial power for a period of six months in the event of extraordinary emergencies.

The senate, like the House of Lords, is to be the highest court for the trial of cases. It is to appoint the lord chancellor and all the other law officers. The county representatives are to serve as justices of the peace. The county magistrates are to try all cases with a jury.

The Presbyterian church government is to be established. The magistrates are to name the minister for each parish. The assembly of all the presbyters of the county is to be the highest ecclesiastical court, but the county magistrates may intervene to decide any ecclesiastical case, and may try, depose, or suspend any presbyter.

The militia is to be established in the Swiss manner.

The aim of Hume's constitution is to provide that the laws and policies of the government shall be the outcome of an accurate appraisal of both human nature and the prevailing condition and circumstances of the state. To meet this requirement the laws and policies must be the product of human intelligence operating at optimum efficiency. Hume's aim in designing this ideal system is twofold: first, to avoid including within the politically powerful group any men who, by reason of their economic and legal standing, might be assumed to be incapable of clear and extensive reasoning; and second, to permit the intelligence of those included to operate unhampered by the distracting possibilities of selfish benefits.

The first branch he sought to accomplish by a high property requirement for participation in the elections and in political office, and by the interposition of the electoral college system. He does not assume, we have seen, that native intelligence varies directly with wealth; rather, he assumes that there is a considerable connection between wealth and education. Some of the wealthy will be so dull that education, no matter how prolonged, would never make them capable of attaining true principles. Some of the wealthy may be badly educated. But, almost certainly, the poor will not be educated. In the first two editions of the essay, both published in 1752, Hume provided: "Let all the freeholders in the country parishes, and those who pay scot and lot in the town parishes, meet annually in the parish church, and chuse, by ballot, some freeholder of the county for their member, whom we shall call the county *representative*." In the five following editions, 1753–54, 1758, 1760, 1764, and 1768, he shifted away from these traditional tests. The provision then read: "Let all the freeholders of ten pounds a year in the country, and all the householders worth 200 pounds in the town parishes, meet annually." The final two editions read: "Let all the freeholders of twenty pounds a-year in the county, and all the householders worth 500 pounds in the town parishes, meet annually." Moreover, even these men are not the electorate for all purposes. They elect the county representatives, who do vote on the proposed laws, but who also are the electors—electing from their own number—of the county magistrates and the senators. Commenting on the senators to be chosen by these colleges, Hume says, in all the editions, that they are elected, "not by an undistinguishing rabble, like the ENGLISH electors, but by men of fortune and education." [43]

The second branch—to permit rational action by those admitted to political power—he sought to attain by devices to exclude the selfish use of power by particular men or groups. What has to be overcome in the case of the primary electorate is the willingness of the "grandees" to exploit the gullibility of the people for their own ends. "The lower sort of people and small proprietors are good judges enough of one not very distant from them in rank or habitation; and therefore, in their parochial meetings, will probably chuse the best, or nearly the best representative: But they are wholly unfit for county-meetings, and for electing into the higher offices of the republic." [44] According to Hume's project they are divided into ten thousand small groups—that is, one hundred parishes in each of the one hundred counties—and elect only county, not national, representatives. At the intermediate or county level, the size and number of the county assemblies again prevent the same danger. The bills are discussed in these county groups, composed of only one hundred representatives, so the representatives are not likely to be whipped into a confused, hysterical mob by a demagogic party orator. Besides, by reason of the extensive division, a local or regional interest, or a successful demagogue can exert an influence only locally, and since the favourable vote of at least fifty-one separate assemblies is necessary to enact laws, probably will be submerged by the rest of the counties.[45]

The one hundred senators must be prevented from forming into one great alliance working for its own interest, and also from breaking up into contending factions. In Hume's scheme, the former tendency is checked, first, by the short term of office and the absence of any claim to power, such as that of the British peers, other than that of election; second, by the small patronage power at their disposal; and third, by the watchfulness of the council of competitors. The latter, the partition of the senate, is prevented by four considerations: first, the small number of senators; second, the popular elections by which the senators will be selected to represent a county, not a special economic or religious interest; third, by their power to expel any senator who manifests a party interest; and fourth, the use of a fixed procedure in selecting the protector and the other high officers.

Evidently it is Hume's belief that political parties are the greatest obstacle to good governance under a free constitution. The state or commonwealth, for him, is a union or group existing to provide common governance. In addition, other natural reasons cause men to establish certain natural groups, families, friendships, neighbourhoods. They also, for economic reasons, ought to establish an economic order, society, in which they would be related to other men as producers and consumers of economic goods. These—the natural groups, the society, and the state—are the three proper kinds of groups. The proper constituent parts of a state are citizens. When parties appear, and those men in whom political power has been vested begin to conduct themselves, not as citizens, but as members of special parts of the commonwealth, both the unity of the state and the possibility of good governance are reduced. The partition of the state into parties, each with its own special narrow interest and its own selfish loyalty, moves the fog banks of confined interest up into governmental deliberation. It is only as an individual, a man independent of partial interests, never as a party supporter, that a citizen has his best chance to discover what is the general or rational good for all citizens. But Hume is not a perfectionist. He sees that human egocentricity inevitably causes different interests, loyalties, and aspirations, and that, consequently, it is better to admit the existence of parties, so that they may restrain each other, than to conceal exploitation behind a veil of homogeneity.

Hume has no dreams about perfecting all ranks of men or about abolishing particular interests.[46] He prefers a representative form of government, provided that it is designed so as not to give power to the vulgar and so as to check and balance into negligible harmfulness the selfish aspirations of those particular interests. But we must always distinguish, he insists, between the ideal form of commonwealth and the best form of government for any particular place and time, because any existing form, even if highly imperfect, has the great advantage of being actual. To be good, a constitution must be one to which men give obedience. To be obeyed, it is not enough to be ideal. Long establishment may be far more important.[47] After all, if men saw their interest clearly, and followed it strictly, the ideal commonwealth would be adopted. Or rather, if men saw their interest clearly, they would adhere stubbornly to the rules of justice, and no government of any kind would be needed.

# IX

## MIXED GOVERNMENT

## IN BRITAIN

Twas under James that the House of Commons began first to raise their Head, & then the Quarrel betwixt Privilege & Prerogative commenc'd. The Government, no longer opprest by the enormous Authority of the Crown, display'd its Genius; and the Factions, which then arose, having an Influence on our present Affairs, form the most curious, interesting, & instructive Part of our History.

*Letters*, I, 168

THE monarchical and the republican are the two simple forms of government. In addition to these, Hume submits, there are two basic kinds of mixed governments, each with a monarchical and a republican element; but in one the former is dominant, while in the other the latter is the greater. The constitution of Rome is an example of the first kind of mixed government. Contemporary Britain, too, he proposes, has a mixed constitution, but of the second kind.

This mixed constitution, he found, was understood inadequately by many Whigs and Tories; and the results of their ignorance were vain criticisms and excessive mutual disgusts, all tending to erode the constitution, and threatening, perhaps not to bring it down, but, at least, to hasten its metamorphosis. And one cause of these misunderstandings, he argued, was that each party had a high, speculative theory of the origin of authority, a theory entirely useless and nonsensical, not applicable to the British or any other constitution.

The Tories try, or at least pretend that they try, to explain the constitution in terms of divine right; but that theory, based as it is on a misconception of authority, is never an adequate guide when we try to discover whom we ought to obey. Theories of divine providence are either general or particular.[1] The former, theories of general providence, lead to an intolerable confusion of might and right, or rather to the submergence of all right in might. Since all that happens is ordained of God, whatever happens is right. Whoever has might has right. All who proclaim a general providence are ready to admit that therefrom it follows that the power of a puissant king is of divine origin. But they will admit also that the power of everybody else, great or small, is also of divine origin. The divine right argument, if based on a theory of general providence, depicts God as the cause of all power, and of all shifts in power. The possession of *de facto* power is the only evidence of the possession of *de jure* power under God. "Whatever actually happens is comprehended in the general plan or intention of providence; nor has the greatest and most lawful prince any more reason, upon that account, to plead a peculiar sacredness or inviolable authority, than an inferior magistrate, or even an usurper, or even a robber or a pyrate." [2] Nor is the divine right argument saved by a shift to the theory of particular providence. If it is claimed that a dynasty or a magistrate has a right given by God, whereas the power of others is only *de facto*, the problem is to ascertain who holds God's commission and who does not. Since divine right is not known intuitively, in solving this puzzle some test, such as long possession, must be used. But when this is done, the test, not providence, is the effective cause of the right of the dynasty or the magistrate.

Against this faulty Tory theory of divine right, the Whigs pose the theory of the original contract. The defect of this theory is that it, like divine right, is not specific enough in designating the rightful ruler. If we think back to a time when there was no political power, we will admit that the first acts of obedience, the acts that created political power, were not caused by political power. If this is what is meant by the original contract, the theory clearly is valid. But it is not now relevant, for once political power had been created, all *de facto* political power, that of the government or that of a band of insurgents, may be said to be the result of the original contract. A particular government may begin with a contract, but this would be, commonly, "so irregular, so confined, or so much intermixed either with fraud or violence, that it cannot have any great authority." [3] Most governments have their origin in a successful exertion of power, either in conquest or usurpation, and habit soon confirms the victor's title.[4]

Hume's view is that each of these two high theories has validity only in that it contradicts the extreme position expounded by the other. Frivolous resistance of the kind encouraged by the theory of the original contract is wrong.[5] Absolute obedience, to which divine right leads, when it is taken seriously, is wrong also.[6]

But these high theories, the one propounded originally to prevent resistance to the anticipated succession of James, Duke of York, and the other elaborated to justify resistance to that succession, by the middle of the eighteenth century, Hume saw, were only the elegant façades on the front of Tory and Whig constitutional thought. Behind them, and much more important because much closer to the truth about the nature of the constitution, were conflicting arguments based on the constitutional history of England. Here again, Hume finds, both parties are in error. In his volumes on the history of Great Britain under the Stuarts (Vol. I, 1754; Vol. II, 1757), by far the most important part of the *History*, he argues that the claims of both the kings and the commons during the seventeenth century, although clashing, were somewhat valid—a paradox that he attributes to the confused, self-contradictory state of the constitution. The next two volumes, on the Tudors (1759), in which he argues that from 1485 to 1603, whatever the theory, the real constitution was strongly monarchical, serve primarily to refute the Whig notion that the first Stuarts were wild innovators. The last two volumes, published in 1762, covering the period from Julius Caesar to the accession of Henry VII, show how in those early centuries the constitution of the government changed from reign to reign, thus providing additional support for his argument that prior to 1689 the constitution was very unsettled. The *History of England* is unified by a twofold thesis: first, that both Whig and Tory constitutional history is highly fictitious; and second, that each party overestimates the importance of its own account because neither knows the genuine nature of a constitution.[7]

The concealed assumption behind the thinking of many Tories and Whigs, when they are not absorbed in beatific contemplation of a divine right constitution or of a constitution created by the people in an original contract, is that once there was an original constitution, the very and true English Constitution, and that it conformed exactly with their own views.[8] The Tories, on the one hand, like to think that the royal authority once was perfect and absolute, and that the wise kings, for pragmatic reasons, not in recognition of rights, conferred certain useful liberties and privileges on the House of Commons, and that they could retract these when they no longer deemed them desirable. The Whigs, on the other hand, fancy that the original constitution was one in which the rights of the House of Commons belonged to it indefeasibly, and that the rights (privileges) of the House were invariably the weapons by which the civil liberty of the people was defended against its principal enemy, the king. Neither of these views, Hume contends, is accurate.

He finds that when we trace the story back to gothic times, we find, indeed, that the king was not then absolute either in theory or practice, but that although authority clearly was not concentrated and absolute in any one officer, it was not divided and assigned in a certain, stable way. The constitution, such as it was, was mixed, but the rights of the several ruling parts varied extremely from one reign to another, especially during the thirteenth, fourteenth, and fifteenth centuries. Prior to the Norman Conquest there had been a good deal of "natural liberty" in England, although not so much as in earlier days when "the ancient Germans" were still close to the State of Nature; but there was great insecurity because the kings lacked the authority and the might to control the increasingly powerful earls and to repel invaders from across the seas.[9] This liberty was largely destroyed when William the Conqueror introduced a new system of ownership, governance, and military organization into England, i.e., feudalism.[10] At first feudalism and royal rule were fairly compatible, for the great barons, being Normans, still felt dependent on the king in this foreign land. After the end of the twelfth century, however, the kings were challenged almost constantly, often were humiliated, and sometimes were even dethroned by the barons.[11] By then the Norman nobility had acquired sufficient authority among the populace to be able to make a weak and foolish king take cognizance, in the Magna Charta, of certain rights of the nobility and certain rights of the freemen (the people). The Charter, however, did not prescribe a constitution; rather, in an age when there was little settled public law, it served merely as a statement of aspirations; the number of times it had to be renewed and reconfirmed shows the limited effect it had on the changeable practice of the age.[12] The actual allocation of authority and the limits of the powers of each of the authorities at any particular time during those centuries were very uncertain, and depended far more on conjunctions of situations and personalities than on a system of well-established rights.

Moreover, argues Hume, the Charter was in part a bad aspiration. The rights of freemen set forth therein, although then relevant to only a few, conform to the principles of governance, and were to become very important in the seventeenth century.[13] But the barons, by reason of their extensive possessions, had great authority, and in the circumstances prevailing in the thirteenth, fourteenth, and fifteenth centuries, the consequent restrictions on the king produced, not an increase, but a decrease in civil liberty. To the extent that the Charter perpetuated the feudal rights of the barons, it worked against equal and predictable liberties for the people. In that age, when the main threat to the peace was not the caprice of kings, but the arbitrary tyranny of imperious, lawless nobles, the chief danger to civilization was not an increase in the king's power, but the partition of the kingdom into barbarous baronies.[14] There were times when the kings were successful in extending their government almost everywhere throughout the realm. There were times when a party of barons, or that entire rank in combination, reduced the king's power to something like a mere fiction.[15] This struggle between baronial liberty and regal authority, between anarchy and order, Hume argues, must not be seen as prefiguring the modern tension between country and court. The barons, far from championing a general, equal liberty, exerted themselves mainly to increase or to retain their own unequal, arbitrary power; it was the kings, who, striving to establish their sway, were working, probably often unwittingly, to produce a secure general liberty for the people. In those tumultuous times the House of Commons, whose origins—contrary to Whig history—can be traced only to 1295, not to an ancient constitution, or even a pre-Conquest constitution, was generally a very minor power.[16]

Since the political struggles of the late middle ages were chiefly between kings who were seeking to establish and maintain centralized, orderly government and barons who were striving to win power against the king and the people, modern ideas on the danger and unconstitutionality of great, even unlimited, royal prerogatives cannot be applied anachronistically to those ages. If the work of the king and the members of his court(s) had involved only the determination of the cases of individuals, there would have been no excuse for great prerogatives. But the kings were concerned to suppress anarchic violence, real or apprehended, against which ordinary procedures would have been quite futile.[17] Accordingly, it is not surprising that, contrary to what Whigs believe, the king's prerogatives in those times generally were as great as the king's might, and that, given the truth that peace and civil liberty depended on the ability of the king to subject those who would fragment the kingdom, even destroy it, complaints that the king was behaving unconstitutionally were far less common than one might expect.[18] The greater the prerogatives in that age, the greater the civil liberty of the people.[19]

The gothic constitution, far from embodying the precise plan and order that both Tories and Whigs attributed to it, was very unsettled. In it, baronial privileges, not the privileges of the House of Commons, were set against and overlapped royal prerogatives. And in this situation, it was prerogative, not privilege, that advanced the interests of the people. Hume's view of "the ancient constitution" is neatly summed up in his estimate of the reign of Edward III. He writes:

There is not a reign among those of the ancient English monarchs, which deserves more to be studied than that of Edward III. nor one where the domestic transactions will better discover the true genius of that kind of mixed government, which was then established in England. The struggles, with regard to the validity and authority of the great charter, were now over: The king was acknowledged to lie under some limitations: Edward himself was a prince of great capacity, not governed by favourites, not led astray by any unruly passion, sensible that nothing could be more essential to his interests than to keep on good terms with his people: Yet on the whole it appears, that the government, at best, was only a barbarous monarchy, not regulated by any fixed maxims, or bounded by any certain undisputed rights, which in practice were regularly observed. The king conducted himself by one set of principles; the barons by another; the commons by a third; the clergy by a fourth. All these systems of government were opposite and incompatible: Each of them prevailed in its turn, as incidents were favourable to it: A great prince rendered the monarchical power predominant: The weakness of a king gave reins to the aristocracy: A superstitious age saw the clergy triumphant: The people, for whom chiefly government was instituted, and who chiefly deserve consideration, were weakest of the whole. But the commons, little obnoxious to any other order; though they sunk under the violence of tempests, silently reared their head in more peaceable times; and while the storm was brewing, were courted by all sides, and thus received still some accession to their privileges, or, at worst, some confirmation of them.[20]

Under the Tudors the constitution had the appearance of an absolute monarchy. The participation of the Lords and the Commons was still required in the making of statutes, but the actual power had passed to the Crown; indeed, probably the old process was retained mainly because the Lords and the Commons never tried to oppose the Crown. In the fifteenth century many of the old baronial families were eradicated, but more important in changing the social structure were the improvements of all the arts and the discovery of America, for while the barons gradually alienated their holdings to acquire the means with which to buy the new luxuries, new men acquired possessions, independence, and importance because of their work as entrepreneurs.[21] Baronial authority waned, and as it did, its old competitor, royal authority, grew. The constitution became simpler and more systematic, but it did so through the concentration of almost unlimited right in the king. The members of the Tudor dynasty, by reason of the propitious circumstances, and their own vigour and prudence, were as absolute, concluded Hume, as any rulers ever were, or ever are likely to be, in England.[22] In both civil and ecclesiastical matters they were almost unquestioned. The House of Commons was obsequious to do the bidding of its royal masters and mistresses; such opposition as there was came not from it, but from religious dissenters.

When the first Stuart kings of England considered the royal office, there were few reasons, therefore, why they should conclude that there were any regular limits on their powers.[23] Under the Tudors, it is true, statutes were made by act of Parliament, but the two Houses always had been ready to follow the royal will. Under the Tudors, contrary to the history cherished by the Whigs, the kings and queens exercised many great prerogatives without being challenged.[24] Back beyond 1485 there was a record of vigorous baronial opposition, but this generally had taken the form of insurrection, not of a regular constitutional constraint, and against this resistance the king had been expected to act at discretion. Moreover, when the Stuarts looked abroad across Europe, they could see almost everywhere that as the gothic constitutions disappeared, they were succeeded by governments in which the king was reputed absolute.

What the Stuarts did not see, indeed, could not be expected to see, however, was that the Tudor constitution was obsoles-

cent at the opening of the seventeenth century. The conditions
that had made that constitution possible were transitional, and
now they were disappearing. Wealth had come to be distributed
widely among the commons. A general enlightenment, not confined to divines and savants, had spread wide among the people.[25] Consequently, the kings were confronted once more by
men of standing; not now, as formerly, by a few, barbarous,
unruly men, but rather by "a middle rank of men," a solid
rank of sober, substantial townsmen and gentry. The conditions in which a constitutional monarchy was possible had developed. The mixed constitution could now take a shape such
that the major parts could constrain each other, not by turbulent rebellion and martial suppression, but by established
constitutional methods.[26]

The precedents supported the conception of the English
monarchy formed by James I and Charles I, but there were
good reasons why that conception no longer could be successfully followed in practice. The Stuarts were a foreign family.
Unlike many European kings they had no standing army at
their command. They were charged with the task of governing
at a time when the costs of administration, of maintaining a
court, and of seconding foreign policy with armies and navies
were rising rapidly because of the influx of gold and silver from
the Americas.[27] Besides, the constitution under which they were
called upon to govern was misaligned: in it power and duty
were not equivalent. It placed the entire onus of governing on
the king, while the House of Commons had no established obligations. Nevertheless, the king could not govern without parliaments, for only parliaments could enact the statutes needed to
finance the operations of the government. In the sixteenth century the cooperation of the Houses had been assured by the
fear and admiration which the Tudors commanded. In the
eighteenth century the cooperation of the Houses would be
assured by the management of elections, by the appointment
of ministers from the Houses, and by parties. The interval between the disappearance of one set of informal controls and
the invention of another set was almost certain to be a time of

troubles.[28] Moreover, the plight of the Stuarts was made especially difficult because just when they came to the throne, a narrow, assured, fierce enthusiasm in religion, the strongest solvent of authority and the most unrestrainable force in politics, was beginning to make itself felt in England. The authority of the king as head of the church in England already was being challenged seriously; the authority of the king as head of the civil government was almost certain to be challenged before the spreading enthusiasm had burned itself out.

It is true, of course, Hume argues, that while the royal prerogatives inherited from the Tudors remained unhedged, a new, fixed plan of government and liberty could not be achieved; still, it must be acknowledged by the Whigs, he insists, that James I and Charles I generally acted constitutionally.[29] It is true that a new, better constitution was the ultimate result of the continual aggrandisement of the House of Commons during the seventeenth century; yet it must be admitted that the House was inspired in its ambition more by jealousy of its money and a desire to enhance its own power than by a perspicuous vision of a better constitution and greater civil liberty.[30] Indeed, Hume argues, many of the most vociferous enemies of the king's authority, far from wishing to increase civil or religious liberty, were moved chiefly by a desire to supplant the king as head of the church and to practice, instead of his discreet toleration, a policy which was utterly abhorrent: the tightest, most zealous control over the religious and moral beliefs and conduct of the people. Paradoxically, it is in large part due to the wild enthusiasm of the Puritans that the achievement of the modern constitution must be attributed. They had little use or understanding of civil liberty and no use for toleration, but it was their blind courage that drove the revolution on.[31]

If, Hume tells his Whig and Tory readers, the Stuarts had understood what was happening, and, in addition to relinquishing many of the old royal prerogatives, as they did reluctantly, had tried to find subtle ways to win the complaisance of the members of the House of Commons, the constitutional readjustment might have taken place without strife. And, more im-

portantly, if the House of Commons had been more realistic
about the nature of governance and its financial costs, and,
accordingly, had been less zealous to destroy royal prerogatives,
and above all, if some of its members had been less ambitious to
dictate the moral and religious beliefs of Englishmen, the readjustment probably would have been made peacefully.[32]

The constitution that had come into existence by the end of
the century, when the struggle finally was over, was not the
ancient constitution restored, but a quite new constitution.
This is a constitution, Hume instructs both Whigs and Tories,
in which the right to govern is shared chiefly by the king and
the House of Commons. Both have authority: the rights of the
king, outside his powers under specific statutes, are his "prerogatives"; similarly, the rights of the House of Commons are
its "privileges." The central tension, the vital tension, in this
new system is between these two, between prerogative and
privilege. If the British constitution were a consistent and logical structure, either the king or the House ultimately would be
absolute, and either the privileges of the House would be
precarious, octroyed rights, or the prerogatives of the king
would be powers delegated temporarily by the House. If the
British constitution were consistent, it would be fundamentally
either a monarchy or a republic. But it is a mixed constitution.
In it authority is divided: neither the king nor the House is
absolute. Moreover, the constitution cannot be described exactly, for, like a perpetual tug-of-war, its continuance depends
on tension and movement, and this is impossible if all is certain
and fixed.[33] If ever the privileges of the House or the prerogatives of the Crown were fixed, precise, and describable,
either the constitution would have become petrified or at least
one of the vital parts would be dead.[34]

The genuine nature of the mixed constitution obviates many
of the Tory criticisms of current practices. In the prevailing
constitution, the power of the House of Commons apparently
is overwhelmingly great. The king and his ministers, although
they govern the country from day to day, seem to do so only
by the generous self-restraint and suffrance of the House. The

king is reputed to have a veto in the making of statutes, but this power has lapsed. The power of the House of Lords, although a support for the Crown in Parliament, has no independence and is important only when it has the support of the Crown. Moreover, the Crown is constantly dependent on the House of Commons for its financial supply. Considering the legal strength of that House and the legal weakness of the Crown, one might wonder how it is possible for the monarchical element to survive at all, or at least how it avoids being reduced to the office of an executive in a republic. The truth, says Hume, is that much of the British constitution is not formal and evident. Although the Crown is powerless vis-à-vis the House, it is able to influence many of the individual members of the House, especially by means of its power of appointment. The Crown is able to win cooperation, and thus the mixed constitution is preserved. The Country party, which denounces this so loudly as "corruption and dependence," should appreciate that however indecorous this may be, it is the method by which the British Constitution, so loudly acclaimed by all, is preserved. It is only because the Crown has so many offices at its disposal, "that, when assisted by the honest and disinterested part of the house, it will always command the resolutions of the whole so far, at least, as to preserve the antient constitution from danger." [35] If the members were tied by the mandates of their electors, as is sometimes proposed, they no longer would be free to yield to the blandishments of the Crown; and this would have the effect of converting the government into a republic.[36] It is by the management of elections, by offices, and by parties that the much-adored British constitution is preserved.

Whigs and Tories alike should realize that the constitution is based on neither divine right nor original contract, but rather, on convention. They should realize that because it is a mixed constitution, it is somewhat vague, and depends for its success on methods that cannot be included in the law of the constitution. And, finally, they should realize that it is the present constitution, not "the original constitution" or "the ancient constitution," that is the authentic constitution.

Hume's historical writing is primarily destructive: his aim
is to annihilate the myth of "the ancient constitution" and to
expose the misunderstanding on which that myth rests. The
Whigs and the Tories, especially the former, he finds, have
been inaccurate in their accounts of past British politics. What
is more important—and it helps explain why they err—is that
neither party understands the nature of a constitution. When
they lay aside their theories of divine right and original contract, they resort to the ancient constitution. This is because
their thinking about authority is not basic enough. They treat
authority as if it were a parcel of land, and think that by tracing back the record of leases and subleases they ultimately can
discover to whom all right(s) to govern originally belonged.
And they think of the heirs of that original owner as the true
rulers. Now, argues Hume, the ancient constitution never can
be discovered. But this need not worry us, for the distribution
of authority is founded basically not on original right, but on
present opinion—which, of course, often is influenced by old
rights. The notion that the task of the civil historian is to discover what the ancient constitution was, and how it was lost,
is one for which Hume has no patience. What he sought to do
in the *History* was to apply his argument set forth in "Of
Morals" to England, and to show the futility and the folly of
such antiquarian enterprises. The final paragraph of the work,
as originally published, reads as follows:

In each of these successive alterations [from the Saxons down],
the only rule of government, which is intelligible or carries any
authority with it, is the established practice of the age, and the
maxims of administration, which are at that time prevalent, and
universally assented to. Those who, from a pretended respect of
antiquity, appeal at every turn to an original plan of the constitution, only cover their turbulent spirit and their private ambition under the appearance of venerable forms; and whatever
period they pitch on for their model, they may still be carried
back to a more antient period, where they will find the measures
of power entirely different, and where every circumstance, by reason of the greater barbarity of the times, will appear still less

worthy of imitation. Above all, a civilized nation, like the English, who have happily established the most perfect and most accurate system of liberty, that ever was found compatible with government, ought to be cautious of appealing to the practice of their ancestors, or regarding the maxims of uncultivated ages as certain rules for their present conduct. An acquaintance with the history of the remote periods of their government is chiefly *useful* by instructing them to cherish their present constitution from a comparison or contrast with the condition of those distant times. And it is also *curious*, by showing them the remote, and commonly faint and disfigured originals of the most finished and most noble institutions, and by instructing them in the great mixture of accident which commonly concurs with a small ingredient of wisdom and foresight, in erecting the complicated fabric of the most perfect government.[37]

Hume does not mean that a present constitution always ought to be accepted. It is conceivable that the Tories might have adequate reasons for not accepting the present constitution and settlement, but, as it happens, he submits, that is not true. Consequently, although other constitutional arrangements and other settlements were possible, since the present constitution and settlement is the prevailing, existing system, the Tories ought to accept it.

Hume makes his view of the implication of constitutional histories quite clear in the essay, "Of the Protestant Succession," published in 1752, just at the time when he was beginning to compose his *History*.[38] Therein he argues that the choice between a Stuart restoration and a Hanoverian importation, at the time of Queen Anne's death, was one on which sane men might disagree. If all the ideological claims, which naturally are absolute and exclusive, are dismissed, and only the practical considerations favouring the Stuarts and Hanoverians are compared, it is easily seen that one "impartial patriot" might have decided for the first family, and that another "impartial patriot" might have decided for the second. But now, he concludes, the time for that choice is past. The House of Hanover is on the throne, and has been on it for many years. The new order is quite satisfactory. Accordingly, any sane, impartial man,

not deceived by wild speculative principles, will feel obliged
to support the Hanoverians. In another essay, "Of the Coalition
of Parties," published in 1758, he makes the same argument
more explicitly. In terms of constitutional law, the King's party
probably was the more correct at the beginning of the seventeenth century. That ancient constitution in terms of which
the Commons protested against the conduct of King James I
and King Charles I, if it ever existed, had long since ceased to
exist. The prevailing constitution then was one of nearly absolute monarchy. But this does not mean that the stubborn
Tories now are in the right. "The true rule of government is
the present established practice of the age." The Whigs have
succeeded conclusively. They have established a new order. If
that new order were not quite satisfactory there might be good
grounds for refusing to acquiesce in it. But it is entirely satis·
factory. The Tories, therefore, should forget their former righteousness, and abandon all their out-dated disgusts. Continued
talk about "the ancient constitution" is entirely silly.[39]

Hume tried to do more than to show that it was their failure
to understand the British constitution that led to the false
political theories and erroneous histories of the Whigs and
Tories. He undertook also to show the cause of the rise and
survival in England of those two parties. Their existence, he
contended, is attributable chiefly to the mixed nature of the
British constitution.

A state, he explains, is an admixture of individual liberty
and authority. When the former increases noticeably, the dissolution of the state and the onset of chaos may seem imminent.
When authority exerts its influence, the speedy establishment
of slavery may seem probable.[40] Moreover, it is impossible to
define the exact point at which individual liberty and authority
are correctly balanced, for what is enough authority in one
situation may be too much or too little in another. The correct
balance is a question on which differences of opinion will arise
perpetually, and on which men of learning and discernment,
not addicted to hysterical speculation, may be expected to dis-

agree. It is possible to see a portent of chaos in every relaxation of authority. It is possible to see a threat of slavery in every reduction of individual liberty. At this point, a basic difference in the characters of men becomes important. The inevitable ambiguity evokes two different reactions: men of cautious, hesitant temperament will worry about chaos, while boisterous, self-reliant men will be fearful of slavery.

The mixed constitution of Great Britain, by providing both kinds of men with standards and champions around which to rally, says Hume, invites the division of the state into two parties. The monarchical element, the Crown, because it is more active and more obvious in its action than the House of Commons, is easily thought of as "the government," the incarnation of authority; and quiet men will tend to think of it with favour as their protector, while the daring will tend to be suspicious of all its policies and acts. The former naturally are supporters of the Court. The latter, who admire the republican element in the British constitution, the House of Commons, and denounce the ministry for reducing its power through corruption and dependence naturally form a Country party. Besides, the mixed constitution works to keep both these parties active. The power to rule is divided between the two parts; and given the nature of governance, no exact definition of privilege and prerogative is possible. The adjustment is always changing and uncertain. The point of division, like the knot that marks the middle of a tug-of-war rope, is always moving, now one way, and now the other, according as the energies of the politicians and the needs of the times vary. This inherent instability constantly provides either the Court party or the Country party with an occasion for alarm or for hope. These causes—a difference between two kinds of men, the need for a combination of individual liberty and authority, and the prevailing mixed constitution—make the existence of two parties inevitable in Great Britain.[41]

These reasonable differences of principle are normally augmented by differences of interest. The monarch turns most readily for advice and ministerial assistance to those who show or declare themselves contented with monarchical government. The original sentiments both of those who get places and those who are excluded are thus confirmed and advanced. Similarly, since liberty of thought and publication erodes the superstition which is their foundation, the clergy, by reason of their interest, if they belong to an established church, may be expected to find their natural place on the side of the Court. Dissenters of all kinds will tend to come down on the side of the Country.

Again, the Court party will be unified by affection for the king or dynasty to whom they are bound by principle and interest. By long association the particular king or dynasty comes to be regarded as the very embodiment of the monarchical principle. The distinction between supporting a monarchy and supporting a certain man or family is lost, at least for all except the foremost leaders. The Country party, on the other hand, will have no particular feeling of warmth for the royal family.

The story of party politics in England, Hume explains, begins at the start of the seventeenth century, and can be traced from 1621. The Tudors had been absolute monarchs. Only Parliament, however, could enact statutes; and various new factors had made the Commons ambitious.[42] Englishmen, understandably, fell into two parties along lines of constitutional principle and ecclesiastical interest. Those who favoured continued strong authority became Cavaliers. Those who demanded more individual liberty became Roundheads. Neither party was so foolish as to deny the value of either individual liberty or authority, but while one exalted the king as the symbol of authority, the other glorified the House of Commons as the champion of freedom. The episcopal priests naturally supported the king, and the nonconformists supported the Commons.[43] These, then, were simply Court and Country parties, such as might have been expected under the mixed constitution. Because methods by which the authority of the king and the authority of the House could be harmonized had not yet been worked out, the partition went as far as civil war.

Hume finds that more subtlety is needed when the nature of

contemporary, eighteenth-century parties is to be analyzed. These are not, as Bolingbroke asserted, merely personal factions; if they were, the mixed constitution would have lost its natural influence. They do not differ in that the Whigs are prepared to follow the doctrine of original contract, while the Tories are prepared to follow the doctrine of divine right, although it is true that a great many Englishmen still prate that kind of nonsense. And, unfortunately, they are not simply Court and Country parties. The political scene, in short, is still distorted by the shift that took place when the Hanoverians were brought in to replace the Stuarts.

When the modern Tories and Whigs first made their appearance, in the election of 1679 and the exertions of the petitioners and abhorrers, they were authentic results of the natural tendency of the constitution to produce a Court and a Country party. The former, it is true, unlike their predecessors, the Cavaliers, went to the extreme in their talk about the most excellent wisdom of the king, the duty of passive obedience, and indefeasible right, and, were "these principles pushed into their most obvious consequences, they imply a formal renunciation of all our liberties, and an avowal of absolute monarchy; since nothing can be a greater absurdity than a limited power, which must not be resisted, even when it exceeds its limitations." [44] Yet the Tories did not believe all they said. They, or at least their leaders, were quite ready to defend the existing mixed constitution in 1688, and to forget James II, whom they may have misled by their declamations. In short, "the *revolution* shewed them to have been, in this respect, nothing, but a genuine *court-party*, such as might be expected in a BRITISH government: That is, *Lovers of liberty, but greater lovers of monarchy.*" After the revolution, they were displeased by the new power taken by the House of Commons, and, by reason of their continued affection for the Stuarts, a sentiment entirely natural in a Court party, they disliked the new settlement. The religion of the Stuarts was no great worry to them as long as the Stuarts were in exile. "A TORY, therefore, since the *revolution*," wrote Hume in 1741, "may be defined in a few words, to be *a lover*

*of monarchy, though without abandoning liberty; and a parti-*
*zan of the family of* STUART." The ultimate loyalty of the
Whigs, too, was to the mixed constitution, although their talk
about original contracts made them seem republicans. They
were an authentic Country party. By reason of their greater
emphasis on individual liberty, their eagerness to displace the
incumbents, and their opposition to the established religion,
they were opposed to the king, and naturally they did not have
the affection for the Stuarts that the Court party felt. A Whig,
then, can be described, as *"a lover of liberty though without
renouncing monarchy; and a friend to the settlement in the*
PROTESTANT *line."* [45] In short, both parties, from 1679 to 1689,
and thereafter, behaved for the most part like typical Court
and Country parties, and their existence is to be traced, not
to a division between the nobles and the people, not to a division between economic competitors, not to a division between
different regions of the country, but to the constitution.

Since 1714 both parties have had a somewhat confused or
ambivalent character. The Whigs, although now playing the
role of a Court party, retain some followers who fear authority,
and still talk about original contract. The Tories, now cast as
a Country party, retain many followers who favour authority,
and have not managed to divest themselves of the theory of
divine right of kings. The most obvious anomaly is that the
Court party is strongly nonconformist in religion, while the
Country party is strongly episcopalian.[46]

Evidently Hume thought that, given the balanced mixed constitution, the existence of a true Court party and a true Country
party would not be bad. That particular combination of individual liberty and authority which allows the most civil liberty
can never be defined for all circumstances, and some sane men
will desire more authority, while other, equally sane men will
desire more individual liberty. If all understood the cause of
this disagreement on practical principles, the result would not
be bad. But the development of such an understanding was
obscured, he believed, by ideological thinking; the Tories going to one impractical extreme, and the Whigs to the other.

Hume, as we have seen, undertook to sweep away those ideologies in his essays, "Of the Original Contract" and "Of Passive Obedience," published in 1748. The understanding of politics in Scotland was much sounder than in England, he reported in 1741 and 1742, and there, because of the absence of a Tory party, men already thought of parties accurately, that is, in terms of Court and Country.[47]

Just as it is to the mixed constitution that Hume traces the two-party system in Great Britain, it is to that mixed constitution, not to any special English predilection for civil liberty, that Hume attributes the extensive liberties, including liberty of the press, and the safeguards against invasions of those liberties by the government that are to be found in Britain. Both the mixed forms of government, unlike the simple ones, he argues in "Of the Liberty of the Press," published in 1741, promote a jealousy among those who share the divided authority. Consequently, where the monarchical element, the part almost everywhere charged with the day-to-day task of preserving the peace and conducting foreign affairs, is dominant, it will seek to achieve full, independent authority, and to the end of destroying any stubborn rival may resort to acts of the greatest cruelty and oppression. This happened in Rome. Where the monarchical element is subordinate, as the Crown in England is subordinate to Parliament, the republican element (in England, the House of Commons) can set limits to the legitimate powers of the king and his ministers, and can also review their *intra vires* conduct. Besides, since it is no secret that the extensive work of the Crown affords many opportunities in which it might extend itself insensibly and surreptitiously, the republican element is almost certain to impose such limits on its rival. This is what has happened in England.

Since 1603 the House of Commons has been, and continues to be, constantly suspicious and jealous of the Crown. This is the normal result of the English type of mixed government. From the desire of the House to hobble the Crown, and not from any unusual innate devotion to liberty, the unique attention shown in Britain to the liberties of the subject is to be traced. The House of Commons seeks to preserve, not the liberties of the subject, but its own position, and consequently, Britons enjoy more liberty than they would have under a republic or even under a civilized monarchy. The House, Hume writes, feels obliged, "for its own preservation, to maintain a watchful *jealousy* over the magistrates, to remove all discretionary powers, and to secure every one's life and fortune by general and inflexible laws. No action must be deemed a crime but what the law has plainly determined to be such: No crime must be imputed to a man but from a legal proof before his judges; and even these judges must be his fellow-subjects, who are obliged, by their own interest, to have a watchful eye over the encroachments and violence of the ministers. From these causes it proceeds, that there is as much liberty, and, even, perhaps, licentiousness in GREAT BRITAIN, as there were formerly slavery and tyranny in ROME." [48]

During the last years of his life, with his philosophic and historical work completed, Hume was drawn into practical politics. For a time he held public office, and subsequently, even during his final illness, he paid close attention to the debates and alarms of the day. While up to this period his letters contain little of interest on contemporary transactions—for example, the rising of 1745, which took place while he was with the Marquis of Annandale in England, is hardly mentioned—in these later years they are full of accounts and comments. He now had time and opportunity to make a first-hand estimate of mixed government in action.

Late in the summer of 1763, while he was debating the wisdom of acceding to the requests of Andrew Millar, his publisher, that he continue the *History* down into the eighteenth century, he was invited by Lord Hertford, newly appointed ambassador to France, to accompany him to Paris. Hume was well prepared for the new way of life now before him. In the *Treatise* he had described the causes of false beliefs and prejudices. In the essays he had explained factiousness. In the *History* he had discovered how ineffectual sound principles are against popular credulity, arrogance, and frenzy, especially when the latter are nurtured and drawn up by reckless demagogues. After a few preliminary weeks spent in London, Hume set out for Paris on October 15, 1763. There he remained—first as personal secretary to Lord Hertford, later as secretary to the embassy, and finally as *chargé d'affaires*—until early in January, 1766, when, accompanied by Rousseau, he recrossed the Channel for the last time. A little more than a year later he was back in office again, this time as under-secretary in the northern department, then headed by General Conway, and there he continued until the General left the government on January 20, 1768. It was not until August of 1769 that he returned to Edinburgh to reestablish his home there. For five years, then, Hume was on or near the political scene, and in the years after he lost office he demonstrated a keen eagerness to hear political news, and profoundly enjoyed pronouncing judgments and imprecations on the politicians and the populace.

His letters after 1763 show that what he saw and heard at first hand did not change his thinking, but instead provided contemporary illustrations for some of his less cheerful insights. It may even be true, as he repeatedly wrote, that he came to expect some great shudder in public life, probably entailing the collapse of the British constitution; but just how seriously he took his own prophecies is hard to say. For him, evidently, the letter was a genre in which, at least when writing to friends, one ought to be good-humoured and diverting even when touching upon the gloomiest topics. One of his favourite devices in his letters is hyperbole. Moreover, he chose to assume, or had fallen into, the pose of a splenetic enemy of the English, and because, therefore, it was the irrepressible folly of the English, bursting forth in innumerable ways, that endangered the delicate constitutional balance, the greater the dangers were depicted, the more adequately was the fatuous, factious wickedness of the English revealed. Since the most important of his political letters were addressed to old friends, all Scots—William Strahan, William Mure of Caldwell, the Reverend Hugh

Blair, Gilbert Elliot of Minto, Adam Smith—he could send off his fulminations, his wholesale denunciations, and his joyous forecasts of calamity without modifications designed to prevent misunderstandings. There is an air of philosophical indifference, too, in some of his letters, especially those written after 1766, which robs them of sting, even of earnestness.

The madness of the English furnished a good paragraph in many a letter. As early as 1741, when he published "Of the Parties of Great Britain," Hume was aware that false principles are especially prevalent in England, among the middling rank of men so extraordinarily numerous there. However, he never took occasion in any of his other works to treat this phenomenon more adequately, although the *History* gives many instances of it. After 1763, however, his letters are full of sallies. The stirring up of anti-Scottish prejudices for use in the campaign against Lord Bute, and the anti-Scottish demagoguery of John Wilkes, a man who for many years had found the company of Scots pleasant, came just at the time when Hume was about to be drawn into political life.[49] His *History* was then completed, and he liked to think, or at least to write, that it would have sold much better had it not been for the anti-Scottish bias south of the border; indeed, here was a convenient excuse for not resuming his labours. Besides, there was the impact of Paris. When Hume arrived there in the fall of 1763, he was appalled by the adulation that he had to endure, and even thought of leaving. Soon, however, as he gained facility in the language and began to make friends in the best circles, to which most of the British, who went about to "Plays, Operas, & Bawdy-houses," [50] never gained access, and as he came to be bantered by the French, he began to enjoy the high standing his literary achievements had won him in that civilized city. It may have been the quality of French society, and its appreciation of genuine worth, that opened his eyes fully to the plight of the English; [51] at least, it was in the frank reports of his successes and new eminence sent to his friends back home that he contrived, and, by frequent use, perfected his favourite words of condemnation for the English.

The effects of English prejudice that concerned him most during the years 1763, 1764, and 1765 were those that touched on his own affairs. Throughout the entire period he was in France he debated with himself and his friends about the best place to settle down, once his duties were ended. All that ever was certain was that he felt that he never could choose London. A few weeks after he arrived at Paris he wrote to William Robertson that he probably would stay on there for some time, for he had, he said, "little inclination to the factious barbarians of London." [52] One year later, and then one year after that, he still had the same opinion.[53]

His official career, also, he felt was bedevilled by the English. He had been offered the post of secretary to the embassy; yet he was allowed to do the work, despite Lord Hertford's efforts, while a dandy in England enjoyed the title and the salary. The delay in his commission, until June, 1765, Hume attributed to a Whig prejudice against him as an historian and a Scot.[54] Then, when Lord Hertford was recalled from Paris, and was made lord lieutenant in Ireland, he wished to have Hume made the secretary for Ireland (with a salary of about £2000 a year, and an assured future, Hume reported with evident satisfaction to his brother), but anti-Scottish prejudice proved too great, so the plan fell through.[55]

Shortly after Hume left office as an under-secretary of state, on January 20, 1768, the "Wilkes and Liberty" riots took place, inaugurating a period of turmoil which continued until Lord North took office, on January 30, 1770, and even thereafter. Hume's numerous comments on the happenings of those years and the ones that followed deal not with his own affairs, but with the fate of the mixed constitution and the country; yet, it is evident that he had become fond of his new activity, and had learned to deal with, even to live with, the English, and that he was not too happy to leave. The folly of this people, he saw, was now expressing itself in mob violence and ministerial slackness. The mixed constitution, in which the republican part had legal preeminence, produced, he now reiterated, an extraordinarily satisfactory combination of individual liberty and authority, a combination which allowed Britons an unusually high degree of civil liberty. But now, without specific goals, and inspired only by a contagious frenzy and a vacuous cry, "Liberty!" the London mob was endangering all. And the politicians were too busy making and unmaking their ministries in their own factious way to rein in the mob or to shock it back to sanity. The result was likely to be either chaos or despotism, or rather, chaos followed by despotism. In the letters of this period Hume writes as an ardent supporter of the mixed constitution, but as one who saw that constitution as endangered, first, by the factiousness of the politicians, which was weakening authority,[56] and, second, by individual liberty, which once having got authority on the run was threatening to destroy all authority, even that of the House of Commons, the republican element in the constitution.

In expressing his impatience with the English throughout these disturbances, Hume sometimes resorted to the device of invoking calamities. On July 22, 1768, in a playful letter written from London to Gilbert Elliot, he says: "I fancy the Ministry will remain; tho' surely their late Remissness or Ignorance or Pusillanimity ought to make them ashamd to show their Faces, were it even at Newmarket. These are fine doings in America. O! how I long to see America and the East Indies revolted totally & finally, the Revenue reduc'd to half, public Credit fully discredited by Bankruptcy, the third of London in Ruins, and the rascally Mob subdu'd. I think I am not too old to despair of being Witness to all these Blessings." [57] Again, writing to Elliot, on October 16, 1769, he informs that gentleman: "I am delighted to see the daily and hourly Progress of Madness and Folly and Wickedness in England. The Consummation of these Qualities are the true Ingredients for making a fine Narrative in History; especially if followd by some signal and ruinous Convulsion, as I hope will soon be the Case with that pernicious People. He must be a very bad Cook indeed, that cannot make a palatable Dish from the whole." [58] But the finest outburst of all came in a letter, dated October 25, 1769, to William Strahan, in which he expresses his fear of severe troubles during the forthcoming session of Parliament. After explaining that his one ambition, to succeed as a man of letters, had expired largely because it had been his "Misfortune to write in the Language of the most stupid and factious Barbarians in the World," so that he now lived in the greatest ease, he writes:

As to my Notion of public Affairs, I think there are very dangerous Tempests brewing, and the Scene thickens every moment. The Government has, no doubt, great Resources, if they employ them with Prudence and Vigour and Unanimity. But have we any reason to think they will do so? The Parliament will certainly be . . . by the Populace every day next winter. If they bear it, they degrade . . . and draw on . . . If they punish, they will still more enrage the Faction, and give a Pretence for the Cry that Liberty is violated. Are we sure, that the popular Discontent may not reach the Army, who have a Pretence for Discontents of their own? The General in chief is a weak man, and fond of low popularity: It is true, you have a very honest Chancellor and a very courageous Chief Justice, who will be a great Ressource in difficult times. But is it certain that Lord Bute will abstain from tampering and trying some more of his pretty Experiments? What if he take it in his head to open the Door to Pitt and his Myrmidons, who will, no doubt, chain the King for ever, and render him a mere Cypher. Our Government has become an absolute Chimera: So much Liberty is incompatible with human Society: And it will be happy, if we can escape from it, without falling into a military Government, such as Algiers or Tunis. The Matter will only be worse, if there be no shooting or hanging next Winter: This Frenzy of the people, so epidemical and so much without a Cause, admits only of one Remedy, which however is a dangerous one, and requires more vigour than has appeard in any minister of late. . . .

You say I am of a desponding Character: On the contrary, I am of a very sanguine Disposition. Notwithstanding my Age, I hope to see a public Bankruptcy, the total Revolt of America, the Expulsion of the English from the East Indies, the Diminution of London to less than a half, and the Restoration of the Government of the King, Nobility, and Gentry of this Realm. To adorn the Scene, I hope also that some hundreds of Patriots will make their

Exit at Tyburn, and improve English Eloquence by their dying Speeches.[59]

By 1769 Hume had come to think that the liberty allowed by the mixed constitution had grown so extreme and rampant that both parts of the system, the monarchical element, the Crown, and the republican element, the House of Commons, which by their tension had fostered that liberty, had lost much of their authority. To this view he adhered to the end of his life. Throughout the last months of 1769 and the first half of 1770 he seems to have regarded a vigorous, discreetly timed stroke against the mobs as a dangerous means, but the only effective means by which to reestablish the authority of the Parliament and the king. On February 21, 1770, after Lord North had survived the first test after taking office, we find Hume writing to Elliot:

I am glad of your Victories; tho' I look upon them all as temporary and imperfect, like the fallacious Recoveries of a hectic Person who is hastening to his Dissolution. Our Government has become a Chimera; and is too perfect in point of Liberty, for so vile a Beast as an Englishman, who is a Man, a bad Animal too, corrupted by above a Century of Licentiousness. The Misfortune is, that this Liberty can scarcely be retrench'd without Danger of being entirely lost; at least, the fatal Effects of Licentiousness must first be made palpable, by some extreme Mischief, resulting from it. I may wish that the Catastrophe shoud rather fall on our Posterity; but it hastens on with such large Strides, as leaves little Room for this hope.[60]

Late in the previous November, he had written: "The Ministry ought to wait with patience till some Violence or personal Insult be offerd to the Parliament, which will not be long, and will give Government great Advantages. I wish only the Army may be faithful, and the Militia quiet: Woud to God we had a Scotch Militia at present. This Country is almost unanimous." [61] Later he was to admit that although Lord North was better than the adventurers and demagogues, he was far too timid in his dealings with the mobs.[62]

In the essay, "Of the Liberty of the Press," (1741), after he had explained why such unusual liberty prevailed in England, Hume went on, in the second part of the essay, to enquire whether this liberty of the press was advantageous or prejudicial to the public. Since liberty of the press is essential to the mixed government, the answer, he found, must be that it is advantageous. But quite aside from its constitutional function in England, this liberty at the worst is quite harmless, and at the best serves to quiet public suspicions and anxieties by dispelling ignorance. His own words are:

Since therefore that liberty is so essential to the support of our mixed government; this sufficiently decides the second question, *Whether such a liberty be advantageous or prejudicial;* there being nothing of greater importance in every state than the preservation of the ancient government, especially if it be a free one. But I would fain go a step farther, and assert, that this liberty is attended with so few inconveniences, that it may be claimed as the common right of mankind, and ought to be indulged them almost in every government: except the ecclesiastical, to which indeed it would prove fatal. We need not dread from this liberty any such ill consequences as followed from the harangues of the popular demagogues of ATHENS and tribunes of ROME. A man reads a book or pamphlet alone and coolly. There is none present from whom he can catch the passion by contagion. He is not hurried away by the force and energy of action. And should he be wrought up to ever so seditious a humour, there is no violent resolution presented to him, by which he can immediately vent his passion. The liberty of the press, therefore, however abused, can scarce ever excite popular tumults or rebellion. And as to those murmurs or secret discontents it may occasion, 'tis better they should get vent in words, that they may come to the knowledge of the magistrate before it be too late, in order to his providing a remedy against them. Mankind, it is true, have always a greater propension to believe what is said to the disadvantage of their governors, than the contrary; but this inclination is inseparable from them, whether they have liberty or not. A whisper may fly as quick, and be as pernicious as a pamphlet. Nay, it will be more pernicious, where men are not accustomed to think freely, or distinguish between truth and falshood.

It has also been found, as the experience of mankind increases, that the *people* are no such dangerous monster as they have been represented, and that it is in every respect better to guide them, like rational creatures, than to lead or drive them, like brute beasts. Before the United Provinces set the example, toleration was deemed incompatible with good government; and it was thought impossible, that a number of religious sects could live together in harmony and peace, and have all of them an equal affection to their common country, and to each other. ENGLAND has set a like example of civil liberty; and though this liberty seems to occasion some small ferment at present, it has not as yet produced any pernicious effects; and it is to be hoped, that men, being every day more accustomed to the free discussion of public affairs, will improve in the judgment of them, and be with greater difficulty seduced by every idle rumour and popular clamour.[63]

In the edition of the essay published in 1770 he dropped this second part of the essay. For the edition brought out in 1777 he added a single final sentence in its place: "It must however be allowed, that the unbounded liberty of the press, though it be difficult, perhaps impossible, to propose a suitable remedy for it, is one of the evils, attending those mixt forms of government." [64]

After 1770 Hume had less occasion to fear that the rampant populace would sweep away all government than that the ministers, weak and contemptible as he found them, would be impelled into foolish policies by the populace, now wildly patriotic. In his letters he refers especially to three topics: foreign policy, the American colonies, and the national debt; on each of these he adheres to the general theories he had put forth in the *Political Discourses* in 1752.

At the end of 1770 and in January, 1771, the government made complete preparations, including an increase in the land tax, for a war with Spain over the title of the Falkland Islands. Such unjust, imprudent conduct by the North ministry, Hume argued, "proceeds entirely from the Timidity of our Ministry, who dread more the contemptible Populace of London than the whole House of Bourbon." [65] Such extreme action over the remote, worthless islands, he contended, was just another instance of the thoughtless patriotism and rant of the English.[66]

It was Hume's opinion from the very start that no effort

whatsoever should be made to retain the restless American colonies. It seemed likely, he held, that the trade of the colonies would continue to come to British ports even if the legal ties were severed. On the other hand, control over the colonies probably could not be long maintained even by the most extraordinary exertions and expenditures. Consequently, the sooner and the more amicably the legal bonds were cut, the better for all. His views, consistent with his general economic theory, were those of a "Little Englander." [67] When he was asked by his friend Mure of Caldwell to draft an address to the king recommending forcible measures against the colonists, to be signed by the gentry of the County of Renfrew, he expressed his opinions on the colonial question and on the zeal of Renfrew quite frankly. He wrote:

Oh! Dear Baron, you have thrown me into Agonies and almost into Convulsions by your Request. You ask what seems reasonable, what seems a mere trifle; yet am I so unfit for it, that it is almost impossible for me to comply. You are much fitter yourself. That Address, by which you gain'd immortal honour, was done altogether without my Knowledge, I mean, that after the Suppression of the late Rebellion. Here is Lord Home teizing me for an Address from the Merse; and I have constantly refus'd him. Besides, I am an American in my Principles, and wish we woud let them alone to govern or misgovern themselves as they think proper: The Affair is of no Consequence, or of little Consequence to us. If the County of Renfrew think it indispensably necessary for them to interpose in public Matters, I wish they woud advise the King first to punish those insolent Rascals in London and Middlesex, who daily insult him and the whole Legislature, before he think of America. Ask him, how he can expect, that a form of Government will maintain an Authority at 3000 Miles distance when it cannot make itself be respected or even treated with common Decency at home. Tell him, that Lord North, tho in appearance a worthy Gentleman, has not a head for these great Operations, and that if fifty thousand Men, and twenty Millions of Money were entrusted to such a lukewarm Coward as Gage, they never coud produce any Effect. These are Objects worthy of the respectable County of Renfrew, not mauling the poor infatuated Americans in the other Hemisphere.[68]

Closely connected with both the Falkland Islands and the colonial questions was his constant worry about the burgeoning national debt, and its consequences for the prevailing mixed constitution. In the essay, "Of Civil Liberty," originally "Of Liberty and Despotism" (1741), he had argued that an absolute monarchy might evade the evil results of financial mismanagement by declaring a bankruptcy, but that in a constitutional government, where the political leaders and the public creditors were likely to be drawn from the same group of men, no such safety device exists. He developed this argument in the essay, "Of Public Credit," in 1752. Now in his letter of March 11, 1771, to Strahan, on the Falkland Islands affair, he writes:

I wish I could have the same Idea with you of the Prosperity of our public Affairs. But when I reflect, that, from 1740 to 1761, during the Course of no more than 21 Years, while a most pacific Monarch sat on the Throne of France, the Nation ran in Debt about a hundred Millions; that the wise and virtuous Minister, Pitt, could contract more Incumbrances, in six months of an unnecessary War, than we have been able to discharge during eight Years of Peace; and that we persevere in the same frantic Maxims; I can forsee nothing but certain and speedy Ruin either to the Nation or to the public Creditors. The last, tho' a great Calamity, woud be a small one in comparison; but I cannot see how it can be brought about, while these Creditors fill all the chief Offices and are the Men of greatest Authority in the Nation. In other Respects the Kingdom may be thriving: The Improvement of our Agriculture is a good Circumstance; tho' I believe our Manufactures do not advance; and all depends on our Union with America, which, in the Nature of things, cannot long subsist. But all this is nothing in comparison of the continual Encrease of our Debts, in every idle War, into which, it seems, the Mob of London are to rush every Minister. But these are all other Peoples Concerns; and I know not why I shoud trouble my head about them.[69]

He followed this, on March 25, 1771, by lamenting that a bankruptcy was unlikely, and that the country would have to endure the grim results. He comments:

When I blame the Insolence of our Ministry with regard to Spain, I must at the same time confess, that we do right to swagger and bounce and bully on the present Occasion: For we have not many Years to do so, before we fall into total Impotence and Langour. You see, that a much greater and more illustrious People, namely the French, seem to be totally annihilated in the midst of Europe; and we, instead of regarding this Event as a great Calamity, are such Fools as to rejoice at it. We see not that the same Catastrophe or a much worse one is awaiting us at no distant Period. The monarchical Government of France (which must be replac'd) will enable them to throw off *their* Debts; ours must for ever hang on our Shoulders, and weigh us down like a Millstone.[70]

Strahan, in his reply, told Hume that if a national bankruptcy came the landlords would not escape entirely unscathed. The creditors would not be prepared to lose everything themselves, while the landlords went unharmed. This contention Hume was unwilling to accept. We find him writing to Strahan on August 19, 1771, as follows:

I am always oblig'd to you for your political Speculations: But I cannot agree with you, that, if matters came to a fair and open Strugle between the Land-holders and the Stock-holders, the latter would be able to reduce the former to any Composition. The Authority of the Land-holders is solidly establishd over their Tenants and Neighbours: But what Stock-holder has any Influence even over his next Neighbour in his own Street? And if public Credit fall, as it must by the least Touch, he woud be reduc'd to instant Poverty, and have authority nowhere. My only apprehensions are, with regard to the public, that this open Struggle will never happen, and that these two Orders of Men are so involvd with each other by Connexions and Interest, that the public Force will be allowd to go to total Decay, before the violent Remedy, which is the only one, will be ventur'd on. But this Event will depend much on Accidents of Men and times; and the Decision will not probably be very distant: The first War will put the Matter to a tryal, I fancy about the third or fourth Year of it, if we exert ourselves with our usual Frenzy.[71]

It is not to be thought that at any time during this entire period Hume advocated an increase in authority simply for its own sake. Liberty in a state requires, he was to argue in his final essay, "Of the Origin of Government" (1777), a combination of individual liberty and authority. The former alone may lead to chaos; but the latter alone may lead to despotism.[72]

He did not participate unreservedly in the prevailing adulation of the British constitution. The partly monarchical and partly republican system had the notable disadvantage of promising far less stability than either of the simple forms. The mixed form was rendered precarious by its very nature: its survival depended on a very nice balance between two entities, the Crown and the House of Commons, each of which inevitably tended at times to grow strong and to subordinate the other.

When he compared the two simple forms, absolute monarchy and a republic, abstractly, he invariably came to the conclusion that a republic is better than a monarchy. The constitution sketched in "Of the Idea of a Perfect Commonwealth," and proposed therein as the goal in "gentle alterations and innovations," is that of a republic. A "free government"—either a republic or a mixed government—he writes in his last essay, is most likely to produce "the perfection of civil society." But both at the beginning and at the end he contends that while a well-made republic is better than an absolute monarchy, a republic produced adventitiously by the atrophy of the British monarchy would almost certainly be bad. In the essay, "Whether the British Government inclines more to Absolute Monarchy, or to a Republic" (1741), he raises the question of whether, now that the troubles of the seventeenth century are at an end, it is the power of the monarchical element or that of the republican element that is likely to increase under the circumstances of the eighteenth century. On the one hand, it can be argued that monarchy is no exciting novelty, and, indeed, that "there has been a sudden and sensible change in the opinions of men within these last fifty years, by the progress of learning and liberty," so that extravagant notions about the celestial origins of kingly power no longer are convincing. On the other hand, it can be said that the enormous part of the nation's annual product—perhaps "a thirtieth part of the whole income and labour of the kingdom"—that passes into the treasury, and then is expended by the Crown inevitably gives the

Crown a vast authority. This second argument Hume finds the weightier: "Durst I venture to deliver my own sentiments amidst these opposite arguments, I would assert, that, unless there happen some extraordinary convulsion, the power of the crown, by means of its large revenue, is rather upon the encrease; though, at the same time I own, that its progress seems very slow, and almost insensible. The tide has run long, and with some rapidity, to the side of popular government, and is just beginning to turn towards monarchy." [73] He then goes on to argue that if the mixed constitution were to deteriorate, a decline into absolute monarchy is the preferable alternative. If the monarchy were to lose its authority, the House of Commons would then remain as the absolute authority. "The inconveniences attending such a situation of affairs, present themselves by thousands. If the house of commons, in such a case, ever dissolve itself, which is not to be expected, we may look for a civil war every election. If it continue itself, we shall suffer all the tyranny of a faction, subdivided into new factions. And, as such a violent government cannot long subsist, we shall, at last, after many convulsions, and civil wars, find repose in absolute monarchy, which it would have been happier for us to have established peaceably from the beginning." [74]

This is almost exactly the view that he sets forth in 1775 in a letter to his nephew, David, then a student at Glasgow, who resided with Professor John Millar, a famous republican. It is to be noted that Hume now thinks that the republican form is suitable only for small countries. He writes:

I cannot but agree with Mr Millar, that the Republican Form of [Government] is by far the best. The antient Republics were somewhat ferocious, and torn [internally] by bloody Factions; but they were still much preferable to the Monarchies or [Aristocracies] which seem to have been quite intolerable. Modern Manners have corrected this Abuse; and all the Republics in Europe, without Exception, are so well governd, that one is at a Loss to which we shoud give the Preference. But what is this general Subject of Speculation to our Purpose? For besides, that an establishd Government [cannot] without the most criminal Imputation,

be disjointed from any Speculation; [Republicanism] is only
fitted for a small State: And any Attempt towards it can in our
[Country], produce only Anarchy, which is the immediate Fore-
runner of Despotism. [Will he] tell us, what is that form of a
Republic which we must aspire to? Or [will the Constit]ution be
afterward decided by the Sword? [One] great Advantage of a
Commonwealth over our mixt Monarchy is, that it [woud con-
sid]erably abridge our Liberty, which is growing to such an Extreme, as to be incom[patible wi]th all Government. Such Fools
are they, who perpetually cry out Liberty: [and think to] augment it, by shaking off the Monarchy.[75]

A good republic or a civilized monarchy would be less likely
to destroy itself than would be the prevailing mixed government.
The republican form is the best form for a small country. An
absolute monarchy would be the best resort if the mixed constitution of Britain were to collapse. But it is the mixed constitution that exists in Britain. This form has the almost in-
superable advantage of being sustained by present opinion.
Accordingly, all men of true principles, men who know that
there is nothing of greater importance in a state than the preservation of the present constitution, if it be reasonably good,
will exert themselves to maintain that constitution.[76]

# X

## GOVERNMENTS AND RELIGION

Religion can never be deemed a point of small consequence in civil government.

*History*, VII, 261

So long as we confine our speculations to trade, or morals, or politics, or criticism, we make appeals, every moment, to common sense and experience, which strengthen our philosophical conclusions, and remove (at least, in part) the suspicion, which we so justly entertain with regard to every reasoning that is very subtle and refined. But in theological reasonings, we have not this advantage; while at the same time we are employed upon objects, which, we must be sensible, are too large for our grasp, and of all others, require most to be familiarised to our apprehension.

*Dialogues*, p. 135

O NE of the two or three topics that writers on morals and politics in the West have constantly found important is the relation between the roles of the individual as a citizen and as a Christian. Conflicts could and often did arise in the ancient world between political or civil obligations and religion, but polytheism, with gods for different places and gods for different activities, was inherently conformable to the mundane interests of each city or people. Christianity came on the scene as a religion which, although it suddenly had been transformed by the acquisition of a new message, a message of universal relevance, retained its original monotheism. Moreover, this new universal monotheism had its institutional embodiment in a universal or catholic church. The advance of Christianity was facilitated, of course, by the previous expansion of Rome, but Christianity spread throughout the Empire both as a system of beliefs alien to indigenous paganism and as an institution independent of the Empire. True religion no longer was merely a matter of political, civil, or national duty. Religious leaders no longer were officers in the public administration. Accordingly, conflicts between civil and religious loyalties hereafter were likely to be much more severe, and instead of appearing as incidents in inevitable, domestic, intramural contentions, were likely to become rending crises in the uneasy coexistences of great and independent organizations, and of separate aspirations within the mind and soul of the individual Christian.

The only period when there was a serious possibility that Christianity in the West would share the eventual fate of Christianity in the East, and become subordinate to the state, was in the fourth and fifth centuries, after Theodosius had made it the established religion of the Empire. But when, about 476 A.D., the Western Empire went down for the last time, the danger of a fusion disappeared. Later, when, under Charlemagne, a new empire began to emerge, the Christian church was well along in its work of raising a mighty edifice of faith encompassing the entire West. Besides, the protagonists of the new empire were never able to make their creation more than a third-rate imitation of the old. The economic and military needs of the populace were accommodated fairly well within the manorial and feudal systems, and where and when these proved inadequate, men turned to the rising royal dynasties or to the growing cities, rather than to the Holy Roman Empire. For us, this makes little difference: free cities, great and even lesser barons, and above all, the ascendant kingdoms, most notably France and England, were just as ready to oppose the church, and often were able to do so far more effectively than the Holy Roman Emperors.

The relations of church and state are displayed in classic simplicity when there is only one church and only one civil body. The plot becomes vastly more complicated when, as in the high and late mediaeval period, the faithful are under the civil governance of many potentates. The extreme of complexity is attained when, as in modern times, there is a plurality of both states and churches. As a result of the Protestant Reformation two great questions became prevalent. First, what ought governments to do about religiously disaffected subjects, or what ought true and faithful Christians to do if their government was either quiescent or militant in heresy? And second, what principle ought to be followed in organizing the members of the true church?

The first question gained in importance initially, chiefly in its second version. On the part of kings and governors of all religious persuasions, the assumption was that their own religion must be the religion of their subjects, and that to allow any latitude, except as a temporary expedient, would be both to encourage treason and to shirk the especial obligation of rulers to sustain true religion. Generally they had power enough to be able to rest on this assumption. Their dissident subjects, however, had to think fast, for the presumption was against them; if they resorted to disobedience or rebellion, they would have to do so against the established current of public life. Passive resistance, active resistance, seditious plotting, deposition of kings, crusades by faithful foreign rulers, and tyrannicide—Protestant and Roman Catholic writers alike moved across this entire spectrum of possibilities, and ordinarily did so in direct relation to their estimate of their own actual power. On the other hand, it was not until their failure to stamp out heretical nonconformity or until distraction from religious matters by more mundane affairs had cooled their zeal, that the governments began to wonder whether there was a need and a possibility of achieving religious uniformity within their lands.

The question of organization was confined to the Protestants, and arose almost at once. The Roman Catholics, despite the uncertainties implied by the Conciliar Movement, can be said to have possessed both a theory of church organization, and an organization in accord with that theory. For them the basic principle was divine right: the church was an institution introduced into this world from on high, and God's officers, arranged in a hierarchy headed by the Pope, had their authority through divine commission. At first, this theory of the church, with the secular ruler in the place of the Pope, was retained by the Protestants in England; but in the late sixteenth century its validity began to be challenged severely. Did God commission the several bishops, or did He commission only the king? It was hard to accept the first alternative, with its implicit federalism, when by statute and in fact the king created the bishops. And it was hard to accept the second alternative when rulers spent most of their time on political or lesser affairs, and gave few signs of religious vocation. In Scotland, the fact that at the crucial moment the reformers regarded their queen as a popish heretic of uncertain moral virtue made even the disjointed English solution unacceptable. In these conditions most Scots and many English began to see the merits of the Presbyterian system. But once the great shift, as a result of which the church was organized from the bottom rather than from the top, had been made, it was difficult to call a halt. In its Presbyterian form the church no longer had the appearance of an historic corporation with titles to power traceable back to Christ; rather, it depended for its unity and authority on the historic Word of God and on constant sustentation by Grace. This reliance on immediate divine operation suggested to many, especially in England, where malcontent with the prevailing settlement prevented the subsidence of such questions, that to enfold the light of inspiration in the dark earthbound wisdom of bishops, councils, or presbyteries, was profoundly hubristic. Here, then, within Protestantism, were a doctrinal view and a theory of organization that made toleration, by private men and by their governments, not the sin of the lukewarm, but a virtue of the true believer.

By the early eighteenth century the church-state question no longer was a fighting issue throughout Great Britain. This does not mean that religion had ceased to be one of the great social and political forces in that country. South of the border, it is true, religion was somewhat weak in the first half of the century, but John Wesley soon worked a revival. And it is probably correct to say that down to the middle of that century, perhaps beyond even to modern times, the Kirk continued to be the most powerful institution influencing and shaping the daily lives of the people of Scotland. Although religion in Scotland, at least in the Lowlands, no longer was entangled in vast political and military disruptions, it retained, probably increased, its influence on ordinary behaviour. Seldom, if ever, was the sabbath safeguarded more cautiously, or the scheme of salvation expounded more exhaustively, or sinners reproved more zealously than in Scotland in the early eighteenth century.[1] It was in this strongly Calvinist atmosphere that Hume was reared.[2]

It was his belief that popular religion is the source of many of the most dangerous crises that governments have to overcome. His recommendations as to the general policy to be followed by a government in relation to religious beliefs result from his own general attitude to popular religion, or, more precisely, from his own definition of popular religion, and not from any contemporary plot, scandal, or uprising. In other words, his proposals are shaped by his philosophical system and his estimate of the multitude, not by political expediency.

Religion was a subject that drew his attention strongly. Any philosopher must at least skirt the margins of theology, but Hume does far more than that. It was no accident that William Warburton, eventually Bishop of Gloucester, found the *Treatise* and the *Enquiry concerning Human Understanding* offensive in the extreme; in both, but particularly in the latter, Hume points out the agnostic implications of his epistemology.[3] The essay, "Of Superstition and Enthusiasm," and the *Natural History of Religion* treat religions as historical or social phenomena to be explained in terms of natural causes; the same concern is obvious in the *History of England*, especially in the volumes on the Tudors and the Stuarts. The work that he revised at the end of his life and for which he sought anxiously to assure posthumous publication, the *Dialogues concerning Natural Religion*, written twenty-five years earlier, deals exclusively and profoundly with the logical or metaphysical evidence for religion.[4]

Further evidence of his interest in religion can be found in the style of his works. Hume's writing is never rushed or murky. The most that can be said by way of criticism is that in the *Treatise* the young author, eager in his adventure, occasionally breaks pace and throws the reader, and that in most of the later works, addressed ostensibly to the conversible rather than the learned part of the literate public, the unvaried courtly measure and high polish of his prose seem incongruent with the earnestness of his thought. But when he is dealing with religion he is at his best. At times, especially when he is trying to show the foundations of "moderate scepticism," he is solemn, even grave. Sometimes, then, in striving to work out his ideas, he achieves a lean, exact prose, encumbered by few, if any, traces of affected elegance. The passages in which he sought to reveal something of the workings of the popular mind are among the most subtle and ingenious that he produced.[5] And at other times, especially when he recalls "the godly facts and words" of ministers and priests, a trace of elfish delight breaks through his urbanity. It is in treating the follies of popular religion— for example, the solemnities performed by Archbishop Laud at the consecration of St. Catherine's Church, the holy fervour shown at *autos-da-fé*, and clerical pranks—that he makes his greatest literary efforts. He disports himself with glee; he takes time to record naughty tales; and he rejoices in whimsies. Probably this is why the earlier parts of his *History*, down to Henry VIII, his first notable man of religion, are duller than his accounts of the Tudor and Stuart periods. When Hume was writing about religion, either seriously, or in an effort to amuse, tease, or outrage, he was ready to strive for success.

When he began to publish he had already arrived at the agnosticism in which he persevered to the end of his life, so we have no record of the course by which he came to that position; yet we may think of his progress in religious thought as something like the beginning of an ocean voyage. Presbyterianism was his point of departure, and while he soon drew away from the particular interpretation and enunciation of the Christian faith accepted within that communion, that this was his home port is always fairly obvious. If he had begun as an Anglican or a Roman Catholic, the presuppositions that he would have had to disown and disprove before arriving at agnosticism would have been quite different. Had he been brought up in a faith and culture that found evidence of authenticity in continuity of tradition, a great shift in viewpoint, such as would have given him a new outlook on the history of Christianity, would have been needed. But since Presbyterianism found continuity of tradition but pale evidence when compared with knowledge of the very grace of God acting providentially, only a revision of his theory of human knowledge was needed to undermine his religious faith. Everything drove towards such a revision.

There appears to have been little in either his character or situation to impede the sceptical thrust of his philosophy. Early, he became addicted to reading and composition, and those vices, although dangerous enough, as his famous letter to an unknown London physician shows, served to crowd out any inclination he may have felt to more dramatic, soul-stirring sins.[6] The classics, with which he spent his formative years, gave him no direct acquaintance with the trials and tribulations of this world; indeed, it is doubtful that either of the two callings his family considered for him, the law and trade, would have been more conducive to spiritual progress in the increasingly prosperous circumstances of the eighteenth century. In recruiting his early friends he seems to have confined his choice to the land and law gentry into which he had been born, and never to have ventured over to the socially inferior, ministerial side of the learned in Scotland; it was precisely this circle of the gentry that, in the early eighteenth century, was beginning to lose, not the staunch moralism, but the dark zeal of the early reformers. Perhaps it is conceivable that if, early, he had found congenial friends among the ministers, he might have been at least less outspoken in his attacks on popular orthodoxy. But as it was, his first adolescent suspicions of the worth and motives of professional men of religion, confirmed by his philosophic studies, renewed by the opposition of the pious to his candidacies for university chairs at both Edinburgh and Glasgow,

and documented by his historical research, remained undisturbed until he took up permanent residence in Edinburgh in
1751, and began to make friends among the Moderate party in
the Kirk.[7] Long before that date his own sentiments had set,
and, in their essentials, had been made public. Moreover, in his
genius there was nothing of the poetic strain that often has sustained religious belief. Always, even when in his youth he
described his ailments and melancholy, or when as a dying man
he composed his autobiography, he retained the role of the
thoughtful, self-conscious observer. He never appears as a man
able to accept, or even willing to accept, enthusiastic involvement. His prose is generally strong; rarely does it have great
vigour. The mind and the words seldom merge. The sentences
march adroitly, the argument is advanced with consummate
skill, but one senses that the writer knows that the whole truth
cannot be trapped in words. Nothing that might be taken for
wild, thoughtless rapture erupts to disturb the urbane equi-
poise, the calculated balance of this circumspect, elegant prose.
Perhaps the one piece in which he strikes out hot, characteristically enough, is the essay on the national debt.[8] His judgment
of poets and playwrights was notably bad, being influenced by
such considerations as the artist's morals, finances, health, and
nationality. The defects of his taste are suggested by his admiration for that uninspired, good man, the blind poet, Black-
lock.[9] The strength of his critical discernment is shown by his
assured, unerring appraisal of James MacPherson and his
poems of Ossian.[10] In short, he seems to have been, at least
until he had begun to relax somewhat under the influence of
Paris—and by that time Edinburgh, too, had changed—except for what his mother had called his uncommon "wake-
minded-ness," a splendid representative of the steady, assiduous, self-reliant, and increasingly prosperous Lowland gentry
from whom he had sprung.

All the major intellectual currents likely to appeal to a young
man such as Hume were flowing away from orthodoxy. His
training in Latin and Greek at the University of Edinburgh
led him to acquire a deep familiarity with pre-Christian an-

tiquity, and to develop a sympathy, not with Christian thought, but with the mental temper common among Hellenistic philosophers. Just then, British philosophy, under the impetus of Locke's discussion of the understanding and of Newton's emphasis on the sharp distinction between knowable nature and the unknown beyond, was pointed towards, and ready for, a new resolute criticism of rationalism.[11] At the same time, the rise of the "moral sense" school of Shaftesbury, Hutcheson, and others, presented an inviting task, that of working out the map of the secondary senses, thus conveniently replacing the task of cultivating the provinces of theological metaphysics, now abandoned. Finally, there was growing up in France and England, and even in Scotland, the American colonies, and Germany, a literate laity, both learnéd and conversible, which would provide a young author with an attentive, sustaining audience, if once its attention could be won.

The tone of the two main works in which Hume argues for "moderate scepticism" is highly serious. "Of the Understanding" is the product of a young man, eager to extend and establish his control over new provinces of learning; it is an aggressive work. In contrast, in the *Dialogues concerning Natural Religion*, Philo (Hume) is an assured, relaxed debater, fully in command, ready to bend and yield, seeking not to expel his opponents, but trying patiently, although patently unsuccessfully, to show them that he already has encompassed the very premises of their arguments.[12] But although an assertive temper has been supplanted by something akin to resignation, the basic theory in the work that last left his hands is the same as that developed in his first published writing. The *Dialogues* is his most carefully composed work. Structurally it is tight, meticulously interwoven, and complete. The exposition is brief, lucid, and exact; yet the work is not very successful. He seems to assume that his readers, unlike Philo's interlocutors, Demea and Cleanthes, already have mastered "Of the Understanding." And unless they have, his terse comments are likely to be as enigmatic for them as they are for Demea and Cleanthes.

In the *Dialogues*, both types of metaphysical argument are

examined.[13] The protagonist of *a priori* arguments is Demea, while the *a posteriori* argument is advanced by Cleanthes. It is Demea's view that the being of God can be demonstrated, can be shown by *a priori* reasoning, without resort to arguments based on the empirically discerned nature of the universe, but that the *nature* of that God is a matter of "adorable mysteriousness" veiled in sacred obscurity. While Philo tends to concur with Demea on the possibility of understanding the Deity, he cannot agree with him that the existence of any being, natural or divine, can be proved by *a priori* arguments. Consequently, he allows Cleanthes to dismiss the bewildered Demea with a succinct statement of Hume's own comment on demonstration in "Of the Understanding": "The words, therefore, *necessary existence*, have no meaning; or, which is the same thing, none that is consistent." [14]

The *a posteriori* argument receives far more attention. Cleanthes contends that the normal eighteenth-century deistic argument from design is valid. The world, we can see, resembles a wonderful machine made up of innumerable extremely complicated lesser machines. Each of these parts is splendidly contrived to mesh into the others, and to perform perfectly a function necessary to the operation of the entire system. Each part is a means in the whole. The world is very much like the product of a craftsman working with a purpose. This being true, from observing the world, Cleanthes submits, we must conclude both that a Creator is in *being*, and that it is His *nature* to act purposefully. Here we have an empirical, *a posteriori* argument, an argument that begins with a description of the observed effect, and then moves back to a cause suitable to that effect.

On this Philo (Hume) has two main comments. The first is that Cleanthes does not know what understanding and explanation are. To understand or to explain any event satisfactorily is to attribute it to its proper causes. As a result of repeated experience, whenever we see an "effect" of a specific kind, we believe that it has been preceded by a "cause" of a specific kind. Explanation always involves kinds or species. To explain any effect is to show the kind of effects to which it belongs, and then to name the kind of causes that produce such effects. In other words, to establish kinds of causal sequences —the only basis for *a posteriori* argument—repetition is absolutely necessary. Now, the universe is one, and only one, universe. We, therefore, are in no position to say that it is an effect of a cause.[15]

The universe is not to be explained: reasoning or causal explanation is not relevant to it. Hume's view here is that causation exists only within the realm of natural time (or change). It does not exist, and argument based on it cannot be applied, within the realm of eternity. This does not mean that there is no relation between eternity and time, between God and His Creation; rather, it means that there is no relation appropriate to the natural human understanding. Moreover, specious explanation of a relation between eternity and time, unless received with "moderate scepticism," inevitably leads to grave errors. Once this relation is treated as analogous to any causal relation, e.g., that between a craftsman and his product, an argument can be made for any other familiar causal relation as the appropriate analogue, e.g., that between an animal and its offspring, that between a parent tree or vegetable and its descendants, or that between a geological cause and its effect. Again, if God is treated as the understandable cause of the world, time and eternity are confused; once this has been done the eternal ostensibly is made susceptible to explanation, with the result that questions about the cause of God, and about the cause of the cause of God, and so on, are raised.[16]

Philo's second comment is practical rather than theoretical. The universe, men can observe, displays many kinds of order. Almost certainly men will wonder why it is and remains orderly. But even to wonder on this is to employ symbolically the categories of human understanding. In short, the "religious hypothesis" is inevitable, and disagreements about it are merely a matter of different words and different emphases.[17] Once men begin to try to treat the natural world as an effect, they find both that many of the operations of nature are analogous to those of man-made devices, and that many are not. The incomprehensibility of the latter suggests the existence of a great cause capable of such effects. The apparent accommodation of the former within human categories suggests that their cause is somewhat like a purposeful human mind. Accordingly, if "we are not contented with calling the first and supreme cause a GOD or DEITY, but desire to vary the expression; what can we call him but MIND or THOUGHT, to which he is justly supposed to bear a considerable resemblance?" [18] Indeed, so inevitable is the "religious hypothesis" for all who seek an explanation that so-called atheists employ it, and may even be prepared to take a more strongly theistic view than many professing theists. The latter, if they be extremely pious, are certain to insist on the incomprehensible difference between the human and the divine mind. The atheist, on the other hand, will admit that nature is orderly, that this natural order does resemble the designed order produced by a purposeful human artisan, and that it is not impossible that the natural order is the effect of a divine mind analogous to the human mind.

At one point in the discussion Cleanthes confuses metaphysical goodness (changelessness or eternality) with moral goodness, and then tries to strengthen his deistic argument by holding that the moral character of the universe shows the perfect moral virtue of the Deity. With this Philo has no patience.[19] If you begin, he argues, to search for an explanation for the distinction between good and evil beyond human nature, and you once admit that there is the slightest evil in the external world, you then must find a cause for the evil as well as a cause for the good. The next step is a descent into a more or less overt Manichaeanism. But this will not do. If we were to remain consistent in the confusion of morals and metaphysics, Manichaeanism would lead us to expect to find metaphysical evil in the world. It would lead us to expect great outbursts of genuine chance, totally uncaused happenings within the causal order of nature. And this expectation would be disappointed. Our conclusion, Philo contends, is that it is a dangerous error to go beyond human nature in any discussion of moral subjects.

But here again, we must be practical. Men are almost certain to try to give ultimate explanations of the moral nature of man. If they do, the only proper observation is that man's moral character is even farther removed than his intellectual character from the perfection of the Deity.[20]

The maximum outcome of the deistic or *a posteriori* argument that Philo is prepared to admit can be stated in the "one simple, though somewhat ambiguous, at least undefined proposition, *that the cause or causes of order in the universe probably bear some remote analogy to human intelligence.*" [21]

Hume's appraisal of efforts to work out *a priori* demonstrations or to find *a posteriori* evidence showing that God is, or that He is of a certain nature, is wholly consistent with his analysis of human understanding. By *a priori* reasoning even knowledge about nature cannot be ascertained—because the system called "Nature," if it is a system, was not created by human fiat. To try to reach outside and beyond nature by *a priori* thought would be presumptuous folly. By *a posteriori* reasoning men can understand the internal relations of the universe—to the extent that they do understand them—only because the universe operates repetitiously, i.e., has a "nature" or "character." The "religious hypothesis" proposes the creation of the universe by a cause independent of the natural universe, and proposes that this creation, as far as men are concerned, took place only once. Hume's contention is that this Creator and this Creation are totally beyond the categories of the human understanding. For the understanding, knowledge of a fact is not evidence unless it has relevant precedents. But God is unique. And the Creation took place only once. This being true, to insist that evidence suitable to the understanding exists is to stumble into the heresy of denying the singular unity or nature of the God of the "religious hypothesis." It is because God is as He is, and because men are His creatures— on the religious hypothesis—that evidence is impossible. Only if God were one of a familiar type of gods and the Creation were a happening in a sequence of similar happenings could either be understood.

The appropriate result is agnosticism, not a denial of the existence of God—it may be that His works are obvious everywhere—but an insistence that the human understanding cannot comprehend God, and that all expressions used in reference to the Deity can never be more than hypothetical and symbolic. For Hume "moderate scepticism" is the only genuine religious attitude. It is the attitude of high self-consciousness. The man who cannot see himself, view himself as an object, is doomed to continue the prisoner of himself, engulfed in all the delusions and misapprehensions appropriate to his self-oriented views and interests. But the route to "moderate scepticism," to the stand of the impartial observer, is long and arduous. To work free from the coils of selfish involvement requires a special moral and intellectual endowment, suitable circumstances, and an imperious philosophic vocation. The notion that true sceptics will ever be more than a select handful lost in the multitude would be a characteristically human error liable to lead to dangerous consequences if taken seriously by men with public power. Three great milestones must be passed on the way: first, the attainment of a conception of the complex order of the universe; second, a comprehension that this unified order is not self-explanatory; and finally, the realization that natural human understanding is constitutionally incapable of advancing beyond nature. Even those deists who do not claim to know more than that God is a Being who works purposefully as do men, show the stubborn traces of *hubris*.

Hume's discussion of "the religious hypothesis," while far from devout, is restrained, respectful, and profoundly sober, in marked contrast with his works on "popular religion," the religion of "the ignorant multitude," which for him is a kind of mental disorder brought on by ignorance and selfishness, and highly dangerous to civil society. For Hume, evidently deeply impressed by the religious element in the conflicts of the previous century, the religious "beliefs" of the vulgar, like a plague, now dormant, now threatening to break out, are a matter that no government can afford to take lightly. The masses cannot be expected, he finds, to achieve "moderate scepticism." At times, fortunately, the hold of their religions on them will be loose, but this will be the result of thoughtless indifference, not of philosophic enlightenment. They are, and will remain, more or less under the influence of popular beliefs. Now, since "moderate scepticism" is the position required by the evidence, or rather by the lack of evidence, these beliefs must be founded on error. Religion of the popular kind is not a guiding instinct original in human nature, such as those that lead to love, gratitude, or resentment. Nor are the beliefs which support religion made up of ideas which derive impressiveness from sensations. Popular religion, consequently, must be the result of a mistake or distortion. Besides, in this case error must be far easier than truth, for popular religion, unlike moderate scepticism, is almost universal, and often is extremely influential. Hume's chief theoretical purpose in *The Natural History of Religion* is to explain the causes and the nature of popular religion. Whereas the *Dialogues concerning Natural Religion* is an exposition of the foundations of moderate scepticism, which always are the same, the *Natural History* is a work in anthropology, not an ecclesiastical history, but a description of the normal and erroneous reactions of ignorant men to certain experiences.

The religious "beliefs" of the masses, Hume finds, originate, not in philosophic attention to nature, but in deep engrossment in the minutiae of everyday life. The involvement of the vulgar in the immediate is the cause of their religion. This explains, he contends, why they are so often filled, not with awful wonder at the vast order of the universe, but with surprise or consternation at the seemingly extraordinary and incomprehensible things that happen. The fabric of causal sequences in which each man or each nation is a part is extremely complicated. The scene spreading around a man at any moment is composed of innumerable, interwoven strands. Many of these are familiar. They have appeared again and again; and they are taken for granted. The regular antecedents of a certain kind of event, and possibly the antecedents of those antecedents, are known, and their names can be given. With them the understanding is easy and satisfied, for beyond the second or third causal step, even curiosity dies away rapidly. But there are other strands which because of their unfamiliarity seem strange and uncanny. Suddenly they emerge from the depths of nature, disrupting the quiet flow of time, astounding the mind. A man suspected of grave impiety chokes on the stone of a plum. Great thunder and lightning storms occur. A fiery comet streaks across the sky. A cat starts up from luxurious slumber, spits a defiant curse at some unseen spectre, and bolts. A worn, all-but-defeated warrior feels a tide of renewing power.

As moderate scepticism is based on wonder and humility, popular religion, Hume explains, springs from a failure to see the order of the universe, a failure which is immediately exploited by the desire for happiness. Most men and women— "the vulgar, that is, all mankind, a few excepted"—conceive the world and history from their own viewpoint, and in relation to their own immediate interests. They accept their own convenience and contentment as the standard by which to evaluate time and eternity. Prompted by their self-oriented desire for the enjoyment of pleasure and the avoidance of pain, they render the natural, but unknown causes of startling events, pleasant or painful, comprehensible by personifying them. And these persons they then proceed to deify. After this has been accomplished, these gods and goddesses become the objects of hopeful, and especially of fearful, solicitation, because they will play with the future, presumably, as they have played with the past. Their devotees feel constrained to employ all kinds of rites and exercises, of gifts and blackmail, of insinuating flattery, of repetitious, importunate beseechings and ululations, going even to the extent of despatching sacrificed emissaries, in efforts to win over or compel the favour of the divinities.[22]

Mass religion, he contends, is the result of a partial view of natural causes, a distortion in understanding, exploited and aggravated by a self-centred desire for happiness. It is based on a misinterpretation of experience. It comes from thinking ideas that have not been derived from impressions according to the proper rules. The effect of this improper derivation on the vividness or impressiveness of the ideas must be appreciated if either the efficacy of religion as a political force or the methods of coping with it are to be understood.

According to Hume's epistemological theory, believing is one of the most important ways of knowing. It has no relevance to our knowledge of demonstrable systems. To say that we believe that the sum of two and two is four is as inept as to say that we believe that green is green. Analytic statements are developed tautologies. The result attained by the development is either consistent (correct) or inconsistent (incorrect) with our system. Instead, the topic or object of believing is the world that we regard as the "real world." We intuit part of it as the present, another part we remember; and beyond, extends the world of proofs and probabilities, the world known by believing. Believing is always a matter of conviction.

To test the validity of our beliefs is one thing; to test their strength is another. Because believing is a way of perceiving "the real world"—the reality in which, and in relation to which, a man acts—it is directly practical. Our acts, by which we venture into the future, depend to a large extent on our beliefs about the future. If our ideas about the future, both tomorrow and the hereafter, for some reason include very vivid ideas of influential gods and goddesses, we are likely to do acts calculated to please them. Now, since the impressiveness necessary to change a mere idea into a believed idea, a belief, is a matter of degree, and is variable, there is no need for us to act consistently. We may sing hymns to the gods, but spend our money for rare comestibles for our tables while neglecting their altars. Most men have a conglomerate of beliefs, and pay a varied deference to all of them. Yet if we observe the general way in which men live and spend their time, we can form a fair notion of their beliefs.

Using this test, Hume comes to the conclusion that popular religious beliefs seldom, if ever, attain the assuring vividness of the beliefs men hold about the regular rising of the sun, the behaviour of falling bodies, the future conduct of their friends and neighbours, or the performance of their pets. Even professional "religionists," he submits, tend to be more ardent in acquiring mundane riches and influence for themselves, than in achieving spiritual advancement. The impressiveness of religious ideas generally is quite low, as one might expect, considering their improper derivation.

Consequently, popular religions are always a source of the greatest danger. Instead of feeling assured and comfortable, prepared to laugh at or to dismiss the dubious, as they are if their beliefs that fire causes heat, poisons cause death, and sleep is refreshing are disputed, men whose religious ideas are questioned tend to become irritable, querulous, persistent, and antagonistic. They are happy in their pretence that their beliefs afford a solid foundation for their avaricious dreams of ease and delectation. They resent everything that weakens their pretence. If it is the unanimous agreement of a community that a particular religious idea represents reality accurately, this unanimity will operate to heighten the conviction of each believer. Divergent views have the opposite effect: and therefore, quite aside from their validity, are abhorred. Moreover, by confronting the orthodox with alternatives, the heterodox arouse the believer's own sleeping doubts. They objectify his own deep infidelity, and since he can neither find peace in the truth nor admit that he has doubts, he strikes out blindly as if thereby he might rid himself of his discomfort. Religion thus produces fierce hostilities, which are liable to explode into holy wars. In addition, the devotees of even the most sordid or selfish causes are liable to take to the field in the armour of righteousness.

Hume's exposition of the causes of popular religion, even if presented with only a theoretical purpose, would be an indictment of it. But the *Natural History*, unlike the *Dialogues*, has a strong polemical quality. In it, as in his essay, "Of Superstition and Enthusiasm," and the *History of England*, he exerts himself to chide, to cajole, to startle his readers, perhaps even to reform them a little. In the *Natural History* he makes no determined frontal attack on the Presbyterians and Anglicans, the communions to which, presumably, most of those he had in mind belonged, but contents himself with one or two thrusts; instead, he seeks to take them quietly from the rear with ingratiating jibes and jokes at the expense particularly of the ancient Romans and Egyptians and the Roman Catholics. His point, however, is never masked: Popular religions, originating in the anxiety caused by ignorance and selfish desire, are always more or less vicious; popular religions did not die out when men stopped worshipping sacred cats and Jupiter; and modern Christianity, even in the Presbyterian form, which greatly resembles that theism which for the sceptic is not ridiculous, is sadly tainted with *hubris*.

Mass religion may be monotheistic as well as polytheistic in its form; indeed, since popular religious thoughts refer to no real being or thing, those thoughts can change freely so that the deity or deities are made suitable to the changing needs of the devout. Consequently, popular religion, Hume finds, tends to move, like a slowly swinging pendulum, from polytheism to monotheism and then back, again and again.[23] These religions are not corrupt forms of an original true religion—if that were their origin, it would be correct to hold that initially they were monotheistic. Because they have their beginning in error, not in truth, we may assume that they took the form most suitable to the generating error, that is, that they were polytheistic, or frankly idolatrous, at first. There was a geographical or functional division of divine power at the beginning. Each city, perhaps each stream and wood, perhaps each nation and each hearth, had its own special presiding deity. Travellers by land, travellers by sea, musicians, warriors, wives and husbands, all these and many others are likely to have been under the attentive care of a god or goddess. But after a while, Hume argues, popular religion tends to move to monotheism. This is never the result of increasing philosophic insight; on the contrary, in their frenzied flights of hyperbole, brought on by their zeal for happiness, the idolators fuse their gods and come at last to the boundary of their own comprehension. They merge the qualities hitherto parcelled out among the several deities into one great, superlative deity. There comes a moment when divinity is concentrated in one omnipotent and omniscient being, and at that juncture popular religion has all the outward and verbal signs of the deism acceptable to moderate sceptics. But this is only accidental. The religionists may, like Demea in the *Discourses*, soar beyond "the notion of a perfect being, the creator of the world," into mysticism. But, in any case, soon the reverse process sets in. The deity has become too pure and exalted for the homely chores, such as assuring fertility, finding lost coins, winning battles, and guarding doors, that must be done. Moreover, such a divinity is not likely to seem sufficiently attentive and friendly. Accordingly, the attributes of the one god or goddess are factored out, and are assigned their particular places and names. This new idolatry, however, is covert. Because a monotheistic peak once has been attained, these beings are counted only as demigods in the theology, although in practice they are the gods of the people. Since these "middle beings" resemble human beings and know their requirements, they naturally occupy the focus of devotion. Eventually the other extreme is reached. And here the process is reversed. The intermediaries have become so familiar, specialized, and trivial that the vulgar no longer respect them, and begin to allow their cults to die out, or to be merged with those of higher and still higher beings. Popular religions, in which devotion is bartered for services, tend to swing back and forth between polytheism and theism—this, Hume finds, is the natural pattern in the history of popular religion. So powerful are the two opposing tendencies here involved that the rulers of some peoples, such as the Jews and Mohammedans, have sought to establish theism permanently by the drastic measure of excluding all statues and pictures from their countries, but even this is not successful, and only slows the swing. The natural understanding cannot be content with the idea that the deity is a pure spirit and perfect intelligence, wholly different from any being ever perceived, and yet the natural terror of the vulgar will not allow them to confine their thinking to the idea of finite gods.

Hume's basic argument here is that popular religion does not begin with truth, and does not lose any of its inherent falsity when it has all the visible signs of truth. Its causes are always ignorance and self-interest. When it seems to approach the truth, it does so not through wisdom, but inadvertently, through transcendent adulation.

At every phase in this swing, popular religions are a cause of worry for a government. They propagate an unseemly, blasphemous idea of divinity by depicting their holy ones as more or less spiteful, vain, incontinent, fickle, and malicious, and for the most vulgar are simply "a species of daemonism." They tend to deprave their devotees by requiring them to practice the gutter arts of bribery, trickery, and hypocrisy. They often lead them to do deeds naturally useless, or even contrary to nature, as an imagined service to the supernatural.

Although all this is true of both polytheism and monotheism, both, Hume contends, are not equally bad and dangerous in all respects. Polytheism needs government supervision because, being founded on the crude notions of the populace, it is not essentially repugnant to corrupt and barbarous opinions and practices, and accordingly, it may have the effect of sanctifying and propagating immorality, subversive of civility and public order. Monotheism, or some close approximation thereto, if correctly inculcated, commends virtue; yet it may be even a greater danger than polytheism, for by reason of being more nearly correct, it is more virulent. While polytheism is transmitted by innumerable vague old tales full of inconsistencies, monotheism is able to make an ally, or rather a captive, of philosophy. The produce of this slave's work is theology, a variety of systems and a maze of specious arguments, all entirely insignificant, made imposing and authoritative by their elaborate mysteriousness and subtle high profundity. The myths that make known the works and jealousies of the gods and goddesses also make them commonplace; in contrast, the dogmas of popular theism produce a narrow, aggressive conviction.

This difference in intensity is made politically important, Hume holds, by the fact that polytheism easily accommodates and indeed encourages diversity of myths, rites, and temples, while monotheism seems to require suspicion, mutual contempt, or strife, even between those who worship the same god or goddess in different ways. Each Christian sect, he finds, prides itself on its true faith and special commission, proclaims grandly that it will not be one among the philosophies, and, at best, dismisses all others as grievous, confounding heresies. Each claims to have a monopoly of not merely the best, but the only, Christianity. When their zeal is high and hot, they slaughter and burn each other to protect the innocent from error. Such devotees always are conspirators against the peace, and often act openly against it. Because, unlike murderers and thieves, they often operate in nation-wide or international bands, they are the most dangerous threat to the civil order with which the civil magistrate has to deal, and as a matter of prudence they should be treated as such.

It is with Christianity as taken up by the masses that Western governments must deal.[24] Hume finds that it has two basic forms, superstition and enthusiasm, but which of the two is the more dangerous he is hard put to say. The basic difference between them is one of mood or temper. Illness, misfortune, calamities, or a sombre disposition tend, he argues, to produce great dreads and terrors. Malignant powers suitable to this fearfulness are then imagined. After this, methods of propitiating the powers of darkness are devised. "Weakness, fear, melancholy, together with ignorance, are, therefore, the true sources of SUPERSTITION." And prosperity, robust health, strong liquors, or a bold disposition tend to produce exuberance, elation, and presumption. Those so inspired soon forget mortal cares and limits, and are swept by glorious raptures, and after a little while, discover that they are distinguished favourites of the Deity. Henceforth, the slightest whim of their fancy suffices to repeal any of the dull ordinances of reason and morality. "Hope, pride, presumption, a warm imagination, together with ignorance, are, therefore, the true sources of ENTHUSIASM." [25]

The superstition of the timorous allows men of special "sanctity of life, or, perhaps, impudence and cunning," to set themselves up as the earthly friends and intimates of divinity, and to take upon themselves the task of serving as mediators between the vulgar and their easily incensed Deity. This is the origin of priests, a set of men, Hume warns, not to be confused with that other most respectable rank, the "*clergymen,* who are set apart *by the laws,* to the care of sacred matters, and to the conducting our public devotions with greater decency and order." [26] But in the enthusiastic sects, "The Fanatick consecrates himself, and bestows on his own Person a sacred Character, much superior to what Forms and ceremonious Institutions can confer on any other." [27] The result is that enthusiasm is even more opposed to priestly power than is sound reason and philosophy. Now, since there is a mixture of enthusiasm and superstition in almost all the churches and sects, there is some degree of "priestly bondage" in almost all. This, Hume finds, is greatest in the Roman Catholic Church. Among the enthusiasts the most egregious, but most innocent, are the Quakers, who have no professional men of religion; then, next to them are the English Independents, whose priests are weak; and next to them are the Presbyterians. In the first two editions (A and B, 1741 and 1742) the Church of England is bulked, along with the Roman Catholic Church and "Modern Judaism," among those in which the authority of the priesthood is high. He wrote therein: "As the Church of ENGLAND may justly be said to retain a strong Mixture of Popish Superstition, it partakes also, in its original Constitution, of a Propensity to Priestly Power and Dominion; particularly in the Respect it exacts to the Priest." In the next editions (D to P, 1748 to 1768) this judgment is modified to read: "As the Church of ENGLAND may justly be said to retain some mixture of Popish superstition, it partakes also, in its original constitution, of a propensity to priestly power and dominion; particularly in the respect it exacts to the sacerdotal character." But in both his last editions (Q and R, 1770 and 1777), the Church of England is not mentioned in the ranks of either the superstitious or enthusiastic.

Hume warns that superstition is pernicious in two ways. First, the priestly order which it sustains, he says, is liable both to acquire an authority challenging or overshadowing that of the civil government, and to disturb peace and prosperity by religious alarms and projects. This is particularly dangerous when that order has an international character, as has the Roman Catholic Church. That church, he holds, is a threat to the government of Roman Catholic countries, and in Protestant and infidel lands it maintains a permanent plot. Second, he contends that it keeps the citizenry suspended in a permanent twilight of rationality and civility, incapable of attaining the self-reliant independence necessary for full human virtue. Moreover, since the priests will work assiduously to prevent any subsidence of popular religion, no natural release from this error can be anticipated, where superstition prevails.[28]

The great danger of enthusiasm is that it produces a fierce, wild, unruly zeal and independence, liable in its misdirected self-confidence to destroy the social order and the established constitution. Here, rationality and civility are overwhelmed by a bigoted fanaticism. It produces a population uneasy, factious, and tumultuous. Besides, it tends to make its adherents grim, dour, and unhappy. Fortunately, enthusiasm, unlike superstition, burns itself out after a time, and then the people emerge cool and careless, liberated from their former feverish exaltations.

Each is bad enough when it holds sway within a country; but when the two compete, or when their factions are competing, the task of civil governments may become almost impossible.

A wise governor, he proposes, will see that religious ideas cannot be eradicated, and therefore should be controlled with greatest care to prevent prejudice to "the civil interests of society." [29] These ideas are as inevitable as their causes, the ignorance of natural causes and the desire for happiness. But he will see also that these ideas play only a small part in the lives of the citizenry unless they are made impressive by circumstances or by the deliberate business of ministers and priests. Most men are far more concerned with the world and the flesh than they ever would think of admitting. This truth should be the foundation of a government's policy on popular religion. Hume makes two principal recommendations. The first is the establishment of one state church with a constitution conforming to the genius of the prevailing form of civil government. There "must be an ecclesiastical order, and a public establishment of religion in every civilized community." [30] The separation of church and state permits the church or churches to wander at large, and religion is far too powerful a force to be left untethered. By establishing one church, the government gains control over religion in two important ways: first, it binds most of the clergy to itself by law and interest, so that they are attentive to the needs of the state, and do not become ambitious or factious; second, it brings the rites and teachings of the clergy under its own regulation and supervision.[31]

Hume writes about the clergy as if they were vendors of a dangerous narcotic to which the multitude is more or less, and permanently, addicted. He believed that they serve an unhealthy appetite, and therefore proposes that they should not be left for the regulation of their activities to the free market; rather, a monopoly should be established.

Most of the arts and professions in a state are of such a nature, that, while they promote the interests of the society, they are also useful or agreeable to some individuals; and in that case, the constant rule of the magistrate, except, perhaps, on the first introduction of any art, is, to leave the profession to itself, and trust its encouragement to those who reap the benefit of it. The artizans, finding their profits to rise by the favour of their customers, encrease, as much as possible, their skill and industry; and as matters are not disturbed by any injudicious tampering, the commodity is always sure to be at all times nearly proportioned to the demand.

But there are also some callings, which, though useful and even necessary in a state, bring no particular advantage or pleasure to any individual; and the supreme power is obliged to alter its conduct with regard to the retainers of those professions. It must give them public encouragement in order to their subsistence;

and it must provide against that negligence, to which they will naturally be subject, either by annexing peculiar honours to the profession, by establishing a long subordination of ranks and a strict dependence, or by some other expedient. The persons, employed in the finances, armies, fleets, and magistracy, are instances of this order of men.

It may naturally be thought, at first sight, that the ecclesiastics belong to the first class, and that their encouragement, as well as that of lawyers and physicians, may safely be entrusted to the liberality of individuals, who are attached to their doctrines, and who find benefit or consolation from their spiritual ministry and assistance. Their industry and vigilance will, no doubt, be whetted by such an additional motive; and their skill in the profession, as well as their address in governing the minds of the people, must receive daily encrease, from their encreasing practice study, and attention.

But if we consider the matter more closely, we shall find, that this interested diligence of the clergy is what every wise legislator will study to prevent; because in every religion, except the true, it is highly pernicious, and it has even a natural tendency to pervert the true, by infusing into it a strong mixture of superstition, folly, and delusion. Each ghostly practitioner, in order to render himself more precious and sacred in the eyes of his retainers, will inspire them with the most violent abhorrence of all other sects, and continually endeavour, by some novelty, to excite the languid devotion of his audience. No regard will be paid to truth, morals, or decency in the doctrines inculcated. Every tenet will be adopted that best suits the disorderly affections of the human frame. Customers will be drawn to each conventicle by new industry and address in practicing on the passions and credulity of the populace. And in the end, the civil magistrate will find, that he has dearly paid for his pretended frugality, in saving a fixed establishment for the priests; and that in reality the most decent and advantageous composition, which he can make with the spiritual guides, is to bribe their indolence, by assigning stated salaries to their profession, and rendering it superfluous for them to be farther active, than merely to prevent their flock from straying in quest of new pastures. And in this manner ecclesiastical establishments, though commonly they arose at first from religious views, prove in the end advantageous to the political interests of society.[32]

He proposes that the established church should be given a seemly, absorbing order of worship designed to sate and pacify, not to excite, the religious emotions of the populace. Any great attention to sermons is ill-advised, as the history of enthusiasm in England and Scotland shows. Speculations in theology, not being susceptible to proof or disproof by easy tests, delight the multitude immensely. They can allow their fancies to gambol at large, and can propound the most astounding theories and interpretations carelessly, for they know no reason to fear the cold shock of conclusive refutation which produces responsibility when more mundane questions are debated. The result is an imperious individualism, fierce and immoderate, totally devoid of scepticism; an individualism that threatens the peace not only by reason of the clash of rival sects, but by propagating its bigoted arrogance into all political debates. In addition, sermons are an invitation to the clerics to sow the people's minds with divisive, subversive thoughts, and to harangue them, and threaten them into action. Instead, priority should be given to rites and procedures, to formulae of adoration, and to spectacles.[33] The assumption behind a simple mode of worship, stripped of worldly operations and rich paraphernalia, is wrong: it makes success in worship, not the act of worshipping, the direct goal. Consequently, since rapturous apprehension of the divine presence is rare, and not to be commanded, the earnest worshipper when deprived of the comfort of a reliable, self-fulfilling ceremony, more often than not, is left uneasy and distraught. The result is that the minds and manners of the people are perverted. There is inculcated among them a dour, fierce disposition, a spirit hard, stubborn, solemn, gloomy, and intent, a frame of mind unconducive to agreeable conformity and the cheerful enjoyment of peace.[34]

He advises that Roman Catholicism, like enthusiastic Protestantism, is to be shunned. It gives the priests an independent public authority, or at least a claim to such authority, which can become a serious challenge to the allegiance due to the civil government, especially when the priests fail to be lukewarm. And it is an international organization with interests that are likely to be contrary to even the most pacific civil government.[35]

The Church of England, Hume seems to have felt more and more strongly, was almost the perfect model of an established church. When the essay, "Of Superstition and Enthusiasm," was first published in 1741, he already was distinguishing between priests and clergymen, but thought that the Church of England had not purged itself sufficiently of "popish superstition." By 1760, he no longer felt it necessary to explain that by "priests" he did not mean those "set apart *by the laws*, to the care of sacred matters, and to the conducting our public devotions with greater decency and order." [36] In 1770 he dropped the Church of England from his list of false religions. Presumably, he had come to think of the clergy of the Church of England as fostering neither superstition nor enthusiasm, but as filling the respectable office of clergyman. In the *History of England* he wrote:

Of all the European churches, which shook off the yoke of papal authority, no one proceeded with so much reason and moderation as the church of England; an advantage, which had been derived partly from the interposition of the civil magistrate in this innovation, partly from the gradual and slow steps, by which the reformation was conducted in that kingdom. Rage and animosity against the catholic religion was as little indulged as could be supposed in such a revolution: The fabric of the secular hierarchy was maintained entire: The ancient liturgy was preserved, so far as was thought consistent with the new principles: Many ceremonies, become venerable from age and preceding use, were retained: The splendor of the Romish worship, though removed, had at least given place to order and decency: The distinctive habits of the clergy, according to their different ranks, were continued: No innovation was admitted merely from spite and opposition to former usage: And the new religion, by mitigating the genius of the ancient superstition, and rendering it more compatible with the peace and interests of society, had preserved itself in that happy medium, which wise men have always sought, and which the people have so seldom been able to maintain.[37]

Hume's second recommendation is that diversity of religious belief be tolerated by the government as a matter of both discretion and principle. The notion that a peaceful state is incompatible with religious liberty is erroneous—this the United Provinces have proved [38]—and there are good reasons why the government should not endeavour to weed out nonconformity. In no place does he discuss the effect of this toleration on the working of his established church, but we may assume he would hold that, given a well-run, relaxed, state church, without compulsory attendance and obedience, there would be no great desire for alternatives.[39] In recounting the clash on the question of toleration in the Council between Bishop Gardiner and Cardinal Pole, during the reign of Queen Mary, a clash in which the politician, Gardiner, and the devout Pole took views opposite to what one might expect—"such is the prevalence of temper above system"—Hume sets forth the arguments for and against toleration.[40] The former he pronounces "entirely satisfactory." Gardiner's position was that since, contrary to the supposition of the advocates of liberty of conscience, the dictates of heaven can be distinguished with certainty from the fictions of overheated imaginations, it is the plain duty of every government to allow and encourage the practice and propagation of only pure, unadulterated truth. It may be that the heretics regained through persecution will be hypocrites, not genuine converts. But does not experience show that habits of hypocrisy tend to settle into reality? And will not the children, innocent of their parents' dissimulation, be likely to grow up in the true faith? Besides, the neutrality or inaction of the government, far from serving the political end of pacifying the sects by suggesting some appreciation for their viewpoints, only encourages them to hope for eventual complete partiality in their favour.

Cardinal Pole's rebuttal, as recounted by Hume, is composed of four points. Fierce zeal in theological questions should never be heeded, for far from being evidence of a deep, assured, solid faith, it is the best, or rather the worst, sign that the zealot himself is tormented by gnawing infidelity. Since he cannot stifle his own doubts and find peace in the truth, he strikes out blindly at those who objectify and confront him with his own doubts. Second, since all men who give any thought to religious questions cannot always have one and the same thought or set of thoughts, the only sure way to prevent diversity in religious beliefs is to destroy all curiosity, and all improvement in science and culture, which spring from curiosity, and in turn prompt curiosity. Again, a society from which all opposition has been purged will produce men of a delicate, infantile disposition, often submissive, but apt to explode in peevish rage at even the most reasonable restraint. And fourth, persecution almost always produces, not the promised disappearance of troublesome sects, but their growth. It bestows an importance on them in the minds of their present and potential members. It tempers the resolution of both the leaders and even wavering adherents. It sweeps all other thoughts from their minds, and concentrates all their attention in a hot, intense zeal.

This final point, that the way to prevent the partition of the state along religious lines is to display a studied, bored, cold indifference to internecine theological disputes, is one that impressed Hume greatly. He found, for example, that the progress of the Presbyterians in Scotland contrary to the law was "a disease dangerous and inveterate; and the government had tried every remedy, but the true one, to allay and correct it. An unlimited *toleration*, after sects have diffused themselves and are strongly rooted, is the only expedient, which can allay their fervour, and make the civil union acquire a superiority above religious distinctions. But as the operations of this regimen are commonly gradual, and at first imperceptible, vulgar politicians are apt, for that reason, to have recourse to more hasty and more dangerous remedies." [41] His stratagem, he notes, is rather new and surprising, and is still inadequately appreciated by many. Not until the late seventeenth century, he finds, did religious leaders in England begin to suspect that toleration of opponents might be bearable, even healthy: before then, all insisted that they themselves must have the benefit of a strictly enforced monopoly.[42] Political leaders, likewise, assumed that the way to be rid of religious parties was to stamp out all diversity. "But it was found by fatal experience, and after spilling an ocean of blood in those theological quarrels, that the evil was of a peculiar nature, and was both enflamed by violent remedies, and diffused itself more rapidly throughout the whole society. Hence, though late, arose the paradoxical principle and salutary practice of toleration." [43]

That Hume's advocacy of toleration is not based merely on a desire to maintain a quiet, prosperous civil society is suggested by his attitude to struggling, new religious groups. Montesquieu had argued that diffused and established nonconformist sects, which could be eradicated only at the cost of great trouble and disruption, should be tolerated, but that new innovators should be repressed. Hume comments that "it is very questionable, whether persecution can in any case be justifyed." [44] This comment, however, he does not explain.

When we examine his harsh, almost scandalous treatment of popular religious beliefs we may at first be astonished. What he has to say seems far less extreme, however, when we remember how smart antireligious thought and anticlericalism were deemed in the eighteenth century, and how far many of the most notable writers of that period went in their attacks. Hume took religion extremely seriously, as the *Dialogues* show, and was made uneasy by the blithe atheism he found in Paris; [45] his "moderate scepticism" made him wary of every kind of absolute dogmatism in matters of religion.

His entire treatment of contemporary religion is controlled by his attitude to revelation, which he puts aside, as above discussion. Thus he deprived himself of all save what could be learned through the natural understanding. And by the natural understanding he was led to "the religious hypothesis." Since he found that only a handful of men are capable of this philosophical view, he was driven to conclude that all popular religion must be idolatry. Moreover, like many other men of the Enlightenment, he was repelled by the disorders caused and aggravated by religious differences during the two previous centuries, and he was worried by the manifestations of popular religion that he found around him. It could be argued that the zeal with which he lays into popular religion springs from a religious sense deeply offended. Be that as it may, any institution made up of men, as Hume well knew, is bound to have bad as well as good aspects and results, and the higher the aspiration, the more certain and obvious will be the shortcomings. That Hume scores many telling blows at popular religion is evident, but that by reason of concentrating on the bad he gives a grievously distorted view is also evident.

What is most important for our analysis of his political theory is his belief that the masses are and will remain ignorant and idolatrous, and therefore will need an established church to reinforce their morality and to tame their spirits.

# XI

## THE PLOT OF TIME

Each generation criticises the unconscious assumptions
made by its parents.

A. N. Whitehead *

IT IS easy to suppose that one cause, possibly among three or
four, that made Hume shift his attention from philosophical to
historical writing was a growing awareness that greater acces-
sions of knowledge could be made by examining man's past than
by philosophizing. The evidence, however, will not sustain this
supposition. Indeed, the argument seems far stronger that
Hume's view of the past was basically negative: he dealt with
the past primarily either to show the progressive character of
his own policy proposals or to exorcise troublesome political
ghosts.

His concentration on the moral activities in which men manifest their nature freed him from major obstacles to the elaboration of a full-fledged theory of history. It led him to insist, in
contrast to Montesquieu, on the independence of the moral
sphere. The ways of life of different nations and of different
times result, he contends, from spiritual (mind) causes, not
from physical causes. He is ready to admit that geographical
and climatic factors exert an influence on men, but he finds incomprehensible the notion that human thoughts, activities, and
institutions are expressions of local circumstances. Moreover,
he is far more interested in the values, the knowledge, and the
techniques of whole societies than in the conduct of individual
men; for him, therefore, biography does not take the place of
history. At the same time, history for him was no mere rope
of sand, no flood of disconnected acts to be grouped according
to the years in which they were done, and recounted as annals,

* *Science and the Modern World* (New York, 1926), p. 36.

but was programmatic. But search as we may, in his writings we shall find no examination of history—no discussion of historical change, and of the course, direction, and patterns of change—in any way comparable with his treatment of epistemology, natural religion, or economics. Yet Hume was far too profound a thinker to have remained oblivious to these questions. Evidently he had concluded that "whereof one cannot speak, thereof one must be silent." [1] Nevertheless, he could could not write without employing certain presuppositions about the course and the importance of historical change, and we can endeavour to disinter those presuppositions.

The declared purpose of the *Treatise* is antihistorical. In the first book Hume's main task is to account for the knowledge we have about "the natural world," and this he seeks to do by contending that our beliefs arise from repeated instances of natural causation. Now, if we say that the physical world and the historical world differ in that the former exhibits constancy, while the latter involves genuine innovation, we are driven to conclude that his theory of the understanding either neglects or misrepresents the historical world. Besides, in the first and second books he is seeking to improve the moral sciences by introducing into them the method employed successfully in the physical sciences. Herein his presupposition is that human nature—both the understanding and the passions—always remains the same. A statement to that effect immediately prompts serious doubts in the reader's mind about the value of histories. Are the changes narrated in histories strictly superficial?

The early essay, "Of the Study of History," published in 1741, springs directly from the *Treatise*. According to the *Treatise*, there are two kinds of judgments: judgments of truth and judgments of value. The former, as we have seen, are based on intuition, remembrance, or imagination. Imagination, in turn, is of three kinds: fancying, the understanding of demonstrable systems, and the understanding of natural systems. Judgments of value are a matter of the feelings, and concern the goodness or badness of the man, poem, or artifact judged.

If, bearing this analysis in mind, we turn to "Of the Study of History," we are driven to conclude that for most people histories are the most edifying kind of reading. Intuition and remembrance concern immediate perception. Demonstrable systems are to be found in books on algebra and geometry. But all the rest of human nature is nurtured by histories. "The advantages found in history seem to be of three kinds, as it amuses the fancy, as it improves the understanding, and as it strengthens virtue." [2]

First, histories are more diverting than romances:

In reality, what more agreeable entertainment to the mind, than to be transported into the remotest ages of the world, and to observe human society, in its infancy, making the first faint essays towards the arts and sciences: To see the policy of government, and the civility of conversation refining by degrees, and every thing which is ornamental to human life advancing towards its perfection. To remark the rise, progress, declension, and final extinction of the most flourishing empires: The virtues, which contributed to their greatness, and the vices, which drew on their ruin. In short, to see all human race, from the beginning of time, pass, as it were, in review before us; appearing in their true colours, without any of those disguises, which, during their life-time, so much perplexed the judgment of the beholders.

Second, histories help us to acquire true beliefs about the past, the present, and the future:

History is not only a valuable part of knowledge, but opens the door to many other parts, and affords materials to most of the sciences. And indeed, if we consider the shortness of human life, and our limited knowledge, even of what passes in our own time, we must be sensible that we should be for ever children in understanding, were it not for this invention, which extends our experience to all past ages, and to the most distant nations; making them contribute as much to our improvement in wisdom, as if they had actually lain under our observation. A man acquainted with history may, in some respect, be said to have lived from the beginning of the world, and to have been making continual additions to his stock of knowledge in every century.[3]

And third, histories refine our sense of what is virtuous and what is vicious: poets stir the feelings too deeply, and philosophers hardly at all, but the "writers of history, as well as the readers, are sufficiently interested in the characters and events, to have a lively sentiment of blame or praise; and, at the same time, have no particular interest or concern to pervert their judgment." [4]

These recommendations seem to forecast a vast encyclopedia in which the general reader could learn the principles of human nature and those of the dependent moral sciences by studying historical cases. The implication is that the acts of one man or of men are so much the same from one time to another that stories about the past are of direct practical relevance to the present and the future. Histories are laboratory reports, records of past experiments and findings, and are directly applicable to the reader and his circumstances.

By attempting to introduce the experimental method into the moral sciences, Hume implies that whatever changes take place in the moral (or historical) sphere are negligible. This view, however, is one which he himself found inapplicable, and even in the *Treatise* we find him shifting to another view, one that takes cognizance of important changes in men's beliefs and values. In "Of Morals," where he is expounding his own theory of the basis of moral standards, Hume, like many moral and political philosophers before him, gives not simply a logical, but a chronological, account of their origin. He has resort, with caveats, to the literary device of an original State of Nature from which men progress to civil society. Since he insists that the civil virtues are not innate, but come to be known and put into operation only through experience, we may say that even in the *Treatise* he gives the rudiments of a theory of history: man's past has been progressive, and this progress has come about chiefly as a result of the challenges involved in the relations among men as producers and consumers of economic goods. He integrates this account with the assumed constancy of human nature by means of the idea of *development*. The potentialities of human nature always are the same, but in the beginning they are not realized, so that civilization may be described as the development of man's attributes. It is quite probable—notice the warnings about believing in a State of Nature—that he did not intend that this account of civilization was to be taken seriously. His aim in "Of Morals" was to show that the virtues, especially the civil virtues, could spring from human nature and man's circumstances, and this development could be shown most easily by providing a fictitious historical account.

But in the *Political Discourses,* published in 1752, he takes civilization or development very seriously, and explains the phases and dynamics of this change. By then his thinking had advanced sufficiently for him to regard the economy as a distinguishable sphere with both its own short-run process and its own process of historical growth. His practical purpose in the *Discourses* was to urge the promotion of national and international commerce. As a basis for his argument, he includes in the various essays sketchy accounts—as if all this were common knowledge—of past civilization. The economic factors contributing to the advance are analyzed extensively, and the process is broken down into three great stages, each higher than its predecessor: first, that of fishing and hunting, second, that of agriculture, and third, that of commerce, and the civil virtues and the commercial civil society in which those virtues find their fullest embodiment are advocated as prerequisites of human excellence. Human needs, chiefly economic needs, are treated by him as the cause for the adoption of a more and more extensive division of labour, which, in turn, entails new social and political arrangements. What we have here, we must notice, is a "speculative history," not a factual history of civilization; in it, the logical steps in man's moral advance, as conceived by Hume, are treated as chronological steps. He does not propose that the realization of civility in any or every country or continent followed this schema exactly; yet, for him, this is the fundamental pattern, of which whatever happens in fact is merely a variation. Again and again throughout the *History of England* he judges the standards of an era by bringing the important men, statutes, and institutions of that era to be measured against the standards provided by his speculative history of civilization.

In contrast with this linear view we have the cyclical theory set forth in "Of the Rise and Progress of Arts and Sciences" (1742) and *The Natural History of Religion* (1757). These are important pieces because both contain theories of change that Hume intended to be taken seriously, and neither can be dismissed as patently polemical. Excellence in the arts and sciences, he submits, might seem so much a matter of particular causes, i.e., of chance, that no general explanation of rises and falls in these fields can be given. But this is not so, for while particular causes give the man of genius his ability to express or to discover, what he expresses or discovers is what has been teasing or haunting the mind of that people in whose midst he appears.

*There is a God within us*, says OVID, *who breathes that divine fire, by which we are animated.* Poets, in all ages, have advanced this claim to inspiration. There is not, however, any thing supernatural in the case. Their fire is not kindled from heaven. It only runs along the earth; is caught from one breast to another; and burns brightest, where the materials are best prepared, and most happily disposed. The question, therefore, concerning the rise and progress of the arts and sciences, is not altogether a question concerning the taste, genius, and spirit of a few, but concerning those of a whole people; and may, therefore, be accounted for, in some measure, by general causes and principles.[5]

The rise and fall of the arts and sciences, in short, can be explained in terms of human nature and men's circumstances.

Here, he says almost nothing about economic causes—in this respect the essay contrasts remarkably with the *Political Discourses*—but concentrates chiefly, as does Plato in explaining the deterioration of a *polis*, on the political and cultural factors that influence the inspiration and ambition of men of genius. The insecurity that prevails in arbitrary monarchies, in contrast to republics, he finds, stifles artistic and scientific achievement. Small, independent states, especially those in close proximity to one another, are likely to be cultural hotbeds, for not only do the citizens of the several states naturally fall into fruitful competition and mutual emulation, but both the sway of potentates and the dominance of old styles and old schools of thought are undermined. Eventually, he finds, a people's will to achieve becomes exhausted, and their art and science deteriorate. When, he writes, *"the arts and sciences come to perfection in any state, from that moment they naturally, or rather necessarily decline, and seldom or never revive in that nation, where they formerly flourished."* [6] Once their elders have created great works and systems, the young men, sensitive of their own inferiority and deprived of the spur of applause, cease to strain for excellence, and consequently their talents, however great, remain undeveloped. "In short, the arts and sciences, like some plants, require a fresh soil; and however rich the land may be, and however you may recruit it by art or care, it will never, when once exhausted, produce any thing that is perfect or finished in the kind." [7]

The potentialities of the human mind remain the same, but changes in morale, brought on by changes in political arrangements and by the maturation of the arts and sciences themselves, cause both rises and subsequent declines in the attainments of nations and cultures. Here we have almost a cyclical theory of history. The declines, of course, are necessary, for they are essential parts of the process. The outbursts, on the other hand, are not inevitable, but depend on the fortuitous constellation of causes.[8] In the part of the *History of England* published in 1762, we find a brief summary of the same argument:

But there is a point of depression, as well as of exaltation, from which human affairs naturally return in a contrary direction, and beyond which they seldom pass either in their advancement or decline. The period, in which the people of Christendom were the lowest sunk in ignorance, and consequently in disorders of every kind, may justly be fixed at the eleventh century, about the age of William the Conqueror; and from that aera, the sun of science, beginning to re-ascend, threw out many gleams of light, which preceded the full morning, when letters were revived in the fifteenth century.[9]

In *The Natural History of Religion* we find a fully articulated theory of recurrence. Once men's minds have become infested by religious beliefs, by their own dialectic those beliefs swing from polytheism to monotheism and back, over and over again, incessantly. The many deities are praised more and more extravagantly by their devotees. In this process, which inevitably entails comparison, many gods and goddesses cease to be distinct personalities, and are merged together until only a few deities remain, and finally, only one, omnipotent god remains. This god, by reason of its majesty and indistinct character, is useless, and a division of labour is begun, so that before long there are various deities and soon, many. Once gods and goddesses have become highly specialized in function and place, they no longer are adequate objects of worship, so the process of "flux and reflux" continues.

The question that rises when we consider these different works is whether Hume regarded historical change as cyclical or linear. Is time repetitious, so that the periods of progress are merely the upswing phase of a cycle? Or are the changes, including any cyclical changes, included as scenes or acts in a great drama that advances from a beginning to an end?

Plato's statement in the *Timaeus*, that time is the moving image of eternity, might be taken as a basic theorem of Greek thinking about social, political, and intellectual change. Since Nature or the World, according to a Greek metaphysical tradition, is the Absolute or the One, beyond which there is nothing, Nature is never changed by an external cause, and therefore is eternal. There are changes within Nature, all the result of natural causes, and the great metaphysical problem is to explain the relation between the One and the Many, the relation between Nature and its many aspects. This concept of variety within unity is the presupposition of the cyclical theory of history, according to which change is viewed as repetitious. Change is not denied, but it brings in nothing genuinely new, only the old; internally, Nature lacks changelessness, but its changeability resembles changelessness in that nothing genuinely new emerges. This is the theory of political change behind Plato's cycle of constitutions. Christian thought breaks radically with this strain of Greek metaphysics by denying the substantiality of Nature. In Christian theology, God, who alone is substantial, created the World out of nothing; because the World is not the One, the Independent, it is liable to great alteration, by both God and man, so that before the End it will not be as it was in the Beginning. It is their belief in the possibility of novelty that has led Christians to conceive of history as resembling a line or a drama, with a beginning, a middle, and an end. Clearly, men's thoughts and acts, and the histories in which these are recorded, take on a new, higher status when they are treated as part of the cumulative drama of human destiny.

In a sense, modern rationalism, against which Hume was protesting, was a revival of Greek metaphysics, and because it emphasized the importance of reason, demonstration, and laws of nature, not of providence and unique historical facts, it was fundamentally antihistorical. Rationalism reverted to the idea that the world is eternal and immutable. This thought Hume found beyond demonstration, and he worked out his own theory to explain how men can have knowledge of a *created* universe. But if Hume is not anti-Christian, in that he does not assert that the universe is substantial, he stops far short of a Christian philosophy of history because his "moderate scepticism" is insufficiently sceptical. He is prepared to entertain a belief in the constancy of nature, a belief contrary to the implications of the doctrines concerning the Creation, Providence, and the End, which for the Christian are the framework of human drama: the beginning, the intervening, and the end of time. Given this belief, we would assume that he either would ignore the fact of important change or would reconcile changelessness and change by resort to a theory of cycles. And as we have seen, he does both these things.

But we have seen, too, in "Of Morals," the *Political Discourses,* and the *History of England,* he also treats change as linear progression. This view, of course, is not necessarily contrary to the other: the linear process could be subsumed as the upswing of a cycle. Still, the thought persists that Hume's study of the past had led him to presuppose that a unique, vast change in men's morals and science had taken place, and that this belief, not the weak logical thought of inclusive cycles, was the foundation of his historical writing.

Perhaps we may say without too much exaggeration that, like most of us, Hume had conflicting ideas. On the one hand, he believed in nature, a repetitious, self-contained causal continuum, and, on the other, he believed in historical change, a process of genuine innovation. He was able to entertain these two ideas—for example, to believe in the changelessness of human nature and at the same time to believe in civilization—in part because of his extensive reliance on the idea of development. Human nature, the implied argument runs, never changes, but initially it is *in potentia*, enveloped, so that civilization may be described as the development of man's attributes. This, however, is an idea that Hume has no right to use because for him the only evidence of the nature of man is the acts of men, i.e., the only knowable human nature is historical human nature. In other words, if the moral (or historical) sphere is highly autonomous, and if human nature is constant, while it may be easy to show the motives behind the conduct of individual public figures, it is hard to explain the great differences between cultures or the transformations that take place within cultures. An epistemologist as strict and parsimonious as Hume must not be allowed the luxury of knowing both a noumenological, essential, unchanging human nature and a phenomonological human nature. We can only conclude that Hume's thinking about historical change and historical knowledge is highly unsatisfactory: the basic aspiration of the *Treatise* makes important change hard to accommodate; the arguments for recurrence in "Of the Rise and Progress of Arts and Sciences" and *The Natural History of Religion* are compatible with this theory, although the scope of the changes they admit seem greater than parts of the *Treatise* would have led us to expect. In his *Political Discourses,* wherein he is concerned to advance civility, either he ignores the decline phase of the civilization-barbarization cycle for polemical reasons, or supplants the cyclical view by a linear view. In addition, in none of these works, not even in the *Discourses,* does he display the true historian's love for the past.

The same must be said of the *History of England,* a work which, like the *Discourses,* was written to teach lessons directly relevant to contemporary politics. No reader can complain that in writing it Hume did not strive to entertain, or that he fails to bring out what he regards as the vices and virtues of the men and women about whom he writes. Both these aspects, however, are subordinate to his desire to impart to his readers a sound understanding of contemporary British politics and governance. The *History* is an occasional work; it was written primarily to exorcise irrational hostility between the Whigs and the Tories. It was primarily a tract for the times: that it has come to be considered a minor historiographical milestone, worthy to be examined briefly in histories of history, is a tribute not to Hume's intentions, but to the patient scholarship, judgment, wit, and stylistic finesse displayed throughout the work. He would have both parties see that their fixation on the past is unfounded, and that it should be given up because it might erode seriously the respect of the vulgar for the present arrangement of economic goods and authority. In the *History* he undertook, first, to dispel the myth of the "ancient constitution" by showing that it had never existed either at the dawn of time or in Tudor or pre-Tudor times. Second, he sought to reduce the animus between the parties by showing both that their predecessors were not to be judged by the standards suitable to the middle of the eighteenth century, but rather were to be regarded as members of two parties, each natural enough under the mixed constitution, between which, given the misalignment of that constitution, conflict had been almost inevitable. And third, he tried to make each party see that, because of the mixed, and therefore, somewhat uncertain, constitution, the other had a part to play in contemporary politics,

and that each should play its part with sedate restraint so as
not to endanger that fabric of vulgar opinion of which the
constitution was chiefly composed. The *History*, in an important sense, is antihistorical. The great stimulus to English
historians, especially in the seventeenth century, had been the
desire to trace up "privilege" or "prerogative" to the "ancient
constitution." By demonstrating the invalidity of such a mode
of argument, Hume annihilates much of the old justification for
studying the past. It is notable that when he had finished his
essentially negative task, he did not undertake another historical work.

The *History* is a political history, not a history of civilization in England. Given his purpose, Hume naturally concentrates his attention on kings, politicians, and political parties.
Only occasionally does he turn aside from public transactions
to examine briefly the deeper current of change; yet it is clear
that he thinks of the political struggles in England in large
part as a manifestation of more fundamental changes: the
decline of an early nomadic, martial way of life, the Norman
attempt to control the conquered country by means of a centralized feudalism and the decline of that system, the rise of
towns, the advance of commerce, new manners, new science, and
a new rank of men. In view of its pragmatic nature, it is not
surprising that he wrote the *History* backwards, treating first
the Stuarts, then the Tudors, and finally the earlier ages. For
Hume the accession of Henry VII marked the beginning in
England of the third phase of civilization. Prior to that date,
politics had been a mere confused tussle of barons and kings,
a chaos harmonious with the dark, primitive condition in which
men then lived.[10] It seems clear that he would not have bothered
to deal with those distasteful centuries if he had not found it
necessary to dispel the myth of the "ancient constitution" and
to cope with the related controversial questions concerning the
origin of the House of Commons, the nature of William's accession, and the popular or feudal nature of Magna Charta. His
treatment of the history of England is controlled by his interest
in promoting domestic peace and cautious progress.

"We wished," wrote Edmund Burke, in his *Reflections on the Revolution in France*, "at the period of the Revolution [of 1688], and do now wish, to derive all we possess as *an inheritance from our forefathers*. Upon that body and stock of inheritance we have taken care not to inoculate any cyon alien to the nature of the original plant. All the reformations we have hitherto made, have proceeded upon the principle of reference to antiquity; and I hope, nay I am persuaded, that all those which possibly may be made hereafter, will be carefully formed upon analogical precedent, authority and example." When English thought on law, politics, and the constitution is examined, it is discovered, he reports, that for generations the controlling, ultimate maxim is the sanctity of tradition.

Our oldest reformation is that of Magna Charta. You will see that Sir Edward Coke, that great oracle of our law, and indeed all the great men who follow him, to Blackstone, are industrious to prove the pedigree of our liberties. They endeavour to prove, that the antient charter, the Magna Charta of King John, was connected with another positive charter from Henry I, and that both the one and the other were nothing more than a re-affirmation of the still more antient standing law of the kingdom. In the matter of fact, for the greater part, these authors appear to be in the right; perhaps not always; but if the lawyers mistake in some particulars, it proves my position still the more strongly; because it demonstrates the powerful prepossession towards antiquity, with which the minds of all our lawyers and legislators, and of all the people whom they wish to influence, have been always filled; and the stationary policy of this kingdom in considering their most sacred rights and franchises as an inheritance.

It is not surprising that a man who wrote so eloquently in favour of traditionalism should have been regarded by Lord Acton as the initiator of the modern historical renaissance.[11]

Hume, too, saw the importance of tradition in British legal and political thought; otherwise, his historical labours would have been unnecessary. Unlike Burke, however, he found that scholars like Spelman and Brady had demonstrated how false was the account transmitted by the great popular oracles and that many of the old constitutional doctrines could be made relevant to modern times only by an unstinting distortion of truth. The past was important—not the remote past of legal fiction, but the immediate past—because most men live chiefly by custom.

Hume's achievements in both speculative and factual history are considerable; but he did not love the past as a retreat from an uncongenial present, neither did he glorify the past, or even justify it to diminish the zeal for economic, social, and political change. He uses history—and this pragmatic intention probably explains the absence of a unified, elaborated theory of history—to promote change. He believed that great advances in thought, in the arts and sciences, and in laws and institutions had been made in Britain and Europe during the previous two centuries. He believed that additional advances still could be made, and he lent his pen to the cause of progress.

# XII

## CIVIL REFORM

*Le mieux est l'ennemi du bien.*
Voltaire, *Dictionnaire philosophique*

It is from habit, and only from habit, that law derives
the validity which secures obedience. But habit can be
created only by the passage of time.
Aristotle, *Politics* 1269a

THE scope and profundity of Hume's thought are excep-
tional; yet when we try to define his position in the history of
modern political philosophy, it seems fair—as fair as such gen-
eralizations ever are—to say that he was a typical eighteenth-
century liberal.

He distinguishes, as we have seen, between family, friendship, and humanity, on the one hand, and the civil relationships,
society and state, on the other. The former are the direct results
of the feelings men have for others, and therefore they can be
called "natural." The latter are artificial: when men are seeking
scarce economic goods the natural relation among them is competition, and society and state are the framework within which
this competition can go on with results most satisfactory for all.
In this chapter, in which we are dealing with Hume as a reformer, our attention will be concentrated on the civil relationships. Since human nature, which is expressed directly in
the family, friendship, and in acts of humanity, remains quite
constant, the noncivil relationships are not susceptible to much
alteration.

From the time of the Sophists the proper civil relationships
among men have been discussed again and again by political philosophers in terms of artifice and nature, and although these
terms have been given a multitude of different meanings—witness Hume's own distinction just referred to—the contrast is

useful still.[1] There are, we may say, two basic (and extreme) ways of viewing these relationships; first, as properly an artificial order, and, second, as properly a natural order. (Few, if any, of the theorists who make this distinction go to either extreme). The former view—emphasizing artifice—presents the relationships as maintained immediately by men, that is, either, first, by one man (or a group of men) deliberately or, second, by the many acting under the influence of accumulated customs and prejudices. It emphasizes, not spontaneous individual conduct, but the limits that must be placed on such conduct if a war of all against all is not to erupt. In contrast, in the latter view—emphasizing nature—the focus is on the efforts of individuals to obtain whatever each deems good; the consequent competition among individuals is extolled; and the emergence without the aid of human laws of a generally good result from this selfish competition is asserted.

The difference between the two kinds of artificial regulation is important. One insists on the need for laws made by a human ruler, i.e., written laws, but does not necessarily prescribe the specific content of those laws. It does not necessarily say what relationships among men—what order of public life—are to be commanded and enforced by the government. But the second theory of artifice, that of "unwritten law," does prescribe the proper relationships for any time, to a great extent. Its basic maxim is that men are to acquire their different places (and rights and duties), not by competition, but by customary rules of inheritance; consequently, the good social and political order is the one received from the past.

Those who contend that Nature should rule, like the proponents of customary law, tell us what the proper social and political relationships for any moment are: there ought to be a free competition, they contend, and each man ought to find his station through competition. This theory emphasizes social mobility. It emphasizes careers for the talented.

These theories—the second theory of artifice and the theory emphasizing nature—which we have stated in their extreme, unmitigated forms, one emphasizing inheritance and the other, individual ability, differ also in two other respects: first, in the ways by which they propose that men may acquire knowledge about the order to be promoted at any time and, second, in their concepts of social change. The advocates of competition are not committed to any particular ranking of specific men and families; rather, they see competition as the best process by which men are to come to the high or low places for which they are fitted. Accordingly, since they are advocating something constantly, not merely temporarily, valid, "the natural process," they say that their theory is scientifically or philosophically valid. It can be known by "reasoning" and without resort to history. Moreover, in a period when the natural process is ignored seriously—when men are corralled into estates, when the transfer of land is prohibited by entail, when mercantilism distorts trade, etc.—they are likely to demand the speedy abolition of such perversions. Once Nature is allowed to rule, they become, of course, opponents of contrived changes. On the other hand, the protagonists of inheritance are committed to the continuation to a high degree of a particular order, namely, the old order. They defend it on the ground that it has passed the test of time; it has worked. A custom, wrote Sir John Davies, "doth never become a Law to bind the people, untill it hath been tried and approved time out of mind, during all which time there did thereby arise no inconvenience: for if it had been found inconvenient at any time, it had been used no longer, but had been interrupted, and consequently it had lost the virtue and force of a Law." [2] They are empiricists: for them endurance is the warrant of the old; similarly, such piecemeal alterations as seem desirable are to be worked out by cautious, tentative trials. Inevitably, social change will be slow.

Just as the proponents of custom rarely have excluded entirely the promotion of the able, the proponents of "the rule of nature" seldom have proposed the survival of the fittest, i.e., that competition should be total. They have desired the elevation of men of ability and virtue within the social and political order and have seen competition as assuring this, but they certainly have not wished to see all order dissolved into fierce, chaotic struggle. In short, almost always they propose to supplement nature with a framework of artifice.

When we think of the debate during the eighteenth century between the proponents of competition and the proponents of custom (those who would have public policy incline to one instead of the other), we often use the terms, "Liberals" and "Conservatives." [3] These terms seem as useful as any, despite obvious disadvantages: few men of that century would have known our meanings of the terms, and we ourselves, now that we have undergone various new liberalisms and various new conservativisms, and have endured the tussles of political parties that call themselves, not necessarily accurately, liberal and conservative (or in some countries, Liberal and Conservative), probably find that they do not mean exactly the same for each of us.[4]

Edmund Burke is perhaps the most outspoken exponent of conservative thought in eighteenth-century Britain. When he looks at the social and political order in Britain or in France, he sees first, not the individual, but a whole "People." For him, this relationship, that by which men are related as a "People," is the cardinal one; and for him, this relationship is a complicated hierarchy of unequal players, at any moment the end product of inheritance. To the maintenance of this great historic relationship, the People, all public policy, both economic and political, should be directed.

In contrast, Hume in his analysis of the structure of the social and political order is antihistorical. Concerned as he is to advance the study of moral subjects by examining human nature, he looks at the whole human scene from the other side: he sees the individual first. Accordingly, it is not surprising that he distinguishes between those relationships that individuals enter because of their inherent value and the civil relationships, society and state, which are merely useful. Moreover, since for Hume, unlike Thomas Hobbes, the usefulness of society and state is chiefly economic, the process and institutions of the former are primary. The first rule of public life is that society (the economy) ought to be allowed to function as fully and as efficiently as possible; it follows, therefore, that no government that either fails to promote the economic process or interferes with the proper activities of the individual can be called a genuine government. When we examine Hume's view of the civil sphere, it becomes clear that he presupposed that competition is the basic process of this sphere. Because he finds that uncontrolled competition frustrates itself, he sets forth the principles of justice, principles entailing three institutions, property, trade, and contract, by which competition can be rendered orderly. And since these institutions probably will not be respected when competition becomes keen, governments are necessary to buttress artifice (justice) with further artifice (human laws). The principles of justice and governance constitute the legal framework within which he would allow competition to fructify. He believed that competition ought not to be left uncontrolled, but at the same time he would have it regulated only in ways, and to the extent, that would permit it to be most fruitful. His theory combines nature (competition) and artifice, but because artifice is to supplement nature, the proper content of the human laws is fixed neither by custom nor by the whim of the government; rather, the content is implied by the natural process which those laws are to supplement.

It might be assumed that, given this beginning, Hume would have proposed a thorough reformation of the existing society and state. It even might be thought that he would have urged the creation of a single system of free, world-wide commerce, based on a world-wide division of labour; second, that he would have advocated the replacement of the old governments by a single world government, or, if one government would have been overworked, by a system of regional governments, each with a jurisdiction scientifically designed, each located conveniently, like a chain of highway service stations; and third, that he would have insisted that this government (or each of these governments) should have the ideally best form of constitution. Such proposals would have been consistent with his analysis of society as a system of relations among owners, traders, and contractors, a system in which the greatest supply of goods would be produced by the natural (world-wide) division of labour and the natural (world-wide) flow of commerce, and it would have been consistent with his analysis of the essential work of government as the enforcement of the rights necessary for fruitful competition. But, although Hume does recommend some very important reforms, he stops far short of anything so unhistorical and rationalistic.

If the principles of justice and governance, which remain the same always, are to be followed, their validity must first become known generally. They can be known in two ways. First, the causal connection between acts of justice and governance and their good results can be traced, so that acts of justice and governance, which otherwise might seem a bother, or even bad, seem good. They are found good because it is believed that they will lead to certain good results. In short, they are found good because of their usefulness. In this case, the obligation to observe the principles is simply "rational." Second, through the mechanism of sympathy men feel the pleasure others feel, and the pain they feel, when their expectations are fulfilled or disappointed, so that without relying on their direct experience, and without tracing the connection between acts and their effects, they come to know, regardless of their private interests, that some acts are morally good, and that others are morally bad. The former they feel obliged to do; the latter they feel obliged to avoid. This obligation is "moral."

It follows from Hume's theory that men may be drawn to somewhat divergent courses of conduct by these two different kinds of obligation. The relation between rational obligation and moral obligation in the civil sphere can be summed up by three points. First, in this area moral duties which are not also generally useful to some degree are impossible, for it is the usefulness of justice and governance that gives rise to the moral virtues of the just man and of the good ruler and subject. Second, conformity to the economic and political standards of a civil society in which the principles of justice and governance are not realized perfectly can be morally obligatory; indeed, since no perfect society or state exists, all moral civil obligations known to us are of this kind. The more civilized men become, the more their economic and political systems will conform to the principles of civility, but at every phase in the process of civilization, even at the earliest, when justice is observed only slightly, and even less attention is given to good governance, men will feel some moral obligation, and so have moral duties. Third, there is an obligation to realize the principles of civility to higher and higher degrees, but this is a rational obligation, not a moral obligation. Moral obligation comes into existence only as a result of expectation, and this, in turn, is an effect of the past. The sense of moral obligation is a cause of many specific (future) acts, but the feeling of moral obligation and the content of moral duty are products of experience. The sense of moral obligation cannot introduce new and higher moral standards.

When we turn to the question of civil reformation, this difference between the two ways of knowing the principles of civility takes on vast importance. For Hume, a proposal that an ideal civil society be established would have to be accompanied by a demonstration that all the participants therein would be self-conscious individuals, that is, men who understand the nature of beliefs and who, consequently, refuse to act on the basis of any belief falling short of proof or high probability. At this point, the difference Hume mentions between "men capable of true principles" and "the vulgar" becomes relevant.

He finds, we have seen, that men fall into various kinds of groups: the nobles and the people, soldiers and civilians, priests and laity, traders and the landed, and so forth. But most important for him, perhaps because he is a philosopher, is the difference between men capable of true principles and the vulgar. The former can distinguish between the several kinds of knowing.[5] They comprehend what belief is, and can employ the rules by which legitimate beliefs are distinguishable from fancies. They can trace the causal connection between justice and governance, on the one hand, and peace and prosperity, on the other, and therefore can know that justice and governance are usefully good. Quite apart from moral obligation, they feel obliged to support civility. The vulgar, in contrast, although they know in the several ways, are incapable of being scrupulous in distinguishing among those ways. They do not test their beliefs against rules based on the nature of belief, so that although many of their beliefs are valid, many are not, or are only partly so. They have undergone civilization, and have learned to live by the principles of civility to some extent; yet they cannot state those principles or explain their basis. They know the principles only in terms of morality. They, in short, are not conscious of the nature of knowing; nor are they self-conscious.

We have seen that it is because he thinks that the vulgar cannot distinguish between true and false beliefs that Hume finds that they tend to run either to superstition or to enthusiasm in their religion. Wise governors, we have been told, will establish procedures by which those religious passions that are dangerous to the civil order can be grounded and dissipated.

The vulgar, or more exactly, those just above the very lowest rank of men, who do little or no thinking whatsoever, because they cannot distinguish between true and false belief are liable to think in terms of ideologies. The attainment of true principles is beyond them; therefore, they fly to simple, impractical theories such as divine right or popular sovereignty.

The vulgar often act on prejudices. No man brought up in a cold climate, however unobservant, would ever expect to be warmed by ice. Nevertheless, that same man, after talking with two lugubrious men from Dublin, may jump to the conclusion that all Irishmen are lugubrious. He forms his judgment of Irishmen before he has had experience with an adequate sample. Cautious, careful men, men of moderate scepticism, consciously make an effort to reserve judgment until they know well what they are talking about.[6]

It may be desirable at this point to observe that although Hume never tries to put down a concise definition of "the vulgar," and, indeed, assumes that his readers need no extensive description, it is obvious that this rank is not very exclusive.[7]

It embraces the vast bulk of the populace. Clearly, it includes many errant divines and philosophers, such as Bishop Warburton and "that bigotted silly Fellow, Beattie." [8] It takes in nearly all Englishmen. The truth is that the separation made by a philosopher such as Hume between cogitative men and the others, inevitably, is never final. Some men may think accurately on some questions; but not so on others. Moreover, the class of cogitative men tends to narrow down until it includes only the writer and his readers. It becomes even smaller when the writer seeks readers among the salon philosophers and "the conversible literate." Ultimately, it contains only the writer and those few who already have read and understood his works. In addition, even the writer and those who learn his lessons are not, inevitably, sufficiently sceptical. When their own short-term interest is not involved, or is not strong, they, unlike the vulgar, will be moved by rational obligation. But when they are deeply interested in gaining a good immediately, rational obligation is likely to prove ineffectual, and, since they understand the genesis of moral obligation, it may influence them less than it does the vulgar. The separation between the cogitative men and the vulgar, in short, is never exact. Nevertheless, this does not mean that we cannot distinguish between the two kinds of thinking, and find that some men are moved more by one kind than by the other.

The principles of civility, we have seen, came to be applied in the past to a large extent because of the insight of neutral observers who required respect for those principles until civil behaviour had become habitual. This is done by parents or chiefs where or when there is no government. Where there is a government, the work of parents and other leaders is taken up to some extent by the rulers. The man who knows the entire set of principles of civility, and knows them as useful, will feel a rational obligation to propose that they be put into operation completely. But he must take into account the existence of the vulgar, and once he has done so he will see that the rational course of action is not what previously he had thought it was.

What he will feel obliged to do because he wishes the greatest prosperity will be different thereafter.

The civilization of men is the process by which they have acquired beliefs about what economic and political conduct is good and bad. Civilization is not something that men have done to themselves; rather, they became civilized by becoming experienced. It is through experience, mainly, bitter experience, that they have acquired their moral beliefs. They were backed into civility. Now, although some men think through the principles of civility, just as some think through the principles of physical nature, it is through the moral sense that most men find justice and governance good. They simply accept their moral judgments, and act according to them. They act in their economic and political affairs very much as they behave in the physical universe. The experienced man, even though he is not a physical philosopher, normally avoids colliding with stoves, stepping into large, dark puddles, and standing near precipices. He has learned what to do and what not to do. Similarly, the highly experienced man normally condemns injustice and misgovernance without the benefit of dissertations from the pens of moral philosophers. In each case, experience has established strong, valid beliefs, and it may be quite as difficult for an ordinary civilized man to bring himself to steal or to revolt as to comport himself without trepidation on a towering height.

But there is an important difference between beliefs about correct behaviour in relation to the physical universe and beliefs about correct conduct in economic and political affairs. Whereas the physical universe does not depend on the opinions of men for its existence, every society and every state does. The principles of justice and governance, insofar as they are embodied in any existing political order, will work, no matter who plays each of the several roles; therefore, in terms of the order, men can be referred to as "individuals." But the men who exist are never mere individuals; rather, they are particular men. If there is to be a working economic and political system, the several roles have to be filled by those particular men; and assuming that all perform reasonably well, although who plays what role makes no appreciable difference in the successful operation of the system, his role—whether as a king, a subject, the owner of this large, fertile field, the owner of that large, stony hill—does makes a difference to each man involved. The principles are the rules of the game. They state the rights of those who play in each different position. But the beginning and the continuation of the game require presupposition or opinion: let Andrew, Robert, and Duncan be the players in each of the positions, and let each have the rights appropriate to his position. Unless this basic, casting presupposition is made there will be rules for a game, but there will be no players, no rights, and, therefore, no game. An economic and political system is founded on presupposition, not on prior right. This does not mean that an economic and political system based on the principles of civility is arbitrary in its form and processes. The principles always are the same, for the way of the greatest utility always is the same, but who will play the particular, different roles is a question not answerable by logic.

Those who know full well that the economic and political orders are good because useful—if indeed there are such men— would be willing to recast the game if the present one were to stop. They would see the need to assign rights and to begin again. In contrast, those who know the principles of civility only as moral beliefs could not possibly begin again deliberately. They might continue to believe that the rights of owners and the rights of rulers ought to be respected, but would find nobody with such rights. Since they would not know the (useful) good of rights, they would not be able to start civil society again by a deliberate act of presupposition. That the vulgar should be helpless if divorced from the present arrangement of possessions and power is inevitable, and it poses a danger to which all reformers should be closely attentive.

It is no accident that in selecting the factual conditions which should be considered when rights to things are to be assigned, the goal Hume set for himself was to discover the assignment that would be least likely to cause protest and objection. The more perfectly the legal relations between men and goods follow the natural association tendencies of the human mind, the better is the distribution of goods. Any gap between these two serves only to reveal the truth that all rights to goods have their origin in opinion. Similarly, it is no accident that in selecting the considerations to be examined when rights to govern are to be assigned, Hume tries to find the most acceptable governor(s).[9] Again and again he reiterates that authority rests finally on opinion.

We may say that as a scientist, Hume feels obliged to promote the full realization of the ideal civil society. How is this obligation to reform both society and state modified by his view that most men are not scientists?

In the case of the principles of justice, the answer is, very little. He seems to have thought that no dangerous shock whatsoever would have been given to popular morality by the elimination of restraints on domestic and foreign trade, and he is prepared to denounce such restraints vigorously. And once the framework of justice has been established, the operation of the economy can be left to the enterprise of individuals. At times, when vast holdings fall into the hands of vicious men, especially misers and laggards, the enlightened man may feel tempted to intervene, but he will see that far, far more would be lost than gained by attempting to transfer such goods to more virtuous men. On the one hand, the success or failure of the economic system does not depend on the felicitous allocation of goods in each instance. On the other, any interference would discover the nature of rights to goods. Justice is blind, and the only way to prevent subjective judgment from wrecking society is to follow the rules of justice.

But when we turn to the principles of governance we come to a far more complex matter. The essential task of governments is to enforce justice. The state is inferior to the economic order: justice is good because it is the means by which competition is made fruitful, but the state, in turn, is a means to justice. Accordingly, any government which cannot or does not do its work, we might think, is liable to be discharged and replaced. But we must not move too fast.

First, are not some governments disqualified by their forms? It is Hume's view that in modern times, when civilized standards prevail, a government of any form can govern well, but that absolute monarchies and mixed governments still have disadvantages, and, consequently, are less likely to govern well over a long period than are well-contrived commonwealths. Yet it is the present government, whatever its form, that has the right to govern, in the opinion of the vulgar. Ordinarily they believe, fortunately, that it would be morally wrong to overthrow that government. Consequently, there always is a *prima facie* rational argument in favour of that ruler or set of rulers whose access to office is most expected. Constitutional changes can be made, often should be made, but such changes should be brought about by such gentle, imperceptible alterations and innovations as will not show that the constitution ultimately is a matter, not of right, but of opinion.

Second, should *national* or *dynastic* governments imposed on the present by the past, governments whose jurisdictions may have no direct relevance to the task of enforcing justice in a world-wide market, be retained? This is a question that Hume himself does not treat, although it is one that rises directly from his analysis of civil society. His answer, clearly, would have been that while some adjustments, such as the union of England and Scotland, are feasible, the obedience of most people is primarily a matter of moral obligation, and that it is their old, familiar rulers whom they feel have a right to be obeyed. A more rational, but novel, scheme probably would become established only after the strenuous exertion of force over a period of three or four generations.

And third, should efforts be made to overthrow bad governments? No constitution, however ingeniously contrived, can be an adequate cause for believing that those in authority under it will always act properly. This is true even in an ideal commonwealth, wherein the due processes of governing have been devised with consummate care to keep rulers from acting to promote either partial or eccentric interests. Obviously, in an absolute monarchy or a mixed government the acumen and industry of the ruler(s), at any time, are extremely important. Rulers are only normal men. Virtue and vice vary as greatly among them as among ordinary men. No dynasty can be relied on to produce a succession of wise and competent governors. Moreover, a man, upon assuming a political office, receives no special access of wisdom and knowledge. The main factor making for good governance is not that rulers, whether they come to office by birth or by election, can be expected to have extraordinary personal virtue, but that they have a neutral, disinterested stand. They are free from many—the more, the better the constitution—of the needs and aspirations that tempt their subjects. They are so placed—unless the constitution is extremely bad—that they are apart from their subjects, and have a more immediate interest in the enforcement of the principles of civility. But rulers do not always adopt the view suitable to their position. The neutral place of the ruler(s) will tend to make him favour justice and the peace, but not invincibly. The character of the ruler(s) may overpower his place: a ruler may be so fully possessed by interested favourites or by ulterior ambitions, or else be so indolent, that he will ignore what lies plain before him, and thus embark upon programs of domestic intervention, either economic or religious, or on military adventures, or waste his time in hunting, carousing, and similar vain pleasures. In short, although rulers in general may be expected to have a greater concern for justice and the peace than ordinary men, the quality of rulers will vary from one to another; and some may be swept by violent passions to such outrages of cruelty and ambition that they, in truth, will cease to perform the office of rulers.

We have seen that in the case of rights to goods, too, we cannot be sure that the general rules will provide the most virtuous men with the greatest, or even with adequate, possessions, but also that it would be wrong to tamper with the assignment of goods produced by those general rules. But here, where we are concerned with the right to govern, Hume lays down no such flat prohibition. These two kinds of rights differ in three ways. First, rights to goods are private and numerous, while rights to govern are public and are limited to a few men, at the most. Second, while in the economic order the character of one man or a few can have only small consequences, in the political order the character of the ruler or rulers may be of the greatest importance. The third difference, the basic one, is that, as we have noticed again and again, the enforcement of justice is the reason for governance. Accordingly, what is not true in the case of economic goods is true in the case of power: from time to time it may be desirable to consider disobedience and rebellion against a king (or a government), and even the overthrow of the constitution, despite his (or their) formal right to rule.

The desirability of rebellion is difficult enough to weigh in an absolute monarchy, but it is even harder, Hume finds, in a constitutional government. An absolute monarch has a complete right to govern, and there never can be a claim that any of his acts is unconstitutional. That his acts are pernicious may be adequate ground for rebellion, but that his acts are *ultra vires*, never. In a constitutional government, in contrast, the right to govern is divided, and occasionally it may be necessary to consider a resort to force to deter one part of the government from altering the constitution by exalting itself permanently. But to ascertain that the acts of any part are *ultra vires* that part, is not easy. First, the right to govern can be allocated to the several parts only in very general language. There are sure to be areas of vagueness and uncertainty, so that different constitutional interpretations are almost inevitable. Second, even if a definite division of powers were possible, insistence on the scrupulous observation of that division at all times, might prove harmful, even disastrous, for the state. It is certain that there will be emergencies, unforeseen events, which can be met expeditiously only if the king and his ministers resort to extraordinary, emergency action, action which may not be provided for in the statutes, or which may even be against the statutes.[10] Now, Hume holds, the emergency power of the day-to-day government should not be defined, for the measures which at one time would be proper and necessary, at another time would be despotic. Any definition of emergency power, therefore, will either make desirable measures illegal or bestow legality on despotism. Emergency power is best left vague. This means that men must use their discretion, and cannot rely on the words of the constitution to discover whether or not the constitution is endangered.

Since no government, whatever its form, always will be perfectly virtuous, and none almost certainly will be entirely vicious, no set of easy tests can be established by which to decide whether or not governors have become "tyrants and public enemies." Many diverse factors should be taken into account by a man as he tries to answer that question. How likely is it that the revolt will succeed? Is it likely that it will issue in a prolonged, bloody civil war? If it is successful, will the new government prove no better, perhaps worse, than the old one? These are questions which should be answered. And malcontents should take up a deeper question, How great will be the corrosive effect of the revolt on the morality of the populace? The vulgar, we know, obey a government chiefly because they think of the established government as having a moral right to be obeyed. A revolt against the established government threatens not only that particular government, but the state, and thus the economic order. Once "the sacred boundaries of the laws" have been violated, nothing remains "to confine the wild projects of zeal and ambition." [11] If the corrosion is extensive, the reestablishment of civility will come to depend largely on the enlightenment of those who, in the event, come to possess coercive power. Besides, not only do rebellions threaten the domestic civil order from top to bottom, but they tend to spread abroad into neighbouring countries, and thus to threaten "universal anarchy and confusion among mankind." [12] There are times when disobedience and even rebellion are proper; obviously, however, one should think seriously of such perilous measures only when tyranny is enormously flagrant and oppressive.[13]

The Tory theory of the divine right of kings is based on a

false notion of the nature of constitutions, and the doctrine of passive obedience, the corollary of that theory, is equally false. The Whig theory of original contract also is based on a false notion of the nature of constitutions, and the doctrine of a right of revolution, likewise, is invalid. The right to govern is not a right delegated to the government by a higher legal body, either God or the people; rather, the right to govern is based on opinion. Revolt is permissible, and sometimes desirable, despite what the Tories say. But whether or not there should be a revolt at any specific juncture is not a question that can be answered by inspecting a list of conditions supposedly laid down by the people in an original contract.

Both parties are wrong in their teachings, but, argues Hume, the error of the Whigs is far more dangerous than that of the Tories. The former, by their theory of popular sovereignty and precarious delegation, tend to destroy the popular belief in the right of the government, and thus they promote a situation in which the only way in which the peace can be maintained is by the constant and fierce exertion of force. If the vulgar were not told constantly that they are the source of all rights, they would not lapse into servile dependence. They are prone enough to disobedience without being told incessantly that the government is only their agent.

This argument is repeated by Hume again and again. Perhaps the most felicitous enunciation of it appears in the *History of England*, at the point where he is reporting on opinions subsequent to the trial and execution of Charles I. He writes as follows:

The tragical death of Charles begat a question, whether the people, in any case, were intitled to judge and to punish their sovereign; and most men, regarding chiefly the atrocious usurpation of the pretended judges, and the merit of the virtuous prince who suffered, were inclined to condemn the republican principle, as highly seditious and extravagant: But there still were a few, who, abstracting from the particular circumstances of this case, were able to consider the question in general, and were inclined to moderate, not contradict, the prevailing sentiment. Such might have been their reasoning. If ever, on any occasion, it were laudable to conceal truth from the populace; it must be confessed, that the doctrine of resistance affords such an example; and that all speculative reasoners ought to observe, with regard to this principle, the same cautious silence, which the laws, in every species of government, have ever prescribed to themselves. Government is instituted, in order to restrain the fury and injustice of the people; and being always founded on opinion, not on force, it is dangerous to weaken, by these speculations, the reverence, which the multitude owe to authority, and to instruct them beforehand, that the case can ever happen, when they may be freed from their duty of allegiance. Or should it be found impossible to restrain the licence of human disquisitions, it must be acknowledged, that the doctrine of obedience ought alone to be *inculcated,* and that the exceptions, which are rare, ought seldom or never to be mentioned in popular reasonings and discourses. Nor is there any danger, that mankind, by this prudent reserve, should universally degenerate into a state of abject servitude. When the exception really occurs, even though it be not previously expected and descanted on, it must, from its very nature, be so obvious and undisputed, as to remove all doubt, and overpower the restraint, however great, imposed by teaching the general doctrine of obedience.[14]

It may be that the young Hume hoped to assist in the general enlightenment of the populace, and thus to speed up the process of civilization. His comments on education as a source of false beliefs and his rules for the testing of beliefs, both in the first book of the *Treatise,* have practical implications. His original comment on the edifying influence of the press on "the people" in "Of the Liberty of the Press" seems hopeful. But not the slightest sign of such thinking is to be found in his later writings; indeed, their general tendency is strongly in the opposite direction. He has no notion that the men of true principles will act as a vanguard leading the vulgar to a new order in which all will be cautious and suitably sceptical, and will understand the principles of civility. These men will try to make some changes, such as the abolition of mercantile laws, the destruction of prejudices against the French, the breaking of the English habit of flying into outrageous wars in the name of the balance of power, and the stopping of the feckless accumulation of a great national debt. They will even try to improve the constitution somewhat, in the light of the idea of a perfect commonwealth. But notions of a vast general enlightenment, such as would emancipate men from dependence on custom and prejudice, are vain and silly. In 1768 he wrote to Turgot:

I know you are one of those, who entertain the agreeable and laudable, if not too sanguine hope, that human Society is capable of perpetual Progress towards Perfection, that the Encrease of Knowlege will still prove favourable to good Government, and that since the Discovery of Printing we need no longer Dread the usual Returns of Barbarism and Ignorance. Pray, do not the late Events in this Country appear a little contrary to your System? Here is a People thrown into Disorders (not dangerous ones, I hope) merely from the Abuse of Liberty, chiefly the Liberty of the Press; without any Grievance, I do not only say, real, but even imaginary; and without any of them being able to tell one Circumstance of Government which they wish to have corrected: They roar Liberty, tho' they have apparently more Liberty than any People in the World; a great deal more than they deserve; and perhaps more than any men ought to have. The same Perfection of our Government, carryed to an Extreme, has a bad Influence on our Ministers: There is too little Difference between the Governors and Governed. A Minister here can amass no Fortune, being checked in every Abuse; he can very little give Employments to his own Friends, Favourites and Flatterers, but must bestow all Offices on those who by their Votes and Credit may support Government; and he can revenge himself on none of his Enemies; because every one is so entrenched in Laws and Privileges, as to be able to set all the World at Defiance. Hence men of great Rank and Fortune are very indifferent about being Ministers; being sensible, that they are more exposed to Obloquy on account of their power, and derive no consideration from it. They either decline high Offices, or behave negligently in them; and express every moment their Wishes of being free of the Trouble and Subjection, attending them. These Sentiments loosen the Attachment of their Inferiors. You will say, perhaps, either that all these Evils are Trifles: So perhaps they are; but they tend to great Mischiefs: Or that they proceed from the still imperfect State of our Knowlege: That is very true; but will Men ever reach a much more perfect State; while the rich have so many more alluring Appetites to gratify than that for Knowlege, and the poor are occupyed in daily Labour, and Industry. I mention not the Disturbances arising from foreign Wars, an incurable Evil, which often springs from the greatest & most unexpected Absurdity, and discourages every Project for serving or improving human Society. You see, I give you freely my Views of things, in which I wish earnestly to be refuted: the contrary Opinion is much more consolatory, and is an Incitement to every Virtue and laudable Pursuit.[15]

Thomas Hobbes, in his *Dialogue of the Common Laws,* contends that human laws, correctly conceived, are the precepts of reason made imperative by the sovereign. Sir Matthew Hale's criticism of this argument is as good a statement of what we have called the conservative viewpoint as is to be found anywhere.[16] Reason does set some limits to human law, but within those limits, Hale argues, there is a vast area for which reason does not prescribe; yet, if men are to live quiet lives of certainty, this area cannot be left void. If we rely on our rulers to originate laws to fill it, the outcome is likely to be unsatisfactory. The life of a civil society is so complex, with remote causes leading to unforseeable results, that the wisest men can neither initiate nor amend with full assurance. The texture of human affairs, we are told, "is not unlike the texture of a diseased body labouring under maladies, it may be of so various nature that such physic as may be proper for the cure of one of the maladies may be destructive in relation to the other, and the cure of one disease may be the death of the patient." [17] Consequently, it is best to rely on the customary laws, even when they are contrary to our own understanding.

With Hale's emphasis on experience Hume would have agreed strongly; indeed, Hume's epistemology could have sprung as directly from the common law tradition as from the philosophy of Locke and Newton, although evidently it did not; yet Hume goes beyond Hale in two very important respects. First, while Hale's theory would admit an idea of progress, this suggestion is not developed. For Hume, however, given the constancy of human nature and the circumstances, the process of experience is progressive: by becoming experienced mankind acquires more and more valid knowledge. Indeed, this advance now has gone so far that some men no longer need rely on custom. No longer are they the mere recipients of experience; rather, cognizant of the nature of knowledge, they can experiment self-consciously to test old knowledge and to acquire new. Proceeding in this way, by "the experimental method," Hume discovers fully the principles of civility, which hitherto were only imperfectly embodied in customs, and thus puts himself in a position to criticize the constitution, laws, and policies of Britain. He, unlike Hale—and this is the second difference—believes that he knows principles that should be used deliberately for the improvement of civil society.

At this point we can do no better than to quote Mr. J. G. A. Pocock. He writes:

Hale follows Selden in implying that the lawyer's knowledge is historical knowledge: in knowing the judgments and statutes of the past, he knows what ills they were designed to remedy and what the state of the law was which they remedied. In this way his understanding of the law's content is deepened, and he comes to see a greater part—never, perhaps, the whole—of the accumulated wisdom with which the refining generations have loaded it.

This is what Hale means by "artificial reason," and it is obvious that he has anticipated and made his own several of the essential points of Burke's philosophy. The distrust of abstract reasoning, the belief that ancient institutions contain a latent wisdom greater than that of the individual, above all the concept of the law as the fruit of a great social process whereby society adapts itself to the consecutive emergencies brought to it by its experience in history—all these are Burke's; but they are foreshadowed, as we have already seen, not by Hale alone, but also by Coke and even by the French sixteenth-century partisans of *droit coutumier*. It is evident that they all arise from the idea of law as custom, or rather from that aspect of the idea of custom which emphasizes its universality and anonymity, the myriad minds who, not knowing the importance of what they do, have, each by responding to the circumstances in which he finds himself, contributed to build up a law which is the sum total of society's response to the vicissitudes of its history and will be insensibly modified tomorrow by fresh responses to fresh circumstances. The philosophy of Burke is descended from the concept of custom worked out in the late Renaissance during the first reaction against Roman law, and Hale marks a definite stage in its development.[18]

Hume differs from Hale, and from the conservative tradition in which Hale stands, in that he believes in progressive civilization—customary artifice has gradually embodied the principles of civility more and more—and in that he presupposes that competition, within the confines of civility, is the best process for shaping the social order.

These differences stem from Hume's epistemology, for while he begins by proclaiming the importance of belief and custom, his purpose is to free men from unexamined beliefs and customs. By "the experimental method," presumably, but not evidently, he finds that all human activities outside the scope of family, friendly, and humanitarian feelings are basically economic, and then, presupposing that limited competition always is the best ordering process, by that same method, he discovers the permanently valid limits to competition.

For Hume, customary law, born of accumulating experience, has been man's guide to civility throughout the past. Now, however, the night of subconscious development is at an end. Men of true principles know that civil society is ordered best by competition, and that since total competition is destructive, the proper framework for competition should be established by deliberate artifice. Because the civility of the vulgar remains mainly a matter of custom, the rules of customary law, especially concerning property and the constitution, are not to be jettisoned, but are to be adopted deliberately; that is, customary artifice is to be swallowed up by deliberate artifice. This concession men of true principle will be ready to make in the interests of stability.

The priority Hume gives to the individual, the preeminence and consequent independence he gives to the economy, his faith in the natural harmony of society, his disinterest in folkish emotions, and his readiness to make performance the test both of forms of government and of particular governments are all notable marks of liberalism. Likewise, the strong emphasis on institutions, sometimes called "constitutionalism," as a means of restraining partial interests and of preventing the vulgar from acquiring a dangerous measure of political power, is an eighteenth-century liberal trait. Hume, of course, save on economic matters, is far from being an ardent reformer; the hold of the vulgar on civility is too precarious to permit quick improvements. But even when he sounds least like a reformer, as when he writes about "the sacred boundaries of the laws," Hume is not a conservative, at least not the same kind of conservative as is Burke. For Burke to talk of rapid change is folly because for him, as for the common lawyers, there is no ideal to pose over against the present. By a slow process of trial, error, and success men work out the best arrangements. For Hume, on the other hand, the present, when it falls short of the ideal, is worthy of no great adulation. When improvement is not to be undertaken, it is not because nothing better is presently conceivable, but because the vulgar, given the nature of their civility, cannot be expected to endure overt reformations.

Hume has transcended conservativism: he had come to know competition framed by artifice as the correct process for ordering civil relations among men. At the same time, he, like many other men of the Enlightenment, was apprehensive of the multitude.

# APPENDIX: THE RECASTINGS

At THE beginning of the volume containing *An Enquiry concerning Human Understanding*, "Of the Passions," and *An Enquiry Concerning the Principles of Morals* in the edition of 1777 (Edition R), there appears an advertisement wherein Hume acknowledges the *Treatise* as his work, and requests that henceforth the pieces in this volume, and not the *Treatise* be regarded as the statement of his philosophical principles and sentiments.[1] How far had Hume abandoned the content of the *Treatise* in these three later works?

The differences between *An Enquiry concerning Human Understanding*, first published in 1748, and the corresponding parts of the *Treatise* do not, I think, show any basic change in Hume's thought. His great and central aim in the first book of the *Treatise* is to reveal the importance and nature of belief. This he accomplishes in "Of knowledge and probability," the third of the four parts which compose the book. Therein he explains that all our thinking about facts and things beyond our intuition and remembrance, but in the real world, is believing, i.e., is the thinking of thoughts or ideas that we find impressive. The two preceding parts and the last part are subordinate. The first is to be read as a preparatory beginning, in which Hume seeks to show how he is using his basic terms, and sets up the problem he proposes to solve. He tries to tell us what the words "ideas" and "impressions" are to indicate. He distinguishes between ideas of memory and those of imagination. He shows that all complexes are systems of relations. He submits that when we think spontaneously, not deliberately, our thoughts are not chaotic, but follow certain principles of association. The next part, "Of the ideas of space and time," is destructive. His aim there is to sweep away the notion that our ideas of space and time, the two basic kinds of relations among our real-world perceptions, are ideas of real things independent of the facts and things we know by feeling impressions. If our ideas of space and time were ideas of independent things with their own constitutions, it would be possible to think reliable thoughts *a priori* about times and places. Hume insists that time and space are only the manner in which the facts and things we know appear.

With these two parts behind him, he is ready to turn to his main task, i.e., to show why we do distinguish between fanciful and reliable thoughts about facts and things neither present to us now nor present to us in the past. His argument, we have seen, is that the reliable thoughts or beliefs are lively and impressive because, unlike our fancies, they are the results of the combined influences of two factors: first, our natural tendency to associate those things and happenings we have found closely related before, and second, the particular relations between things or happenings that we have observed in the past.[2]

The concluding part, "Of the sceptical and other systems of philosophy," is commentary and comparison. Hume already has given his account of human understanding. Now he compares his own account, which he regards as adequate, with the sceptical, the ancient, and the modern philosophies. He finds that all these, having failed to see that knowing is a familiar operation to be described as a result of observation and one which always involves two aspects, feeling and thinking, i.e., having begun by putting too much emphasis on thinking, soon find themselves in the deplorable plight of claiming in their theories to know perfectly what they know, but of knowing little that is worth knowing.

The implications of Hume's theory for whatever subjects are under discussion become obvious when we shift our attention from knowing to the known, i.e., from an account of believing to a description of the relations presupposed among real facts and things. These relations are causal. We can have beliefs only if we presuppose that the subject matter is orderly, either that it does not change, or that if changes do occur, they happen according to due process or necessity. Free (or chaotic) changes are unknowable, and therefore cannot be described in either moral or physical subjects. In the *Treatise* this implication is not made plain in the first book; nor do we find it applied openly in the second book, "Of the Passions" until the last part, where, having already introduced us to the most important passions, Hume is ready to declare that there is a causal link between the passions felt by a man and the acts done by him.[3] He then argues that human acts are the outcome of whatever causes, including passions, are influential, and that there is no mysterious change—called "free will"—between moral causes and moral effects.

"Of the Understanding" sets forth not a partial, but a general theory of knowing. With a few minor alterations, to expunge signs that it was written to carry the principles of the physical sciences into the moral sciences, the book could have served equally well as an introduction to a study of physical subjects. As the epistemologists have demonstrated repeatedly by concentrating exclusively on it, Hume's theory of knowing is not inseparably tied to the contents of the other books in the *Treatise*.

Between this book, "Of the Understanding," and *An Enquiry concerning Human Understanding*, there are three notable differences. First, the latter work is shorter and more simply organized. The first and second sections serve, in place of the first part of the original book, to introduce the argument.[4] No replacement is provided for the difficult discussion in "Of the ideas of time and space." Six sections—three through nine, excluding the eighth—are given over to the argument in "Of knowledge and probability." The final section supplants the entire last part. The second difference is that the eighth section of *Enquiry*, entitled, "Of Liberty and Necessity," has no equivalent in "Of the Understanding." And third, the tenth and eleventh sections of *Enquiry*, treating of supernatural topics, are also new.

What Hume has done is clear. The central argument of the two works is exactly the same, i.e., the thoughts we believe, our beliefs, are ideas made impressive by the influence of past observation on our imaginations.[5] But in the *Enquiry* he presents this argument as simply as he can, and as an independent work. In the original work the crucial third part, "Of knowledge and probability," does not stand out, but in the *Enquiry* two of its neighbours have been cut back severely, and the third has been rooted out entirely. Then, because the *Enquiry* is to stand as an independent work, the implications of this theory of knowing for whatever subject, moral, physical, or religious, happens to be under discussion are revealed at once in the eighth section, "Of Liberty and Necessity." In the tenth and eleventh sections he illustrates the kind of ideas which, because they refer to the unnatural, chaotic, and inexplicable, can never be true beliefs. Instead of using physical "chances" or acts of "free will" as his examples, he deals with ideas of supernatural happenings and conditions.[6] This choice, which does not influence the argument, may be the result of a desire to stir up a storm of outraged opposition, or it may be additional evidence that about this time he was shaping up the views on religion plainly implied in the *Treatise* and later published in *The Natural History of Religion* and the *Dialogues concerning Natural Religion.*

The first recasting, *An Enquiry concerning Human Understanding*, merely presents the basic argument in "Of the Understanding" in a simplified, elegant version designed to win approval, or at least attention, where the *Treatise* had failed.[7] The second, *An Enquiry concerning the Principles of Morals*, presents far more difficult problems. If the *Treatise* did not exist, so that we had to rely entirely on this work, published in 1751, the explanation attributed to Hume of the nonselfish basis of standards of conduct would have to be much vaguer than that given in the foregoing account.[8]

Philosophic ardour, evident throughout the *Treatise*, never disturbs the smooth progress of *An Enquiry concerning the Principles of Morals*. The former work resembles the log-book of a daring voyage of discovery. The voyage is often rough, and the log, often terse. At times the ship seems to drift without a fixed course. At its best it moves ahead steadily and inquisitively, rounding capes, exploring rivers and their tributaries, and opening up new, surprising scenes on every quarter. The *Enquiry* is the work of an experienced captain, a man who, because he already knows both the port for which he is bound and all the inviting estuaries, the spectacular dangers, and pirates near his track, brings his land-lubbers to their destination by the quietest, safest route. The *Treatise* is a philosophical work, while the *Enquiry* is a masterpiece of elegant exposition. Furthermore, it is an error to think that *An Enquiry concerning the Principles of Morals* is the third book of the *Treatise*, the book entitled, "Of Morals," refined, tamed, and improved. This enquiry is not related to "Of Morals" in the same way that *An Enquiry concerning Human Understanding* is related to "Of the Understanding." In this case, although much of the same metal has been used again, the product is quite different. The sadder, wiser Hume of 1751 would be pleased to make one point, namely, that the difference between virtue and vice is not to be learned simply by ratiocination. Although reasoning is often involved, the ultimate distinction in morals is a matter of feeling, a matter of "moral sense." In the *Treatise* this argument is only one step, albeit an indispensable one, in an endeavour in which the standards of artistic achievement, the structure of society, and much of our language are all traced back to the impressive aspect of perception.

Consequently, the mere omission from *An Enquiry concerning the Principles of Morals* of parts of the moral theory set forth in the *Treatise*, although enough to alert us, does not constitute even *prima facie* evidence that Hume has abandoned those parts as delusions. Now, it is the account of the process of sympathy, which plays a central role in the *Treatise* and in my interpretation of Hume's theory, that is most noticeably absent in this later work; although he uses the word "sympathy" many times in it, he does so casually and ambiguously. Moreover, the second section of this enquiry is entitled, "Of Benevolence." It is tempting to think that Hume has decided that sympathy is not the source or foundation of the feeling involved in moral evaluation, and has replaced it by an instinctive feeling of good will for all men. This temptation, I think, must be resisted. An impartial spectator might reach three conclusions: first, that it is palpably true that Hume, after the failure of even friendly readers to follow him in the *Treatise*, had lowered his sights as a writer; second, that his interest in the theory of the *Treatise* probably had waned somewhat since the time when, in the spring of 1729, he had begun to investigate his "new scene of thought"; and third, that there is no conclusive evidence in *An Enquiry concerning the Principles of Morals* on which to base a guess that if pressed for an explanation of the moral sense, Hume would not have resurrected his original account of sympathy. Because what he says about sympathy in the *Enquiry* does not contradict what he says in the *Treatise*, and is far vaguer, I conclude that he is simply trying to propagate his views on the relative contributions to moral judgments of reason and the moral sense, and is trying to do so without asking his readers to endure an elaborate explanation of how a moral sense is possible.

The third book of the *Treatise*, entitled, "Of Morals," the one with which *An Enquiry concerning the Principles of Morals* is frequently compared, is divided into three parts. In the first of these Hume reverts to a topic already treated briefly when he discussed the causes of acts, namely, the efficacy of reason. His prior argument was that feeling, not reasoning, is the ultimate cause of action. He now argues that when it is a matter of distinguishing between virtuous and vicious acts, the difference is detected by moral feeling, by "moral sense," not by reasoning. In the second and third parts he proceeds to show how this particular kind of feeling, "moral sense," which produces evaluations independent of our particular or selfish interests, arises in both the sphere of artificial relations and the sphere of natural relations. It is caused, as we have noticed, by the expression and recognition of feelings, by what he calls "sympathy." Hume's chief purpose in "Of Morals" is not to argue that virtue and vice are distinguished by the moral sense, but, going one stage further, to show that sympathy is the cause of the moral sense.

In the *Enquiry* the main question concerns the comparative contributions of the moral sense and reason to our moral judgments. It is, in other words, a more politic and more leisurely treatment of the topic dealt with in the first part of the book, "Of Morals." Hume's answer here is substantially the same as the one given in the earlier work, i.e., the ultimate distinction between virtue and vice is made by the moral sense. But instead of stopping with a stark answer to the basic question, he brings in the separate and essential role of reasoning in the making of judgments. He thus comes to a conclusion which does not contradict what he said in the *Treatise*, but which, being less startling, is more likely to win the approval of the reader. Instead of asking the reader to assent to the proposition, "Reason is, and ought only to be the slave of the passions, and can never pretend to any other office than to serve and obey them," [9] a proposition put forth in explaining the causes of acts, which in "Of Morals" he applies to the causes of moral judgments, he here comments: "But though reason, when fully assisted and improved, be sufficient to instruct us in the pernicious or useful tendency of qualities and actions; it is not alone sufficient to produce any moral blame or approbation. Utility is only a tendency to a certain end; and were the end totally indifferent to us, we should feel the same indifference towards the means. It is requisite a *sentiment* should here display itself, in order to give a preference to the useful above the pernicious tendencies." [10] Besides, his method of presentation is different. In "Of Morals" he states, in twenty brilliant pages written in a polemical mood, that the difference is discerned by a moral sense, but in the *Enquiry*, after launching upon the question gently, he adheres faithfully to "the experimental method," and comes to his balanced verdict only gradually, after an edifying review of the fourfold catalogue of the virtues.

Sir L. A. Selby-Bigge, in introducing the *Enquiry*, suggests that this work shows that between 1740 and 1751 Hume had become discontented with the moral theory set forth in the *Treatise*, and, specifically, that he had come to think that "a love of simplicity" had misled him. In explaining the moral sense, he had used sympathy too freely as a solvent. Accordingly, says Selby-Bigge, in the *Enquiry*, no use is made of sympathy to provide the individual with a basis of evaluation broader than his own particular feelings; rather, the argument of this later work is that each individual naturally has an independent instinct of benevolence, and that this is really his moral sense. The word "sympathy" appears often in the *Enquiry*, but it is now "another name for social feeling, humanity, benevolence, natural philanthropy, rather than the name of the process by which the social feeling has been constructed out of non-social or individual feeling." [11] Selby-Bigge argues that, while in the *Treatise* benevolence is mentioned only incidentally, in the *Enquiry* it is treated as "the chief of the social virtues, and though a main object of its treatment is to show its 'utility,' its independence is fully recognized." [12] This entire interpretation, based on the view that in the *Enquiry* communication of feelings (sympathy) has been abandoned, and that its place has been taken by benevolence (sympathy), seems wrong to me.

Let us consider benevolence first. Hume's aim in the *Enquiry* is to show that both moral sense and reason make a contribution to most of our moral judgments. To this end, he turns to the fourfold classification of the virtues mentioned briefly in the *Treatise*, the classification according to which a virtue is a quality "fitted to be useful to others, or to the person himself, or which is agreeable to others, or to the person himself," [13] and examines each of the four kinds separately. Thereby, he is able to show that reason is very important where a judgment has to be passed on a useful quality, and that in all cases the ultimate judgment is a result of the moral sense. The work, as originally published,[14] was divided into nine sections and two appendices, as follows:

I.     Of the general Principles of Morals
II.    Of Benevolence
III.   Of Justice

The first section raises the main question: whether morals be "derived from Reason, or from Sentiment; whether we attain the knowledge of them by a chain of argument and induction, or by an immediate feeling and finer internal sense; whether, like all sound judgment of truth and falsehood, they should be the same to every rational intelligent being; or whether, like the perception of beauty and deformity, they be founded entirely on the particular fabric and constitution of the human species." [15] Hume proceeds, in the next three sections, to survey three kinds of conduct regarded as virtuous because useful. The fifth section explains why we call useful qualities and acts virtuous. In short, the second, third, fourth, and fifth sections are devoted to explaining the first of the four kinds of virtue. Each of the next three sections, as the titles show, deals with one of the three remaining kinds. The ninth section explains that there are only these four kinds of virtue, that for various reasons they are commended by men, and that since virtue is best for ourselves, we ought to act virtuously. The first appendix gives Hume's answer, already quoted in part, to the main question.

When we examine the second section, "Of Benevolence," we find that in it Hume states only one point directly related to his argument.[16] This is that a considerable part of the merit of benevolent acts arises from the utility of those acts to the persons benefited. The rest, we are told in the seventh section, arises from the agreeableness to the benefactor of doing benevolent acts.[17] Hume is not saying that benevolent acts are regarded as virtuous because they are caused by an instinct called "benevolence"; rather, his whole point is that benevolent acts are regarded as good to a great extent because they are useful. Why useful acts, whether done from benevolence, from a sense of justice, or from a sense of allegiance, are regarded as virtuous, he has to explain later, in the fifth section. Clearly, his explanation there, cannot be that useful acts are regarded as good because they show benevolence. The section, "Of Benevolence," is of primary importance only if we assume that Hume is putting forth a new system in which benevolence is itself the touchstone of virtue. If this were true, he would not undertake to explain the virtue of benevolence.

Again, the truth that in his explanation he can accommodate benevolence in the fourfold classification of the virtues already set forth in the *Treatise*, implies that benevolence is not a great, independent principle now first discovered. When we turn to the *Treatise* to test this implication, we find that it is correct. The organization of both "Of the Passions" and "Of Morals" is no more perspicuous than that of the first book, "Of the Understanding." In all three Hume overestimates the reader's ability to follow the main line of the argument through its turns and switch-backs. But, given the organization, when we look for references to benevolence, we find them exactly where we would expect them. Let us turn first to "Of the Passions." There Hume uses the words "love" and "hatred" as inclusive terms signifying our feelings for other persons, and undertakes to explain the causes of love and hatred. Now, love and hatred, like joy and sorrow, are feelings that do not inevitably lead to wilful action. Love will lead to good will (benevolence) and hatred to ill will (anger or malevolence), when by our action goods or evils may be visited upon those whom we love or hate. This condition is usually present in ordinary life. We can almost say that one of Hume's aims in "Of the Passions" is to explain benevolence by explaining the prior emotion, love. He writes:

The passions of love and hatred are always followed by, or rather conjoin'd with benevolence and anger. 'Tis this conjunction, which chiefly distinguishes these affections from pride and humility. For pride and humility are pure emotions in the soul, unattended with any desire, and not immediately exciting us to action. But love and hatred are not compleated within themselves, nor rest in that emotion, which they produce, but carry the mind to something farther. Love is always follow'd by a desire of the happiness of the person belov'd, and an aversion to his misery: As hatred produces a desire of the misery and an aversion to the happiness of the person hated.[18]

In "Of Morals" his general purpose is to explain how, through sympathy, we come to evaluate both the motives (will) and acts of men as morally virtuous or vicious. One sphere, that of civil society, is the sphere of acts done because they are useful to the actor. We should not expect to find a discussion of good will and benevolent acts there. The other sphere, that of the family, friendships, and humanity, however, is a sphere in which acts are done because of the love or hatred, and consequently, the good will or ill will of the actor for the other person. It is precisely at the end of Hume's discussion of natural moral virtue, in the crowning position, where we should expect to find it, that his explanation of why we give our approval to good will and benevolent acts appears. Benevolence or good will is the motive behind virtuous conduct in the sphere of natural moral relations.[19] In short, just as the third and fourth sections of the *Enquiry*, when combined with the fifth section, are a restatement of the explanation of *artificial* moral virtues given in "Of Morals," the second section, "Of Benevolence," when combined with the fifth and seventh sections, is merely a restatement of the explanation of *natural* moral virtues given in "Of Morals." It is impossible to show that utility is either less or more important in the *Enquiry* as an explanation of the virtue of good will than in the *Treatise*.

If we notice the kinds of acts considered as benevolent acts, we come to the same conclusion, namely, that insofar as benevolence is concerned, the *Enquiry* makes no advance on the *Treatise*. In a footnote to "Of Benevolence"—now somewhat lost as a footnote to the appendix for "Of Self-love"—Hume distinguishes between two kinds of benevolent acts. He writes:

Benevolence naturally divides into two kinds, the *general* and the *particular*. The first is, where we have no friendship or connexion or esteem for the person, but feel only a general sympathy with him or a compassion for his pains, and a congratulation with his pleasures. The other species of benevolence is founded on an opinion of virtue, on services done us, or on some particular connexions. Both these sentiments must be allowed real in human nature: but whether they will resolve into some nice considerations of self-love, is a question more curious than important. The former sentiment, to wit, that of general benevolence, or humanity, or sympathy, we shall have occasion frequently to treat of in the course of this enquiry; and I assume it as real, from general experience, without any other proof.[20]

Here we are told that acts done, not from a sense of civil duty, but from good will for the person benefited, are of two kinds. The particular acts are those done for persons regularly related to the actor. The general acts are those done for any eligible person who happens to come our way, e.g., acts of charity done for passing strangers. Both these kinds of acts, as distinguished from acts of justice and acts of political obedience, are also recognized in the *Treatise*. These are the acts which result from the natural moral virtues. In that work Hume mentions particular benevolent acts, i.e., acts done from good will for friends, neighbours, and relatives. He also mentions general benevolent acts, i.e., acts done from good will for the poor and for strangers, and even goes so far as to recognize acts of good will done for animals.[21]

Given Selby-Bigge's argument that the new prominence of benevolence shows that Hume had changed his attitude, it is not surprising to find that he is inaccurate in his comment on the treatment of "self-love" in the *Treatise*. He says: "He had declined, even in the Treatise, with excellent good sense, to accept the popular reduction of benevolence as given by the selfish school, but he certainly tried to reduce benevolence to something which was neither selfish nor unselfish, but rather physical." [22] Hume did not merely "decline" to accept the theory of the selfish school *even* in the *Treatise*. He goes so far as to deny that the term "self-love" has any real meaning.[23] His whole exposition of sympathy and of the consequent moral sense would have been unnecessary to a selfish theory. I do not know in what way the word "physical" is used in this comment on Hume's theory of moral subjects.[24]

It may be worthwhile to notice here that Selby-Bigge's comment on Hume's discussion of justice is misleading also. He says: "In the Treatise he insisted vigorously, though not very intelligibly, that justice was not a natural but only an artificial virtue, and it is pretty plain that he meant to be offensive in doing so. His argument in the Treatise was, to say the least, awkward, and he may have been glad to get rid of an ungainly and unnecessary discussion. In the Enquiry he dismisses the question [of whether or not justice is "artificial"] in a few words as a vain one." [25] Hume's aim in distinguishing between the artificial virtues and the natural virtues, as we have seen, is not to deride the former. Stated briefly, his view is that acts of natural virtue result from good will, and that just acts and acts of civil obedience are conventional acts based ultimately on utility. In *An Enquiry concerning the Principles of Morals* itself, for example, he says that,

"The necessity of justice to the support of society is the sole foundation of that virtue." [26] If in the *Enquiry* he was not still distinguishing between natural and artificial virtues—although, for obvious reasons, he was not content with the words "natural" and "artificial" as the marks of the distinction,[27] he would not have treated benevolent acts in a section separate from the third and fourth sections, in which he treats of civil acts.

If the word "benevolence," in the *Enquiry*, marks no newly found feeling or passion which might serve as a foundation for moral judgments, and there is no other alternative, we must ask whether "sympathy" or the communication of feelings, the foundation used in the *Treatise*, is not used here too. The answer, I think, must be affirmative.[28] Hume undoubtedly stands away cautiously. He does not explore the communication of feelings. He does not announce the presence of sympathy to his readers in unmistakable terms. He even goes so far as to hush the curious.[29] But when we turn to the crucial passages—the ones in sections 5, 6, 7, and 8, where he tells why qualities useful to others and to ourselves, and qualities agreeable to ourselves and to others are regarded as virtuous—we find the word "sympathy" used with an ambiguity that can hardly be the result of carelessness. Sometimes it seems to mean the communication of feelings, and at other times "humanity," "friendliness," "charity," or "generosity," the feelings brought on by the communication of feelings.

Have we any difficulty to comprehend the force of humanity and benevolence? Or to conceive, that the very aspect of happiness, joy, prosperity, gives pleasure; that of pain, suffering, sorrow, communicates uneasiness? The human countenance, says Horace, borrows smiles or tears from the human countenance.[30]

There seems here a necessity for confessing that the happiness and misery of others are not spectacles entirely indifferent to us; but that the view of the former, whether in its causes or effects, like sunshine or the prospect of well-cultivated plains (to carry our pretensions no higher), communicates a secret joy and satisfaction; the appearance of the latter, like a lowering cloud or barren landscape, throws a melancholy damp over the imagination.[31]

In general, it is certain, that, wherever we go, whatever we reflect on or converse about, everything still presents us with the view of human happiness or misery, and excites in our breast a sympathetic movement of pleasure or uneasiness. In our serious occupations, in our careless amusements, this principle still exerts its active energy.[32]

Others enter into the same humour, and catch the sentiment, by a contagion or natural sympathy; and as we cannot forbear loving whatever pleases, a kindly emotion arises towards the person who communicates so much satisfaction. He is a more animating spectacle; his presence diffuses over us more serene complacency and enjoyment; our imagination, entering into his feelings and disposition, is affected in a more agreeable manner than if a melancholy, dejected, sullen, anxious temper were presented to us.[33]

Another passage reads like a quotation from the most technical account of sympathy in the *Treatise:* "The idea, which we form of their effect on his acquaintance, has an agreeable influence on our imagination, and gives us the sentiment of approbation." [34]

It is difficult to believe that so astute a thinker could use a word to which he already had given a precise meaning ambiguously, without knowing that he was using it ambiguously. Furthermore, it is hard to believe that he would use it ambiguously, unless he wished to do so. The explanation seems to be that in the *Enquiry* Hume was trying to win one argument, and that, quite properly, he does not complicate his task by gratuitously veering into a difficult strait in which at the time he probably was not much interested. Our conclusion, then, is that if we had to rely on *An Enquiry concerning the Principles of Morals* alone, our account would have to be different. But there is nothing in the *Enquiry* that requires that a theory attributed to Hume on the basis of what he says in the *Treatise* be modified.

The last of the recastings, "Of the Passions," published in 1757, is much less important, and raises no important problems. It is made up entirely of quotations from Book II of the *Treatise* and of summaries of passages in that book. It is best read as a partial outline of the original, for it draws the material together, and shows the function of some of the most obscure parts. When read alone, it is interesting enough, but falls far short of the standard set in the two *Enquiries*. Unlike them, it is composed of a train of short descriptive pieces without an adequate unifying argument. The first of the six sections traces the direct passions to original painful or pleasant impressions. The next two describe the rise, through double association, of the two major sets of indirect passions: pride and humility, and love and hatred. The fourth shows the influence of the individualistic focus of perception on the indirect passions. In the fifth, the notion that reason can be a motive for or against action is rebutted. The last section shows how the passions are made calm or violent by certain factors. The dissertation begins abruptly, without a word of explanatory introduction. It ends with a kind of postscript: "I pretend not to have here exhausted this subject. It is sufficient for my purpose, if I have made it appear, that, in the production and conduct of the passions, there is a certain regular mechanism, which is susceptible of as accurate a disquisition, as the laws of motion, optics, hydrostatics, or any part of natural philosophy." [35] This dissertation has neither a proper beginning nor a proper end.

The explanation seems obvious. In shaping the material in the first and third books of the *Treatise* into the two *Enquiries*, Hume had robbed the connecting book of the unifying themes which had run through it. The postscript summarizes the basic argument in Book II, "Of the Passions," but this argument had been carried off, and presented in general terms, as "Of Liberty and Necessity," in *Enquiry* I. Thereafter, what remains in "Of the Passions" can be only an example of his contention, argued elsewhere, that only orderly relations can be known. Even then, approaching the material on another level, something important might have been made of the controversy over the relative efficacy of reason or passion. Hume, however, had already carried away his best thoughts on that question, and had recommitted them in *Enquiry* II, leaving only the meagre one-page fifth section in the dissertation. Selby-Bigge, in his introduction, calls attention to the omission in this work of most of the discussion of sympathy contained in Book II, "Of the Passions." This omission, however, cannot be used as evidence for his opinion that Hume had modified his moral theory. Since the dissertation is not a discussion of the origins of moral standards, nor an introduction to a discussion of the origin of moral standards, any extensive discussion of sympathy in it would have been superfluous. Moreover, in the one passage in the dissertation where sympathy is relevant, the one in which Hume treats of the love of fame, his explanation relies on sympathy in the same way that the earlier explanation in the *Treatise* did.[36]

But, in addition to comparing the contents of the three recastings with the *Treatise*, it is necessary to read the advertisement of 1777 carefully. Hume had busied himself in revising the first two books of the *Treatise* until the moment when they went to the press. About a year later he wrote to Francis Hutcheson: "I wait with some Impatience for a second Edition principally on Account of Alterations I intend to make in my Performance. . . . Our Conversation together has furnish'd me a hint, with which I shall augment the 2d Edition." [37] About that time he seems to have been trying to arrange with a Dublin bookseller for the publication of a pirated, corrected edition of the two books.[38] Apparently this effort failed, and no revised edition was ever published. When "Of Morals" was published, late in 1740, he added an appendix, "Wherein some passages of the foregoing volumes are illustrated and explain'd." In it he writes candidly: "I have not yet been so fortunate as to discover any very considerable mistakes in the reasonings deliver'd in the preceding volumes, except on one article: But I have found by experience, that some of my expressions have not been so well chosen, as to guard against all mistakes in the readers; and 'tis chiefly to remedy this defect, I have subjoin'd the following appendix." [39] All the comments and additions in this appendix refer to "Of the Understanding." Evidently, then, Hume was discontented with the *Treatise* from the beginning, but this discontent was mainly with his failure to achieve the felicitous enunciation that his argument deserved, and his discontent centered on the first book.[40]

It is notable that in the advertisement Hume makes it plain that he regards the "victories" of the critics—Dr. Reid and "that bigotted silly Fellow, Beattie"—as more apparent than real, and that even at that they are due only to the stubborn insistence of those critics on misinterpreting his youthful prose.

# NOTES

## I: INTRODUCTION

1. Robert Rait and G. S. Pryde, *Scotland* (London, 1954), pp. 84–109.

2. Scotland was represented in the House of Commons by forty-five members. Fifteen of these were chosen by the town councils of the royal burghs—one by the town council of Edinburgh, and the others by fourteen assemblies of delegates from groups of burghs. Since the town councils were co-opted, and since many royal burghs were only decayed relics, it is hardly surprising that, as Holden Furber says, "In practice, the burgh electors . . . were in almost every case the mere tools of some great noble, political manager, or man of wealth." Thirty members were elected in the counties; and the county vote was even less independent than that of the burghs. There were two franchise qualifications: either "a forty shilling land of old extent held of the king" or properties assessed at £400. The phrase "old extent" was interpreted as referring to an evaluation made in the thirteenth century; consequently, as land values rose and money became devalued, the franchise was narrowed. By 1793, according to Mathieson, the rent of land valued for electoral purposes at 40*s.* was computed at from £70 to £130 sterling. W. L. Mathieson, *The Awakening of Scotland* (Glasgow, 1910), pp. 17–18, 20. Moreover, the law was phrased in a way that permitted great landholders to multiply their votes by bestowing paper titles and "superiorities" to freeholds on their reliable friends and dependents. In 1790 there were fewer than 3,000 county electors, and about 1,500 of these possessed only fictitious qualifications. "With a population well over a million in 1800, [Scotland] had less than four thousand voters and less than four hundred inhabitants who had any real influence on election returns." Holden Furber, *Henry Dundas, First Count Melville* (London, 1931), pp. 187–88.

3. The interpretation of the relationship between the Crown and the House of Commons implied by the practice of the Scottish politicians was not as cynical or mistaken, or even as extraordinary, as we might think. Neither the idea of loyal, but systematic opposition to the ministries, nor the idea of an alternation in office of parties had become common. Consequently, it was reasonable to assume that every right-

minded member of Parliament would support the government unless it became dangerously corrupt or unwise, and to assume that any persistent opposition must be prompted by selfish or disloyal motives, and probably by both. The Scots were distinguished mainly by their early and perspicuous understanding of the British constitution. Cf. L. H. Namier, *The Structure of Politics at the Accession of George III* (London, 1929), I, c. iv.

4. Wallace Notestein, *The Scot in History* (New Haven, 1946), pp. 183–91.

5. Henry Grey Graham, *The Social Life of Scotland in the Eighteenth Century* (London, 1950), pp. 508–11.

6. Henry Hamilton, *The Industrial Revolution in Scotland* (Oxford, 1932), pp. 4–5. Later in the century the manufacture of cotton goods was to surpass linen. Cf. Hamilton, p. 146.

7. In 1707 the Scottish merchant marine was less than 100 ships, with a total tonnage under 6,000. By 1770 there were about 1,500 Scots ships, and the tonnage totalled nearly 90,000. Agnes Mure Mackenzie, *Scotland in Modern Times, 1720–1939* (London, 1947), p. 26. Cf. the detailed account of the revival in James Mackinnon, *The Social and Industrial History of Scotland* (London, 1921), pp. 19–20.

8. James E. Handley, *Scottish Farming in the Eighteenth Century* (London, 1953), pp. 117–75, especially 153–57.

9. *Letters,* I, 88.

10. This work later, in 1758, was given the new title, *An Enquiry concerning Human Understanding.*

11. G. W. F. Hegel, *The Philosophy of History* (New York, 1944), pp. 16–20.

12. *Essays,* I, 244.                    13. *Treatise,* pp. xvii–xviii.

14. "You must know then that from my earliest Infancy, I found alwise a strong Inclination to Books & Letters. As our College Education in Scotland, extending little further than the Languages, ends commonly when we are about 14 or 15 Years of Age, I was after that left to my own Choice in my Reading, & found it encline me almost equally to Books of Reasoning & Philosophy, & to Poetry & the polite Authors. Every one, who is acquainted either with the Philosophers or Critics, knows that there is nothing yet establisht in either of these two Sciences, & that they contain little more than endless Disputes, even in the most fundamental Articles. Upon Examination of these, I found a certain Boldness of Temper, growing in me, which was not enclin'd to submit to any Authority in these Subjects, but led me to seek out some new Medium, by which Truth might be establisht. After much Study, & Reflection on this, at last, when I was about 18 Years of Age, there seem'd to be open'd up to me a new Scene of Thought, which transported me beyond Measure, & made me, with an Ardor

natural to young men, throw up every other Pleasure or Business to apply entirely to it. The Law, which was the Business I design'd to follow, appear'd nauseous to me, & I cou'd think of no other way of pushing my Fortune in the World, but that of a Scholar & Philosopher." *Letters,* I, 13.

15. " 'Tis evident, that all the sciences have a relation, greater or less, to human nature; and that however wide any of them may seem to run from it, they still return back by one passage or another. Even *Mathematics, Natural Philosophy, and Natural Religion,* are in some measure dependent on the science of MAN; since they lie under the cognizance of men, and are judged of by their powers and faculties. 'Tis impossible to tell what changes and improvements we might make in these sciences were we thoroughly acquainted with the extent and force of human understanding, and cou'd explain the nature of the ideas we employ, and of the operations we perform in our reasonings. And these improvements are the more to be hoped for in natural religion, as it is not content with instructing us in the nature of superior powers, but carries its views farther, to their disposition towards us, and our duties towards them; and consequently we ourselves are not only the beings, that reason, but also one of the objects, concerning which we reason.

"If therefore the sciences of Mathematics, Natural Philosophy, and Natural Religion, have such a dependence on the knowledge of man, what may be expected in the other sciences, whose connexion with human nature is more close and intimate? The sole end of logic is to explain the principles and operations of our reasoning faculty, and the nature of our ideas: morals and criticism regard our tastes and sentiments: and politics consider men as united in society, and dependent on each other. In these four sciences of *Logic, Morals, Criticism, and Politics,* is comprehended almost every thing, which it can any way import us to be acquainted with, or which can tend either to the improvement or ornament of the human mind." *Treatise,* pp. xix–xx.

16. "I found that the moral Philosophy transmitted to us by Antiquity, labor'd under the same Inconvenience that has been found in their natural Philosophy, of being entirely Hypothetical, & depending more upon Invention than Experience. Every one consulted his Fancy in erecting Schemes of Virtue & of Happiness, without regarding human Nature, upon which every moral Conclusion must depend. This therefore I resolved to make my principal Study, & the Source from which I wou'd derive every Truth in Criticism as well as Morality." *Letters,* I, 16.

17. *Treatise,* pp. xxii–xxiii, 175.　　　　18. *Treatise,* p. xx.

19. In his *Abstract,* published in 1740, Hume writes about the first two books as follows: "This treatise therefore of human nature seems

intended for a system of the sciences. The author has finished what regards logic, and has laid the foundation of the other parts of his account of the passions." *Abstract,* p. 7.

20. *Treatise,* p. 456.                    21. *Essays,* II, 368.
22. *Enquiry* I, 8.                    23. *Letters,* I, 25.

## II: BELIEF: FALSE AND AUTHENTIC

1. Understanding embraces demonstrative reasoning and believing. Why these particular terms have been used in this chapter is explained in note 31. In the *Abstract,* pp. 7–8, Hume draws attention to the effort of the writer of the *Treatise* to deal adequately with "probabilities, and those other measures of evidence on which life and action entirely depend, and which are our guides even in most of our philosophical speculations."

The reader will find it most helpful to notice that in this chapter, I do not use the terms "knowledge," "to know," and "knowing" with the same meanings that these terms have in the *Treatise.* Hume uses the terms narrowly to refer to demonstrative reasoning. I have used the terms to refer to the five ways of perceiving, i.e., intuiting, remembering, fancying, demonstrative reasoning, and believing.

2. See Norman Kemp Smith's explanation of Part I in *The Philosophy of David Hume* (London, 1949), pp. 10–12, 110–16, and 205–26.

3. "All the perceptions of the human mind resolve themselves into two distinct kinds, which I shall call IMPRESSIONS and IDEAS. The difference betwixt these consists in the degrees of force and liveliness with which they strike upon the mind, and make their way into our thought or consciousness. Those perceptions, which enter with most force and violence, we may name *impressions;* and under this name I comprehend all our sensations, passions and emotions, as they make their first appearance in the soul. By *ideas* I mean the faint images of these in thinking and reasoning; such as, for instance, are all the perceptions excited by the present discourse, excepting only, those which arise from the sight and touch, and excepting the immediate pleasure or uneasiness it may occasion. I believe it will not be very necessary to employ many words in explaining this distinction. Every one of himself will readily perceive the difference betwixt feeling and thinking." *Treatise,* pp. 1–2.

4. *Treatise,* pp. 17–25.

5. See the passage from the *Abstract,* pp. 19–20, quoted at p. 43.

6. *Treatise,* p. 19.

7. *Treatise,* p. 3. Later in the same work (p. 96), he writes: "All

the perceptions of the mind are of two kinds, *viz.* impressions and ideas, which differ from each other only in their different degrees of force and vivacity. Our ideas are copy'd from our impressions, and represent them in all their parts. When you wou'd any way vary the idea of a particular object, you can only encrease or diminish its force and vivacity."

8. *Treatise,* pp. 6–7.

9. The statement of the distinction given by Hume in *Enquiry* I is far more satisfactory. Therein (p. 18), he says: "Here therefore we may divide all the perceptions of the mind into two classes or species, which are distinguished by their different degrees of force and vivacity. The less forcible and lively are commonly denominated *Thoughts* or *Ideas.* The other species want a name in our language, and in most others; I suppose, because it was not requisite for any, but philosophical purposes, to rank them under a general term or appellation. Let us, therefore, use a little freedom, and call them *Impressions;* employing that word in a sense somewhat different from the usual. By the term *impression,* then, I mean all our more lively perceptions, when we hear, or see, or feel, or love, or hate, or desire, or will. And impressions are distinguished from ideas, which are the less lively perceptions, of which we are conscious, when we reflect on any of those sensations or movements above mentioned."

10. "Every one will readily allow, that there is a considerable difference between the perceptions of the mind, when a man feels the pain of excessive heat, or the pleasure of moderate warmth, and when he afterwards recalls to his memory this sensation, or anticipates it by his imagination. These faculties may mimic or copy the perceptions of the senses; but they never can entirely reach the force and vivacity of the original sentiment. The utmost we say of them, even when they operate with greatest vigour, is, that they represent their object in so lively a manner, that we could *almost* say we feel or see it: But, except the mind be disordered by disease or madness, they never can arrive at such a pitch of vivacity, as to render these perceptions altogether undistinguishable. All the colours of poetry, however splendid, can never paint natural objects in such a manner as to make the description be taken for a real landskip. The most lively thought is still inferior to the dullest sensation." *Enquiry* I, p. 17. See also quote on p. 43.

11. Locke, *An Essay concerning Human Understanding* (Oxford, 1894), vol. I, chap. XXX, p. 497.

12. *Treatise,* p. 86.

13. *Treatise,* p. 7, and *Abstract,* pp. 9–10.

14. *Treatise,* pp. 17–25.     15. *Treatise,* pp. 199–201.

16. Complex ideas, Hume found, traditionally were grouped under

three headings: Relations, Modes, and Substances. Modes and Substances he dismisses; so that for him complex ideas are made up of simple ideas related in one or more of the seven ways he mentions. *Treatise,* pp. 13–17.

17. *Treatise,* pp. 14–15 and p. 69.          18. *Treatise,* p. 70.

19. "Thro' this whole book, there are great pretensions to new discoveries in philosophy; but if any thing can intitle the author to so glorious a name as that of an *inventor,* 'tis the use he makes of the principle of the association of ideas, which enters into most of his philosophy. Our imagination has a great authority over our ideas; and there are no ideas that are different from each other, which it cannot separate, and join, and compose into all the varieties of fiction. But notwithstanding the empire of the imagination, there is a secret tie or union among particular ideas, which causes the mind to conjoin them more frequently together, and make the one, upon its appearance, introduce the other. Hence arises what we call the *apropos* of discourse: hence the connection of writing: and hence that thread, or chain of thought, which a man naturally supports even in the loosest *reverie.* These principles of association are reduced to three, *viz. Resemblance;* a picture naturally makes us think of the man it was drawn for. *Contiguity;* when *St. Dennis* is mentioned, the idea of *Paris* naturally occurs. *Causation;* when we think of the son, we are apt to carry our attention to the father. 'Twill be easy to conceive of what vast consequence these principles must be in the science of human nature, if we consider, that so far as regards the mind, these are the only links that bind the parts of the universe together, or connect us with any person or object exterior to ourselves. For as it is by means of thought only that any thing operates upon our passions, and as these are the only ties of our thoughts, they are really *to us* the cement of the universe, and all the operations of the mind must, in a great measure, depend on them." *Abstract,* pp. 31–32.

20. "All the objects of human reason or enquiry may naturally be divided into two kinds, to wit, *Relations of Ideas,* and *Matters of Fact.* Of the first kind are the sciences of Geometry, Algebra, and Arithmetic; and in short, every affirmation which is either intuitively or demonstratively certain. . . .

"Matters of fact, which are the second objects of human reason, are not ascertained in the same manner; nor is our evidence of their truth, however great, of a like nature with the foregoing. The contrary of every matter of fact is still possible; because it can never imply a contradiction, and is conceived by the mind with the same facility and distinctness, as if ever so conformable to reality. *That the sun will not rise to-morrow* is no less intelligible a proposition, and implies no more contradiction than the affirmation, *that it will rise*. We should in vain, therefore, attempt to demonstrate its falsehood. Were it demonstratively false, it would imply a contradiction, and could never be distinctly conceived by the mind." *Enquiry* I, pp. 25–26.

21. *Treatise*, pp. 73–74; *Enquiry* I, pp. 26–27.

22. *Abstract*, p. 11.                   23. *Enquiry* I, p. 61.

24. *Treatise*, p. 89.                    25. *Treatise*, pp. 10–11.

26. *Enquiry* I, pp. 54–55.           27. *Enquiry* I, p. 43.

28. *Treatise*, p. 96. See also pp. 94, 97, 103; *Enquiry* I, p. 46.

29. *Abstract*, pp. 19–20.

30. "I conclude, by an induction which seems to me very evident, that an opinion or belief is nothing but an idea, that is different from a fiction, not in the nature, or the order of its parts, but in the *manner* of its being conceiv'd. But when I wou'd explain this *manner*, I scarce find any word that fully answers the case, but am oblig'd to have recourse to every one's feeling, in order to give him a perfect notion of this operation of the mind. An idea assented to *feels* different from a fictitious idea, that the fancy alone presents to us: And this different feeling I endeavour to explain by calling it a superior *force*, or *vivacity*, or *solidity*, or *firmness*, or *steadiness*. This variety of terms, which may seem so unphilosophical, is intended only to express that act of the mind, which renders realities more present to us than fictions, causes them to weigh more in the thought, and gives them a superior influence on the passions and imagination." *Treatise*, pp. 628–29.

31. Although Hume himself does not list the several ways of knowing, he does compare five ways of knowing, and the terms I have employed herein to designate those five ways seem as satisfactory as any available.

For his use of "intuition," see the *Treatise*, p. 70. In that work (pp. 8–10), he distinguishes between "remembering" and "imagining." See also *Enquiry* I, p. 25.

"Imagining," he finds, has three meanings in common usage. "In general we may observe, that as our assent to all probable reasonings is founded on the vivacity of ideas, it resembles many of those whimsies and prejudices, which are rejected under the opprobrious character of being the offspring of the imagination. By this expression it appears that the word, imagination, is commonly us'd in two different senses; and tho' nothing be more contrary to true philosophy, than this inaccuracy, yet in the following reasonings I have often been oblig'd to fall into it. When I oppose the imagination to the memory, I mean the faculty, by which we form our fainter ideas. When I oppose it to reason, I mean the same faculty, excluding only our demonstrative and probable reasonings. When I oppose it to neither, 'tis indifferent whether it be taken in the larger or more limited sense, or at least the context will sufficiently explain the meaning." *Treatise,* pp. 117–18, footnote.

Naming these three kinds of imagination—"When I oppose it to reason, I mean the same faculty, excluding only our demonstrative and probable reasonings"—is quite difficult. The first, imagination as contrasted to both kinds of "reasonings," can be called "fancying," but the other two cause trouble.

The book, "Of the Understanding," is primarily an analysis of what Hume calls, "the reasoning faculty." "The understanding," he submits (*Treatise,* p. 413), "exerts itself after two different ways, as it judges from demonstration or probability; as it regards the abstract relations of our ideas, or those relations of objects, of which experience only gives us information." "Probable reasoning," the second of these two branches of understanding, he finds, has been treated inadequately by philosophers; and the main purpose of his own book is to explain how we understand in this second way. See the *Abstract,* pp. 7–8.

His argument is that each of these two ways of understanding— reasoning about a logical system, and reasoning about a natural system —is legitimate, and that the two must not be confused. But since the two generally have been confused, he has no entirely satisfactory term to use for the second. Sometimes he speaks of it as "probable reasoning," but the word "reasoning" is likely to retain its old deceptive connotation. And sometimes he speaks of it as "believing," but the trouble here is that our perceptions of the present and the past also are beliefs. I have followed the last usage because, despite the somewhat wider meaning of the word, it seems better than "imagining" or "probable reasoning."

In both the *Treatise* and the *Enquiry concerning Human Understanding* he changes his use of the words "understanding" and "reasoning." At first, following the prevailing practice, he uses these words to refer only to judgment from demonstration, so that, for example, we find him contrasting imagination and understanding. But towards the ends of the books, when he assumes that the reader now knows that understanding (or reasoning) is of two distinct kinds and can ascertain from the context which of the two meanings is intended, he uses these words ("understanding" and "reasoning") with both meanings.

32. *Treatise,* p. 89.

33. *Enquiry* I, p. 46.     34. *Treatise,* p. 131; *Enquiry* I, p. 55.

35. "But allow me to tell you, that I never asserted so absurd a Proposition as *that any thing might arise without a Cause:* I only maintain'd that our Certainty of the Falshood of that Proposition proceeded neither from Intuition nor Demonstration; but from another Source. *That Caesar existed, that there is such an Island as Sicily;* for

these Propositions, I affirm, we have no demonstrative nor intuitive Proof. Woud you infer that I deny their Truth, or even their Certainty? There are many different kinds of Certainty; and some of them as satisfactory to the Mind, tho perhaps not so regular, as the demonstrative kind." *Letters*, I, 187.

36. *Treatise*, p. 183. "Custom, then, is the great guide of human life. It is that principle alone which renders our experience useful to us, and makes us expect, for the future, a similar train of events with those which have appeared in the past. Without the influence of custom, we should be entirely ignorant of every matter of fact beyond what is immediately present to the memory and senses. We should never know how to adjust means to ends, or to employ our natural powers in the production of any effect. There would be an end at once of all action, as well as of the chief part of speculation." *Enquiry* I, pp. 44–45.

37. *Treatise*, p. 124; *Enquiry* I, p. 56, footnote.

38. *Treatise*, p. 132.          39. *Treatise*, p. 142.

40. *Treatise*, p. 143.          41. *Treatise*, pp. 143–44.

42. *Treatise*, pp. 144–46.          43. *Treatise*, pp. 146–53.

44. In the essay, "Of the Study of History," Hume says: "I must add, that history is not only a valuable part of knowledge, but opens the door to many other parts, and affords materials to most of the sciences. And indeed, if we consider the shortness of human life, and our limited knowledge, even of what passes in our own time, we must be sensible that we should be for ever children in understanding, were it not for this invention, which extends our experience to all past ages, and to the most distant nations; making them contribute as much to our improvement in wisdom, as if they had actually lain under our observation. A man acquainted with history may, in some respect, be said to have lived from the beginning of the world, and to have been making continual additions to his stock of knowledge in every century." *Essays*, II, 390.

45. *Treatise*, p. 113.          46. *Treatise*, p. 117.

47. *Treatise*, pp. 116, 118.

48. "In every judgment, which we can form concerning probability, as well as concerning knowledge, we ought always to correct the first judgment, deriv'd from the nature of the object, by another judgment, deriv'd from the nature of the understanding. 'Tis certain a man of solid sense and long experience ought to have, and usually has, a greater assurance in his opinions, than one that is foolish and ignorant, and that our sentiments have different degrees of authority, even with ourselves, in proportion to the degrees of our reason and experience." *Treatise*, pp. 181–82.

49. *Treatise*, pp. 173–74.

50. *Abstract*, p. 25. See the important discussion of "identity" in the

*Treatise,* pp. 200–1, and notice the distinction between numerical and specific identity in the *Treatise,* pp. 257–58.

51. *Treatise,* p. 261.               52. *Treatise,* pp. 234, 250.
53. *Treatise,* pp. 188–92.           54. *Treatise,* p. 193.
55. *Treatise,* pp. 195–210, especially p. 199.
56. *Treatise,* p. 215.               57. *Treatise,* p. 218.
58. *Enquiry* I, pp. 152–53.          59. *Enquiry* I, pp. 41–42, 159.
60. *Enquiry* I, p. 161.

61. *Enquiry* I, pp. 12, 30–31, 162. In the *History,* VIII, 334, we read that: "While Newton seemed to draw off the veil from some of the mysteries of nature, he shewed at the same time the imperfections of the mechanical philosophy; and thereby restored her ultimate secrets to that obscurity, in which they ever did and ever will remain."

62. "For rightly is truth called the daughter of time, not of authority." Bacon, Book I, LXXXIV.

63. *Treatise,* pp. 149–50.           64. *Treatise,* pp. 175, 271–73.


# III: PASSION AND ACTION

1. The relation between passion, on the one hand, and good and evil, on the other, is of two kinds, according to Hume. First, some sensations originate externally, when objects come into contact with the external organs. These sensations are found either pleasant or painful, and appropriate passions result. Second, other sensations are of internal origin, arising from the constitution of the body or from the animal spirits. These give rise to passions. And then objects are found pleasant or painful according as they suit those passions.

He writes: "Beside good and evil, or in other words, pain and pleasure, the direct passions frequently arise from a natural impulse or instinct, which is perfectly unaccountable. Of this kind is the desire of punishment to our enemies, and of happiness to our friends; hunger, lust, and a few other bodily appetites. These passions, properly speaking, produce good and evil, and proceed not from them, like the other affections." *Treatise,* p. 439; see also p. 275.

In "Of the Passions," *Essays,* II, 139, he makes the same analysis: "Some objects produce immediately an agreeable sensation, by the original structure of our organs, and are thence denominated GOOD; as others, from their immediate disagreeable sensation, acquire the appellation of EVIL. Thus moderate warmth is agreeable and good; excessive heat painful and evil.

"Some objects again, by being naturally conformable or contrary to passion, excite an agreeable or painful sensation; and are thence called *Good* or *Evil.* The punishment of an adversary, by gratifying revenge, is good; the sickness of a companion, by affecting friendship, is evil."

2. *Treatise,* pp. 440–41.          3. *Treatise,* pp. 283–84.

4. In *Enquiry* II, p. 314, Hume explains that he does not use the word "pride" with its common meaning. By "pride" he designates "the *sentiment* of conscious worth, the self-satisfaction proceeding from a review of a man's own conduct and character; it seems certain, I say, that this sentiment, which, though the most common of all others, has no proper name in our language, arises from the endowments of courage and capacity, industry and ingenuity, as well as from any other mental excellencies." In a footnote he expatiates: "The term, pride, is commonly taken in a bad sense; but this sentiment seems indifferent, and may be either good or bad, according as it is well or ill founded, and according to the other circumstances which accompany it." See also *Treatise,* pp. 297–98.

5. *Treatise,* pp. 281–82.          6. *Treatise,* pp. 290–94.

7. *Treatise,* pp. 317–20.

8. Adam Smith presented Hume with a copy of his first book, *The Theory of Moral Sentiments,* published in 1759. On July 28, 1759, Hume wrote to Smith as follows: "I wish you had more particularly and fully prov'd, that all kinds of Sympathy are necessarily Agreeable. This is the Hinge of your System, & yet you only mention the Matter cursorily in p. 20. Now it woud appear that there is a disagreeable Sympathy, as well as an agreeable: And indeed, as the Sympathetic Passion is a reflex Image of the principal, it must partake of its Qualities, & be painful where that is so. Indeed, *when we converse with a man with whom we can entirely sympathize,* that is, where there is a warm & intimate Friendship, the cordial openness of such a Commerce overpowers the Pain of a disagreeable Sympathy, and renders the whole Movement agreeable. But in ordinary Cases, this cannot have place. An ill-humord Fellow; a man tir'd & disgusted with every thing, always *ennuié;* sickly, complaining, embarass'd; such a one throws an evident Damp on Company, which I suppose wou'd be accounted for by Sympathy; and yet is disagreeable.

"It is always thought a difficult Problem to account for the Pleasure, receivd from the Tears & Grief & Sympathy of Tragedy; which woud not be the Case, if all Sympathy was agreeable. An Hospital woud be a more entertaining Place than a Ball. I am afraid that in p. 99 and 111 this Proposition has escapd you, or rather is interwove with your Reasonings in that place. You say expressly, *it is painful to go along with Grief & we always enter into it with Reluctance.* It will probably be requisite for you to modify or explain this Sentiment, & reconcile it to your System." *Letters,* I, 313.

9. *Treatise,* p. 363.

10. *Treatise,* pp. 363, 365; *Enquiry* II, p. 220.

11. *Treatise,* p. 117.        12. *Treatise,* pp. 316–17.

13. See p. 100.        14. *Treatise,* p. 316.

15. The vulgar, Hume tells us, overestimate the importance of riches. Experience, as well as philosophy, may free a man from this folly. *Enquiry* II, p. 248.

16. *Treatise,* pp. 339–40.

17. "Those, who take a pleasure in declaiming against human nature, have observ'd, that man is altogether insufficient to support himself; and that when you loosen all the holds, which he has of external objects, he immediately drops down into the deepest melancholy and despair. From this, say they, proceeds that continual search after amusement in gaming, in hunting, in business; by which we endeavour to forget ourselves, and excite our spirits from the languid state, into which they fall, when not sustain'd by some brisk and lively emotion. To this method of thinking I so far agree, that I own the mind to be insufficient, of itself, to its own entertainment, and that it naturally seeks after foreign objects, which may produce a lively sensation, and agitate the spirits. On the appearance of such an object it awakes, as it were, from a dream: The blood flows with a new tide: The heart is elevated: And the whole man acquires a vigour, which he cannot command in his solitary and calm moments." *Treatise,* pp. 352–53.

18. *Treatise,* p. 348.        19. *Treatise,* p. 375.

20. *Treatise,* p. 381.        21. *Treatise,* p. 377.

22. *Treatise,* pp. 386–87, 594–95.

23. "DESIRE arises from good consider'd simply, and AVERSION is deriv'd from evil. The WILL exerts itself, when either the good or the absence of the evil may be attain'd by any action of the mind or body." *Treatise,* p. 439. See Hume's definition of "Will," at *Treatise,* p. 399.

24. It may be objected, Hume comments, that while necessity is regular and certain, human conduct is irregular and uncertain. But we must bear in mind, he says, that although many of our beliefs are weak, we do not therefore abandon the idea of natural necessity. Below proofs "there are many inferior degrees of evidence and probability, nor does one single contrariety of experiment entirely destroy all our reasoning. The mind ballances the contrary experiments, and deducting the inferior from the superior, proceeds with that degree of assurance or evidence, which remains. Even when these contrary experiments are entirely equal, we remove not the notion of causes and necessity; but supposing that the usual contrariety proceeds from the operation of contrary and conceal'd causes, we conclude, that the chance or indifference lies only in our judgment on account of our imperfect knowledge, not in the things themselves, which are in every case equally necessary, tho' to appearance not equally constant or cer-

tain. No union can be more constant and certain, than that of some actions with some motives and characters; and if in other cases the union is uncertain, 'tis no more than what happens in the operations of body, nor can we conclude any thing from the one irregularity, which will not follow equally from the other." *Treatise,* pp. 403–4.

25. *Treatise,* pp. 348–50, 412.

26. Much of the disagreement on this topic, Hume submits, results from the confusion of two kinds of liberty. When "we have perform'd any action; tho' we confess we were influenc'd by particular views and motives; 'tis difficult for us to perswade ourselves we were govern'd by necessity, and that 'twas utterly impossible for us to have acted otherwise; the idea of necessity seeming to imply something of force, and violence, and constraint, of which we are not sensible. Few are capable of distinguishing betwixt the liberty of *spontaniety,* as it is call'd in the schools, and the liberty of *indifference;* betwixt that which is oppos'd to violence, and that which means a negation of necessity and causes. The first is even the most common sense of the word; and as 'tis only that species of liberty, which it concerns us to preserve, our thoughts have been principally turn'd towards it, and have almost universally confounded it with the other." *Treatise,* pp. 407–8.

27. *Treatise,* p. 414.  28. *Treatise,* p. 459.
29. *Treatise,* pp. 418–19.  30. *Treatise,* p. 276.
31. *Treatise,* p. 417.  32. *Treatise,* pp. 276, 417–18.

33. "What is commonly, in a popular sense, called reason, and is so much recommended in moral discourses, is nothing but a general and a calm passion, which takes a comprehensive and a distant view of its object, and actuates the will, without exciting any sensible emotion. A man, we say, is diligent in his profession from reason; that is, from a calm desire of riches and a fortune. A man adheres to justice from reason; that is, from a calm regard to public good, or to a character with himself and others.

"The same objects, which recommend themselves to reason in this sense of the word, are also the objects of what we call passion, when they are brought near to us, and acquire some other advantages, either of external situation, or congruity to our internal temper; and by that means excite a turbulent and sensible emotion. Evil, at a great distance, is avoided, we say, from reason: Evil, near at hand, produces aversion, horror, fear, and is the object of passion." "A Dissertation of the Passions," *Essays,* II, 161–62.

34. *Treatise,* pp. 420–22.  35. *Treatise,* pp. 424–27.
36. *Treatise,* pp. 427–32, 536.

37. "A Dissertation of the Passions," *Essays,* II, 162; *Treatise,* p. 418; *Enquiry* II, p. 239.

38. *Treatise,* p. 437.

## IV: MORAL DUTIES

1. *Treatise,* p. 455.

2. Whether or not there is a difference between virtue and vice is not the question. That there is a difference, Hume submits, is easily seen from our common language and conduct. *Enquiry* II, pp. 174, 214, 228.

3. Hume suggests this in "My Own Life," *Essays,* I, 3–4. See the Appendix, p. 325, footnote 1.

4. "We shall call *every quality or action of the mind,* virtuous, *which is attended with the general approbation of mankind:* and we shall denominate vicious, *every quality which is the object of general blame or censure." Enquiry concerning the Principles of Morals, Essays,* II, 173, footnote.

5. "If any *action* be either virtuous or vicious, 'tis only as a sign of some quality or character. It must depend upon durable principles of the mind, which extend over the whole conduct, and enter into the personal character. Actions themselves, not proceeding from any constant principle, have no influence on love or hatred, pride or humility; and consequently are never consider'd in morality." *Treatise,* p. 575.

6. This would not be true in the case of moral laws based on the right of a superior Being to command mankind.

7. *Treatise,* p. 478.          8. *Treatise,* p. 480.

9. Francis Hutcheson read "Of Morals" in manuscript, and commented on it. In his reply, dated September 17, 1739, to Hutcheson's comments, Hume wrote:

"I cannot forbear recommending another thing to your Consideration. Actions are not virtuous nor vicious; but only so far as they are proofs of certain Qualitys or durable Principles in the Mind. This is a Point I shou'd have establish'd more expressly than I have done. Now I desire you to consider, if there be any Quality, that is virtuous, without having a Tendency either to the public Good or to the Good of the Person, who possesses it. If there be none without these Tendencys, we may conclude, that their Merit is derivd from Sympathy. I desire you wou'd only consider the Tendencys of Qualitys, not their actual Operation, which depends on Chance. *Brutus* riveted the Chains of *Rome* faster by his Opposition; but the natural Tendency of his noble Dispositions, his public Spirit & Magnanimity, was to establish her Liberty.

"You are a great Admirer of *Cicero,* as well as I am. Please to review the 4th Book, *de finibus bonorum & malorum;* where you find him prove against the *Stoics,* that if there be no other Goods but Virtue, tis impossible there can be any Virtue; because the Mind woud then want all Motives to begin its Actions upon: And tis on the Goodness or Badness of the Motives that the Virtue of the Action depends. This proves, that to every virtuous Action there must be a Motive or impelling Passion distinct from the Virtue, & that Virtue can never be the sole Motive to any Action. You do not assent to this; tho' I think there is no Proposition more certain or important." *Letters,* I, pp. 34–35.

10. Hume himself used this tactic. See Chapter IV, note 34.

11. On March 16, 1740, while preparing "Of Morals" for the printer, Hume wrote to Francis Hutcheson as follows: "I must consult you in a Point of Prudence. I have concluded a Reasoning with these two Sentences. *When you pronounce any Action or Character to be vicious, you mean nothing but that from the particular Constitution of your Nature you have a Feeling or Sentiment of Blame from the Contemplation of it. Vice & Virtue, therefore, may be compar'd to Sounds, Colours, Heat & Cold, which, according to modern Philosophy, are not Qualitys in Objects but Perceptions in the Mind: And this Discovery in Morals, like that other in Physicks, is to be regarded as a mighty Advancement of the speculative Sciences; tho' like that too, it has little or no Influence on Practice.* Is not this laid a little [too stro]ng?" *Letters,* I, 39–40.

The two sentences quoted by Hume appear in the *Treatise,* p. 469, with only two minor changes. The word *particular* is omitted, and *considerable* is used instead of *mighty.*

12. *Treatise,* pp. 465–66.

13. Hume did not claim that his argument that the distinction between virtue and vice is based on the feelings was original. The ancients, especially Aristotle, and moderns such as Lord Shaftesbury and Mr. Hutcheson had preceded him. *Enquiry* II, pp. 170–71.

It is interesting to notice that Hume includes Montesquieu among the rationalists. He praised him in the first two editions of *Enquiry* II (1751 and 1753–54) as the author of "the best system of political knowledge, that, perhaps, has ever yet been communicated to the world" but goes on to comment in a footnote: "This illustrious writer, however, sets out with a different theory, and supposes all right to be founded on certain *rapports* or relations; which is a system, that, in my opinion, never will be reconciled with true philosophy. Father MALEBRANCHE, as far as I can learn, was the first that started this abstract theory of morals, which was afterwards adopted by CUD-WORTH, CLARKE, and others; and as it excludes all sentiment, and pretends to found every thing on reason, it has not wanted followers in this philosophic age." *Essays,* II, 190–91.

Professor J. A. Passmore suggests that the fact that both Cudworth and Malebranche were Cartesian Platonists may be sufficient to explain their similarities, but that if there is any indebtedness, Malebranche is the borrower. *Hume's Intentions* (Cambridge, 1952), p. 88, footnote.

14. *Treatise,* p. 471.        15. *Treatise,* pp. 575–76, 618.

16. *Treatise,* pp. 471–72.

17. It is certain, he writes, that "self-love, when it acts at its liberty, instead of engaging us to honest actions, is the source of all injustice and violence; nor can a man ever correct those vices, without correcting and restraining the *natural* movements of that appetite." *Treatise,* p. 480; see also pp. 486–87.

18. *Enquiry* II, pp. 218–19, 243.        19. *Treatise,* p. 472.

20. *Treatise,* p. 581; *Enquiry* II, p. 272.

21. *Treatise,* p. 591; also pp. 582–83, 602–3.

22. *Treatise,* p. 472.

23. "In general, all sentiments of blame or praise are variable, according to our situation of nearness or remoteness, with regard to the person blam'd or prais'd, and according to the present disposition of our mind. But these variations we regard not in our general decisions, but still apply the terms expressive of our liking or dislike, in the same manner, as if we remain'd in one point of view. Experience soon teaches us this method of correcting our sentiments, or at least, of correcting our language, where the sentiments are more stubborn and inalterable." *Treatise,* p. 582. Hume restates this argument felicitously in the *Enquiry* II, p. 229.

24. *Treatise,* pp. 483–84, and pp. 478, 532. See also *Enquiry* II, p. 225, footnote.

25. *Treatise,* pp. 589–90.        26. *Treatise,* p. 587.

27. *Treatise,* p. 591.

28. *Enquiry* II, p. 278. Hume devotes a separate discussion to each of these four kinds of virtue in the *Enquiry.* Those useful to others are treated at pp. 218–32; those useful to the possessor in Section VI; those agreeable to others in Section VIII; and those agreeable to the possessor in Section VII. Notice his listing of the four kinds of virtues in that work, pp. 277–78.

29. *Treatise,* p. 610. In *Enquiry* II he examines extensively, pp. 312–23, the distinction between virtues and talents. In his letter to Hutcheson, September 17, 1739, he says: "Whether natural Abilitys be Virtues is a Dispute of Words. I think I follow the common Use of Language. *Virtus* signify'd chiefly Courage among the *Romans.* I was just now reading this Character of Alexander the 6th in Guicciardin. In Alessandro Sesto fu solertia & sagacita singulare: consiglio eccellente, efficacia a persuadere maravigliosa, & a tutte le facende gravi, sollicitudine & destrezza incredible. Ma erano queste virtù avanzate di grande intervallo da vitii &c. Were Benevolence the

only Virtue no Characters cou'd be mixt, but wou'd depend entirely
on their Degrees of Benevolence. Upon the whole, I desire to take
my Catalogue of Virtues from *Cicero's Offices,* not from the *Whole
Duty of Man.* I had, indeed, the former Book in my Eye in all my
Reasonings." *Letters,* I, 33–34.

30. *Treatise,* pp. 614–15; *Enquiry* II, pp. 244–45.

31. *Treatise,* p. 479. In "The Sceptic," which, of the four essays
entitled after ancient schools of philosophy, seems to present his
own viewpoint best, Hume submits that no philosophic doctrine can
remedy a man's character. The chief benefit of philosophy is indirect.

"It is certain, that a serious attention to the sciences and liberal arts
softens and humanizes the temper, and cherishes those fine emotions,
in which true virtue and honour consists. It rarely, very rarely happens, that a man of taste and learning is not, at least, an honest man,
whatever frailties may attend him. The bent of his mind to speculative
studies must mortify in him the passions of interest and ambition, and
must, at the same time, give him a greater sensibility of all the de-
cencies and duties of life. He feels more fully a moral distinction in
characters and manners; nor is his sense of this kind diminished, but,
on the contrary, it is much encreased, by speculation.

"Besides such insensible changes upon the temper and disposition,
it is highly probable, that others may be produced by study and application. The prodigious effects of education may convince us, that the
mind is not altogether stubborn and inflexible, but will admit of many
alterations from its original make and structure. Let a man propose to
himself the model of a character, which he approves: Let him be well
acquainted with those particulars, in which his own character deviates
from this model: Let him keep a constant watch over himself, and
bend his mind, by a continual effort, from the vices, towards the
virtues; and I doubt not but, in time, he will find, in his temper, an
alteration for the better.

"Habit is another powerful means of reforming the mind, and im-
planting in it good dispositions and inclinations." *Essays,* I, 223.

32. "The intercourse of sentiments, therefore, in society and conversation, makes us form some general inalterable standard, by which
we may approve or disapprove of characters and manners." *Treatise,*
p. 603.

33. *Treatise,* p. 415.

34. "Thus the distinct boundaries and offices of *reason* and of *taste*
are easily ascertained. The former conveys the knowledge of truth
and falsehood: the latter gives the sentiment of beauty and deformity,
vice and virtue. The one discovers objects as they really stand in nature, without addition or diminution: the other has a productive faculty,
and gilding or staining all natural objects with the colours, borrowed

from internal sentiment, raises in a manner a new creation. Reason being cool and disengaged, is no motive to action, and directs only the impulse received from appetite or inclination, by showing us the means of attaining happiness or avoiding misery: Taste, as it gives pleasure or pain, and thereby constitutes happiness or misery, becomes a motive to action, and is the first spring or impulse to desire and volition. From circumstances and relations, known or supposed, the former leads us to the discovery of the concealed and unknown: after all circumstances and relations are laid before us, the latter makes us feel from the whole a new sentiment of blame or approbation. The standard of the one, being founded on the nature of things, is eternal and inflexible, even by the will of the Supreme Being: the standard of the other, arising from the eternal frame and constitution of animals, is ultimately derived from that Supreme Will, which bestowed on each being its peculiar nature, and arranged the several classes and orders of existence." *Enquiry* II, p. 294; note also p. 173.

## V: NATURAL RELATIONSHIPS AND CIVIL SOCIETY

1. The importance of the family in Hume's thought is shown by his strong arguments against polygamy and divorce. *Essays,* I, 231–39.
2. *Treatise,* p. 481.
3. In *Enquiry* II, he makes the same distinction between feelings for others that cause continuing relationships and those that cause only occasional acts. "Benevolence naturally divides into two kinds, the *general* and the *particular.* The first is, where we have no friendship or connexion or esteem for the person, but feel only a general sympathy with him or a compassion for his pains, and a congratulation with his pleasures. The other species of benevolence is founded on an opinion of virtue, on services done us, or on some particular connexions. Both these sentiments must be allowed real in human nature: but whether they will resolve into some nice considerations of self-love, is a question more curious than important. The former sentiment, to wit, that of general benevolence, or humanity, or sympathy, we shall have occasion frequently to treat of in the course of this enquiry; and I assume it as real, from general experience, without any other proof" (p. 298, footnote).
4. *Treatise,* p. 578.  5. *Treatise,* p. 603.
6. *Treatise,* p. 485.  7. *Treatise,* pp. 486–87.
8. On January 10, 1743, Hume wrote as follows to Francis Hutcheson: "You sometimes, in my Opinion, ascribe the Original of Property & Justice to public Benevolence, & sometimes to private Benevo-

lence towards the Possessors of the Goods, neither of which seem to me satisfactory. You know my Opinion on this head. It mortifies me much to see a Person, who possesses more Candour & Penetration than any almost I know, condemn Reasonings, of which I imagine I see so strongly the Evidence. I was going to blot out this after having wrote it, but hope you will consider it only as a Piece of Folly, as indeed it is." *Letters,* I, 47–48.

9. *Treatise,* pp. 503–13.

10. "Some philosophers account for the right of occupation, by saying, that every one has a property in his own labour; and when he joins that labour to any thing, it gives him the property of the whole: But, 1. There are several kinds of occupation, where we cannot be said to join our labour to the object we acquire: As when we possess a meadow by grazing our cattle upon it. 2. This accounts for the matter by means of *accession;* which is taking a needless circuit. 3. We cannot be said to join our labour in any thing but in a figurative sense. Properly speaking, we only make an alteration on it by our labour. This forms a relation betwixt us and the object; and thence arises the property, according to the preceding principles." *Treatise,* pp. 505–6, footnote.

11. *Treatise,* p. 505.     12. *Treatise,* p. 503.

13. *Treatise,* pp. 506–9; *Enquiry* II, p. 196.

14. *Enquiry* II, p. 196.     15. *Treatise,* p. 509.

16. *Enquiry* II, pp. 309–10.

17. *Treatise,* pp. 530–31; *Enquiry* II, pp. 308–9. "It must, indeed, be confessed, that nature is so liberal to mankind, that, were all her presents equally divided among the species, and improved by art and industry, every individual would enjoy all the necessaries, and even most of the comforts of life; nor would ever be liable to any ills, but such as might accidentally arise from the sickly frame and constitution of his body. It must also be confessed, that, wherever we depart from this equality, we rob the poor of more satisfaction than we add to the rich, and that the slight gratification of a frivolous vanity, in one individual, frequently costs more than bread to many families, and even provinces. It may appear withal, that the rule of equality, as it would be highly *useful,* is not altogether *impracticable;* but has taken place, at least in an imperfect degree, in some republics; particularly that of Sparta; where it was attended, it is said, with the most beneficial consequences. Not to mention that the Agrarian laws, so frequently claimed in Rome, and carried into execution in many Greek cities, proceeded, all of them, from a general idea of the utility of this principle.

"But historians, and even common sense, may inform us, that, however specious these ideas of *perfect* equality may seem, they are really, at bottom, *impracticable;* and were they not so, would be extremely *pernicious* to human society. Render possessions ever so equal, men's different degrees of art, care, and industry will immediately break that equality. Or if you check these virtues, you reduce society to the most extreme indigence; and instead of preventing want and beggary in a few, render it unavoidable to the whole community. The most rigorous inquisition too is requisite to watch every inequality on its first appearance; and the most severe jurisdiction, to punish and redress it. But besides, that so much authority must soon degenerate into tyranny, and be exerted with great partialities; who can possibly be possessed of it, in such a situation as is here supposed? Perfect equality of possessions, destroying all subordination, weakens extremely the authority of magistracy, and must reduce all power nearly to a level, as well as property.

"We may conclude, therefore, that, in order to establish laws for the regulation of property, we must be acquainted with the nature and situation of man; must reject appearances, which may be false, though specious; and must search for those rules, which are, on the whole, most *useful* and *beneficial.* Vulgar sense and slight experience are sufficient for this purpose; where men give not way to too selfish avidity, or too extensive enthusiasm." *Enquiry* II, pp. 193–95.

18. In a letter, December 8, 1775, to his nephew, then a student at Glasgow, Hume commented: "[Ha]rrington is an Author of Genius; but chimerical. No Laws, however rigorous, [would ma]ke his Agrarian practicable." *Letters,* II, 306.

19. *Treatise,* p. 502; *Enquiry* II, pp. 192–93, 305.

20. "In general we may observe that all questions of property are subordinate to the authority of civil laws, which extend, restrain, modify, and alter the rules of natural justice, according to the particular *convenience* of each community. The laws have, or ought to have, a constant reference to the constitution of government, the manners, the climate, the religion, the commerce, the situation of each society." *Enquiry* II, p. 196.

After the first edition of the *Enquiry* Hume added several paragraphs at this point, among them the following: "How great soever the variety of municipal laws, it must be confessed, that their chief out-lines pretty regularly concur; because the purposes, to which they tend, are everywhere exactly similar. In like manner, all houses have a roof and walls, windows and chimneys; though diversified in their shape, figure, and materials. The purposes of the latter, directed to the conveniences of human life, discover not more plainly their origin from reason and reflection, than do those of the former, which point all to a like end." *Enquiry* II, pp. 202–3.

21. *Treatise,* pp. 514–16.     22. *Treatise,* pp. 516–25.

23. *Treatise,* p. 520.                    24. *Treatise,* pp. 521–22.

25. It is important to notice how Hume at this point makes a transition from traditional moral theory to modern economic thought. He has made three rules of competition the fundamental principles of society; and he is quite prepared to say that, insofar as social life, as distinct from the family, friendship, and humanity, is concerned these three rules of competition are the true content of what traditionally was called the "Laws of Nature." He writes: "We have now run over the three fundamental laws of nature, *that of the stability of possession, of its transference by consent,* and *of the performance of promises.* 'Tis on the strict observance of those three laws, that the peace and security of human society entirely depend; nor is there any possibility of establishing a good correspondence among men, where these are neglected. Society is absolutely necessary for the well-being of men; and these are as necessary to the support of society." *Treatise,* p. 526.

26. Adam Smith, *The Wealth of Nations* (London, 1950), I, 16.

27. *Treatise,* p. 537.

28. At this point, and at several others in later chapters, I have found it helpful to use the analogy of a play—sometimes in the sense of a game and sometimes in the sense of a drama—in my attempt to open up the implications of Hume's thought. This is my device, not his. It is justified, I think, for, first, in his principles of society and state, we have a set of rules of conduct; second, in precivilization men we have potential members of casts or teams; and, third, in "civilization" we have a casting process in which particular men attain specific roles, thus bringing the rules down into the world of action.

29. *Treatise,* pp. 537–38.

30. "If the ideas of justice, sometimes, do not follow the dispositions of civil law; we shall find, that these cases, instead of objections, are confirmations of the theory delivered above. Where a civil law is so perverse as to cross all the interests of society, it loses all its authority, and men judge by the ideas of natural justice, which are conformable to those interests. Sometimes also civil laws, for useful purposes, require a ceremony or form to any deed; and where that is wanting, their decrees run contrary to the usual tenour of justice; but one who takes advantage of such chicanes, is not commonly regarded as an honest man. Thus, the interests of society require, that contracts be fulfilled; and there is not a more material article either of natural or civil justice: But the omission of a trifling circumstance will often, by law, invalidate a contract, *in foro humano,* but not *in foro conscientiae,* as divines express themselves. In these cases, the magistrate is supposed only to withdraw his power of enforcing the right, not to have altered the right. Where his intention extends to the right, and

is conformable to the interests of society; it never fails to alter the right; a clear proof of the origin of justice and of property, as assigned above." *Enquiry* II, p. 197, footnote.

31. "Man, born in a family, is compelled to maintain society, from necessity, from natural inclination, and from habit. The same creature, in his farther progress, is engaged to establish political society, in order to administer justice; without which there can be no peace among them, nor safety, nor mutual intercourse. We are, therefore, to look upon all the vast apparatus of our government, as having ultimately no other object or purpose but the distribution of justice, or, in other words, the support of the twelve judges. Kings and parliaments, fleets and armies, officers of the court and revenue, ambassadors, ministers, and privy-counsellors, are all subordinate in their end to this part of administration. Even the clergy, as their duty leads them to inculcate morality, may justly be thought, so far as regards this world, to have no other useful object of their institution." *Essays*, I, 113–14.

32. "No one can doubt, that the convention for the distinction of property, and for the stability of possession, is of all circumstances the most necessary to the establishment of human society, and that after the agreement for the fixing and observing of this rule, there remains little or nothing to be done towards settling a perfect harmony and concord. All the other passions, beside this of interest, are either easily restrain'd, or are not of such pernicious consequence, when indulg'd." *Treatise*, p. 491.

33. *History*, IV, 30–31.          34. *Treatise*, pp. 538–39.

35. *Essays*, I, 185; *History*, VI, 143–44.

36. *Essays*, I, p. 180.          37. *History*, I, 207–8.

38. *History*, II, 86–88.          39. *Treatise*, pp. 553–63.

40. "The *first* of those principles I shall take notice of, as a foundation of the right of magistracy, is that which gives authority to all the most establish'd governments of the world without exception: I mean, *long possession* in any one form of government, or succession of princes. 'Tis certain, that if we remount to the first origin of every nation, we shall find, that there scarce is any race of kings, or form of a commonwealth, that is not primarily founded on usurpation and rebellion, and whose title is not at first worse than doubtful and uncertain. Time alone gives solidity to their right; and operating gradually on the minds of men, reconciles them to any authority, and makes it seem just and reasonable." *Treatise*, p. 556.

41. *Treatise*, p. 559; *History*, I, 199–200; II, 39.

42. *Treatise*, p. 561; *Essays*, I, p. 456.

43. *Enquiry* II, p. 196.          44. *Treatise*, p. 558.

45. *Treatise*, pp. 551–52.          46. *Treatise*, p. 563.

47. "Whoever considers the history of the several nations of the world; their revolutions, conquests, increase, and diminution; the manner in which their particular governments are establish'd, and the successive right transmitted from one person to another, will soon learn to treat very lightly all disputes concerning the rights of princes, and will be convinc'd, that a strict adherence to any general rules, and the rigid loyalty to particular persons and families, on which some people set so high a value, are virtues that hold less of reason, than of bigotry and superstition. In this particular, the study of history confirms the reasonings of true philosophy; which, shewing us the original qualities of human nature, teaches us to regard the controversies in politics as incapable of any decision in most cases, and as entirely subordinate to the interests of peace and liberty. Where the public good does not evidently demand a change; 'tis certain, that the concurrence of all those titles, *original contract, long possession, present possession, succession,* and *positive laws,* forms the strongest title to sovereignty, and is justly regarded as sacred and inviolable. But when these titles are mingled and oppos'd in different degrees, they often occasion perplexity; and are less capable of solution from the arguments of lawyers and philosophers, than from the swords of the soldiery." *Treatise,* p. 562.

48. *Enquiry* II, p. 184.          49. *Enquiry* II, pp. 186–87, 196.

50. *Enquiry* II, pp. 183–84.

51. *Treatise,* pp. 497, 531–32; *Enquiry* II, pp. 305–6.

52. In the *Treatise,* p. 526, Hume speaks of the three principles of justice as being "of human invention." By this he does not mean that these principles are a matter of arbitrary choice; rather, he means that the principles will not operate unless they have been discovered. Provided that it is understood that the principles are not self-evident and are different from the principles that govern the natural relationships, he is quite ready to have them called "natural." See, for example, the *Treatise,* p. 484; *Letters,* I, 33; and the passages quoted in Chapter V, footnotes 25 and 30.

In *Enquiry* II, p. 307, he writes: "The word *natural* is commonly taken in so many senses and is of so loose a signification, that it seems vain to dispute whether justice be natural or not. If self-love, if benevolence be natural to man; if reason and forethought be also natural; then may the same epithet be applied to justice, order, fidelity, property, society. Men's inclination, their necessities, lead them to combine; their understanding and experience tell them that this combination is impossible where each governs himself by no rule, and pays no regard to the possessions of others: and from these passions and reflections conjoined, as soon as we observe like passions and reflections in others, the sentiment of justice, throughout all ages, has infallibly and certainly had place to some degree or other in every individual of the human species. In so sagacious an animal, what necessarily arises from the exertion of his intellectual faculties may justly be esteemed natural."

## VI: PAST CIVILIZATION

1. *Treatise,* p. 486.    2. *Treatise,* p. 493.

3. "But suppose the conjunction of the sexes to be established in nature, a family immediately arises; and particular rules being found requisite for its subsistence, these are immediately embraced; though without comprehending the rest of mankind within their prescriptions. Suppose that several families unite together into one society, which is totally disjoined from all others, the rules, which preserve peace and order, enlarge themselves to the utmost extent of that society; but becoming then entirely useless, lose their force when carried one step farther. But again suppose, that several distinct societies maintain a kind of intercourse for mutual convenience and advantage, the boundaries of justice still grow larger, in proportion to the largeness of men's views, and the force of their mutual connexions. History, experience, reason sufficiently instruct us in this natural progress of human sentiments, and in the gradual enlargement of our regards to justice, in proportion as we become acquainted with the extensive utility of that virtue." *Enquiry* II, p. 192.

4. *Treatise,* p. 490.    5. *Treatise,* p. 499.
6. *Treatise,* pp. 500, 523.    7. *Treatise,* pp. 493–94.
8. *Treatise,* p. 486.    9. *Treatise,* p. 535.
10. *Treatise,* p. 540.    11. *Treatise,* p. 541.
12. *Treatise,* p. 554.
13. *Essays,* I, 444–45. * Added in Edition Q.
14. *Essays,* I, 445–46.    15. *Essays,* I, 115–16.
16. *Treatise,* pp. 545–46.    17. *Essays,* I, 293.
18. *Essays,* I, 322.    19. *Essays,* I, 306.
20. *Essays,* I, 322.

21. "The bulk of every state may be divided into *husbandmen* and *manufacturers.* The former are employed in the culture of the land; the latter work up the materials furnished by the former, into all the commodities which are necessary or ornamental to human life. As soon as men quit their savage state, where they live chiefly by hunting and fishing, they must fall into these two classes; though the arts of agriculture employ *at first* the most numerous part of the society. Time and experience improve so much these arts, that the land may easily maintain a much greater number of men, than those who are imme-

diately employed in its culture, or who furnish the more necessary manufactures to such as are so employed." *Essays,* I, 289.

22. "If we consult history, we shall find, that, in most nations, foreign trade has preceded any refinement in home manufactures, and given birth to domestic luxury. The temptation is stronger to make use of foreign commodities, which are ready for use, and which are entirely new to us, than to make improvements on any domestic commodity, which always advance by slow degrees, and never affect us by their novelty. The profit is also very great, in exporting what is superfluous at home, and what bears no price, to foreign nations, whose soil or climate is not favourable to that commodity. Thus men become acquainted with the *pleasures* of luxury and the *profits* of commerce; and their *delicacy* and *industry,* being once awakened, carry them on to farther improvements, in every branch of domestic as well as foreign trade. And this perhaps is the chief advantage which arises from a commerce with strangers. It rouses men from their indolence; and presenting the gayer and more opulent part of the nation with objects of luxury, which they never before dreamed of, raises in them a desire of a more splendid way of life than what their ancestors enjoyed. And at the same time, the few merchants, who possess the secret of this importation and exportation, make great profits; and becoming rivals in wealth to the ancient nobility, tempt other adventurers to become their rivals in commerce." *Essays,* I, 295–96.

23. *Essays,* I, 317.

24. "Every thing useful to the life of man arises from the ground; but few things arise in that condition which is requisite to render them useful. There must, therefore, beside the peasant and the proprietors of land, be another rank of men, who receiving from the former the rude materials, work them into their proper form, and retain part for their own use and subsistence. In the infancy of society, these contracts between the artisans and the peasants, and between one species of artisans and another are commonly entered into immediately by the persons themselves, who, being neighbours, are easily acquainted with each other's necessities, and can lend their mutual assistance to supply them. But when men's industry encreases, and their views enlarge, it is found, that the most remote parts of the state can assist each other as well as the more contiguous, and that this intercourse of good offices may be carried on to the greatest extent and intricacy. Hence the origin of *merchants,* one of the most useful races of men, who serve as agents between those parts of the state, that are wholly unacquainted, and are ignorant of each other's necessities." *Essays,* I, 324.

25. *Treatise,* p. 539.                26. *Treatise,* p. 541.

27. *Essays,* I, 298–99.                28. *Essays,* I, 322.

29. In the course of a long description of feudalism, Hume writes:

"If the feudal government was so little favourable to the true liberty even of the military vassal, it was still more destructive of the independence and security of the other members of the state, or what in a proper sense we call the people. A great part of them were *serfs,* and lived in a state of absolute slavery or villainage: The other inhabitants of the country paid their rent in services, which were in a great measure arbitrary; and they could expect no redress of injuries, in a court of barony, from men, who thought they had a right to oppress and tyrannize over them: The towns were situated either within the demesnes of the king, or the lands of the great barons, and were almost entirely subjected to the absolute will of their master. The languishing state of commerce kept the inhabitants poor and contemptible; and the political institutions were calculated to render that poverty perpetual. The barons and gentry, living in rustic plenty and hospitality, gave no encouragement to the arts, and had no demand for any of the more elaborate manufactures: Every profession was held in contempt but that of arms: And if any merchant or manufacturer rose by industry and frugality to a degree of opulence, he found himself but the more exposed to injuries, from the envy and avidity of the military nobles." *History,* II, 111–12.

See also the paragraphs on commerce and interest rates in the thirteenth century in *History,* II, 224–26, 494–98, and in the reigns of Henry VII and Elizabeth in *History,* III, 83–84; V, 472.

30. He concludes the first part of the *History* as follows: "Thus have we pursued the history of England through a series of many barbarous ages; till we have at last reached the dawn of civility and science. . . . Such a state of society was very little advanced beyond the rude state of nature: Violence universally prevailed, instead of general and equitable maxims: The pretended liberty of the times, was only an incapacity of submitting to government: And men, not protected by law in their lives and properties, sought shelter, by their personal servitude and attachments under some powerful chieftain, or by voluntary combinations.

"The gradual progress of improvement raised the Europeans somewhat above this uncultivated state; and affairs, in this island particularly, took early a turn, which was more favourable to justice and to liberty. Civil employments and occupations soon became honourable among the English: The situation of that people rendered not the perpetual attention to wars so necessary as among their neighbours, and all regard was not confined to the military profession: The gentry, and even the nobility, began to deem an acquaintance with the law a necessary part of education: They were less diverted than afterwards from studies of this kind by other sciences; and in the age of Henry VI. as we are told by Fortescue, there were in the inns of court about two thousand students, most of them men of honourable birth, who gave application to this branch of civil knowledge: A circumstance which proves, that a considerable progress was already made in the science of government, and which prognosticated a still greater." *History,* III, 296–302.

31. "In the first ages of the world, when men are as yet barbarous and ignorant, they seek no farther security against mutual violence and injustice, than the choice of some rulers, few or many, in whom they place an implicit confidence, without providing any security, by laws or political institutions, against the violence and injustice of these rulers." *Essays,* I, 178.

32. *Essays,* I, 178.          33. *Essays,* I, 179.

34. *Essays,* I, 307. Earlier in the same essay, Hume says: "In rude unpolished nations, where the arts are neglected, all labour is bestowed on the cultivation of the ground; and the whole society is divided into two classes, proprietors of land, and their vassals or tenants. The latter are necessarily dependent, and fitted for slavery and subjection; especially where they possess no riches, and are not valued for their knowledge in agriculture; as must always be the case where the arts are neglected. The former naturally erect themselves into petty tyrants; and must either submit to an absolute master, for the sake of peace and order; or if they will preserve their independency, like the ancient barons, they must fall into feuds and contests among themselves, and throw the whole society into such confusion, as is perhaps worse than the most despotic government. But where luxury nourishes commerce and industry, the peasants, by a proper cultivation of the land, become rich and independent; while the tradesmen and merchants acquire a share of the property, and draw authority and consideration to that middling rank of men, who are the best and firmest basis of public liberty. These submit not to slavery, like the peasants, from poverty and meanness of spirit; and having no hopes of tyrannizing over others, like the barons, they are not tempted, for the sake of that gratification, to submit to the tyranny of their sovereign. They covet equal laws, which may secure their property, and preserve them from monarchical, as well as aristocratical tyranny." *Essays,* I, 306.

35. "This industry is much promoted by the knowledge inseparable from ages of art and refinement; as, on the other hand, this knowledge enables the public to make the best advantage of the industry of its subjects. Laws, order, police, discipline; these can never be carried to any degree of perfection, before human reason has refined itself by exercise, and by an application to the more vulgar arts, at least, of commerce and manufacture. Can we expect, that a government will be well modelled by a people, who know not how to make a spinning-wheel, or to employ a loom to advantage? Not to mention, that all

ignorant ages are infested with superstition, which throws the government off its bias, and disturbs men in the pursuit of their interest and happiness." *Essays,* I, 303.

36. *Essays,* I, 179.    37. *Essays,* I, 180.    38. *Essays,* I, 161.

## VII: ECONOMIC POLICY AND CIVILITY

1. "Those who employ their pens on political subjects, free from party-rage, and party-prejudices, cultivate a science, which, of all others, contributes most to public utility, and even to the private satisfaction of those who addict themselves to the study of it. I am apt, however, to entertain a suspicion, that the world is still too young to fix many general truths in politics, which will remain true to the latest posterity. We have not as yet had experience of three thousand years; so that not only the art of reasoning is still imperfect in this science, as in all others, but we even want sufficient materials upon which we can reason. It is not fully known, what degree of refinement, either in virtue or vice, human nature is susceptible of; nor what may be expected of mankind from any great revolution in their education, customs, or principles." *Essays,* I, 156.

2. Hume begins the essay "Of the Rise and Progress of the Arts and Sciences" by stating that to refer to an event as the result of "chance" is merely to admit that we cannot discover its causes. He continues: "The distinguishing between chance and causes must depend upon every particular man's sagacity, in considering every particular incident. But, if I were to assign any general rule to help us in applying this distinction, it would be the following, *What depends upon a few persons is, in a great measure, to be ascribed to chance, or secret and unknown causes: What arises from a great number, may often be accounted for by determinate and known causes.*" *Essays,* I, 175.

3. Similarly, says Hume, it is easier "to account for the rise and progress of commerce in any kingdom, than for that of learning; and a state, which should apply itself to the encouragement of the one, would be more assured of success, than one which should cultivate the other. Avarice, or the desire of gain, is an universal passion, which operates at all times, in all places, and upon all persons: But curiosity, or the love of knowledge, has a very limited influence, and requires youth, leisure, education, genius, and example, to make it govern any person." *Essays,* I, 176.

4. *Essays,* I, 288.

5. J. A. Passmore, *Hume's Intentions* (Cambridge, 1952), pp. 10–11, 15.

6. The original titles of the twelve discourses first published in 1752 are:

1. Of Commerce
2. Of Luxury (later: Of Refinement in the Arts)
3. Of Money
4. Of Interest
5. Of the Balance of Trade
6. Of the Balance of Power
7. Of Taxes
8. Of Public Credit
9. Of some Remarkable Customs
10. Of the Populousness of Antient Nations
11. Of the Protestant Succession
12. Idea of a perfect Commonwealth

It may appear strange that Hume should place "Of the Balance of Power" among the discourses on "economic" matters; but, as we shall see, his aim was to stop bad economic practices caused in part by a blind belief in the balance of power. In 1758 a new discourse, "Of the Jealousy of Trade," was inserted between the fifth discourse and the original sixth discourse.

7. *Essays,* I, 327.     8. *Essays,* I, 322–23.     9. *Essays,* I, 325.

10. "Commerce encreases industry, by conveying it readily from one member of the state to another, and allowing none of it to perish or become useless. It encreases frugality, by giving occupation to men, and employing them in the arts of gain, which soon engage their affection, and remove all relish for pleasure and expense. It is an infallible consequence of all industrious professions, to beget frugality, and make the love of gain prevail over the love of pleasure. Among lawyers and physicians who have any practice, there are many more who live within their income, than who exceed it, or even live up to it. But lawyers and physicians beget no industry; and it is even at the expence of others they acquire their riches; so that they are sure to diminish the possessions of some of their fellow-citizens, as fast as they encrease their own. Merchants, on the contrary, beget industry, by serving as canals to convey it through every corner of the state: And at the same time, by their frugality, they acquire great power over that industry, and collect a large property in the labour and commodities, which they are the chief instruments in producing. There is no other profession, therefore, except merchandize, which can make the monied interest considerable, or, in other words, can encrease industry, and, by also encreasing frugality, give a great command of that industry to particular members of the society. Without commerce, the state must consist chiefly of landed gentry, whose prodigality and expence make a continual demand for borrowing; and of peasants, who have no sums to supply that

demand. The money never gathers into large stocks or sums, which can be lent at interest. It is dispersed into numberless hands, who either squander it in idle show and magnificence, or employ it in the purchase of the common necessaries of life. Commerce alone assembles it into considerable sums; and this effect it has merely from the industry which it begets, and the frugality which it inspires, independent of that particular quantity of precious metal which may circulate in the state." *Essays*, I, 325–26.

11. *Essays*, I, 293.    12. *Essays*, I, 302.    13. *Essays*, I, 294.

14. Hume is strongly in favour of taxes "levied upon consumptions, especially those of luxury." Such taxes, if not exorbitant, he contends, do not diminish industry, and indeed may serve to foster this spirit among the people. *Essays*, I, 356, 358.

15. "There may be some circumstances, where the commerce and riches and luxury of individuals, instead of adding strength to the public, will serve only to thin its armies, and diminish its authority among the neighbouring nations. Man is a very variable being, and susceptible of many different opinions, principles, and rules of conduct. What may be true, while he adheres to one way of thinking, will be found false, when he has embraced an opposite set of manners and opinions." *Essays*, I, 289.

16. Governors cannot return to ancient policy, because it "was violent, and contrary to the more natural and usual course of things. It is well known with what peculiar laws SPARTA was governed, and what a prodigy that republic is justly esteemed by every one, who has considered human nature as it has displayed itself in other nations, and other ages. Were the testimony of history less positive and circumstantial, such a government would appear a mere philosophical whim or fiction, and impossible ever to be reduced to practice. And though the ROMAN and other ancient republics were supported on principles somewhat more natural, yet was there an extraordinary concurrence of circumstances to make them submit to such grievous burthens. They were free states; they were small ones; and the age being martial, all their neighbours were continually in arms. Freedom naturally begets public spirit, especially in small states; and this public spirit, this *amor patriae*, must encrease, when the public is almost in continual alarm, and men are obliged, every moment, to expose themselves to the greatest dangers for its defence. . . . Not to mention the great equality of fortunes among the inhabitants of the ancient republics, where every field, belonging to a different proprietor, was able to maintain a family, and rendered the numbers of citizens very considerable, even without trade and manufactures." *Essays*, I, 291–92.

17. *Essays*, I, 292.        18. *Essays*, I, 294–95.

19. *Essays*, I, 315–16.        20. *Essays*, I, 319–20.

21. Hume describes the effect of currency inflation in "Of Money."
He writes: "From the whole of this reasoning we may conclude, that it
is of no manner of consequence, with regard to the domestic happiness
of a state, whether money be in a greater or less quantity. The good
policy of the magistrate consists only in keeping it, if possible, still
encreasing; because, by that means, he keeps alive a spirit of industry
in the nation, and encreases the stock of labour, in which consists all
real power and riches. A nation, whose money decreases, is actually, at
that time, weaker and more miserable than another nation, which possesses no more money, but is on the encreasing hand. This will be easily
accounted for, if we consider, that the alterations in the quantity of
money, either on one side or the other, are not immediately attended
with proportionable alterations in the price of commodities. There is
always an interval before matters be adjusted to their new situation;
and this interval is as pernicious to industry, when gold and silver are
diminishing, as it is advantageous when these metals are encreasing.
The workman has not the same employment from the manufacturer
and merchant; though he pays the same price for everything in the
market. The farmer cannot dispose of his corn and cattle; though he
must pay the same rent to his landlord. The poverty, and beggary, and
sloth, which must ensue, are easily foreseen." *Essays*, I, 315.

Hume showed a draft of the essay, "Of the Balance of Trade," to
James Oswald of Dunnikier, who wrote (*Caldwell Papers*, II, i, 93–
107) proposing some amendments. One of the points on which he commented was Hume's insistence that bullionist measures always fail. In
his reply, Hume wrote: "I never meant to say that money, in all
countries which communicate, must necessarily be on a level, but only
on a level proportioned to their people, industry, and commodities.
That is, where there is double people, &c. there will be double money,
and so on; and that the only way of keeping or increasing money is, by
keeping and increasing the people and industry; not by prohibitions of
exporting money, or by taxes on commodities, the methods commonly
thought of. I believe we differ little on this head. You allow, that if all
the money in England were increased four-fold in one night, there
would be a sudden rise of prices; but then, say you, the importation of
foreign commodities would soon lower the prices. Here, then, is the
flowing out of the money already begun. But, say you, a small part of
this stock of money would suffice to buy foreign commodities, and
lower the prices. I grant it would for one year, till the imported commodities be consumed. But must not the same thing be renewed next
year? No, say you; the additional stock of money may, in this interval,
so increase the people and industry, as to enable them to retain their
money. Here I am extremely pleased with your reasoning. I agree with
you, that the increase of money, if not too sudden, naturally increases

people and industry, and by that means may retain itself; but if it do not produce such an increase, nothing will retain it except hoarding." *Letters*, I, 142–43.

22. In 1758 he inserted "Of the Jealousy of Trade" before "Of the Balance of Power," thus making the argument of these five essays even more obvious.

23. *Essays*, I, 354.             24. *Essays*, I, 354.

25. See the footnote quoted in chapter 8, from "Of the Balance of Power," *Essays*, I, 355.

26. Hume is decidedly and openly opposed to the physiocratic theory that all taxes should be on the possessors of land. He denies the accuracy of the view that "all taxes fall ultimately on land." He does not prohibit taxes upon possessions in addition to taxes on consumptions: "Taxes upon possessions are levied without expence; but have every other disadvantage. Most states, however, are obliged to have recourse to them, in order to supply the deficiencies of the other." *Essays*, I, 358–59.

27. *Essays*, I, 366.

28. "If, on the contrary, the consent of the annuitants be requisite for every taxation, they will never be persuaded to contribute sufficiently even to the support of government; as the diminution of their revenue must in that case be very sensible, would not be disguised under the appearance of a branch of excise or customs, and would not be shared by any other order of the state, who are already supposed to be taxed to the utmost. There are instances, in some republics, of a hundredth penny, and sometimes of the fiftieth, being given to the support of the state; but this is always an extraordinary exertion of power, and can never become the foundation of a constant national defence. We have always found, where a government has mortgaged all its revenues, that it necessarily sinks into a state of languor, inactivity, and impotence." *Essays*, I, 369.

29. *Essays*, I, 369. Later in the same essay Hume writes that where a national bankruptcy is declared, thousands are sacrificed to the safety of millions. "But we are not without danger, that the contrary event may take place, and that millions may be sacrificed for ever to the temporary safety of thousands. Our popular government, perhaps, will render it difficult or dangerous for a minister to venture on so desperate an expedient, as that of a voluntary bankruptcy. And though the house of Lords be altogether composed of proprietors of land, and the house of Commons chiefly; and consequently neither of them can be supposed to have great property in the funds; yet the connections of the members may be so great with the proprietors, as to render them more tenacious of public faith, than prudence, policy, or even justice, strictly speaking, requires. And perhaps too, our foreign enemies may

be so politic as to discover, that our safety lies in despair, and may not, therefore, show the danger, open and barefaced, till it be inevitable. The balance of power in EUROPE, our grandfathers, our fathers, and we, have all deemed too unequal to be preserved without our attention and assistance. But our children, weary of the struggle, and fettered with incumbrances, may sit down secure, and see their neighbours oppressed and conquered; till, at last, they themselves and their creditors lie both at the mercy of the conqueror. And this may properly enough be denominated the *violent death* of our public credit." *Essays*, I, 373–74.

30. *Essays*, I, 367–68.          31. *Essays*, I, 343–44.

32. Writing to Lord Kames, on March 4, 1758, Hume, probably referring to Josiah Tucker's *The Elements of Commerce & Theory of Taxes,* said:

"The author, conformable to the character both of a divine and a philosopher, draws an argument from the goodness of Providence; but I think it may be turned against him. It was never surely the intention of Providence, that any one nation should be a monopolizer of wealth: and the growth of all bodies, artificial as well as natural, is stopped by internal causes, derived from their enormous size and greatness. Great empires, great cities, great commerce, all of them receive a check, not from accidental events, but necessary principles.

"There is a hint thrown out in the papers, which gave me great satisfaction, because it concurs with a principle which I have thrown out to your Lordship, and which you seemed not to disapprove of. I was indeed so pleased with it, that, as I told you, I intended to make it the subject of a political discourse, as soon as I should have occasion to give a new edition of that work. My principle is levelled against the narrow malignity and envy of nations, which can never bear to see their neighbours thriving, but continually repine at any new efforts towards industry made by any other nation. We desire, and seem by our absurd politics to endeavour to repress trade in all our neighbours, and would be glad that all Europe were reduced to the same state of desolation as Turkey: the consequence of which must be, that we would have little more than domestic trade, and would have nobody either to sell or buy from us. I remember, that in a conversation of this head with your Lordship, I asked whether a man who opened a shop in Tartary was likely to meet with many customers. This narrow spirit of nations, as well as individuals, ought carefully to be repressed; and I am glad to find that Mr. Tucker is likely to employ his talents and abilities in so useful a manner." *Letters,* I, 271–72.

A few months later Hume published his essay, "Of the Jealousy of Trade."

33. *Essays,* I, 343.

34. *Letters,* I, 143–44. In the discourse, "Of Money" (*Essays,* I,

311), and the discourse, "Of the Balance of Trade" (*Essays*, I, 333), he reiterates his argument that the balance of trade tends to reverse itself naturally.

35. *Essays*, I, 346–47.

36. *Essays*, I, 347.

37. *Essays*, I, 296.

38. *Essays*, I, 221.

39. *Essays*, I, 300.

40. *Essays*, I, 296–97.

41. *Essays*, I, 325.

42. *Essays*, I, 300.

43. Hume does not seem to have worried much about the influence of specialization and professionalism on the minds and bodies of all who participate in a division of labour, although he was well aware of the influence. This was a consideration that concerned Adam Smith greatly. See Joseph Cropsey, *Polity and Economy: An Interpretation of the Principles of Adam Smith* (The Hague, 1957), pp. 88–92.

44. "Whatever we may imagine concerning the usual truth and sincerity of men, who live in a rude and barbarous state, there is much more falsehood, and even perjury among them, than among civilized nations: Virtue, which is nothing but a more enlarged and more cultivated reason, never flourishes to any degree, nor is founded on steady principles of honour, except where a good education becomes general; and where men are taught the pernicious consequences of vice, treachery, and immorality." *History*, I, 222.

45. *Essays*, I, 302–5.

46. *Essays*, I, 306.

47. Hume is not prepared to say that luxury is entirely good. The desire for luxury may become excessive. But if you propose to banish this desire, you must be careful to banish all other vices also, for it is this desire that makes the economy work. "By banishing *vicious* luxury, without curing sloth and an indifference to others, you only diminish industry in the state, and add nothing to men's charity or their generosity." The magistrate "cannot cure every vice, by substituting a virtue in its place. Very often he can only cure one vice by another; and in that case, he ought to prefer what is least pernicious to society. Luxury, when excessive, is the source of many ills; but is in general preferable to sloth and idleness, which would commonly succeed in its place, and are more hurtful both to private persons and to the public." *Essays*, I, 308–9.

Nor is he prepared to say that an industrious society has no vices. The virtue of frugality easily may become the vice of avarice. In his early essay, "Of Avarice" (1741) he writes: "There is only one vice, which may be found in life with as strong features, and as high a colouring as needs be employed by any satyrist or comic poet; and that is AVARICE. Every day we meet with men of immense fortunes, without heirs, and on the very brink of the grave, who refuse themselves the most common necessaries of life, and go on heaping possessions on possessions, under all the real pressures of the severest poverty." *Essays*, II, 392.

VIII: MONARCHIES AND REPUBLICS

1. *Essays*, I, 222–24.                    2. *Essays*, I, 94.
3. *Treatise*, p. 322.                     4. *Essays*, I, 245.
5. *Essays*, I, 245.                       6. *Essays*, I, 287–88.
7. *Essays*, I, 97, 113, 365, 376.         8. *Essays*, I, 127–28.
9. *Essays*, I, 128.

10. "There has been an attempt in ENGLAND to divide the *landed* and *trading* part of the nation; but without success. The interests of these two bodies are not really distinct, and never will be so, till our public debts encrease to such a degree, as to become altogether oppressive and intolerable." *Essays*, I, 130.

11. *Essays*, I, 298.                    12. *Essays*, I, 130.

13. "When two orders of men, such as the nobles and people, have a distinct authority in a government, not very accurately balanced and modelled, they naturally follow a distinct interest; nor can we reasonably expect a different conduct, considering that degree of selfishness implanted in human nature. It requires great skill in a legislator to prevent such parties; and many philosophers are of opinion, that this secret, like the *grand elixir,* or *perpetual motion,* may amuse men in theory, but can never possibly be reduced to practice. In despotic governments, indeed, factions often do not appear; but they are not the less real; or rather, they are more real and more pernicious, upon that very account. The distinct orders of men, nobles and people, soldiers and merchants, have all a distinct interest; but the more powerful oppresses the weaker with impunity, and without resistance; which begets a seeming tranquillity in such governments." *Essays*, I, 130.

14. This second meaning of "interest" comes out in "Of the Parties of Great Britain" and in the *History*.

15. *Essays*, I, 130.

16. "Two men travelling on the highway, the one east, the other west, can easily pass each other, if the way be broad enough: But two men, reasoning upon opposite principles of religion, cannot so easily pass, without shocking; though one should think, that the way were also, in that case, sufficiently broad; and that each might proceed, without interruption, in his own course. But such is the nature of the human mind, that it always lays hold on every mind that approaches it; and as it is wonderfully fortified by an unanimity of sentiments, so is it shocked and disturbed by any contrariety. Hence the eagerness, which

most people discover in a dispute; and hence their impatience of opposition, even in the most speculative and indifferent opinions." *Essays*, I, 131.

17. *Essays*, I, 132.    18. *Essays*, I, 142.

19. "I must be understood to mean this of persons who have motives for taking party on any side. For, to tell the truth, the greatest part are commonly men who associate themselves they know not why; from example, from passion, from idleness. But still it is requisite, that there be some source of division, either in principle or interest; otherwise such persons would not find parties, to which they could associate themselves." *Essays*, I, 135 (Editions A to P).

20. *Essays*, I, 142.    21. *Essays*, I, 144.

22. *History*, I, 253.    23. *Essays*, I, 116.

24. *Essays*, I, 161.

25. "However perfect, therefore, the monarchical form may appear to some politicians, it owes all its perfection to the republican; nor is it possible, that a pure despotism, established among a barbarous people, can ever, by its native force and energy, refine and polish itself. It must borrow its laws, and methods, and institutions, and consequently its stability and order, from free governments. These advantages are the sole growth of republics. The extensive despotism of a barbarous monarchy, by entering into the detail of the government, as well as into the principal points of administration, for ever prevents all such improvement.

"In a civilized monarchy, the prince alone is unrestrained in the exercise of his authority, and possesses alone a power, which is not bounded by any thing but custom, example, and the sense of his own interest. Every minister or magistrate, however eminent, must submit to the general laws, which govern the whole society, and must exert the authority delegated to him after the manner, which is prescribed. The people depend on none but their sovereign, for the security of their property. He is so far removed from them, and is so much exempt from private jealousies or interests, that this dependence is scarcely felt. And thus a species of government arises, to which, in a high political rant, we may give the name of *Tyranny,* but which, by a just and prudent administration, may afford tolerable security to the people, and may answer most of the ends of political society." *Essays*, I, 186.

26. *Treatise*, p. 537.    27. *Essays*, I, 101.

28. But in "Of Civil Liberty," he wrote: "It must, however, he confessed, that, though monarchical governments have approached nearer to popular ones, in gentleness and stability; they are still inferior. Our modern education and customs instil more humanity and moderation than the ancient; but have not as yet been able to overcome entirely the disadvantages of that form of government." *Essays*, I, 161–62.

29. *Essays,* I, 98.     30. *Essays,* I, 105.     31. *Essays,* I, 99.

32. "Durst I deliver my opinion in an affair of so much uncertainty, I would assert, that, notwithstanding the efforts of the FRENCH, there is something hurtful to commerce inherent in the very nature of absolute government, and inseparable from it: Though the reason I should assign for this opinion, is somewhat different from that which is commonly insisted on. Private property seems to me almost as secure in a civilized EUROPEAN monarchy, as in a republic; nor is danger much apprehended in such a government, from the violence of the sovereign; more than we commonly dread harm from thunder, or earthquakes, or any accident the most unusual and extraordinary. Avarice, the spur of industry, is so obstinate a passion, and works its way through so many real dangers and difficulties, that it is not likely to be scared by an imaginary danger, which is so small, that it scarcely admits of calculation. Commerce, therefore, in my opinion, is apt to decay in absolute governments, not because it is there less *secure,* but because it is less *honourable.* A subordination of ranks is absolutely necessary to the support of monarchy. Birth, titles, and place, must be honoured above industry and riches. And while these notions prevail, all the considerable traders will be tempted to throw up their commerce, in order to purchase some of those employments, to which privileges and honours are annexed." *Essays,* I, 160.

"In most countries of Europe, family, that is, hereditary riches, marked with titles and symbols from the sovereign, is the chief source of distinction. In England, more regard is paid to present opulence and plenty. Each practice has its advantages and disadvantages. Where birth is respected, unactive, spiritless minds remain in haughty indolence, and dream of nothing but pedigrees and genealogies: the generous and ambitious seek honour and authority, and reputation and favour. Where riches are the chief idol, corruption, venality, rapine prevail: arts, manufactures, commerce, agriculture flourish. The former prejudice, being favourable to military virtue, is more suited to monarchies. The latter, being the chief spur to industry, agrees better with a republican government." *Enquiry* II, pp. 248–49.

33. "The poverty of the common people is a natural, if not an infallible effect of absolute monarchy; though I doubt, whether it be always true, on the other hand, that their riches are an infallible result of liberty. Liberty must be attended with particular accidents, and a certain turn of thinking, in order to produce that effect. Lord BACON, accounting for the great advantages obtained by the ENGLISH in their wars with FRANCE, ascribes them chiefly to the superior ease and plenty of the common people amongst the former; yet the government of the two kingdoms was, at that time, pretty much alike. Where the labourers and artisans are accustomed to work for low wages, and

to retain but a small part of the fruits of their labour, it is difficult for them, even in a free government, to better their condition, or conspire among themselves to heighten their wages. But even where they are accustomed to a more plentiful way of life, it is easy for the rich, in an arbitrary government, to conspire against *them,* and throw the whole burthen of taxes on their shoulders." *Essays,* I, 297–98.

34. *Essays,* I, 179.                    35. *Essays,* I, 186–87.

36. See the passage quoted at pp. 184–85. See also *Essays,* I, 374 and *History,* III, 215.

37. *Essays,* I, 162–63. This passage, with slight changes in the data on the Greeks, appeared in the 1741 volume in these words.

38. *Essays,* I, 119.                    39. *Essays,* I, 99.

40. *Essays,* I, 99–100.                 41. *Essays,* I, 119.

42. "As one form of government must be allowed more perfect than another, independent of the manners and humours of particular men; why may we not enquire what is the most perfect of all, though the common botched and inaccurate governments seem to serve the purposes of society, and though it be not so easy to establish a new system of government, as to build a vessel upon a new construction? The subject is surely the most worthy curiosity of any the wit of man can possibly devise. And who knows, if this controversy were fixed by the universal consent of the wise and learned, but, in some future age, an opportunity might be afforded of reducing the theory to practice, either by a dissolution of some old government, or by the combination of men to form a new one, in some distant part of the world? In all cases, it must be advantageous to know what is most perfect in the kind, that we may be able to bring any real constitution or form of government as near it as possible, by such gentle alterations and innovations as may not give too great disturbance to society." *Essays,* I, 480–81.

43. *Essays,* I, 488. Holden Furber in *Henry Dundas, First Count Melville* (London, 1931), p. 188, estimates that, because of the control of the councils in the selection of the members of Parliament from the burghs and of the landowners in the county elections, in 1800 Scotland "had less than four thousand voters and less than four hundred inhabitants who had any real influence on election returns."

44. *Essays,* I, 487.

45. Hume's views on parties and his semi-federal scheme for confining them seem to be echoed in James Madison's *Federalist Paper,* No. 10.

46. "HARRINGTON's Oceana was well adapted to that age, when the plans of imaginary republics were the daily subjects of debate and conversation; and even in our time it is justly admired as a work of genius and invention. The idea, however, of a perfect and immortal

commonwealth will always be found as chimerical as that of a perfect and immortal man." *History*, VII, 347.

47. *Essays*, I, 480.

## IX: MIXED GOVERNMENT
## IN BRITAIN

1. In the essay, "Of the Original Contract" (1748), Hume sought to refute both the theory of divine right and the theory of original contract. In "Of Passive Obedience" (1748), he demonstrated the practical consequences drawn by the Tories and Whigs with regard to obedience and resistance from these theories.

2. *Essays*, I, 444.    3. *Essays*, I, 450.

4. "When a new government is established, by whatever means, the people are commonly dissatisfied with it, and pay obedience more from fear and necessity, than from any idea of allegiance or of moral obligation. The prince is watchful and jealous, and must carefully guard against every beginning or appearance of insurrection. Time, by degrees, removes all these difficulties, and accustoms the nation to regard, as their lawful or native princes, that family, which, at first, they considered as usurpers or foreign conquerors." *Essays*, I, 450–51.

5. *Treatise*, pp. 553–54.    6. *Treatise*, pp. 550, 563–64.

7. *History*, VI, 117–20.

8. "It was the fashion," writes Sir William Holdsworth, "amongst the lawyers of the seventeenth century to minimize the effects of the Norman Conquest, and to derive English law and English institutions from an Anglo-Saxon, or from an even more remote past. The publication of Lambard's *Archaionomia* in 1568 had restored the Anglo-Saxon laws to the students of the common law; and in the seventeenth century they were used as a basis upon which pedigrees of English laws and institutions could be constructed, and from which theories as to existing laws and institutions could be deduced. Coke, somewhat naively, said in the Preface to his Third Institute, 'to speak what we think, we would derive from the Conqueror as little as we could;' and this attitude of mind no doubt helped him to swallow whole all the fables told by that curious legal romance, *The Mirror of Justices*. Hale, too, in his *History of Common Law*, devotes a whole chapter [Chapter V] to minimizing the effects of the Conquest—'in truth,' he said, 'it was not such a conquest as did or would alter the laws of this kingdom.' In the eighteenth and nineteenth centuries this idea passed from the lawyers to the historians. Montesquieu found the origin of the English constitution in the *Germania*. Freeman went back to the institutions of

Uri and Appenzell, denounced 'the slavish subtleties of Norman law-yers,' and 'the arbitrary influence of the lawyers,' and considered that some of the legislation of his own day marked a return to 'those simpler principles which the untutored wisdom of our forefathers never thought of calling in question.' " *The Influence of the Legal Profession on the Growth of the English Constitution* (Oxford, 1924), pp. 8–9.

9. *History*, I, 16, 197–99, 212–13, 215. Hume had no admiration for Anglo-Saxon England. He writes: "On the whole, notwithstanding the seeming liberty or rather licentiousness of the Anglo-Saxons, the great body even of the free citizens, in those ages, really enjoyed much less true liberty, than where the execution of the laws is the most severe, and where subjects are reduced to the strictest subordination and de-pendance on the civil magistrate. The reason is derived from the excess itself of that liberty. Men must guard themselves at any price against insults and injuries; and where they receive not protection from the laws and magistrate, they will seek it by submission to superiors, and by herding in some private confederacy, which acts under the direc-tion of a powerful leader. And thus all anarchy is the immediate cause of tyranny, if not over the state, at least over many of the individuals." *History*, I, 207–8; see also pp. 205 and 229.

10. Hume had no doubt whatsoever that William I acquired the crown of England as a conqueror. *History*, I, 281–84. Similarly, he had no doubt but that it was William I who introduced feudalism into England. *History*, I, 253–54; II, 108.

11. *History*, I, 224–25, 253, 465–66, and *History*, II, 77–78.

12. *History*, II, 488.

13. Evidently Hume thought that these rights of freemen could be traced back to Edward the Confessor, and beyond him to Alfred, and beyond Alfred to early Anglo-Saxon times. After he had detailed the privileges granted to the barons by the Magna Charta he outlined the concessions made to the freemen. See pp. 127–29. He then continued: "We may, now, from the tenor of this charter, conjecture what those laws were of king Edward, which the English nation, during so many generations, still desired, with such an obstinate perseverance, to have recalled and established. They were chiefly these latter articles of *Magna Charta;* and the barons, who, at the beginning of these com-motions, demanded the revival of the Saxon laws, undoubtedly thought, that they had sufficiently satisfied the people, by procuring them this concession, which comprehended the principal objects, to which they had so long aspired." *History*, II, 88–89.

Earlier he had written: "The better to guide the magistrates in the administration of justice, Alfred framed a body of laws; which, though now lost, served long as the basis of English jurisprudence, and is generally deemed the origin of what is denominated the COMMON LAW.

. . . The similarity of these institutions to the customs of the ancient Germans, to the practice of the other northern conquerors, and to the Saxon laws during the Heptarchy, prevents us from regarding Alfred as the sole author of this plan of government; and leads us rather to think, that, like a wise man, he contented himself with reforming, extending, and executing the institutions, which he found previously established." *History,* I, 95.

14. *History,* II, 112.            15. *History,* II, 368.

16. *History,* I, 201–3; II, 116–21, 265–79; VI, 15, 552.

17. *History,* II, 137, 234, 273.

18. *History,* II, 490; II, 42–43.        19. *History,* VI, 228–29.

20. *History,* II, 499–500.        21. *History,* III, 58–60, 119, 400–4.

22. "In Sir John Fortescue's treatise of absolute and limited monarchy, a book written in the reign of Edward the IVth, the word *absolute* is taken in the same sense as at present; and the government of England is also said not to be absolute. They were the princes of the house of Tudor chiefly, who introduced that administration, which had the appearance of absolute government. The princes before them were restrained by the barons; as those after them by the house of commons. The people had, properly speaking, little liberty in either of these ancient governments, but least, in the more ancient." *History,* VI, 550; see also *History,* III, 396–97; VI, 551–52, 561.

23. On April 12, 1755, Hume wrote to Andrew Millar as follows: "The second Volume of my History I can easily find a way of conveying to you, when finishd & corrected, & fairly copy'd. Perhaps I may be in London myself about that time. I have always said to all my Acquaintance that if the first Volume bore a little of a Tory Aspect, the second wou'd probably be as grateful to the opposite Party. The two first Princes of the House of Stuart were certainly more excusable than the two second. The Constitution was in their time very ambiguous & undetermin'd, & their Parliaments were, in many respects, refractory & obstinate: But Charles the 2d knew, that he had succeeded to a very limited Monarchy: His long Parliament was indulgent to him, & even consisted almost entirely of Royalists; yet he cou'd not be quiet, nor contented with a legal Authority. I need not mention the Oppressions in Scotland nor the absurd Conduct of K. James the 2d. These are obvious & glaring Points. Upon the whole, I wish the two Volumes had been publishd together. Neither one Party nor the other, wou'd in that Case, have had the least Pretext of reproaching me with Partiality." *Letters,* I, 217–18.

24. *History,* V, 452–72.

25. "About this period, the minds of men, throughout Europe, especially in England, seem to have undergone a general, but insensible revolution. Though letters had been revived in the preceding age, they

were chiefly cultivated by those sedentary professions; nor had they, till now, begun to spread themselves, in any degree, among men of the world. Arts, both mechanical and liberal, were every day receiving great improvements. Navigation had extended itself over the whole globe. Travelling was secure and agreeable. And the general system of politics, in Europe, was become more enlarged and comprehensive.

"In consequence of this universal fermentation, the ideas of men enlarged themselves on all sides; and the several constituent parts of the gothic governments, which seem to have lain long unactive, began, every where, to operate and encroach on each other. On the continent, where the necessity of discipline had begotten standing armies, the princes commonly established an unlimited authority, and overpowered, by force or intrigue, the liberties of the people. In England, the love of freedom, which, unless checked, flourishes extremely in all liberal natures, acquired new force, and was regulated by more enlarged views, suitably to that cultivated understanding, which became, every day, more common, among men of birth and education. A familiar acquaintance with the precious remains of antiquity excited in every generous breast a passion for a limited constitution, and begat an emulation of those manly virtues, which the Greek and Roman authors, by such animating examples, as well as pathetic expressions, recommend to us. The severe though popular, government of Elizabeth had confined this rising spirit within very narrow bounds: But when a new and a foreign family succeeded to the throne, and a prince less dreaded and less beloved; symptoms immediately appeared of a more free and independent genius in the nation." *History*, VI, 21–22.

26. *History*, V, 488–89; VI, 48, 170–71.

27. *History*, VI, 47, 171.          28. *History*, VI, 173.

29. *History*, VI, 160.

30. *History*, V, 451–52. "In that great revolution of manners, which happened during the sixteenth and the seventeenth centuries, the only nations, who had the honourable, though often melancholy advantage, of making an effort for their expiring privileges, were such as, together with the principles of civil liberty, were animated with a zeal for religious parties and opinions. Besides the irresistible force of standing armies, the European princes possessed this advantage, that they were descended from the ancient royal families; that they continued the same appellations of magistrates, the same appearance of civil government; and restraining themselves by all the forms of legal administration, could insensibly impose the yoke on their unguarded subjects. Even the German nations, who formerly broke the Roman chains, and restored liberty to mankind, now lost their own liberty, and saw with grief the absolute authority of their princes firmly established among them. In their circumstances, nothing but a pious zeal, which disre-

gards all motives of human prudence, could have made them entertain
hopes of preserving any longer those privileges, which their ancestors,
through so many ages, had transmitted to them." *History*, VI, 100–1;
see also V, 154–55, 182–83; VI, 562–63.

31. Hume wrote about his *History:* "I have the impudence [in it]
to pretend that I am of no party, and have no bias. Lord Elibank says,
that I am a moderate Whig, and Mr Wallace that I am a candid Tory."
*Letters*, I, 185. The Right Reverend William Warburton found him
more colourful: "He is an atheistical Jacobite, a monster as rare with
us as a hippogriff." E. C. Mossner, *The Life of David Hume* (Edinburgh, 1954), p. 309.

32. "Thus have we seen, through the course of four reigns,
a continual struggle maintained between the crown and the people:
Privilege and prerogative were ever at variance: And both parties, beside the present object of dispute, had many latent claims, which, on
a favourable occasion, they produced against their adversaries. Governments too steady and uniform, as they are seldom free, so are they,
in the judgment of some, attended with another sensible inconvenience: They abate the active powers of men; depress courage, invention, and genius; and produce an universal lethargy in the people.
Though this opinion may be just, the fluctuation and contest, it must
be allowed, of the English government were, during these reigns,
much too violent both for the repose and safety of the people. Foreign
affairs, at that time, were either entirely neglected, or managed to
pernicious purposes: And in the domestic administration there was
felt a continued fever, either secret or manifest; sometimes the most
furious convulsions and disorders. The revolution forms a new epoch
in the constitution; and was probably attended with consequences more
advantageous to the people, than barely freeing them from an ex-
ceptionable administration. By deciding many important questions in
favour of liberty, and still more, by that great precedent of deposing
one king, and establishing a new family, it gave such an ascendant to
popular principles, as has put the nature of the English constitution
beyond all controversy. And it may justly be affirmed, without any
danger of exaggeration, that we, in this island, have ever since enjoyed,
if not the best system of government, at least the most entire system
of liberty, that ever was known amongst mankind.

"To decry with such violence, as is affected by some, the whole line
of Stuart; to maintain, that their administration was one continued
encroachment on the *incontestible* rights of the people; is not giving
due honour to that great event, which not only put a period to their
hereditary succession, but made a new settlement of the whole constitution. The inconveniencies, suffered by the people under the two
first reigns of that family (for in the main they were fortunate) pro-

ceeded in a great measure from the unavoidable situation of affairs; and scarcely any thing could have prevented those events, but such vigour of genius in the sovereign, attended with such good fortune, as might have enabled him entirely to overpower the liberties of his people. While the parliaments, in those reigns, were taking advantage of the necessities of the prince, and attempting every session to abolish, or circumscribe, or define, some prerogative of the crown, and innovate in the usual tenor of government: What could be expected, but that the prince would exert himself, in defending, against such inveterate enemies, an authority, which, during the most regular course of the former English government, had been exercised without dispute or controversy? And though Charles II. in 1672, may with reason be deemed the aggressor, nor is it possible to justify his conduct; yet were there some motives surely, which could engage a prince, so soft and indolent, and at the same time so judicious, to attempt such hazardous enterprizes. He felt, that public affairs had reached a situation, at which they could not possibly remain without some farther innovation. Frequent parliaments were become almost absolutely necessary to the conducting of public business; yet these assemblies were still, in the judgment of the royalists, much inferior in dignity to the sovereign, whom they seemed better calculated to counsel than controul. The crown still possessed considerable power of opposing parliaments; and had not as yet acquired the means of influencing them. Hence a continual jealousy between these parts of the legislature: Hence the inclination mutually to take advantage of each other's necessities: Hence the impossibility, under which the king lay, of finding ministers, who could at once be serviceable and faithful to him. If he followed his own choice in appointing his servants, without regard to their parliamentary interest, a refractory session was instantly to be expected: If he chose them from among the leaders of popular assemblies, they either lost their influence with the people, by adhering to the crown, or they betrayed the crown, in order to preserve their influence. Neither Hambden, whom Charles I. was willing to gain at any price; nor Shaftesbury, whom Charles II. after the popish plot, attempted to engage in his counsels, would renounce their popularity for the precarious, and, as they esteemed it, deceitful favour of the prince. The root of their authority they still thought to lie in the parliament; and as the power of that assembly was not yet uncontroulable, they still resolved to augment it, though at the expence of the royal prerogatives.

"It is no wonder, that these events have long, by the representations of faction, been extremely clouded and obscured. No man has yet arisen, who has payed an entire regard to truth, and has dared to expose her, without covering or disguise, to the eyes of the prejudiced public. Even that party amongst us, which boasts of the highest regard to liberty, has not possessed sufficient liberty of thought in this particular; nor has been able to decide impartially of their own merit, compared with that of their antagonists. More noble perhaps in their ends, and highly beneficial to mankind; they must also be allowed to have often been less justifiable in the means, and in many of their enterprizes to have payed more regard to political than to moral considerations. Obliged to court the favour of the populace, they found it necessary to comply with their rage and folly; and have even, on many occasions, by propagating calumnies, and by promoting violence, served to infatuate, as well as corrupt that people, to whom they made a tender of liberty and justice. Charles I. was a tyrant, a papist, and a contriver of the Irish massacre: The church of England was relapsing fast into idolatry: Puritanism was the only true religion, and the covenant the favourite object of heavenly regard. Through these delusions the party proceeded, and, what may seem wonderful, still to the encrease of law and liberty; till they reached the imposture of the popish plot, a fiction which exceeds the ordinary bounds of vulgar credulity. But however singular these events may appear, there is really nothing altogether new in any period of modern history: And it is remarkable, that tribunitian arts, though sometimes useful in a free constitution, have usually been such as men of probity and honour could not bring themselves either to practice or approve. The other faction, which, since the revolution, has been obliged to cultivate popularity, sometimes found it necessary to employ like artifices.

"The Whig party, for a course of near seventy years, has, almost without interruption, enjoyed the whole authority of government; and no honours or offices could be obtained but by their countenance and protection. But this event, which, in some particulars, has been advantageous to the state, has proved destructive to the truth of history, and has established many gross falsehoods, which it is unaccountable how any civilized nation could have embraced with regard to its domestic occurrences. Compositions the most despicable, both for style and matter, have been extolled, and propagated, and read; as if they had equalled the most celebrated remains of antiquity (such as Rapin Thoyras, Locke, Sidney, Hoadley, &c.). And forgetting that a regard to liberty, though a laudable passion, ought commonly to be subordinate to a reverence for established government, the prevailing faction has celebrated only the partizans of the former, who pursued as their object the perfection of civil society, and has extolled them at the expence of their antagonists, who maintained those maxims, that are essential to its very existence. But extremes of all kinds are to be avoided; and though no one will ever please either faction by moderate opinions, it is there we are most likely to meet with truth and certainty." *History*, VIII, 319–23.

33. *History*, VI, 459, 555, 577.

34. "All questions concerning the proper medium between extremes are difficult to be decided; both because it is not easy to find *words* proper to fix this medium, and because the good and ill, in such cases, run so gradually into each other, as even to render our *sentiments* doubtful and uncertain. But there is a peculiar difficulty in the present case, which would embarrass the most knowing and most impartial examiner. The power of the crown is always lodged in a single person, either king or minister; and as this person may have either a greater or less degree of ambition, capacity, courage, popularity, or fortune, the power, which is too great in one hand, may become too little in another. In pure republics, where the authority is distributed among several assemblies or senates, the checks and controuls are more regular in their operation; because the members of such numerous assemblies may be presumed to be always nearly equal in capacity and virtue; and it is only their number, riches, or authority, which enter into consideration. But a limited monarchy admits not of any such stability; nor is it possible to assign to the crown such a determinate degree of power, as will, in every hand, form a proper counterbalance to the other parts of the constitution. This is an unavoidable disadvantage, among the many advantages, attending that species of government." *Essays*, I, 121–22.

35. *Essays*, I, 120. See also *History*, VI, 41, 71–72.

36. *Essays*, I, 112.

37. This passage, slightly modified, appears in the *History*, III, 305–6; also II, 451–52.

38. On February 9, 1748 Hume wrote to Henry Home that his new essay, "Of the Protestant Succession," showed him "a Whig, but a very sceptical one." *Letters*, I, 111. A few days later, on February 13, 1748, he wrote to Lord Tinwald that he proposed to add three new essays to the forthcoming edition of the *Essays Moral and Political*. "One is against the original Contract, the System of the Whigs, another against passive Obedience, the System of the Tories: A third upon the Protestant Succession, where I suppose a Man to deliberate, before the Establishment of that Succession, which Family he shou'd adhere to, & to weigh the Advantages & Disadvantages of each. I hope I have examin'd this Question as coolly & impartially as if I were remov'd a thousand Years from the present Period: But this is what some People think extremely dangerous, & sufficient, not only to ruin me for ever, but also throw some Reflection on all my Friends." Hume proceeds to ask Tinwald's advice on whether or not to publish "Of

the Protestant Succession." *Letters,* I, 112–13. The essay was not published until Edition H (1752).

39. *Essays,* I, 469–70. It is worth noting that in "Of the Coalition of Parties," first published in Edition M (1758), Hume has sloughed off some of his original Whig prejudices. In "Of the Parties of Great Britain," first published in 1741, he makes James I an innovator who stirred up the House of Commons by trying to revoke privileges and disregarding the liberties of his subjects. *Essays,* I, 136. In 1758, when he published "Of the Coalition of Parties," he added a footnote to the earlier essay, which reads: "Some of the opinions delivered in these Essays, with regard to the public transactions in the last century, the Author, on more accurate examination, found reason to retract in his *History* of GREAT BRITAIN. And as he would not enslave himself to the systems of either party, neither would he fetter his judgment by his own preconceived opinions and principles; nor is he ashamed to acknowledge his mistakes. These mistakes were indeed, at that time, almost universal in this kingdom." *Essays,* I, 141.

40. *Essays,* I, 116.

41. "Were the British Government proposed as a subject of speculation, one would immediately perceive in it a source of division and party, which it would be almost impossible for it, under any administration, to avoid. The just balance between the republican and monarchical part of our constitution is really, in itself, so extremely delicate and uncertain, that, when joined to men's passions and prejudices, it is impossible but different opinions must arise concerning it, even among persons of the best understanding. Those of mild tempers, who love peace and order, and detest sedition and civil wars, will always entertain more favourable sentiments of monarchy, than men of bold and generous spirits, who are passionate lovers of liberty, and think no evil comparable to subjection and slavery. And though all reasonable men agree in general to preserve our mixed government; yet, when they come to particulars, some will incline to trust greater powers to the crown, to bestow on it more influence, and to guard against its encroachments with less caution, than others who are terrified at the most distant approaches of tyranny and despotic power. Thus are there parties of PRINCIPLE involved in the very nature of our constitution, which may properly enough be denominated those of COURT and COUNTRY. The strength and violence of each of these parties will much depend upon the particular administration. An administration may be so bad, as to throw a great majority into the opposition; as a good administration will reconcile to the court many of the most passionate lovers of liberty. But however the nation may fluctuate between them, the parties themselves will always subsist, so long as we are governed by a limited monarchy." *Essays,* I, 133–34. See also

his comment on mixed forms of government in his letter of April 10, 1749 to Montesquieu. *Letters,* I, 138.

42. *Essays,* I, 469–70.

43. *Essays,* I, 136–37. See also *History,* VI, 563.

44. *Essays,* I, 138.

45. *Essays,* I, 139. In "Of the Parties of Great Britain" (1741), Hume goes far towards attributing the contentions leading up to 1688 to the arbitrary designs of Charles II. In his *History,* however, he lays more emphasis on the continued disharmonies of the mixed constitution, and to the immoderate practices of the Whigs. Nothing is said in the essay about James II, so the idea is conveyed that he carried to an extreme the policies of his brother. But in the *History* he is depicted as an outsider, one who by reason of his constitutional ideas and his religion was simply irrelevant to the tension between the court and country parties, and who, therefore, was forgotten by both Tories and Whigs. The Tories retained their loyalty to the Stuarts, and subsequently would sigh for their return, but James II they regarded as one put aside on account of madness. *History,* VIII, 283–84. Notice the contrast Hume draws between the deposition of James II and that of Richard III in *History,* III, 43–46.

46. *Essays,* I, 140–41.

47. In Scotland, he writes in the essay, "Of the Parties of Great Britain," editions A through P (1741 through 1768), there are no true Tories, but only Jacobites. "A JACOBITE seems to be a TORY, who has no regard to the constitution, but is either a zealous partizan of absolute monarchy, or at least willing to sacrifice our liberties to the obtaining the succession in that family to which he is attached. The reason of the difference between ENGLAND and SCOTLAND, I take to be this: Political and religious divisions in the latter country, have been, since the *revolution,* regularly correspondent to each other. The PRESBYTERIANS were all WHIGS without exception: Those who favoured *episcopacy,* of the opposite party. And as the clergy of the latter sect were turned out of the churches at the *revolution,* they had no motive for making any compliances with the government in their oaths, or their forms of prayers, but openly avowed the highest principles of their party; which is the cause why their followers have been more violent than their brethren of the TORY party in ENGLAND."

In editions A and B only (1741 and 1742) Hume concludes the essay with this paragraph: "As violent Things have not commonly so long a Duration as moderate, we actually find, that the *Jacobite* Party is almost entirely vanish'd from among us, and that the Distinction of *Court* and *Country,* which is but creeping in at LONDON, is the only one that is ever mention'd in this *kingdom.* Beside the Violence and Openness of the JACOBITE party, another Reason has, perhaps,

contributed to produce so sudden and so visible an Alteration in this part
of BRITAIN. There are only two Ranks of Men among us; Gentlemen,
who have some Fortune and Education, and the meanest slaving Poor;
without any considerable Number of that middling Rank of Men, which
abounds more in ENGLAND, both in Cities and in the Country, than in
any other Part of the World. The slaving Poor are incapable of any
Principles: Gentlemen may be converted to true Principles, by Time
and Experience. The middling Rank of Men have Curiosity and
Knowledge enough to form Principles, but not enough to form true
ones, or correct any Prejudices that they may have imbib'd: And 'tis
among the middling Rank, that TORY Principles do at present prevail
most in ENGLAND." *Essays*, I, 143–44.

48. *Essays*, I, 96.

49. *Letters*, I, 391.

50. *Letters*, I, 435.

51. *Letters*, I, 497–98.

52. *Letters*, I, 417.

53. *Letters*, I, 470.

54. *Letters*, I, 502.

55. *Letters*, I, 516–17.

56. *Letters*, II, 161, 180–81.

57. *Letters*, II, 184.

58. *Letters*, II, 208–9.

59. The praise of the Chancellor (Lord Camden) and the Chief
Justice (Lord Mansfield) is ironical. *Letters*, II, 209–10.

60. *Letters*, II, 216.

61. *Letters*, II, 211–12.

62. *Letters*, II, 244–45.

63. *Essays*, I, 97.

64. *Essays*, I, 97–98.

65. *Letters*, II, 241. Earlier in this letter, which is addressed to
William Strahan, he speaks of the revision of his *Essays*, and comments: "This power, which Printing gives us, of continually improving and correcting our Works in successive Editions, appears to me
the Chief Advantage of that Art. For as to the dispersing of Books,
that Circumstance does perhaps as much harm as good: Since Nonsense flies with greater Celerity, and makes greater Impression than
Reason; though indeed no particular Species of Nonsense is so durable. But the several Forms of Nonsense never cease succeeding one
another; and Men are always under the Dominion of some one or
other, though nothing was ever equal in Absurdity and Wickedness to
our present Patriotism." *Letters*, II, 239.

66. *Letters*, II, 234, 236–37.

67. In a letter, written on October 26, 1775, to William Strahan,
Hume said: "I must, before we part, have a little Stroke of Politics
with you, notwithstanding my Resolution to the contrary. We hear
that some of the Ministers have propos'd in Council, that both Fleet
and Army be withdrawn from America, and these Colonists be left
entirely to themselves. I wish I had been a Member of His Majesty's
Cabinet Council, that I might have seconded this Opinion. I shoud
have said, that this Measure only anticipates the necessary Course of

Events a few Years; that a forced and every day more precarious Monopoly of about 6 or 700,000 Pounds a year of Manufactures, was not worth contending for; that we shoud preserve the greater part of this Trade even if the Ports of America were open to all Nations; that it was very likely, in our method of proceeding, that we shoud be disappointed in our Scheme of conquering the Colonies; and that we ought to think beforehand how we were to govern them, after they were conquer'd. Arbitrary Power can extend its oppressive Arm to the Antipodes; but a limited Government can never long be upheld at a distance, even where no Disgusts have interven'd: Much less, where such violent Animosities have taken place. We must, therefore, annul all the Charters; abolish every democratical Power in every Colony; repeal the Habeas Corpus Act with regard to them; invest every Governor with full discretionary or arbitrary Powers; confiscate the Estates of all the chief Planters; and hang three fourths of their Clergy. To execute such Acts of destructive Violence twenty thousand Men will not be sufficient; nor thirty thousand to maintain them, in so wide and disjointed a Territory. And who are to pay so great an Army? The Colonists cannot at any time, much less after reducing them to such a State of Desolation: We ought not, and indeed cannot, in the over-loaded or rather over-whelm'd and totally ruin'd State of our Finances. Let us, therefore, lay aside all Anger; shake hands, and part Friends. Or if we retain any anger, let it only be against ourselves for our past Folly; and against that wicked Madman, Pitt; who has reduced us to our present Condition. *Dixi." Letters,* II, 300–1.

68. *Letters,* II, 302–3. See also his letter, dated November 13, 1775, to William Strahan in *Letters,* II, 304–5.

69. *Letters,* II, 237.          70. *Letters,* II, 241–42.

71. *Letters,* II, 248.

72. In that essay he wrote: "The government, which, in common appellation, receives the appellation of free, is that which admits of a partition of power among several members, whose united authority is no less, or is commonly greater than that of any monarch; but who, in the usual course of administration, must act by general and equal laws, that are previously known to all the members and to all their subjects. In this sense, it must be owned, that liberty is the perfection of civil society; but still authority must be acknowledged essential to its very existence: and in those contests, which so often take place between the one and the other, the latter may, on that account, challenge the preference. Unless perhaps one may say (and it may be said with some reason) that a circumstance, which is essential to the existence of civil society, must always support itself, and needs be guarded with less jealousy, than one that contributes only to its perfection, which the indolence of men is so apt to neglect, or their ignorance to overlook." *Essays,* I, 116–17.

Something of the same concern for liberty is shown in a letter of October 26, 1772, to William Strahan, wherein Hume writes: "It pleases me to hear, that Affairs settle in London, and that the Mob are likely to be no longer predominant. I wish, that People do not take a Disgust at Liberty; a word, that has been so much profand by these polluted Mouths, that men of Sense are sick at the very mention of it. I hope a new term will be invented to express so valuable and good a thing." *New Letters,* p. 196.

73. *Essays,* I, 125.     74. *Essays,* I, 126.

75. *Letters,* II, 306. A strip has been torn off the edge of the letter. "Or [will the Constit]ution be . . ." is my guess; Grieg's reconstruction is, "Or [will the Revol]ution be. . . ." Hume's two last sentences, although consistent with what he had written in "Of the Liberty of the Press," may have been included for the advantage of Professor John Millar. *Letters,* II, 306.

76. *Letters,* II, 260–61.

## X: GOVERNMENTS AND RELIGION

1. See H. G. Graham's *The Social Life of Scotland in the Eighteenth Century* (4th ed.: London, 1950), pp. 267–416.

2. Hume's experience with Calvinism is examined by Professor Norman Kemp Smith in the Introduction to his edition (Edinburgh, 1947) of the *Dialogues concerning Natural Religion.*

3. E. C. Mossner, *The Life of David Hume* (Edinburgh, 1954), pp. 289–90, 325–26.

4. The times at which the *Dialogues* were composed and revised are discussed in Smith's Introduction, pp. 87–96.

5. See his discussion of popular religious conviction in *Natural History,* p. 60.

6. *Letters,* I, pp. 12–18.

7. Mossner, *Life of Hume,* pp. 272–85.

8. Notice especially the final paragraph of this essay at *Essays,* I, 374.

9. E. C. Mossner, *The Forgotten Hume* (New York, 1943), pp. 13–37.

10. *Ibid.,* pp. 83–102; and *Essays,* II, 415–24.

11. *History,* VIII, 334.

12. That the views of Philo were those most acceptable to Hume himself is far from being the unanimous verdict of Humian scholars. See Smith's Introduction in *Dialogues,* pp. 58–59.

13. *Dialogues,* pp. 45–75.

14. See the paragraph that concludes with these words in *Dialogues,* pp. 189–90.

15. "The case is not the same with our reasonings from the works of nature. The Deity is known to us only by his productions, and is a single being in the universe, not comprehended under any species or genus, from whose experienced attributes or qualities, we can, by analogy, infer any attribute or quality in him. As the universe shews wisdom and goodness, we infer wisdom and goodness. As it shews a particular degree of these perfections, we infer a particular degree of them, precisely adapted to the effect which we examine. But farther attributes or farther degrees of the same attributes, we can never be authorised to infer or suppose, by any rules of just reasoning. Now, without some such licence of supposition, it is impossible for us to argue from the cause, or infer any alteration in the effect, beyond what has immediately fallen under our observation." *Enquiry* I, pp. 144–45; see also pp. 143–44, 145–46.

16. Notice how close Cleanthes comes to temporalizing the eternal in the *Dialogues*, p. 159.

17. Already, in *Enquiry* I, pp. 135–36 Hume refers to and explains "the religious hypothesis" in the same way. See also the beginning of his Introduction to *Natural Religion*, p. 21.

18. *Dialogues*, p. 217.          19. *Dialogues*, pp. 203–13.

20. *Dialogues*, p. 219.          21. *Dialogues*, p. 227.

22. Hume's comments on popular religions here are strongly reminiscent of Plato. Notice his teasing comment on William Leechman in *Letters*, I, 50.

23. *Natural History*, pp. 45–47.

24. Hume thought that it was the plain duty of any historian of Great Britain to lay bare, without distortions contrived to mollify the overly sensitive, the malign influence of popular religion on British politics; and he was somewhat surprised that certain passages in his first volume on the Stuarts stirred up critics. Consequently, he wrote a preface for the second volume, in which he declared his views on the historian's task. This preface was not printed, but its argument was set forth in a footnote in that volume. The original draft is in Mossner, *Life of Hume*, pp. 306–7. The footnote reads as follows:

"This sophism, of arguing from the abuse of any thing against the use of it, is one of the grossest, and at the same time, the most common, to which men are subject. The history of all ages, and none more than that of the period, which is our subject, offers us examples of the abuse of religion; and we have not been sparing, in this volume more than in the former, to remark them: But whoever would thence draw an inference to the disadvantage of religion in general would argue very rashly and erroneously. The proper office of religion is to reform men's lives, to purify their hearts, to inforce all moral duties, and to secure obedience to the laws and civil magistrate. While it pursues these salutary purposes, its operations, tho' infinitely valuable, are secret and silent, and seldom come under the cognizance of history. That adulterate species of it alone, which inflames faction, animates sedition, and prompts rebellion, distinguishes itself on the open theatre of the world, and is the great source of revolutions and public convulsions. The historian, therefore, has scarce occasion to mention any other kind of religion; and he may retain the highest regard for true piety, even while he exposes all the abuses of the false. He may even think, that he cannot better show his attachment to the former than by detecting the latter, and laying open its absurdities and pernicious tendency.

"It is no proof of irreligion in an historian, that he remarks some fault or imperfection in each sect of religion, which he has occasion to mention. Every institution, however divine, which is adopted by men, must partake of the weakness and infirmities of our nature; and will be apt, unless carefully guarded, to degenerate into one extreme or the other. What species of devotion so pure, noble, and worthy the Supreme Being, as that which is most spiritual, simple, unadorned, and which partakes nothing either of the senses or imagination? Yet it is found by experience, that this mode of worship does very naturally, among the vulgar, mount up into extravagance and fanaticism. Even many of the first reformers are exposed to this reproach; and their zeal, tho', in the event, it proved extremely useful, partook strongly of the enthusiastic genius: Two of the judges in the reign of Charles the second scrupled not to advance this opinion even from the bench. Some mixture of ceremony, pomp, and ornament may seem to correct the abuse; yet will it be found very difficult to prevent such a form of religion from sinking sometimes into superstition. The church of England itself, which is perhaps the best medium among these extremes, will be allowed, at least during the age of archbishop Laud, to have been somewhat infected with a superstition, resembling the popish; and to have payed a higher regard to some positive institutions, than the nature of the things, strictly speaking, would permit. It is the business of an historian to remark these abuses of all kinds; but it belongs also to a prudent reader to confine the representations, which he meets with, to that age alone of which the author treats. What absurdity, for instance, to suppose, that the Presbyterians, Independants, Anabaptists, and other sectaries of the present age partake of all the extravagancies, which we remark in those, who bore these appellations in the last century? The inference indeed seems juster; where sects have been noted for fanaticism during one period, to conclude, that they will be very moderate and reasonable in the subsequent. For as it is the nature of fanaticism to abolish all slavish submission to priestly power; it follows, that as soon as the first ferment is abated, men are naturally in such sects left to the free use of their reason, and shake off the fetters of custom and authority." *The History of Great Britain* (1st ed.; London, 1756), II, 449–50.

25. *Essays*, I, 145.

26. This caveat appears in the essay, "Of Superstition and Enthusiasm" in these words, in Editions D to N (1748 to 1760). Similar words were added first in Edition B (1742). The warning is dropped in Editions O to R (1764 to 1777). *Essays*, I, 147 and 146.

27. *Essays*, I, 147, footnote.        28. *Essays*, I, 149.

29. *History*, VII, 71.                     30. *History*, IV, 29.

31. Hume would not agree with the argument attributed by Professor Joseph Cropsey to his friend, Adam Smith, that "liberal, humane society requires to be rid of authoritative rule by civil governors, which it can accomplish only by ridding itself at the same time of authoritative ecclesiastical government." *Polity and Economy: An Interpretation of the Principles of Adam Smith* (The Hague, 1957), p. 86. Hume's explanation of the role of an established church and his statement of "the proper office of religion" (see note 24) lead me to believe that he would subscribe to a position put forth in an argument incorporated in *Enquiry* I. It reads: "You conclude, that religious doctrines and reasonings *can* have no influence on life, because they *ought* to have no influence; never considering, that men reason not in the same manner you do, but draw many consequences from the belief of a divine Existence, and suppose that the Deity will inflict punishments on vice, and bestow rewards on virtue, beyond what appear in the ordinary course of nature. Whether this reasoning of theirs be just or not, is no matter. Its influence on their life and conduct must still be the same. And, those, who attempt to disabuse them of such prejudices, may, for aught I know, be good reasoners, but I cannot allow them to be good citizens and politicians; since they free men from one restraint upon their passions, and make the infringement of the laws of society, in one respect, more easy and secure." *Enquiry* I, p. 147.

32. *History*, IV, 30–32; also I, 201 and 389.

33. *History*, IV, 309–10; and see VI, 13–14.

34. *History*, VI, 84–85.        35. *History*, IV, 31–32; VIII, 72.

36. *Essays*, I, 147.

37. *History*, V, 149–50; and see VII, 41–42.

38. *Essays*, I, 97.

39. "Whence comes it then, that, in fact, the utmost a wise magistrate can propose with regard to popular religions, is, as far as possible, to make a saving game of it, and to prevent their pernicious consequences with regard to society? Every expedient which he tries for so humble a purpose is surrounded with inconveniences. If he admits only one re-

ligion among his subjects, he must sacrifice, to an uncertain prospect of tranquillity, every consideration of public liberty, science, reason, industry, and even his own independency. If he gives indulgence to several sects, which is the wiser maxim, he must preserve a very philosophical indifference to all of them, and carefully restrain the pretensions of the prevailing sect; otherwise he can expect nothing but endless disputes, quarrels, factions, persecutions, and civil commotions." *Dialogues,* p. 223.

40. *History,* IV, 406–10.

41. *History,* VIII, 49–50; see also VI, 91.

42. *History,* VII, 20.          43. *History,* VI, 165.

44. *History,* VII, 515–16.    45. Mossner, *Life of Hume,* p. 485.

## XI: THE PLOT OF TIME

1. Ludwig Wittgenstein, *Tractatus Logico-Philosophicus* (London, 1955), p. 189.

2. *Essays,* II, 389.          3. *Essays,* II, 389–90.

4. *Essays,* II, 391.          5. *Essays,* I, 177.

6. *Essays,* I, 195.           7. *Essays,* I, 197.

8. *Essays,* I, 170.           9. *History,* III, 298.

10. *History,* III, 296, 406–7.

11. "History issues from the Romantic School. Piecing together what the Revolution snapped. It hails from Burke, as Education from Helvetius, or Emancipation from the Quakers." This comment by Acton is quoted by Herbert Butterfield, *Man on his Past* (Cambridge, 1955), p. 70. See Butterfield's own discussion of Burke, pp. 68–72.

## XII: CIVIL REFORM

1. Our concentration on the civil relationships in this chapter requires that in the following pages we use the term "natural" to mean "competitive." Clearly, in the noncivil sphere the term would not have this meaning.

2. As quoted by J. G. A. Pocock in *The Ancient Constitution and The Feudal Law* (Cambridge, 1957), pp. 32–33.

3. The idea that custom is genuine law can lead to two conflicting views on the proper order. First, custom can be regarded as changeable, not so completely changeable as to be chaotic, but sufficiently changeable to meet emerging needs, provided they do not come too fast. It is not exact and narrow, allowing a judge no room to innovate somewhat. The past that guides (limits) him is the immediate

past: he looks back only so far as he and his brothers think "reasonable." This view makes the customary law-courts the legislatures of the land. It exposes them as the mediators between the past and the future. But a claim to power based only on special education is too inconclusive to serve in hot polemics; besides, most men are afraid of the responsibility that political power entails, so while they are ready enough to seek and use power, they hide it in a cloud of words lest they themselves be made uneasy and their associates be made vigilant. Accordingly, it is not surprising that common lawyers often resort to a second view of custom, one that ignores, as the first does not, the legislative work of the courts, and concentrates on the rules of law which guide them. These rules, in turn, are not regarded as man-made, but are said to be immemorial. Custom thus becomes the ancient, or original law, and any change that is not merely an enunciation of that law is a nullity. The social and political order of the immemorial past is the good order. The courts, of course, continue to innovate, but they do so under the pretense of discovering the good, old law.

It is not surprising that in the English constitutional disputes of the seventeenth century resort was had to this view that custom (genuine law) is the ancient law, and that all subsequent changes must be regarded as illegitimate. This view furnished an ultimate argument. While there might be disagreements as to who had (the) power under the ancient law—consequently the argument was used by all major contestants—whoever had held (the) power had had an indefeasible right to it.

"If the idea that law is custom implies anything," writes Mr. Pocock, "it is that law is in constant change and adaptation, altered to meet each new experience in the life of the people; and it might seem that there was no theory more likely to lead to a historical conception of the nature of law. Yet the fact is that the common lawyers, holding that law was custom, came to believe that the common law, and with it the constitution, had always been exactly what they were now, that they were immemorial: not merely that they were very old, or that they were the work of remote and mythical legislators, but that they were immemorial in the precise legal sense of dating from time beyond memory—beyond, in this case, the earliest historical record that could be found. This is the doctrine or myth of the ancient constitution." *Ancient Constitution*, p. 36.

Already we have seen (pp. 233–34) that Hume dismisses the argument that it is the immemorial law that is genuine as dismally false. But the view of customary law as experimental adaptation cannot be dismissed summarily; and it is the proponents of this view of custom whom I have called "conservatives."

4. More often than not, we may assume, the reasons why men are

liberals or conservatives are quite selfish, and have little or nothing to do with theoretical arguments about the proper way to place men in the social and political order. Those who in any existing order are wealthy and powerful, together with their heirs, tend to be pleased with that order; therefore, they are likely to be conservatives. Similarly, the perpetuation of the existing order by inheritance is likely to be ridiculed by those who think that they themselves would be advanced by competition. Our present inquiry, however, concerns the substance of liberalism and conservativism, not the many factors that happen to cause men to join parties and movements that are called "liberal" or "conservative."

5. See p. 198.

6. At *Enquiry* I, p. 107, Hume lists some of the causes that make for differences in the validity of the beliefs of different men. In addition to all the other factors, the temper and disposition of these few, unlike those of the vulgar, will have been modified by philosophic study. See Chapter IV, footnote 31.

7. Those in the middle station of life "form the most numerous Rank of Men, that can be suppos'd susceptible of Philosophy; and therefore, all Discourses of Morality ought principally to be address'd to them. The Great are too much immers'd in Pleasure; and the Poor too much occupy'd in providing for the Necessities of Life, to hearken to the calm Voice of Reason. . . .

"Those, who are plac'd among the lower Ranks of Men, have little Opportunity of exerting any other Virtue, besides those of Patience, Resignation, Industry and Integrity. Those, who are advanc'd into the higher Stations, have full employment for their Generosity, Humanity, Affability and Charity. When a Man lyes betwixt these two Extremes, he can exert the former Virtues towards his *Superiors,* and the latter towards his *Inferiors.* . . .

"We may also remark of the middle Station of Life, that it is more favourable to the acquiring of *Wisdom* and *Ability,* as well as of *Virtue,* and that a man so situate has a better Chance for attaining a Knowledge both of Men and Things, than those of a more elevated Station. . . . And here I cannot forbear communicating a Remark, which may appear somewhat extraordinary, *viz.* That 'tis wisely ordain'd by Providence, that the middle Station, shou'd be the most favourable to the improving our natural Abilities, since there is really more Capacity requisite to perform the Duties of that Station, than is requisite to act in the higher Spheres of Life. There are more nattural Parts, and a stronger Genius requisite to make a good Lawyer or Physician, than to make a great Monarch." *Essays,* II, 376–78.

8. *Letters,* II, 301.

9. See p. 131. In the essay, "Of the Protestant Succession," he

writes: "He [a member of Parliament considering the problem of the succession, early in the eighteenth century] would easily perceive the great advantage resulting from the restoration of the STUART family; by which we should preserve the succession clear and undisputed, free from a pretender, with such a specious title as that of blood, which, with the multitude, is always the claim, the strongest and most easily comprehended. It is in vain to say, as many have done, that the question with regard to *governors,* independent of *government,* is frivolous, and little worth disputing, much less fighting about. The generality of mankind never will enter into these sentiments; and it is much happier, I believe, for society, that they do not, but rather continue in their natural prepossessions. How could stability be preserved in any monarchical government, (which, though, perhaps, not the best, is, and always has been, the most common of any) unless men had so passionate a regard for the true heir of their royal family; and even though he be weak in understanding, or infirm in years, gave him so sensible a preference above persons the most accomplished in shining talents, or celebrated for great atchievements? Would not every popular leader put in his claim at every vacancy, or even without any vacancy; and the kingdom become the theatre of perpetual wars and convulsions?" *Essays,* I, 471.

10. *History,* VI, 421; VIII, 10–17. In the *Treatise,* pp. 563–64, he writes: "We have already remark'd, that in the case of enormous tyranny and oppression, 'tis lawful to take arms even against supreme power; and that as government is a mere human invention for mutual advantage and security, it no longer imposes any obligation, either natural or moral, when once it ceases to have that tendency. But tho' this *general* principle be authoriz'd by common sense, and the practice of all ages, 'tis certainly impossible for the laws, or even for philosophy, to establish any *particular* rules, by which we may know when resistance is lawful; and decide all controversies, which may arise on that subject. This may not only happen with regard to supreme power; but 'tis possible, even in some constitutions, where the legislative authority is not lodg'd in one person, that there may be a magistrate so eminent and powerful, as to oblige the laws to keep silence in this particular. Nor wou'd this silence be an effect only of their *respect,* but also of their *prudence;* since 'tis certain, that in the vast variety of circumstances, which occur in all governments, an exercise of power, in so great a magistrate, may at one time be beneficial to the public; which at another time wou'd be pernicious and tyrannical. But notwithstanding this silence of the laws in limited monarchies, 'tis certain, that the people still retain the right of resistance; since 'tis impossible, even in the most despotic governments, to deprive them of it. The same necessity of self-preservation, and the same motive of public good,

give them the same liberty in the one case as in the other. And we may farther observe that in such mix'd governments, the cases, wherein resistance is lawful, must occur much oftener, and greater indulgence be given to the subjects to defend themselves by force of arms, than in arbitrary governments. Not only where the chief magistrate enters into measures, in themselves, extremely pernicious to the public, but even when he wou'd encroach on the other parts of the constitution, and extend his power beyond the legal bounds, it is allowable to resist and dethrone him; tho' such resistance and violence may, in the general tenor of the laws, be deem'd unlawful and rebellious. For besides that nothing is more essential to public interest, than the preservation of public liberty; 'tis evident, that if such a mix'd government be once suppos'd to be establish'd, every part or member of the constitution must have a right of self-defence, and of maintaining its antient bounds against the encroachment of every other authority."

11. *History,* VII, 82.                    12. *Treatise,* p. 553.

13. *Treatise,* pp. 549–53. In the essay, "Of Passive Obedience," he writes: "Resistance, therefore, being admitted in extraordinary emergencies, the question can only be among good reasoners, with regard to the degree of necessity, which can justify resistance, and render it lawful or commendable. And here I must confess, that I shall always incline to their side, who draw the bond of allegiance very close, and consider an infringement of it, as the last refuge in desperate cases, when the public is in the highest danger, from violence and tyranny. For besides the mischiefs of a civil war, which commonly attends insurrection, it is certain, that, where a disposition to rebellion appears among any people, it is one chief cause of tyranny in the rulers, and forces them into many violent measures which they never would have embraced, had every one been inclined to submission and obedience. Thus the *tyrannicide* or assassination, approved of by ancient maxims, instead of keeping tyrants and usurpers in awe, made them ten times more fierce and unrelenting; and is now justly, upon that account, abolished by the laws of nations, and universally condemned as a base and treacherous method of bringing to justice these disturbers of society." *Essays,* I, 461–62.

14. *History,* VII, 148–49. See also *History,* VII, 373–74 and VIII, 13; and also *Essays,* I, 462.

15. *Letters,* II, 180–81.

16. Hale's *Reflections* on Hobbes' *Dialogue* is printed by Sir William Holdsworth in *A History of English Law* (London, 1952), V, 500–13.

17. Holdsworth, V, 503.                    18. Pocock, p. 173.

## APPENDIX: THE RECASTINGS

1. On October 26, 1775, Hume wrote to William Strahan as follows: "There is a short Advertisement, which I wish I had prefix'd to the second Volume of the Essays and Treatises in the last Edition. I send you a Copy of it. Please to enquire at the Warehouse, if any considerable Number of that Edition remain on hands; and if there do, I beg the favour of you, that you woud throw off an equal Number of this Advertisement, and give out no more Copies without prefixing it to the second volume. It is a compleat Answer to Dr Reid and to that bigotted silly Fellow, Beattie." *Letters,* II, 301. This Advertisement, now famous, reads as follows:

"Most of the principles, and reasonings, contained in this volume, were published in a work in three volumes, called *A Treatise of Human Nature:* A work which the Author had projected before he left College, and which he wrote and published not long after. But not finding it successful, he was sensible of his error in going to the press too early, and he cast the whole anew in the following pieces, where some negligences in his former reasoning and more in the expression, are, he hopes, corrected. Yet several writers, who have honoured the Author's Philosophy with answers, have taken care to direct all their batteries against that juvenile work, which the Author never acknowledged, and have affected to triumph in any advantages, which, they imagined, they had obtained over it: A practice very contrary to all rules of candour and fair-dealing, and a strong instance of those polemical artifices, which a bigotted zeal thinks itself authorized to employ. Henceforth, the Author desires, that the following Pieces may alone be regarded as containing his philosophical sentiments and principles."

In a letter written in 1754 Hume had said: "That you may see I wou'd no way scruple of owning my Mistakes in Argument, I shall acknowledge (what is infinitely more material) a very great Mistake in Conduct, viz my publishing at all the Treatise of human Nature, a Book, which pretended to innovate in all the sublimest Parts of Philosophy, & which I compos'd before I was five & twenty. Above all, the positive Air, which prevails in that Book, & which may be imputed to the Ardor of Youth, so much displeases me, that I have not Patience to review it. But what Success the same Doctrines, better illustrated & exprest, may meet with, *Ad huc sub judice lis est.* The Arguments have been laid before the World, and by some philosophical Minds have been attended to. I am willing to be instructed by the Public; tho' human Life is so short that I despair of ever seeing the Decision. I wish I had always confin'd myself to the more easy Parts of Erudition;

but you will excuse me from submitting to a proverbial Decision, let it even be in Greek." *Letters*, I, 187.

2. In the *Abstract* he writes: "To ease the reader's memory I shall briefly resume them. No matter of fact can be proved but from its cause or its effect. Nothing can be known to be the cause of another but by experience. We can give no reason for extending to the future our experience in the past; but are entirely determined by custom, when we conceive an effect to follow from its usual cause. But we also believe an effect to follow, as well as conceive it. This belief joins no new idea to the conception. It only varies the manner of conceiving, and makes a difference to the feeling or sentiment. Belief, therefore, in all matters of fact arises only from custom, and is an idea conceived in a peculiar *manner*." *Abstract*, p. 19.

3. *Treatise*, pp. 399–418.

4. The four parts in "Of the Understanding" are:

  I. Of ideas; their origin, composition, abstraction, connexion, etc.
  II. Of the ideas of space and time
  III. Of knowledge and probability
  IV. Of the sceptical and other systems of philosophy

The twelve sections in *Enquiry* I are:

  I. Of the different Species of Philosophy
  II. Of the Origin of Ideas
  III. Of the Association of Ideas
  IV. Sceptical Doubts concerning the Operations of the Understanding
  V. Sceptical Solution of these Doubts
  VI. Of Probability
  VII. Of the Idea of necessary Connexion
  VIII. Of Liberty and Necessity
  IX. Of the Reason of Animals
  X. Of Miracles
  XI. Of a particular Providence and of a future State
  XII. Of the academical or sceptical Philosophy

5. In the spring of 1751 Hume wrote to Gilbert Elliot as follows: "I believe the philosophical Essays contain every thing of Consequence relating to the Understanding, which you woud meet with in the Treatise; & I give you my Advice against reading the latter. By shortening & simplifying the Questions, I really render them much more complete. *Addo dum minuo*. The philosophical Principles are the same in both: But I was carry'd away by the Heat of Youth & Invention to publish too precipitately. So vast an Undertaking, plan'd before I

was one and twenty, & compos'd before twenty five, must necessarily be very defective. I have repented my Haste a hundred, & a hundred times." *Letters*, I, 158.

6. He probably had these sections in good shape before the *Treatise* was published. On December 2, 1737, he wrote to Henry Home about pruning the manuscript. *Letters*, I, 24; see also p. 361.

7. A different view is set forth and examined thoroughly by Anthony Flew in *Hume's Philosophy of Belief: A Study of his First Inquiry* (London, 1961).

8. In examining the relation between the *Treatise* and *Enquiry* II, I have undertaken to reply to some of the comments made by L. A. Selby-Bigge in his edition of the *Enquiries*. I have done this, not because his introduction is notably good, but because for over half a century it has stood as the introduction to the standard edition of these works. See pp. xxii–xxxi in *Enquiries concerning the Human Understanding and concerning the Principles of Morals* (2d ed.; Oxford, 1902).

9. *Treatise*, p. 415.     10. *Enquiry* II, p. 286.

11. *Enquiries*, p. xxvi.     12. *Enquiries*, p. xxvi.

13. *Treatise*, p. 591.

14. In 1764 (Edition O) the first part of the seventh section was made into a new appendix entitled, "Of Some Verbal Disputes." In 1777 (Edition R) the first of the three parts into which "Of Benevolence" was divided previously became an appendix under the title, "Of Self-love."

15. *Enquiry* II, p. 170.

16. In the first part of the section, the part which in 1777 became the appendix, "Of Self-love," Hume criticizes those who describe morality as a product of self-love. He writes that those writers are wrong who "from that love of *simplicity* which has been the source of much false reasoning in philosophy" have sought to reduce benevolence to self-love by tricky philosophical chemistry. This comment on the "love of simplicity" is read as a confession by Selby-Bigge. This reading is possible only if it is assumed that in the *Treatise* Hume was inclined to the self-love theory of morality. *Enquiry* II, p. 298.

17. "The merit of benevolence, arising from its utility, and its tendency to promote the good of mankind, has been already explained, and is, no doubt, the source of a *considerable* part of that esteem, which is so universally paid to it. But it will also be allowed, that the very softness and tenderness of the sentiment, its engaging endearments, its fond expressions, its delicate attentions, and all that flow of mutual confidence and regard, which enters into a warm attachment of love and friendship: it will be allowed, I say, that these feelings, being delightful in themselves, are necessarily communicated to the spectators,

and melt them into the same fondness and delicacy." *Enquiry* II, p. 257.

18. *Treatise,* p. 367. See also *Treatise,* p. 382 and "A Dissertation of the Passions" in *Essays,* II, 156.

19. After explaining why we call certain kinds of conduct in the sphere of noncivil or natural relations "good" or "virtuous," Hume goes on to say: "From these principles we may easily account for that merit, which is commonly ascrib'd to *generosity, humanity, compassion, gratitude, friendship, fidelity, zeal, disinterestedness, liberality,* and all those other qualities, which form the character of good and benevolent." *Treatise,* p. 603; see also p. 478.

20. *Enquiry* II, p. 298. See also the passage, *Enquiry* II, pp. 303–4, in which he contrasts particular and general benevolence with the "artificial" virtues of justice and fidelity.

21. *Treatise,* p. 481.          22. *Enquiries,* p. xxvii.

23. *Treatise,* p. 329.          24. See p. 11.

25. *Enquiries,* pp. xxvii–xxviii.          26. *Enquiry* II, p. 203.

27. *Treatise,* p. 484. See also *Enquiry* II, p. 305.

28. Professor Norman Kemp Smith disagrees with this interpretation. See his *The Philosophy of David Hume* (London, 1949), p. 151.

29. Hume writes: "It is needless to push our researches so far as to ask, why we have humanity or a fellow-feeling with others. It is sufficient, that this is experienced to be a principle in human nature. We must stop somewhere in our examination of causes; and there are, in every science, some general principles, beyond which we cannot hope to find any principle more general. No man is absolutely indifferent to the happiness and misery of others. The first has a natural tendency to give pleasure; the second, pain. This every one may find in himself. It is not probable, that these principles can be resolved into principles more simple and universal, whatever attempts may have been made to that purpose. But if it were possible, it belongs not to the present subject; and we may here safely consider these principles as original: happy, if we can render all the consequences sufficiently plain and perspicuous!" *Enquiry* II, pp. 219–20, footnote.

This passage is not as heavy against me as it may seem to be. Throughout the *Enquiry* Hume engages in a running fight with those who "from a love of simplicity" would explain all standards of conduct in terms of "self-love." This passage is a footnote to one of his broadsides; and therefore ostensibly is directed against simple, self-love systems. Probably it is wise to accept it as meaning what it ostensibly means. Hume, we must remember, did not have to write with an eye to covering his stern; to the public at large he was a writer without a past, a writer with nothing to retract.

30. *Enquiry* II, p. 220.          31. *Enquiry* II, pp. 243–44.

32. *Enquiry* II, p. 221.

33. *Enquiry* II, p. 251. See also *Enquiry* II, p. 229.

34. *Enquiry* II, p. 267. And see the passage in the *Dissertation, Essays,* II, 152, which was published six years after *Enquiry* II. In 1759 Adam Smith published his *Theory of Moral Sentiments:* notice Hume's comment, p. 351, on Smith's treatment of sympathy.

35. *Essays,* II, 166.          36. *Essays,* II, 152.

37. *Letters,* I, 38–39.          38. *Abstract,* pp. xix–xxii.

39. *Treatise,* p. 623.

40. See the letters quoted in notes 1 and 5. In his autobiography he wrote: "I had always entertained a notion, that my want of success in publishing the Treatise of Human Nature, had proceeded more from the manner than the matter; and that I had been guilty of a very usual indiscretion, in going to the press too early." *Essays,* I, 3.

# HUME'S PRINCIPAL WORKS:
## EDITIONS PUBLISHED DURING
## HIS LIFETIME *

1739     *A Treatise of Human Nature: Being An Attempt to introduce the experimental Method of Reasoning into* MORAL SUBJECTS. Book I, "Of the Understanding." London.

1739     *A Treatise of Human Nature: Being An Attempt to introduce the experimental Method of Reasoning into* MORAL SUBJECTS. Book II, "Of the Passions." London.

1740     *An Abstract of A Book lately Published; entituled, a Treatise of Human Nature, &c. Wherein The Chief Argument of that Book is farther Illustrated and Explained.* London. (Reprinted with an Introduction by J. M. Keynes and P. Straffa. Cambridge, 1938.)

1740     *A Treatise of Human Nature: Being An Attempt to introduce the experimental Method of Reasoning into* MORAL SUBJECTS. Book III, "Of Morals." London.

1741     *Essays Moral and Political.* Edinburgh.    EDITION A
      1. Of the Delicacy of Taste and Reason
      2. Of the Liberty of the Press
      3. Of Impudence and Modesty
      4. That Politics may be reduc'd to a Science
      5. Of the first Principles of Government
      6. Of Love and Marriage (omitted in 1764)
      7. Of the Study of History (omitted in 1764)
      8. Of the Independency of Parliament
      9. Whether the British Government inclines more to Absolute Monarchy or to a Republic
      10. Of Parties in general
      11. Of the Parties of Gt. Britain
      12. Of Superstition and Enthusiasm

---

* In lettering the editions of the Essays the system used by T. H. Green and T. H. Grose, *Essays* (London, 1875), I, 85–86, has been followed.

13. Of Avarice (omitted in 1770)
14. Of the Dignity of Human Nature
15. Of Liberty and Despotism

1742    *Essays Moral and Political.* Edinburgh. Second edition
of A.                                              EDITION B

1742    *Essays Moral and Political.* Vol. II. Edinburgh.
                                                   EDITION C
1. Of Essay Writing (omitted in 1748)
2. Of Eloquence
3. Of Moral Prejudices (omitted in 1748)
4. Of the Middle Station of Life (omitted in 1748)
5. Of the Rise and Progress of Arts and Sciences
6. The Epicurean
7. The Stoic
8. The Platonist
9. The Sceptic
10. Of Polygamy and Divorces
11. Of Simplicity and Refinement
12. A Character of Sir Robert Walpole (reduced to
a footnote in 1748)

1748    *Essays Moral and Political.* Third edition, corrected
with Additions. London and Edinburgh.    EDITION D
1. Of the Original Contract (added)
2. Of Passive Obedience      (added)
3. Of National Characters   (added)

1748    *Philosophical Essays concerning Human Understanding.* London.                                    EDITION E

1751    *Philosophical Essays concerning Human Understanding.* Second edition, corrected with Additions. London.
                                                   EDITION F

1751    *An Enquiry concerning the Principles of Morals.* London.                                              EDITION G

1752    *Political Discourses.* Edinburgh.         EDITION H
1. Of Commerce
2. Of Luxury
3. Of Money
4. Of Interest

5. Of the Balance of Trade
6. Of the Balance of Power
7. Of Taxes
8. Of Public Credit
9. Of Some Remarkable Customs
10. Of the Populousness of Antient Nations
11. Of the Protestant Succession
12. Idea of a Perfect Commonwealth

1752    *Political Discourses.* Second edition. Edinburgh.
                                                    EDITION I

1753–54 *Essays and Treatises on Several Subjects.* London and
        Edinburgh.                                  EDITION K

1754    *The History of Great Britain.* Vol. I containing the
        Reigns of James I. and Charles I. Edinburgh.

1756    *The History of Great Britain.* Vol. II containing the
        Commonwealth, and the Reigns of Charles II. and James
        II. London.

1757    *Four Dissertations.* London.               EDITION L
        I.    The Natural History of Religion
        II.   Of the Passions
        III.  Of Tragedy
        IV.   Of the Standard of Taste

1758    *Essays and Treatises on Several Subjects.* London.
                                                    EDITION M
        Part I.  Essays, Moral, Political, and Literary
        Part II. Essays, Moral, Political, and Literary (Po-
        litical Discourses)
        An Enquiry concerning Human Understanding
        An Enquiry concerning the Principles of Morals
        The Natural History of Religion
        Of the Jealousy of Trade   (added late, as pp. 187–89)
        Of the Coalition of Parties (added late, as pp. 265–69)

1759    *The History of England under the House of Tudor.* 2
        volumes. London.

1760    *Essays and Treatises on Several Subjects.* London
        and Edinburgh.                              EDITION N

1762     *The History of England from the Invasion of Julius Caesar to the Accession of Henry VII.* London.

1764     *Essays and Treatises on Several Subjects.* London and Edinburgh.        EDITION O

1768     *Essays and Treatises on Several Subjects.* London and Edinburgh.        EDITION P

1770     *Essays and Treatises on Several Subjects.* London and Edinburgh.        EDITION Q

1777     *Essays and Treatises on Several Subjects.* (Of the Origin of Government added.) London and Edinburgh.        EDITION R

1777     *The Life of David Hume, Esq.: Written by Himself.* London.

1779     *Dialogues concerning Natural Religion.* London.

The following pieces were not published, or were published only once, or were published and then suppressed:

Of the Immortality of the Soul

Of Suicide

Of the Authenticity of Ossian's Poems

Letter concerning Wilkie's Epigoniad

Dedication of the *Four Dissertations* to the Reverend Mr. John Home

Fragments describing the descent on the coast of Brittany in 1746

A Concise and Genuine Account of the Dispute between Mr. Hume and Mr. Rousseau

A True Account of the Behaviour and Conduct of Archibald Stewart, Esq; late Lord Provost of Edinburgh, In a Letter to a Friend

Petition of the Grave and Venerable Bellmen, Or Sextons, of the Church of Scotland, To the Honourable House of Commons